GWYNEDD
INHERITING A REVOLUTION

The Archaeology of Industrialisation in North-West Wales

At work in Dinorwic quarry.

GWYNEDD
INHERITING A REVOLUTION

The Archaeology of Industrialisation in North-West Wales

DAVID GWYN

PHILLIMORE

> Praise for *Gwynedd: Inheriting A Revolution*
>
> Winner of the Peter Neaverson Award for Outstanding Scholarship
>
> Dr Dafydd Roberts, *Transactions of the Merionethshire Historical and Record Society*
> 'eruditely written and profusely illustrated by an author who understands people, society, technology industry and the surrounding landscape.'

First published in 2006 by
PHILLIMORE & CO. LTD

Reprinted in paperback in 2007

Reprinted in 2015 by Phillimore, an imprint of
The History Press
The Mill, Brimscombe Port
Stroud, Gloucestershire, GL5 2QG
www.thehistorypress.co.uk

The right of David Gwyn to be identified as the Author
of this work has been asserted in accordance with the
Copyrights, Designs and Patents Act 1988.

All rights reserved. No part of this book may be reprinted
or reproduced or utilised in any form or by any electronic,
mechanical or other means, now known or hereafter invented,
including photocopying and recording, or in any information storage or retrieval
system, without the permission in writing from the Publishers.

© David Gwyn, 2006, 2015

ISBN 978 1 8607 7515 4

Printed and bound in Great Britain

To Dr Marian Gwyn

CONTENTS

List of Maps and Illustrations ix
Acknowledgements xiii
Foreword xv
Conventions xvii

1 Introduction 1

2 Approaches to the Industrial Past 11
   2.1 Origins 11
   2.2 Industrial Archaeology 15
   2.3 Heritage Management 16
   2.4 Defining the Discipline 17
   2.5 Wales and Gwynedd. 20
   2.6 Summary and Conclusion 27

3 Topographical, Cultural and Economic Context 29
   3.1 Topography 29
   3.2 Cultural Context. 30
      3.2.1 Pre-modern history 30
   3.3 Economic Context 34
      3.3.1 Pre-modern industry. 34
      3.3.2 Urban development 36
      3.3.3 Landed estates and economic development. 38

4 Industrial Archaeology of Gwynedd 41
   4.1 Extractive Industries 42
      4.1.1 Quarrying for slate 42
      4.1.2 Quarrying for stone 70
      4.1.3 Metalliferous mining. 78
      4.1.4 Mining for coal 92
      4.1.5 Agriculture in the industrial period 96
      4.1.6 Forestry and the timber trade 110
      4.1.7 Brick-making and ceramics 115
   4.2 Processing industries 118
      4.2.1 Textiles 118
      4.2.2 Metal processing. 123
      4.2.3 The food industry 127

- 4.3 Ancillary Industries .. .. .134
  - 4.3.1 Foundries, ironworks, engineering .. .. .134
  - 4.3.2 Chemicals and explosives .. .. .137
- 4.4 Public Utilities .. .. .139
  - 4.4.1 Public water supply .. .. .139
  - 4.4.2 Gas and electricity supply .. .. .142
- 4.5 Transport and Communications .. .. .146
  - 4.5.1 Roads. .. .. .146
  - 4.5.2 Railways .. .. .153
  - 4.5.3 Docks, quays and harbours .. .. .166
  - 4.5.4 Water-control systems, canals .. .. .175
  - 4.5.5 Telegraphy and wireless .. .. .179
- 4.6 Settlement .. .. .182
  - 4.6.1 Housing .. .. .182
  - 4.6.2 Social infrastructure and communal buildings .. .. .. .195
  - 4.6.3 Artefacts and interiors .. .. .210
  - 4.6.4 The morphology of settlement .. .. .212
- 4.7 The Twentieth Century .. .. .221
  - 4.7.1 Warfare, industrialisation, the command economy and beyond .221

5 Perspectives 227
- 5.1 An Industrial Revolution? .. .. .227
- 5.2 Archaeology or Heritage Management?. .. .. .229
- 5.3 A Period Discipline or a Thematic Discipline? .. .. .231
- 5.4 Industrial Archaeology, Post-medieval Archaeology, Historical Archaeology, an Archaeology of Capitalism or an Archaeology of Industrial Society? .. .. .233

Appendix 1: Bateman's Classifications of Landholding .. .. .241
Appendix 2: Growth of Retailing .. .. .243
Bibliography .. .. .245
Index .. .. .255

LIST OF MAPS AND ILLUSTRATIONS

Maps
1. Topography .. 30
2. Industry and settlement pre-1700. .. 35
3. Slate quarries .. 43
4. Stone quarries.. .. 70
5. Metalliferous mines .. 79
6. Coal mining area .. 93
7. Agriculture .. 99
8. Forestry .. 112
9. Textiles .. 120
10. Roads .. 149
11. Railways (i) – railways built to serve regional needs .. 154
12. Railways (ii) – the national railway network .. 155
13. Harbours .. 167
14. Water control systems .. 176
15. Settlement after 1700 .. 213

Illustrations
    At work in Dinorwic quarry .. *frontispiece*
1. A chapel congregation at Drws y Coed in the Nantlle valley. .. 2
2. Cayo Evans at a Tryweryn protest rally .. 3
3. Iorwerth Jones as an engine driver in Penrhyn quarry .. 4
4. Iorwerth looking after the Penrhyn Castle Industrial Railway Museum .. 5
5. Georgius Agricola – woodcut diagram of a *wassergopel* .. 12
6. The former quarryman William Williams. .. 23
7. Early days on the Talyllyn Railway .. 25
8. Aberfan – discovering bodies. .. 26
9. Llanrwst bridge .. 38
10. Penrhyn quarry in the 1940s .. 44
11. A 'landscaped' quarry environment at Dinorwic.. .. 45
12. A powder magazine at Hafodlas quarry .. 46
13. An Easton and Amos water-pressure engine at Penrhyn quarry. .. 46
14. Dorothea in the Nantlle group .. 46
15. Dinorwic quarry .. 48
16. Underground chambers at Blaenau Ffestiniog .. 48
17. Slate tipping at Alexandra quarry.. .. 50
18. Trackwork at Maenoffroad quarry .. 51

19. *Chaloner* on the Leighton Buzzard Railway 51
20. *Vaenol* at Dinorwic quarry. 52
21. An overhead wire locomotive at Llechwedd quarry 52
22. Incline at Maenofferen quarry 53
23. A transporter incline at Vivian quarry 54
24. Water-balance shaft head-frame at Penrhyn quarry 55
25. Water-wheel and ropeway at Rhos quarry 55
26. A chain incline and a blondin ropeway at Pen yr Orsedd quarry. 57
27. *Gwaliau* at Foel quarry. 58
28. Ynys y Pandy slate mill 58
29. Slate-splitting and a saw table. 59
30. Gilfach Ddu workshops 62
31. Suspension water-wheel at Penrhyn quarry 63
32. Hydro-station at Llechwedd quarry 63
33. Cornish engine at Dorothea quarry 64
34. Rhiwbach quarry 66
35. Oakeley hospital at Blaenau Ffestiniog 67
36. Barracks at Pen y Bryn quarry 67
37. Penmaenmawr quarry in the 1950s 71
38. Inclines at Penmaenmawr. 73
39. Penmon quarry 74
40. Limestone kiln at Lledwigan 75
41. Mochdre quarry 76
42. Loading chutes at Penmaenmawr station. 77
43. Parys copper mines 81
44. Gyrn and Egryn manganese mines 83
45. Parys mine precipitation pits, sulphur kilns and sublimation chambers 84
46. Stamp mill at Drws y Coed copper mine.. 85
47. Lliwedd mine 85
48. Smelters at Porth Amlwch 86
49. Glasdir mine 87
50. Ty Gwyn level. 88
51. Ropeway at Cwm Bychan. 89
52. Cwm Ciprwth.. 90
53. Engine house at Penrhyn Du. 90
54. Medieval and later coal-mining at Tyddyn Mawr.. 94
55. Berw colliery 95
56. Penrhyn estate map of 1769 .. .. .100
57. Pen isa'r Nant.. .. .. .101
58. Glynllifon estate workshops .. .. .102
59. Vaynol barn .. .. .103
60. Merioneth hay-barn .. .. .104
61. Sheepfold.. .. .. .108
62. Holyhead brickworks .. .. .115
63. Porth Wen brickworks .. .. .117
64. Woollen mill at Llandderfel .. .. .118

LIST OF ILLUSTRATIONS

65. Madocks' loom-house. .. .. .121
66. Dolgarrog aluminium works 126
67. Glanbia cheese factory .. .. .130
68. Warehouse at Ty Gwyn y Gamlas. .. .. .132
69. Market hall at Bala. .. .. .133
70. DeWinton's Union ironworks, Caernarfon .. .. .136
71. Ornamental hand-pump, Llanuwchllyn. .. .. .140
72. Aqueduct over the Conwy river. .. .. .141
73. Maentwrog power station. 143
74. Pipelines and transmission lines at Dolgarrog 143
75. Llyn Ystradau pumped storage scheme 145
76. Proposed bridge at Trefriw .. .. .147
77. The *lôn felen* on Parys mountain .. .. .147
78. Roads and railways at Penmaenmawr. .. .. .148
79. *Mona Inn* complex. .. .. .150
80. Waterloo bridge .. .. .151
81. Menai bridge .. .. .151
82. Tollhouse on the Telford road .. .. .152
83. Garage at Llanuwchllyn .. .. .153
84. *Fire Queen* .. .. .157
85. Stable-depot on the Padarn Railway .. .. .157
86. Single Fairlie locomotive on the Festiniog Railway .. .. .158
87. The Darjeeling Himalayan Railway .. .. .158
88. A Beyer Garrett locomotive on the Welsh Highland Railway .. .. .160
89. Swiss-style station building on the Snowdon Mountain Railway. .. .. .161
90. Preserved section of tube with the reconstructed Britannia bridge .. .. .163
91. Stephenson's tubular bridge across the St Lawrence in Canada .. .. .. .164
92. Llandudno Junction shed.. .. .. .165
93. Porth Amlwch. .. .. .168
94. Port Dinorwic/y Felinheli. .. .. .169
95. Port Penrhyn .. .. .170
96. Tyddyn Isa wharf .. .. .171
97. The hotel at Holyhead harbour .. .. .174
98. The Marine yard at Holyhead. .. .. .174
99. The sluice bridge at Malltraeth .. .. .177
100. Telegraph station on the Great Orme .. .. .180
101. Marconi station at Waunfawr.. .. .. .181
102. The classic vernacular cottage – Ty'n Llwyn near Rhosgadfan .. .. .183
103. Abergynolwyn. .. .. .183
104. One of a former row at Porth Amlwch .. .. .186
105. A row at Drws y Coed copper mine .. .. .187
106. An estate-built dwelling near Trefriw.. .. .. .188
107. 'One-chimney' house in Ffestiniog .. .. .188
108. Dublin Street, Tremadoc .. .. .189
109. Treddafydd, Pen y Groes .. .. .190
110. A Porthmadog terrace and a Ffestiniog terrace in Penrhyndeudraeth .. .191

111.	'The American style'.	.191
112.	St David's Street, Penmaenmawr	.191
113.	Cottages and town houses in Bala.	.192
114.	Cottages in Bontnewydd.	.194
115.	Glanogwen church, Bethesda.	.197
116.	Hen Gapel in Ffestiniog	.198
117.	Capel Peniel, Tremadoc	.199
118.	Peniel, Porth Amlwch.	.200
119.	Richard Westmacott's memorial	.201
120.	Chapel and shop, Tal y Sarn, 1820s	.202
121.	Gogerddan Stores at Tal y Sarn	.203
122.	Staircase in Kerfoot's, Porthmadog	.204
123.	Star Stores, Dolgellau.	.205
124.	The Cwmorthin quarry reading room of *c.*1841	.206
125.	*Queen's Hotel*, Porthmadog.	.207
126.	Williams and Hughes' bank in Caernarfon	.209
127.	The Bryn Twrw astronomical slates	.211
128.	Map of Caellwyngrydd	.218
129.	Map of Bethesda	.218
130.	Changing technology	.226

Map acknowledgements

I am indebted to David Longley, formerly Director of the Gwynedd Archaeological Trust, for preparing the maps.

Illustration acknowledgements

Illustrations 10, 14-17, 34, 38, 44, 54, 59, 61-64, 75, 79 and 122 are Crown Copyright. I am grateful to the RCAHMW for permission to reproduce them. Nos 1-3, 6 and 7 are published courtesy of the National Library of Wales. No 8 forms part of the collection of the National Library and is published courtesy of Bryn Campbell. Nos 13, 25, 30, 49, 76, 78, 89, 115 and 123 are published courtesy of Gwynedd Archives Service, 100 courtesy of Conwy Archives Service, and 27, 32 and 39 courtesy of the Gwynedd Archaeological Trust. I am grateful to Andrew Hurrell for permission to reproduce 19, 24, 31 and 87, to the Rev. Michael Outram for the frontispiece, 20 and 23, to Michael Messenger for 21, to Bryan Hope for 48, to Tom Parry and the Great Orme Exploration Society for 50, to Chris Lester for 51, to Peter Crew for 52, to the Rev. Dr Richard Hills for 53, to Eric Lander for 84, to John Dobson for 68, 86 and 88, to Dr Barrie Trinder for 92, to Tim Smith for 96, to Judith Alfrey for 106 and to Jeremy Yates for 127, a copy of his rubbing of the Bryn Twrw stone.

Nos 12, 28, 33, 47, 65, 80, 81, 90, 103 and 107 derive from a collection passed on to me by my late friend Dr Tony Rawlins. Nos 11, 40-2, 55, 57, 58, 67, 77, 85, 99, 105, 111, 112, 114, 118, 121 and 126 were taken for the book by Geoff Gornall, whose skills as a photographer are infinitely greater than mine. Other photographs derive from the author's own collection.

ACKNOWLEDGEMENTS

I owe thanks to the very many people who have contributed in one way or another to this study, either by passing on information, discussing its issues directly or for having helped me formulate my thoughts more generally. My late father, Professor Rhys Gwyn, to whom I dedicated the first 2006 printing, would recognise many of his own interests and priorities in this volume. So would my grandparents, each of whom, in their different ways, had a keen eye for the past and for social change. My mother and brother's support and encouragement have been all-important.

To the late Dr Gwynfor Pierce Jones and to Dr Michael Lewis I am particularly indebted, for sharing with me the fruits of their own very detailed research over many years. Rev. Dr Richard Buxton, Professor Barrie Trinder and Rosemary Sutton have not only proof-read the text but made a number of invaluable suggestions about the broader issues raised. Dr Ron Fitzgerald, Dr Mike Nevell of the University of Salford, Professor Marilyn Palmer of the University of Leicester and Dr Colin Rynne of University College, Cork have discussed with me the vexed question of 'whither industrial archaeology' and what Gwynedd might tell us about its future. For general discussion of the process of industrialisation in Gwynedd I thank Dr Wil Griffith, formerly of the University of Wales, Bangor, Rev. Dr Richard Hills, Stephen Hughes of the Royal Commission on the Ancient and Historic Monuments of Wales, Professor R. Merfyn Jones, former Vice-Chancellor of the University of Wales, Bangor and Dr Peter Wakelin. Andrew Davidson of the Gwynedd Archaeological Trust has helped me particularly in understanding the relationship between agriculture and industry. On historic landscape issues, Richard Kelly, formerly of the Countryside Council for Wales has been a great help, as has Judith Alfrey of Cadw on housing matters.

For all-important specific matters of information or access to sites, I am indebted to John Bennett of the Welsh Mines Preservation Trust, John Cave of Holyhead, Ian Cuthertson of the Parys Mine, R. Hefin Davies of J.W. Greaves Welsh Slate, Dr Diane Drummond of Trinity and All Saints' College, Leeds, Margaret Dunne, Bryan Hope, Peredur Hughes, Dr David Jenkins, Bill Jones, Eric Lander, Emily LaTrobe-Bateman of Gwynedd Archaeological Trust, Professor Patricia Layzell-Ward, John Lloyd of Wincilate Ltd, Aberllefenni, Dr Pam Michael and Bob Morris, both of the University of Wales, Bangor, Steffan ab Owain, Alun John Richards, John Roberts of the Snowdonia National Park, Sion Roberts, formerly of McAlpine's Welsh Slate, Jeff Spence of the Clwyd Powys Archaeological Trust, Nina Steele of the Gwynedd Archaeological Trust, Brian Sutton, Dr Robert Vernon, David Wagstaffe, Elfed Williams, Dr John Llewelyn Williams, Richard Williams, Vivian Parry Williams, Gareth Haulfryn Williams and Terry Williams.

Amongst those who are no longer with us, I name Dafydd Price of Dolau Las, Tan y Grisiau, quarryman, scrap-merchant, archaeologist, raconteur, leg-puller, Peter M. Hughes, a locomotive fireman at Holbeck shed before he became a schoolteacher, Griff R. Jones, Fellow of Bangor University, Iorwerth Jones, a Penrhyn quarry driver and guardian of the Penrhyn Castle Industrial railway Museum, and John Keylock of the Welsh Highland Railway. We shall not see their like again – nor, sadly, the like of Dr Tony Rawlins, a stalwart of the Plas Tan y Bwlch industrial archaeology courses from their earliest days. Some of Tony's archaeological photographs appear in this volume.

Other friends to who I am indebted for permission to use visual and photographic material are Judith Alfrey, Sarah Gasbé-Cochrane, the Rev. Michael Outram, Tom Parry and Jeremy Yates. Geoff Gornall's skills with the camera are evident in many of the photographs which appear in this volume.

For assistance with archival matters, the staff of the National Library, and the Llangefni, Caernarfon and Dolgellau record offices have been, as ever, extremely helpful, as has Einion Thomas, now retired from the university's Department of Manuscripts, and his predecessor Tomos Roberts. Dr Peter Wakelin, sometime Secretary of the Royal Commission on the Ancient and Historic Monuments of Wales, Aberystwyth, gave this book every encouragement from its inception.

I need hardly add that any errors of fact or interpretation are to be laid at my door and not those of these friends and colleagues who have been so generous with their assistance.

Finally, this book would have been impossible without the help and support of Dr Marian Gwyn, not only for proof-reading the draft and her observations on it, but also because her own research into the issues of British slavery has enabled me better to understand how the industrial revolution came about, and how ambiguous its legacy actually is. It is therefore to her that I dedicate this reprint.

FOREWORD

By the Rt Hon. Dafydd Wigley PC AM
Member of Parliament for Caernarfon, 1974-2001

A much-loved, and often-recited, poem by Pembrokeshire poet Waldo Williams – *'Cofio'* ('Remembering') touches the heart and mind as it evokes our yearning to learn about 'the long-forgotten relics of the family of mankind'.

In every part of Wales, there are relics of our industriousness. They remain evident – if not entirely comprehensible – because of the terrain of Wales. Some were set in stone, because that was the available material. Some, such as standing stones, are carved out of rock and retain their visibility if not their significance. Some are carved through rock, as are the many railway and tramway 'cuts' of the 19th century.

In Gwynedd, this is especially true. The rock-hard environment and the harsh climate made the people what they are – rock-solid, reliable and enduring; *Cadernid Gwynedd* ('the dependability of Gwynedd') is the motto of the county; a place where there is an abundance of cornerstones on which to build our community. Amongst the treasures of antiquity in the county is the dramatic hilltop fort of Tre Ceiri, with its remnants of more than 100 huts, still standing after thousands of years.

I often felt uneasy to be described at Westminster as representing a 'rural area'. Certainly Penrhyn Llŷn had agriculture as a major part of its economy. But so was tourism, and maritime activities were, historically, equally important. The Arfon area, where I lived as a child – and still do – was very much an industrial area, with the trappings of the receding slate industry as a dominant feature of our landscape as well as our social consciousness.

Slate, dragged out of the bowels of our earth, and hewn by sweat, blood and silicotic lungs, was the all-purpose material of our community. It not only roofed our homes; the offcut waste provided ready-made walling blocks. Placed on end, slate slabs – *crawia* – were the natural field dividers. Even water-troughs on farms and were constructed from carefully mortised slate. The doorsteps of our homes were of slate, as were our gateposts, the slabs on which we walked and the name-plates by our doors; not to mention our gravestones. These were the by-products of an industry which, before the First World War, employed 20,000 people in Gwynedd.

The industrial archaeology in Gwynedd clearly goes beyond the blue-grey shadow of slate, with its all-too evident spoil tips, gouged out mountainsides and residual tracks and inclines where busy trucks once hurtled towards the nearest port with the product of our hills to roof the world.

My village of Bontnewydd today still has a massive watermill building, and the overgrown channels are still discernible which a century ago directed water from the nearby Afon Gwyrfai to drive the huge waterwheel which sadly is long since gone: a mill which still ground flour from locally grown oats when I was a child.

Around the county there is evidence of age-old workings – for gold, silver, copper, lead and manganese. Engineering sheds, printing works, woollen mills, tanneries – they are all there, if now heavily disguised. Docksides, today trampled by yachtsmen, still bear evidence of half-hidden railtracks. Even the farms show testimony to the ingenuity of blacksmiths, whose hands created more than horseshoes, as the rusting metal scrap heaps adjacent to many a farm building visibly demonstrate.

Engineering technology was an essential part of our old industrial world. It is so appropriate that recently Techniquest, the science and technology experience centre in Cardiff, opened an offshoot at Llanberis, just across the lake from the outstanding Slate Museum and the Dinorwig slate quarry.

Sharing as I do with David Gwyn an upbringing in the shadows of mountains, language crises and submerged valleys, I could not help but be aware of the redundant relics of a recent age that was, before my eyes, passing into history. I therefore welcome this timely publication. It comes as the world around us moves into another era, which has only the incongruous industrial scars to link the younger generation – and incomers – to our busy industrial past.

David Gwyn and I both lived here as children; left to live and work in English conurbations; and returned to appreciate the physical witness borne by our environment to the history of our communities. For me, that consciousness was heightened from having lived for some years in Merthyr Tydfil, the birthplace of the industrial revolution, whose physical and social scars tell their own story of the impact of coal and iron on those valleys.

R.S. Thomas, in his splendid poem 'A Welsh Testament', lets an archetypal rural native speak of the present being entrapped in the past, complaining of being required to pander to voyeuristic visitors, by playing a role of 'keeper of the heart's relics, blowing the dust in my own eyes'. Understanding our industrial heritage is not for the purpose of developing niche products to feed a ravenous tourist market – though this may be a beneficial side-product. It is primarily to enable us who live here to understand ourselves better – and for other people to do so.

There is always a danger, in an area like Gwynedd, that the indigenous population is conditioned to believe that our communities were always rather backward, lacking in both inventiveness and diligence. Our industrial story tells us otherwise. That is just one of many good reasons why we should know more about it and appreciate its significance.

DAFYDD WIGLEY

CONVENTIONS

First of all, the limits of *Gwynedd* need to be explained. The medieval kingdom of Gwynedd changed in size and shape as its princes' fortunes waxed and waned, and the name ceased to have any official validity until 1974, when it was revived as a local government unit. It stretched from the east bank of the Conwy as far south as the Dulas, and included Anglesey. These are the boundaries of the present study, even though in 1996 Gwynedd was much reduced in size. It seems easier to use this attractive and ancient name rather than clumsily repeating 'north-west Wales' each time. From the 13th century until 1974 the study area formed Caernarvonshire and Anglesey, the greater part of Merionethshire, and part of Denbighshire.

In this volume, the phrase *Atlantic isles* is used to mean Britain and Ireland. It is assumed that these islands form part of *Europe*, and that *continental Europe* is a convenient way of referring to the European land-mass without these islands.

The Welsh words for certain natural features are generally retained. I refer to *Penrhyn Llŷn* rather than to the *Llŷn peninsula*, and, for instance, to the *Afon Dwyryd* rather than to the *Dwyryd river*. Otherwise, where there is an accepted English word for a place or an area, that is the one used – *Anglesey* rather than *Ynys Môn*, the *Great Orme* rather than *Pen y Gogarth*. Though the contemporary form of Welsh place-names is used elsewhere, where official bodies have retained earlier forms of spelling this is of course retained in the text, therefore the *Caernarvonshire Historical Society* though the town of *Caernarfon*, the *Festiniog Railway* though the parish of *Ffestiniog*.

I also employ a limited number of Welsh words. A *plas* (pl: *plasau*) is the home of the owner of a landed estate, but 'manor house' is not an accurate translation in that the manorial system was never properly applied to Wales. Neither is a *plas* a 'stately home', as anyone visiting the Lloyds of Cwm Bychan found out very quickly.

I have endeavoured to use as neutral as possible a vocabulary to describe social groupings. Following E.P. Thompson, I prefer *patrician* to 'gentry' or 'upper class', as a useful catch-all word for the wealthy and the powerful, though for distinctions within the category of *landholder*, I go to the other end of the political spectrum, and borrow the terminology of that irascible Tory, John Bateman, which does at least have the advantage again of being neutral and unloaded – Bateman reserved his polemic for his footnotes (see **Appendix 1**).*

I feel that Thompson's *plebeians* cannot on the whole do justice to the complexity of class relations in a culture such as Gwynedd (and that 'working class' and 'proletariat' are much wider of the mark) so I tend to refer to people simply by what they did,

---

* Thompson, E.P., *Customs in Common* (London: Merlin Press, 1991), pp. 16-96; John Bateman, *The Great Landowners of Great Britain* (New York: Leicester University Press, 1971 – original London, 1883).

as quarrymen, labourers, farmers, railwaymen. It is difficult also to do justice to the complexity of gender roles. The vast majority of industrial workers in Gwynedd in this period, in the sense of people who were paid for working in a particular industry, were men. Where women were employed, as in the copper mines, strong traditions survive about them but very little documentation, probably because payments were made to the male head of a work-team who distributed them (probably within a family unit) as he saw fit. Women clearly did work for money, in shops and as seamstresses, domestic servants, in health-care. The phrase 'farmer's wife' does scant justice to the labours of women on agricultural holdings, particularly the smaller ones where the margins of productivity were less and where the men in the family might be working in a quarry for much of the day. We know hardly more about the employment of women in war-time in the area, whether through the material record or from archaeology[*].

Specific technical terms are explained in the appropriate sub-chapters.

Though some sections are illustrated with indicative maps, grid references are given for most of the post-1700 features located within Gwynedd that are mentioned in the text.

Principal dimensions and distances are given in metric measurements followed by their imperial equivalents where this is likely to be helpful.

The following abbreviations are employed throughout:
CBA: Council for British Archaeology
CRO: Caernarfon Record Office
DRO: Dolgellau Record Office
DNB: Dictionary of National Biography (London: Oxford University Press, 1963-1990) and supplements
DWB: Dictionary of Welsh Biography down to 1940 (London: The Honourable Society of the Cymmrodorion, 1959)
IAR: Industrial Archaeology Review
JMHRS: Journal of the Merioneth Historical and Record Society
LlRO: Llangefni Record Office
NLW: National Library of Wales (Aberystwyth)
NMGW: National Museum and Galleries of Wales
NMR: National Monuments Record (maintained by RCAHMW)
PRO: Public Record Office (Kew)
RCHAMW: Royal Commission on the Ancient and Historic Monuments of Wales
RCAHMW *Caernarvonshire: Inventory of Caernarvonshire* (volume 1 – East [1956]; volume 2 – Central [1960]; Volume 3 – West [1964])
SAM: Scheduled Ancient Monument
TAAS: Transaction of the Anglesey Antiquarian Society
TCHS: Transaction of the Caernarvonshire Historical Society
UWB: University of Wales, Bangor (formerly University College of North Wales, now Bangor University)
WEA: Workers' Educational Association

---

[*] Gwyn, M., *Continuity and Change in Women's Lives in Gwynedd 1937-1947* (Bangor: Women's Studies Monograph Series, 2002).

Chapter 1

INTRODUCTION
To The 2015 Reprint

The opportunity to update this book, nine years after it first appeared in 2006, has prompted me to think about how far things have or have not changed in the intervening period. In the first printing I set myself the task of describing the archaeological evidence for how the industrial revolution had played out in my native Gwynedd (North-West Wales), and on this basis to make what I hope were useful observations both on the archaeology of the recent past and on heritage management, as they apply here and in other parts of the world as well. Since then, there has been an interesting change in perceptions of the industrial past at several levels, but I am not persuaded that the intellectual basis of the discipline has been much advanced, despite some hard work by a number of individuals.

I had come to the conclusion that the industrial revolution in North-West Wales was sudden and transformative but that the same was not necessarily true of other parts of the United Kingdom, and suggested that other regional studies might shed more light on this. I also found myself asking how parts of the world that did not industrialise on the British model fitted into this equation, and what that might tell us.

These are the questions which were being discussed by professional colleagues a number of years ago and which prompted me first to write and now to update this book. It comes with all the academic apparatus of footnotes and references which readers may consult or ignore as they choose, but its inspiration comes not from the lecture-hall or seminar room but from memory, family and friendship, and it is with these that I would like to begin.

The world of a childhood spent half a century ago is always going to be a remote and distant place but it is probably true to say that Gwynedd in the early 1960s was very old-fashioned indeed, both in terms of its social relations and of the way in which people earned their living. Very few people in Wales now attend church or chapel, but fifty years ago it was still formally at least a deeply religious society, and of markedly Protestant hue. In Llanrwst, my grandparents' market town in the Conwy valley, the Calvinist and the Wesleyan chapels were (and indeed are) on opposite sides of the road, one Romanesque and the other a muted Gothic. But Seion would disgorge its Calvinists five minutes or so before the Wesleyans emerged from Horeb, among them my grandfather, his twill suit contrasting with the chalk-stripe of his contemporaries, and subtly hinting at notions more heterodox than theirs. The two congregations would gather on their own bit of pavement to discuss among themselves the sermons they

1 A world that seems impossibly remote – a chapel congregation at Drws y Coed in the Nantlle valley after the service (courtesy National Library of Wales: GC/Y/2201/5).

had just heard, with no animosity or rancour between them but only the most cursory acknowledgement of the friends and neighbours on the other side of the road, before drifting off home – Sunday was a day that belonged to God and to one's own tribe. Where we lived went one better, in that it even had rival establishments of the same denomination – Congregationalists making their way to Bethania on a Sunday morning would pass their co-religionists hurrying to Bethesda at the other end of High Street.

Bethesda chapel had given its name to this small town, built in the 19th century as a dormitory for the huge Penrhyn slate quarry on the opposite side of the Ogwen valley. Its population was still traumatised by a strike that had taken place there sixty years earlier, when a mainly Liberal, nonconformist workforce had taken on the owner, George Sholto Gordon Douglas Pennant, second Baron Penrhyn, and had been comprehensively defeated. The quarry was a mysterious, overwhelming place, where lines of narrow gauge railway snaked around piles of slate rubble in threepenny bit curves, and compressed air pipes hissed ominously. Once, I was allowed to travel down to the bottom of the pit in a water-balance shaft, something that would now cause apoplexy in an inspector of quarries. Steam locomotives with names like *Winifred*, *Linda* and *Blanche* shunted the quarry and took the slate down to the harbour, their plumes of smoke moving rapidly through the trees on the far side of the valley as I came home from school.

My mother's parents lived near the village of Cerrigydrudion, the highest point on Thomas Telford's post road between London and Holyhead. Their links were with the

Dee valley and with Corwen, Llangollen and Wrexham, itself an area with a remarkable industrial past, but they had been brought up in Liverpool. From them I heard completely different stories – about growing up in a big city, about the 'Overhead', about getting one's bicycle wheels stuck in tram tracks, about quarrels between Catholics and Protestants, and about 'battling Bessie' Braddock. When I was seven, we as a family made the move to a big English city, in our case to Manchester.

Leaving where I had been brought up, but returning frequently during the school holidays, both conferred some objectivity on the scenes of my childhood and ultimately prompted me to think about their significance. The chapel-going culture, I learnt, was not unique to Wales but had powerfully affected the country's culture and history. Its legacy was by no means universally benign, but it had encouraged literacy and learning, and ensured the survival of the Welsh language into the 20th century. How much longer either chapel

2 Neither *kaiserliche* nor *königliche*, despite the Danubian inspiration; Cayo Evans (1937-95) at a Tryweryn protest rally in the uniform he designed for an officer of the Free Wales Army (courtesy NLW: GC/M/78).

or language would last was unclear; Welsh was in severe decline even in these north-western heartlands. On 13th February 1962 the elderly Saunders Lewis, who had been imprisoned in 1936-7 for making a dramatic pacifist-nationalist protest, emerged from silence to broadcast *Tynged yr Iaith* ('The Fate of the Language') on BBC radio, in which he argued for more assertive methods of upholding the language and which led to the creation of the Welsh Language Society/Cymdeithas yr Iaith Gymraeg. Liverpool Corporation's decision to create a reservoir which involved the removal of an entire Welsh community at Tryweryn in Merionethshire had confirmed once again the institutional powerlessness of Wales. In the spirit of protest which inspired young people from Prague to Los Angeles, Welsh cultural and political nationalism took a more radical turn. Graffiti urged resistance to English rule in the name of the Free Wales Army (Figure 2), and for a while Wales seemed a greater potential threat to law and order in the United Kingdom than quiescent Ulster. As it happened, it was on the streets of Belfast and Derry, not Caernarfon and Cardiff, that troubles loomed, and Wales remained largely loyal to its traditions of peaceful protest. Yet its heroes were now people like Dafydd Iwan, a young folk-singer and republican nationalist (and, typically, a minister's son), whose anti-royalist satire no less than his long hair and prominent side-burns marked him out as a man of the modern world.

Dafydd Iwan's protest song *Carlo* railed against the investiture of Charles as Prince of Wales in Caernarfon in 1969 – itself a tradition of no long standing, devised not by Edward I but by David Lloyd George, who represented the town in Parliament and who saw an opportunity to boost tourist revenue and to proclaim his own respectability at a time when he was busy destroying the political power base of the landed interest. Charles was invested on a throne of Welsh slate, so there was a sad irony that a fortnight later the great Dinorwic quarry near Llanberis, whence the slate had come, closed down. Other giants of the industry had already closed or were to do so within a year – Dorothea in the Nantlle valley, and the Oakeley slate mine in Blaenau Ffestiniog. This once-mighty industry, which had roofed the world, was passing out of existence, another blow to the intensely literate, cultured society of the men it employed. By 1970 it was on the brink of extinction.

In fact, the industry survived, due partly to the capital reserves of Alfred McAlpine, who took over the Penrhyn quarry, and partly to the determination and canny business sense of the remaining Welsh proprietors, but between modernisation and closure, 19th century technology soon began to disappear. Economic decline was to some extent cushioned by nuclear power stations at Wylfa on Anglesey and at Trawsfynydd near Blaenau Ffestiniog, pumped storage hydro schemes at Llanberis and at Tan y Grisiau, and the huge Anglesey Aluminium smelter which went into production in 1970.

This was the transitional year, not only because it was the nadir of the old patterns of work and the dawn of the new, but also when attitudes to industrial heritage began visibly to change, in several different ways. Dr Michael Lewis of the University of Hull set up an adult education course to carry out archaeological recording of the slate quarries, which has continued to this day, based at the Snowdonia National Park Study Centre at Plas Tan y Bwlch in Maentwrog. The Welsh Slate Museum opened in the former Dinorwic Quarry's huge quadrangular workshop, and Llechwedd Slate Mines in Blaenau Ffestiniog turned an early level into a visitor attraction. The time was ripe for industrial tourism throughout Britain. In England, the Beamish Open Air Museum opened as a visitor attraction in 1970, the Ironbridge Gorge Museum in 1973, and the Black Country Museum was to follow. The industrial past of North West Wales had, it is true, already

3 Changing times – Iorwerth Jones as an engine driver in Penrhyn quarry, January 1959 (courtesy NLW: GC/Y/271/4-5).

been presented to the visitor for nearly twenty years, from the time when Tom Rolt rescued the Talyllyn Railway in Merionethshire from closure in 1951 and when the Festiniog Railway commenced its gradual process of reopening from 1955 onwards. Yet somehow, these were joy-rides, threading their way through beautiful scenery and then stopping in the middle of nowhere. It was only when the Festiniog finally managed to return to its original upper terminus in the slate-quarry town of Blaenau Ffestiniog in May 1982 that it became a real railway again, linking quarry to port. This had involved building the 'deviation', a completely new section, using volunteer labour and what were effectively Victorian methods, but other projects to revive local railways I dismissed as totally fanciful. Surveying the grass-grown hillside ledge which was all that remained of the old Beddgelert station, at a time when the Festiniog was still struggling to build its new length of track, my twelve-year old self loftily concluded that trains would never run again on the Welsh Highland Railway. Not only was I wrong, but in 2009 it was I, as the Welsh-speaking member of the Company board, who formally requested the Presiding Officer of the newly-established Welsh Assembly Government, Dafydd Elis-Thomas, to perform the honours at Beddgelert once our train of invited guests had drawn to a halt alongside the platform and they had disembarked.

Given my interests, it might have seemed obvious that I should read History at university, but in the event I studied English Literature, then taught it in the south of England for eleven years. However agreeable a life this was, it was increasingly clear to me that I wanted to return. In my spare time, I found myself reading the books which were coming out on the slate industry – above all, Michael Lewis and John Denton's archaeological description of Rhosydd slate quarry and Merfyn Jones' powerful and eloquent 1981 Marxist study *The North Wales Quarrymen 1874-1922* (about which I say more in Chapter 2). Here, at least, were ways of writing about the past that were not condescending and which acknowledged the experience of working people. *Rhosydd*

4 Changing times – engine driver to heritage professional – Iorwerth looking after the Penrhyn Castle Industrial Railway Museum.

told a compelling story of local ingenuity and hard work, in a concern that had remained in Welsh hands. Michael Lewis brought a classically-trained archaeologist's eye and academic rigour to industrial sites, but also encouraged the attendees on his summer course to bring their own understanding and judgement to bear, to carry out research and to draw their own conclusions. Under his guidance, they soon began to build up a detailed knowledge-base of the industry, returning year after year to the glorious scenery of the Vale of Ffestiniog and the friendly environment of Plas Tan y Bwlch. Merfyn Jones was by then lecturing at Bangor University; his gift as a writer was to make Bethesda seem somehow far more real to me than Berkshire, and the plight of long-dead quarrymen more relevant than the concerns of the stockbroker belt.

Another influence was Gwynfor Pierce Jones (1953-2013). Like the polyglot Dic Aberdaron and the lexicographer Sgolor Mawr, he amassed more knowledge and understanding than is permitted to those who are more assiduous in their pursuit of worldly advancement, reflected in what ultimately became his PhD thesis, *The Economic and Technological Development of the Slate Quarrying Industry in the Nantlle Valley, Gwynedd*. He had close links with the Plas Tan y Bwlch group and also respected the work of 'Dr Merfyn', though as a good Gladstonian Liberal, Gwynfor considered his approach too programmatically socialist and too constrained by its Marxism. Brought up a Calvinist, his sympathies lay with the older non-respectable, pre-nonconformist past of his native valley, a part of the world where the pretensions of visiting preachers counted for marginally less than in the conservative rural areas where my Welsh roots lay. It was here that I clearly had to make my home. At the end of the summer term in 1993 I packed my books and my grandfather clock into a trailer, drove back to Wales and set about looking for work.

I was lucky enough to find employment with the Gwynedd Archaeological Trust, who took me on as a project officer despite having no training or formal qualification in the discipline, and before long I was also co-opted as a tutor on the Plas Tan y Bwlch course. I was able to make a start on several major projects recording the slate industry and metalliferous mining, as well as on cross-period initiatives such as coastal archaeology and on assessments, all of which meant I had to think seriously about matters which I had no previous opportunity to consider in any depth.

One thing led to another. In 2002 I was asked to take over the editorship of *Industrial Archaeology Review* from Peter Neaverson and Professor Marilyn Palmer, and had to give further thought, and a much wider context, to these issues. The previous editors had urged that a discipline which was 'technocentric' had to become 'social' – that even at its narrowest definition it should encompass housing and places of worship as well as functional sites such as factories and mines. This made sense to me, though I had no quarrel with the archaeology of technology *per se*, as one of the defining characteristics of an industrial revolution, and could not go along with the arguments advanced by some members of the Society for Post-Medieval Archaeology that anything later than the medieval period was *ipso facto* 'post-medieval', and industrial archaeology was therefore a sub-section of this period discipline. An arid intellectual turf-war perhaps, but I could not convince myself that either I or my Gwynedd ancestors of the 19th century lived in a Post-Medieval environment, certainly those of the later Victorian period, shipwrights, farmers, building contractors, blacksmiths in Penmachno, Eglwysbach and Glan Conwy, as they stared out at me from photographs in the National Library of Wales. There had been, in other words, a distinct change at some stage, and technology was crucial to it. Writing the book you are now reading was an attempt to set out this point of view and to invite challenges to it. A conference held at Leicester in 2008 held under the joint auspices of the Society for Post-Medieval Archaeology and the Association for Industrial Archaeology, published as *Crossing Paths or Sharing Tracks?*, explored both the *longue durée* and the paradigmatic change, and urged 'unity in diversity'*. There the matter should perhaps rest for now, but instinctively, I continue both to emphasise the 18th century disjunction, and to place industrial 'take-off' (the time when technological, economic and political change combines to bring about rapid, self-sustained growth) towards the beginning of the century, rather than around 1750, the date which archaeologists normally regard as the start of the 'Industrial/Modern' period. True, it was the Seven Years War (1756-63) which confirmed Britain as a world power, but I was intrigued that political change from 1688 to 1707 coincided with innovations like the Savery pump, the Newcomen engine and coke-smelting of iron. I would now add that the banking systems on the Dutch model established in London after 1688 were also highly significant, in that they both financed Britain's transition from an agrarian and handicraft society to one based on winning and processing mineral resources, and also ensured military victory by providing the government with access to credit.

Furthermore, it is now clear that this also made possible the enormous development of the British slave economy, which was in turn fundamental to the industrial revolution, matters which barely surfaced in 2006. The role of slavery is now much better known due to an initiative of the Labour government in 2007, which encouraged Heritage Lottery funding to commemorate the bicentenary of the end of the British slave trade. This ignited a debate and prompted a reconsideration of what the three hundred-year-long British traffic in human beings had actually done and who had profited from it. The Caribbean scholar Dr Eric Williams (1911-1981; Prime Minister of Trinidad and Tobago) had argued in 1944 that 'The commercial capitalism of the eighteenth century developed the wealth of Europe by means of slavery and monopoly.'† Most historians of the period would now go further and say that without slavery, Britain and other participating European countries would not have been able to develop their banking systems and capital reserves, their markets for textiles and other products, and their world-wide supply chains.‡ Additionally, before 2007 most well-informed people would have been happy to identify a handful of rich families as the beneficiaries, natural oppressors who also no doubt mistreated their white dependants – locally, the Penrhyn family's links with Jamaica had long been a matter of public knowledge so it seemed to make sense that these were the people who were also accused of mistreating the quarrymen of Bethesda. It has since become clear that money from the slave economy fed directly or indirectly into the coffers of the poor

---

* Horning, A. and Palmer, M. (eds), *Crossing Paths or Sharing Tracks? Future directions in the archaeological study of post-1550 Britain and Ireland* (Woodbridge: Boydell and Brewer, 2009), p. 406.

† Williams, E., *Capitalism and Slavery* (Chapel Hill: University of North Carolina Press, 1944), p. 210.

‡ As well as the British, the main players were the Dutch and the French. Portuguese and Spanish slave-trading was in decline by the mid-18th century but the Danes and the Swedes also participated, and research is now revealing how neighbouring countries also supported the trade.

and the middling as well as of the rich – Merionethshire weavers who sold 'Welsh plains' to Liverpool factors for onward sale to the Indies, Parys miners whose copper sheathed sailing ships and went to make slaves' cooking pots. It also became apparent that Penrhyn was not the only slate-producing area with close links to slavery; the list had to be extended to include the Liverpool interests who invested in Merionethshire quarries and in the Nantlle Railway, and the Huguenot bankers from Dublin who paid for the Festiniog Railway, whose wealth had come from the trade in meat and lactuals with the West Indies.

Another factor which has encouraged me to retain a focus on technical issues has been working on bids to nominate World Heritage sites, a UNESCO designation that recognises 'Outstanding Universal Value', a concept which derives from a distinctly French and enlightenment yearning for *universalisme*. If nothing else, identifying the unique 'OUV' to industrial site bids concentrates the mind wonderfully on the transformative nature of technological innovation. As Chapter 2 describes, in 2000 the Blaenavon industrial landscape in South Wales became a World Heritage Site on the basis of its international importance in iron making and coal mining, joining a dozen or so industrial sites world-wide. Two enthusiastic officers at Wrexham County Borough Council championed the claims of the Pontcysyllte and Chirk aqueducts and the Llangollen canal; a commission from the authority to evaluate its chance of becoming a World Heritage site, on which I worked with Professor Barrie Trinder and Dr Ron Fitzgerald, led us to endorse a bid based on the canal's heroic ambition and on the aqueducts' innovative use of cast-iron. It was duly inscribed in August 2009. Within days, Gwynedd Council had dusted off an earlier proposal to put the slate industry of North Wales forward for nomination, and discussion was under way as how best to achieve this. Not entirely co-incidentally, I was already at work on my next writing project after *Inheriting a Revolution*, a study of the slate industry of Wales, ultimately published in 2015.*

A successful World Heritage bid does not come with a cash prize but can be a factor in economic regeneration through increased visitor numbers and better access to grant-aid. Blaenavon, until recently a blighted and desperately impoverished town, was beginning to reap the indirect benefits of its citation, and Gwynedd saw the opportunity to work the same alchemy on Blaenau Ffestiniog and Bethesda. Other potential benefits are cultural confidence and nation-building, especially in countries which have only recently acquired their own institutions. In 1998, by the very narrowest of margins, Wales had voted for the creation of its own Assembly, ultimately established in Cardiff's Tiger Bay, once despised by respectable Welsh opinion as a multi-ethnic ghetto, now a symbol of urban regeneration and cultural diversity. The slate industry of North Wales represents an opportunity to tell not only the story of ordinary men and women's resilience in difficult circumstances but also their ability to create their own way of life, to say nothing of the inventiveness of an industry which gave the world (for instance) the narrow gauge railway. Scotland has recently (2015) shown the way, with the inscription of the Forth bridge, enthusiastically supported both by former United Kingdom Prime Minster Gordon Brown and the former First Minster of Scotland, Alex Salmond. Another inscription of the same year was the

---

* Gwyn, D., *Welsh Slate: Archaeology and History of an Industry* (Aberystwyth: RCAHMW, 2015).

Meiji-era iron, steel, colliery and shipbuilding sites in Japan, the first successful transfer of Western industrialisation to a non-Western nation, though Chinese and Korean representatives insisted that the inscription included a reference to the use of enforced labour in the 20th century.

The following chapters are exactly as they were published in 2007. Chapter 2 outlines the ways in which – in Wales, England and in the wider world – the archaeology of the industrial past has been studied so far. Chapter 3 provides a context for understanding the historical evolution of Gwynedd as an industrialising area, and Chapter 4 examines the archaeology of the productive landscape from approximately 1700 onwards under various sub-headings. In each case, particular monument types and landscapes are discussed not only in terms of their archaeology and their survival but also in terms of how and to what extent they have been studied, and what assumptions have been brought to bear on them. This is important to understand the archaeological resource at both micro and macro level – railways, for instance, have been studied and conserved by very different individuals and groups from those who interest themselves in water mills.

I included agriculture as an industry even though it has not traditionally been considered 'i.a.', and has its origins many millennia before the modern period. I argued that it should go in because industry also dates to the Neolithic, and both industry and agriculture are forms of exploitation of the natural environment that only gradually grew apart. I now see the argument as even more compelling in that I have a better understanding of how changes in farming practice fed a growing industrial workforce and in addition how closely linked these were with the way in which British colonies functioned. There could hardly be a better example than Gwynedd's Richard Pennant, Lord Penrhyn, who managed his pastures, sheep-walks and slate quarries in the Ogwen valley in the same hands-on way as his Jamaican estate, building not only roads, railways and a harbour but also dairies, mills, model farmsteads, and cottages for labourers and quarrymen as well. If these formed part of industrial archaeology – and it seemed clear that they did – then so did settlements that were not sponsored by the wealthy and powerful. These might be squatter smallholdings on mountain commons like Rhosgadfan, or they might be towns built by speculators or by working people's own investment in a building society like Bethesda and Blaenau Ffestiniog. If houses were to be included, then so must churches and chapels, shops and market halls.

The conclusion, Chapter 5, asks a number of questions. Can we speak of an 'industrial revolution' in an area that remained to a great extent rural? What is the relationship between the process of industrialisation within Gwynedd and industrialisation as it was experienced in other parts of the world? To what extent is it possible to see a distinction between industrial archaeology and the other forms of archaeological inquiry set out in this chapter? If there is a distinction, is it one of period or of theme? Should we distinguish between academic understanding of archaeology and the vocational nature of heritage management? It seems to me that these questions are still germane, but were I writing the book anew, I would ask others as well – above all, what reasonable prospect is there of industrial archaeology surviving as a discipline? As early as 2000, Neil Cossons, then Chairman of English Heritage, pointed out that industrial archaeology was facing the same problems as 'folk life' studies – both had grown from a mourning for a recent past, both were inherently 'generational', and neither seemed to know how best to sustain itself*.

There have been some worthwhile initiatives in recent years such as the growth in 'contemporary archaeology' and the archaeology of digital technology, yet traditional industrial archaeology is withering away. To grow, or even to survive, it probably needs both its 'hobby' enthusiasts, who are becoming elderly, as well as academic support, yet even fewer university courses now offer any training in it than in 2006. Coming to terms with the difficult legacy of global economic divergence, on which I briefly touch in chapter 4.2.1, and with European countries' involvement with slavery, would enable us better to understand both what industrialisation means and how technology brings it about, and also encourage a more reflective view of our recent past, and of our present place in the world.

To repeat: this book is not a history, of engineering or of anything else. Boardroom battles, acts of parliament, quarrels between savants – such as Stephenson's falling-out with Fairbairn over the Britannia bridge – are not particularly germane to an archaeological study. The archaeological past is a 'people story', but its actors are as likely to be from humble walks of life as to be managers or owners. I have tried to give appropriate weight both to iconic and internationally-recognised structures such as the Menai bridges and also to small-scale and unremarkable but once-common or distinctive features. I have necessarily had to be broad-brush, and to ignore many exceptions and qualifications. In every case I have provided references, to secondary works or to original documentation as appropriate, and those who wish for fine details may seek them there. If a site, a building or a machine is not explicitly mentioned here, that does not necessarily mean that it is not important.

Neither is this book a gazetteer, nor a guide. There is no public access to many of these sites, and nothing in this book should be taken as implying that there is.

Finally, the use of metric measurements – I already anticipate the irritation of railway historians, for whom standard gauge will always be a Stephensonian 4' 8½", not 1.435m, and can only plead that the metric system is here to stay, whereas rising generations will not instinctively think in terms of feet and inches. Children's encyclopaedias, after all, now impart a very different type of information in a very different way, and Victorian Wales is passing from sight.

---

* Cossons, N., (ed.), *Perspectives on Industrial Archaeology* (London: The Science Museum, 2000), 13.

Chapter 2

APPROACHES TO THE INDUSTRIAL PAST

The concept of 'industrial archaeology' is commonly assumed to date from the 1950s, when the term was first coined. This chapter argues that if we are to understand industrial archaeology we need to understand how it has been studied so far; that we need to trace its roots back much earlier than its commonly-accepted beginnings in the mid-20th century, and also that we need to see it in terms of broader patterns of intellectual change and industrial decline which vary within different cultures. The experience of Wales in this respect, and of north-west Wales in particular, is contrasted with the experience of Britain as a whole and of the wider world. It suggests that, though study of the industrial past has become accepted at a hobby level and by archaeological units, it has failed to find common ground with other forms of investigating the recent past, both archaeological and document-based; that it has not established a university presence; and that its intellectual basis has so far failed to advance sufficiently.

2.1 Origins

From the 16th century, the process of industrialisation was the subject of intense contemplation by contemporaries, whether economists or statisticians, capitalists or workers. When Georgius Agricola published his great *De Re Metallica* in 1556, with its many woodcuts of machines and devices that were then coming into use in the mining areas of central Europe (Figure 5), he stated that:

> I have hired illustrators to delineate their forms, lest descriptions which are conveyed by words should either not be understood by men of our own time, or should cause difficulty to posterity.[*]

Later writers who studied the impact of industrialisation did not always share Agricola's perception that future generations would wish to understand the historical significance of what he had witnessed and described, but were well aware that they were observing a phenomenon that implied social and economic change. Many of them, such as Reinhold Angerstein, who made his way to England in 1753 to observe the new manufactures, were effectively industrial spies.[†] The *Encyclopédie* of his contemporary Diderot, published from 1751 to 1765, by contrast, combined detailed descriptions of technical developments with irreverent digs at the Church, in order to promote a 'philosophic spirit' in the name of Enlightenment anti-clericalism.[‡] Abraham Rees's

---

[*] Agricola, G., trans. Hoover H. and Hoover, L.H., *De Re Metallica* (New York: Dover, 1950), p. xvi.
[†] R.R. *Angerstein's Illustrated Travel Diary, 1753-1755* (trans. Torsten and Peter Berg) (London: Science Museum, 2001).
[‡] Doyle, W., *The Oxford History of the French Revolution* (OUP, 1990), pp. 51-2.

5 Georgius Agricola – woodcut diagram of a *wassergopel*, probably based on a sketch by Basileus Wefring, 'lest descriptions which are conveyed by words should either not be understood by men of our own time, or should cause difficulty to posterity'.

Cyclopaedia, or Universal Dictionary of Arts and Sciences, published between 1802 and 1819, promoted a spirit of rational Protestant dissent.*

All of these individuals were, of course, fascinated by the novelty of industrialisation. So, in their very different ways were Samuel Smiles, who saw in the changing social relations of industrialisation the opportunity for the determined and the hard-working

---

* Rees, A., *Cyclopaedia, or Universal Dictionary of Arts and Sciences* (Newton Abbot: David and Charles, repr. 1972).

to better themselves, and authors of fiction – Charles Dickens (whose *Hard Times* was set in a barely-disguised Preston), Benjamin Disraeli and Elizabeth Gaskell. The only other major European novelist directly to confront the traumas of industrialisation was Émile Zola, whose *La Bête Humaine* and *Germinal* are set respectively on the Paris to Le Havre railway and in the coalfields of north-eastern France. Ruskin deplored the invasion of the Lake District by the railway, but was fascinated by the steam locomotive.*

Industrialisation was seized on polemically by economists and economic historians, though without any clear party line. 'Pessimists' (those who believed that industrialisation fundamentally impoverished and disempowered plebeian experience) included Friedrich Engels and the 'New Liberal' husband-and-wife team John Lawrence Hammond (1872-1949) and Barbara Hammond (1873-1961).† 'Meliorists' could trace their intellectual ancestry to Macaulay (1800-59) but owed most to Sir John Clapham (1873-1946), who challenged the Hammonds' interpretation from the chair of Economic History at Cambridge, to which he was appointed in 1929. A later meliorist was Professor T.S. Ashton of the London School of Economics (1889-1968), and the debate rages still. It flared up most famously with the 'standard of living' controversy between E.J. Hobsbawm and Max Hartwell.‡

Though the work of these individuals shaped social and political agenda on the left and on the right, none denied the traumas of industrialisation, the violent changes in living standards and the reality of bitter social conflict. In this context, it is painful to record that the preservation of the material remains of industrialisation in Britain begins with sentiment, and with that most powerfully anthropomorphic of machines, the steam locomotive. In 1840 Stephenson's *Rocket* was 'laid up in ordinary' rather than scrapped because its owner had conceived an affection for it. *Rocket* found a home when the London Patent Office Museum opened in 1857, through the efforts of Bennet Woodcroft (1803-79), Assistant to the Commissioner of Patents,§ a passionate but discriminating collector of industrial artefacts. These went to the South Kensington Museum, out of which grew the Victoria and Albert Museum (1909) and the Science Museum (1928).¶

The example was noticed elsewhere in the world. The Deutsches Museum von Meisterwerken der Naturwissenschaft und Technik was opened in 1903. The Smithsonian Museum also exhibited some industrial items, mainly as a consequence of the 1876 centennial exhibition in Philadelphia, though the most significant industrial collection in the USA was the museum established by Henry Ford in Dearborn, Michigan as a tribute to his mentor Thomas Alva Edison. From 1929 it included a long-

---

* Hilton, T., *John Ruskin: The Later Years* (New Haven and London: Yale University Press, 2000), pp. 83-4 (quoting from *The Cestus of Aglaia*) and p. 335 (preface to Robert Somervell's pamphlet *A Protest against the Extension of Railways in the Lake District*).

† Hammond, J. and B., *The Village Labourer 1760-1832* (London: Green, 1911), *The Town Labourer 1760-1832* (London: Longmans, Green and Co., 1917) and *The Skilled Labourer 1760-1832* (London: Longmans, Green and Co., 1919).

‡ Clapham, J., *Economic History of Modern Britain* (Cambridge: Cambridge University Press, three vols, 1926-38); Ashton, T.S., *The Industrial Revolution* (London: Oxford University Press, 1948).

§ Bailey, M.R. and Glithero, J.P., *The Engineering and History of Rocket* (London and York: National Railway Museum, 2000), p. 40.

¶ More recently, fascination with this particular machine has led to an excellent archaeological study, arguably the first of a railway locomotive, by Dr Michael Bailey and Dr John Glithero, *op.cit*.

disused Newcomen engine from Fairbottom near Ashton-under-Lyne in Tameside.* Dedicated societies also came into being, such as the Newcomen Society, founded in 1920 in the United Kingdom to encourage the study of the history of engineering,† and some important local initiatives such as the Sheffield Trades Historical Society were inaugurated.‡

A handful of prescient amateurs began to record historic industrial sites in the early 20th century but it was in the 1940s that attitudes began to change markedly. A technically-driven war had revealed just how out-of-date much British industry actually was – or, to put it another way, just what extraordinary survivors there were. Central to the change in perceptions was an engineer from an Anglo-Irish family, Lionel Thomas Caswall (Tom) Rolt (1910-74), the most significant of the first generation of industrial archaeologists. Rolt describes visiting Ironbridge on the River Severn during the war and being amazed to see plateways delivering materials to craftsmen building barges for the Normandy landings, to watch horses working gin-pits, and to talk to a man who made coracles.§ In 1944 an account of his canal travels, *Narrow Boat*, became an instant success, and made possible the establishment of the Inland Waterways Association, of which he became Honorary Secretary. Charles Hadfield (1909-96), a civil servant and a prolific author of canal histories, served as Vice Chairman. Internal politics soon forced both out of the Association, allowing Rolt to publish *The Inland Waterways of England* in 1949 and to rescue the near-moribund Talyllyn Railway in what is now Gwynedd from closure in 1951. This provided the inspiration for one of Ealing Studios' best comedy films (the first to be made in Technicolor), *The Titfield Thunderbolt*, shot on the former Great Western branch between Limpley Stoke and Camerton in Somerset. The story revolves around a nationalised branch line facing closure, which is rescued by a triumvirate of local worthies (the squire, the vicar and the town clerk), with the capital of a friendly local dipsomaniac and the support of the community as a whole. Only the 'bus company opposes reopening, and they contrive to derail the line's locomotive and carriage the night before the government inspection. The line's original engine, the eponymous *Thunderbolt*, comes to the rescue from having slumbered long in the town museum, an ancient carriage is rescued from a field, and, sure enough, honour is saved.¶ In Titfield, the traditional rural elite still leads a timeless community at odds with the command economy embodied in 'the man from the Ministry'; but the railway has now become part of old England.

How much this was the case was demonstrated by the first major industrial archaeology conservation battle, to save the Doric arch at Euston station in 1962. Harold Macmillan, the Prime Minister, was utterly bemused that anyone should want to preserve such a thing, and the developers were victorious. This conservation failure catalysed later attempts to preserve industrial-era sites and artefacts, and soon provided

---

* Cossons, N., 'A Perspective on the Nature of Industrial Collections', in Dollery, D. and Henderson, J. (eds), *Industrial Collections: Care and Conservation* (Cardiff and London: Council of Museums in Wales and The United Kingdom Institute for Conservation, 1997), pp. 9-15; Nevell, M., Roberts, J. and Champness, B., 'Excavating the Iconic: The Rediscovery of the Fairbottom Bobs Colliery Pumping Engine', *IAR* 26 2 (November 2004), pp. 83-93.

† Cannadine, D., 'Engineering History, or the History of Engineering? Rewriting the Technological Past', *Transactions of the Newcomen Society* 74 2 (2004), pp. 163-180.

‡ This organisation was initiated in 1933, and arose out of Sheffield Trades Technical Societies, established in 1918 under the aegis of the Faculty of Engineering of the University of Sheffield. It was instrumental in the preservation of several important industrial sites within the area.

§ Rolt, L.T.C., *Landscape with Canals* (London: Allen Lane, 1977), pp. 54-7.

¶ Huntley, J., *Railways on the Screen* (Shepperton: Ian Allan, 1993), pp. 180-2.

many people, from very different backgrounds, with an interesting and challenging hobby. Crucial to this were university extra-mural classes, such as those at Birmingham organised by Michael Rix, who, if he did not invent the term 'industrial archaeology', certainly made it current.* Not the least consequence of the social dislocations of the war and the years which followed was the craving for a particular kind of authenticity, whereby the beneficiaries of the post-1945 consensus, typically the products of a grammar school and university education, could feel that they both understood and had kept faith with the generations that had gone before. For some this was 'folk-life', for others the gradually vanishing world of the steam railway, the mill and the mine.†

2.2 Industrial Archaeology

Before long there were grounds for cautious optimism that industrial archaeology might move out of the extra-mural classes to become a recognised university discipline. A few academic appointments were made in the UK in the 1960s and 1970s – at Bath University, Professor Angus Buchanan established the Centre for Study of the History of Technology, where the card-index National Record of Industrial Monuments was housed. The Centre was also host to the meetings which led to the establishment in 1973 of the Association for Industrial Archaeology, whose house-journal, *Industrial Archaeology Review* (1976 to date) effectively superseded *The Journal of Industrial Archaeology* (1964 to 1980). It also encouraged Robert Vogel of the Smithsonian to establish the (American) Society for Industrial Archaeology which held its first annual meeting in 1971. This organisation reflected Angus Buchanan's focus on technology and hardware, although its own journal‡ also reflects stronger American links with engineering rather than archaeology and with initiatives such as the Historic American Engineering Record. This was established in 1969 as part of the federal National Park Service in order to document engineering and industrial heritage; their records (initially a rather more sophisticated card-index) became part of the archive of the Library of Congress. A longer-established American journal is *Technology and Culture*, published by the Society for the History of Technology since 1958.

It was a sign of how quickly the idea became established that several book-length studies were soon published in the UK. The first regional study was Green's *The Industrial Archaeology of County Down* (1963). Others followed – the David and Charles series and the Batsford guides, the Longman series edited by Rolt himself and other thematic or regional studies. Barrie Trinder's remarkable *The Industrial Revolution in Shropshire*, initially published by Phillimore in 1973, proved so durable in conception and scope as to lead to revised incarnations in 1981 and 2000,§ and Colin Rynne's study of Cork has shown how the genre can be developed.¶ A number of important thematic studies were published. Michael Lewis' *Early Wooden Railways*, an overview that extended from

---

* Trinder, B., *'The Most Extraordinary District in the World': Ironbridge and Coalbrookdale* (Chichester: Phillimore, 2005), p. 142.
† The connection is rarely made explicit but underlies more than industrial archaeology and folk-life; see, for instance, Seamus Heaney's poem 'Digging', the first poem in his first collection, *Death of Naturalist*, published in 1966. See Symonds, J., 'Experiencing Industry: Beyond Machines and the History of Technology' in Casella, E. and Symonds, J. (eds), *Industrial Archaeology: Future Directions* (New York: Springer, 2005), pp. 33-57.
‡ This is *IA The Journal of the Society for Industrial Archaeology*, published from Michigan Technical University.
§ Trinder, B., *The Industrial Revolution in Shropshire* (Chichester: Phillimore, 1973,1981, 2000).
¶ Rynne, C., *The Industrial Archaeology of Cork City and its Environs* (Dublin: Stationery Office, 1999).

County Tyrone to the Urals, not only analysed an important industrial site-type but offered a model for how the archaeologist can integrate material and documentary evidence for a period when archival sources are becoming common.* Geoffrey Timmins' work on handloom weavers' cottages established patterns of growth and of economic and technical change in the Lancashire cotton industry.†

Even so, by the 1990s 'i.a.' remained obstinately stuck in the 'hobby' bracket and had failed to sustain the position it had created for itself in the academies a generation earlier. There were encouraging signs; in the USA, a master's programme was established at Michigan Technological University, and in England Dr Marilyn Palmer was awarded a chair in industrial archaeology at Leicester University in 2001. In the UK industrial archaeology made greatest progress in archaeological contracting units. Legislation by this time forced practitioners to come to terms with the archaeology of the industrial period. The adoption of Planning Policy Guidance (PPG) notes 15 and 16 expanded the opportunities for developer-funded recording, whilst English Heritage's Monument Protection Programme (MPP) was initiated in 1991. Scotland was quicker off the mark, with the work of John Hume and the Scottish Industrial Archaeology Survey at the University of Strathclyde, which had already carried out extensive thematic surveys before the SIAS was formally transferred to the Scottish Royal Commission in 1985.

Just as one English organisation encouraged industrial archaeology in the United States, another encouraged it in continental Europe. Neil Cossons, Barrie Trinder and Stuart Smith – all from the newly opened Ironbridge Gorge Museum – hosted the First International Conference on the Conservation of Industrial Monuments (FICCIM) in 1973. This became TICCIH (The International Committee for the Conservation of the Industrial Heritage), a body which *inter alia* provided UNESCO with guidance as to which sites should merit World Heritage status. The emphasis TICCIH placed on British sites reflected the belief that industrialisation was Britain's gift to the world, that it was the child of free trade and that as such its younger sibling was parliamentary democracy.‡ But TICCIH's global role gave its members a global perspective. Once communism collapsed, and delegates could make their way to remote places like the Urals – to Ekaterinburg, where an ancient Bessemer converter still roared away, and to Nizhny-Tagil, where Peter the Great's multi-furnace ironworks survives – it began to appear that Britain's industrial revolution was one of several, and that the parent might as well have been a stern autocrat in a baroque palace as a Hanoverian merchant in a Liverpool counting-house.

2.3 Heritage Management

As industrial archaeology found a voice, its message that industrial heritage should be preserved and managed began to fall on more receptive ears, reflecting a growing feeling that this had less to do with sentiment than with quality of life, as the western

---

* Lewis, M.J.T., *Early Wooden Railways* (London: Routledge and Kegan Paul, 1970).
† Timmins, G., *The Last Shift: the Decline of Handloom Weaving in Nineteenth Century Lancashire* (Manchester: Manchester University Press, 1993).
‡ The connection is made explicit in Trinder, B. and Cossons, N., *The Iron Bridge* (Chichester: Phillimore, 2002), p. 55. The Ironbridge Conservation Area became a World Heritage Site in 1986.

world moved from an industrial to a service economy.* The restoration of the cast-iron Napoleonic *Pont des Arts* in Paris in 1981 and the conservation in the United States of the Troy gasholder in New York State, the Du Pont black powder factory in Delaware and the textile mill town of Lovell in Massachusetts were all notable achievements. In Britain, industrial, or industrial period, structures were increasingly being scheduled as Ancient Monuments or listed from the 1960s. At Beamish, the North of England Open Air Museum, opened in 1970, drew on the Scandinavian 'Skansen' ideal of the open-air folk museum, but gave equal emphasis to the industrial past.† After the Ironbridge Conservation Area was declared a World Heritage Site by UNESCO in 1986, the Blaenavon industrial landscape followed in 2000, the Derwent Valley textile mills and Saltaire in 2001 and the Liverpool waterfront in 2004.

The management of heritage was becoming increasingly professionalised, industrial heritage in particular. This development was partly recognised, partly fostered, by the establishment, in Britain and Ireland at least, of university courses to integrate informed study of the archaeology of industrialisation with cultural resource management, a need recognised by Marilyn Palmer,‡ of which the longest-established and the best-known was initiated at the Ironbridge Institute in 1981. These courses have enjoyed varying fortunes and have for the most part not been established within history or archaeology faculties but within vocational schools of tourism, museum-management or regional development. Partly because of the possibilities for economic regeneration which tourism offers, industrial heritage has had an impact in continental Europe in a way that industrial archaeology has not.§

2.4 Defining the Discipline

Preparing inventories of industrial sites greatly augmented knowledge but did not progress a theoretical basis beyond the David and Charles regional series, with their front-cover photographs of forlorn monuments in the middle of a field. In the meantime, historians and archaeologists had redefined the study of landscape, as the perspective and context which gave monuments their meaning – William Hoskins (1908-92) and Maurice Beresford (1920-2006), more recently Trevor Rowley (b. 1942) and Michael (Mick) Aston (b. 1946). Though none focused particularly on industry, it was as a result of Hoskins' and Beresford's work that articles on industry began to appear in the Victoria County Histories and in 'The Making of the English Landscape' series. In 1982 Barrie Trinder published *The Making of the Industrial Landscape*, which focused on 'mines and manufactures and their immediate surroundings' but which also argued that agriculture and landscapes of recreation need to be regarded as products of industry.¶ Dr Trinder took as his starting point the England and Wales of Celia Fiennes and Daniel Defoe at the turn of the 17th and 18th centuries, half a century before the industrial revolution is commonly assumed to have begun, and traced the

---

* Public support for industrial archaeology eerily paralleled the declining fortunes of British industry – see Hewison, R., *The Heritage Industry: Britain in a Climate of Decline* (Methuen, 1987), p. 31.

† Anon. (George Muirhead), *Beamish; The North of England Open-Air Museum* (Jarrold Publishing, 2003 – museum guidebook).

‡ Palmer, M. and Neaverson, P., *Industrial Archaeology: Principles and Practice* (London and New York: Routledge, 1998), pp. 141-63.

§ Alfrey, J. and Putnam, T., *The Industrial Heritage: managing resources and uses* (London and New York: Routledge, 1992).

¶ Trinder, B., *The Making of the Industrial Landscape* (London: J.M. Dent and Sons, 1982), p. 5.

process of industrialisation within this 'landscape of busy-ness'. The longue durée also informed an extensive landscape survey of the Ironbridge Gorge by Judith Alfrey and Catherine Clark, published in 1993 as The *Landscape of Industry*.* This examined, plot by plot, the landscape evidence for the industrial evolution of this area, tracing its origins to the activities of Wenlock Priory. The book was, however, more than a study of the Gorge; it was an attempt to develop techniques of landscape-based study which might be applicable to other industrial areas.

The landscape context of industrialisation was developed by two scholars associated with the School of Archaeology at the University of Leicester, Peter Neaverson and Marilyn Palmer, in *Industry in the Landscape 1700-1900*,† and by the University of Manchester Archaeological Unit, under two successive directors, John Walker and Dr Michael Nevell. The Unit developed a research strategy which examines the process of transition from an agrarian to an industrial society through the emergence of new site-types and the pattern of their introduction, as they relate to the sphere of influence of *lord, freeholder* and *tenant*. The Unit's work has focused on Tameside, a metropolitan authority within Greater Manchester, during the period 1640-1870, where the social distribution of these sites indicates that the main thrust of industrialisation came from the tenant farmers who were seeking ways of expanding their income, whilst the local land-owners continued to invest in areas they traditionally controlled, such as mineral rights. By these means, a thinly-populated and marginal area in the 17th century became a major industrial region serving a world economy in the 19th.‡ This methodology has been tested and questioned in other areas, and a note of caution sounded. Industry was not the dominant form of economic activity in many areas even of western Europe during the classic industrial period, though areas that remained rural serviced industrial economies.§ Furthermore, it has been argued that within areas that did industrialise, evidence is qualitative as well as quantitative; monument types need to be understood in terms of morphology, growth and decline as well as first appearance.¶

In 1998 Neaverson and Palmer published *Industrial Archaeology: Principles and Practice*, in which they argued strongly that industrial archaeology needed to define its relationship with other forms of archaeological inquiry that looked at the more recent past.** Just as folk life studies had proved to be a one-generation discipline, 'second generation' industrial archaeologists like Neaverson and Palmer noted the failure to build an adequate theoretical base on the foundations laid by pioneers. The failure lay, they suggested, in the limited number of academic posts and a consequent absence of theoretical models. Industrial archaeology had remained largely untouched by the 'new

---

* Alfrey, J. and Clark, C., *The Landscape of Industry: Patterns of Change in the Ironbridge Gorge* (Routledge, 1993).
† Palmer, M. and Neaverson, P., *Industry in the Landscape 1700-1900* (London: Routledge, 1994).
‡ The theoretical framework for this approach has been set out in several volumes, such as Nevell, M. (ed.), *From Farmer to Factory Owner: Models, Methodology & Industrialisation. Archaeological Approaches to the Industrial Revolution in North West England* (Council for British Archaeology, University of Manchester Archaeology Unit and Chester Archaeology, 2003). It has its origins in closure theory, whereby individuals bolster their position by acting as a group which then makes use of exclusion (the exercise of power downwards to control or restrict others) and usurpation (where lower groups wrest rights from more powerful groups). This approach is discussed in Gwyn, D., 'The Landscape Archaeology of the Vale of Ffestiniog', *IAR* 27 1 (May 2004), pp. 129-36.
§ Rynne, C., Hurley, F. and Lyttleton, J., 'The Archaeology of Industrialisation: An Exploration in the Application of the Manchester Methodology to County Offaly' (unpublished report for the Heritage Council, Ireland, November 2003), pp. 20-3.
¶ Gwyn, D., *op. cit.* and 'Publishing and Priority in Industrial Archaeology' in Eleanor Casella and Jim Symonds (eds), *op. cit.*, pp. 121-34.
** Palmer, M. and Neaverson, P., *Industrial Archaeology: Principles and Practice*.

archaeology' of the 1960s and 1970s and its emphasis on culture process, with the result that too many practitioners adhered strictly to the functional interpretation of 'industrial remains'. Social landscape and cultural interaction were still largely ignored.* Others argued that the strength of industrial archaeology lay in its independence from the academies, and that it was fortunate to be sustained by so many informed and active amateurs.†

Other archaeologies of the recent past had grown since the 1950s. Post-Medieval Archaeology had its own society from 1967 and later published its own journal and research agenda. As it established its tenuous foothold in some universities, it borrowed some of the theoretical assumptions of the historical archaeology that had evolved in the USA, where the majority definition is that it is the archaeology of the post-Columbian period. If nothing else, archaeology in the USA has been characterised by a readiness to embrace and argue over theoretical models in a way that many practitioners in Europe find uncongenial. Even before Palmer and Neaverson committed to print the view that industrial archaeology was slow to come to terms with the language of 'processual' archaeology, American journals and monographs were publishing papers challenging its rationalising and deterministic methodology in favour of approaches that stress historical context and change, social and physical environments, active material culture – and the active archaeologist. Post-processual (or 'contextual') archaeology has drawn on Anthony Giddens' structuration theory, with its emphasis on the dynamic interrelationship between human agency and social structure, and on the French anthropologist Pierre Bourdieu's explanation of *habitus* as the interaction of unconscious and the physical world.‡

The post-Columbian period in America marked a shift from a non-literate to a literate or at least partly literate culture, and a premise of historical archaeology is that written evidence has to be integrated with the material evidence. The equivalent period in Europe does not represent a sudden adoption of literacy, but does encompass a major paradigmatic change, in the reformation of the Church, the counter-reformation, and, in the Atlantic isles, a major transfer of land to the secular elite as a result of the dissolution of the monasteries. On this basis some scholars have argued that an equally meaningful 'historical' period of archaeology can be regarded as beginning at much the same time on both sides of the Atlantic, and that in a European context 'historical archaeology', with its potential for a broad chronological sweep, was preferable to the negative associations of 'Post-Medieval' archaeology.§ Some have argued that 'Post-Medieval' is (or should be) the period from the reformation to the industrial revolution – say, 1540 to 1750. This leaves Industrial Archaeology as the archaeology of the period from 1750 to the present day, in which case the argument is advanced that it should encompass the archaeology of consumption as well as of production.¶ Some

---

* Gould, S., review of Cossons, N., *Perspectives on Industrial Archaeology* (2000), *IAR* 23 1 (May 2001), p. 67.
† Clark, K., unpublished paper at joint AIA/Society for Post-Medieval Archaeology, Bristol, 1998.
‡ Structuration argues that it is the repetition of the acts of individual agents which reproduces social structure. Social structure, embodied in traditions, institutions and moral codes can be changed when people start to ignore them, replace them, or reproduce them differently. *Habitus* is similarly reinforced through interaction and the creation of symbolic meanings which sustain ideologies of power.
§ Newman, R., *The Historical Archaeology of Britain c.1540-1900* (Stroud: Sutton, 2001).
¶ Palmer, M., 'Industrial Archaeology: a thematic or a period discipline?', *Antiquity* 64 (1990), pp. 275-85. Here (p. 281) Professor Palmer defines industrial archaeology as 'a period study embracing the tangible evidence of social economic and technological development in the period since industrialization'.

practitioners have claimed the 19th century as 'Post-Medieval', and have suggested that Industrial Archaeology is a thematic study rather than a period one.[*] Another suggestion has been that it should be understood as the archaeology of production within the broader sub-discipline of historical archaeology. To confuse matters still further, other categories again such as '20th-century archaeology' and 'later second millennium archaeology' have been coined.[†]

Though this is largely an academic dispute, the argument is not just about semantics, and it seems likely that, over the next few years, industrial archaeologists will need to find common ground with Post-Medievalists and with historical archaeologists, though precisely how these respective disciplines will define or re-define themselves within this process remains to be seen. It is also unclear whether and in what way a redefined archaeology of the modern period will find favour in university departments. University faculties in Britain are also under pressure to produce results of 'international' significance on 'international' topics, and preferably in 'international' journals. Regional studies do not find favour with grant-awarding bodies nor become priorities within departmental 'mission statements'. Yet it is clear from the archaeological record that industrialisation was a very regional phenomenon – there were profound variations from place to place. It is also clear that the intellectual basis of the archaeology of the period we can associate with industrialisation (to be no more dogmatic than that about it) is in need of re-assessment. Under these circumstances, there is a strong case for looking again at a definable 'region' to focus study *a priori* of its modern archaeology.

2.5 Wales and Gwynedd

To what extent can a regional study such as this do more than add to the overall inventory of monuments? Inventories, after all, there have been in plenty, each one adding its mite to knowledge of the resource. Is it possible that one more could offer something new to say about not only what there is to see 'out there' but the way in which we view the material evidence for the historic but recent past?

Gwynedd offers intriguing possibilities. Politically linked with the rest of Britain and Ireland as a constituent part of the UK (whether or not as an economic colony), economically linked with banking systems in England, and with a wider world through its exports of copper ore and roofing slate, it was (and is) very far from being an anachronistic fief within what some scholars persist in seeing as a Celtic periphery. Yet at the same time, it was little involved with the leading sectors of coal, iron and textiles that distinguished the text-book industrial revolution of England, South Wales and central Scotland.

On this basis Gwynedd might offer a corrective to a view of industrial archaeology written from the standpoint of scholars whose assumptions are those of England and the eastern United States, places where industrialisation did become the dominant economic activity and which led the world. Neither Wales as a whole nor Gwynedd in particular could be described as being purely and simply an exploited colony, a 'robber economy'. Products did not have to go, as Indian cotton did, to the imperial centre for processing before they reached the market-place. Welsh exports circulated within

---

[*] Raistrick, A., *Industrial Archaeology: An Historical Survey* (London: Eyre Methuen, 1972).
[†] Cranstone, D., 'After Industrial Archaeology', in Casella E. and Symonds, J. (eds), *op. cit.*, pp. 77-92.

the same free-trade area as England; Welsh workers were free, not bond. Cultural continuities between Wales and England in the 19th century (and for that matter, with the United States) were strong – the same traditions prevailed, of Protestant Christianity and of the work ethic, and of a social elite open to merchants and engineers. Yet there were also discontinuities – the rocky terrain of Wales, and the Welsh language not least. Partly for these reasons, it is possible to identify in Wales ways of looking at the past, perhaps particularly the industrial past, which are not present in England, or which emerge in different forms and with different emphases.

One view of the Welsh historical past that is still to some extent current, sees it as a matter that saturates the present, and that the people of Wales *are* history rather than enactors or social agents of historical forces. Ever since Chrétien de Troyes in the 12th century redacted tales of King Arthur and his war-band that were already ancient and located them firmly in North Wales, it has seemed easier to believe that gods and heroes rested in Gwynedd's mountains than that miners and quarrymen worked there, and that the long inlets facing the sunset were more apt to row a dying king to Avalon than to speed a trim schooner to Germany or Africa. Matthew Arnold voiced this perception most powerfully in his essay *On the Study of Celtic Literature*, where he identified the 'Celtic genius' as lacking 'The skilful and resolute appliance of means to ends which is needed both to make progress in material civilisation, and also to form powerful states ...' – this on the basis of a visit to Llandudno in 1864, where he evidently remained impervious to activities as varied as copper-mining and house-building going on all around him.[*] Fortunately, historical study (in the sense of document- or memory-based accounts) of the region's industries was already commonplace in many parts of Wales. Village and chapel *eisteddfodau* frequently sponsored competitions on local history topics from the mid-19th century onwards, often with publication in book form as one of the prizes. They were common to both rural and industrial parishes. Such competitions enabled budding writers to hone their skills on documentary sources such as the parish records or company minute books without going to any prohibitive expense, though a show of learning drawn from beyond the parochial boundary always went down well. For all their limitations, they convey the sense of what it must have felt like to be part of the transforming power of modernisation. Nearly all have preserved details which would otherwise have been completely lost, and some are significant works of scholarship in their own right.[†]

This intense sense of belonging to a tight-knit community, inevitable perhaps in a mountainous country, fed into the development of folk-studies in Wales in the early 20th century, which has taken root in a stronger way than it has done in England. The key figure was Dr Iorwerth Cyfeiliog Peate (1901-82) whose achievement was the transformation of the 'Museum of Welsh Bygones' within the National Museum of Wales into a Welsh 'Skansen' at St Ffagans in Glamorgan in which historic buildings could be relocated and conserved. He and other scholars employed by the Museum would make the journey up to the University College of North Wales in Bangor to lecture on folk-life – in the Welsh department, rather than in History or Sociology – as well as to the colleges at Aberystwyth and Swansea, though never to the one on their

---

[*] Arnold, M., *The Study of Celtic Literature* (London: Smith, Elder and Co., 1891), pp. 4, 84.
[†] Examples can be multiplied, though see for instance, 'Sylwedydd', *Chwarelau Dyffryn Nantlle a Chymdogaeth Moel Tryfan* (Cylchwyl Lenyddol Rhostryfan, *c*.1889).

doorstep, in cosmopolitan anglicised Cardiff. Peate drew on the notion of the *gwerin*, the supposedly classless democratic folk-culture of Welsh-speaking Wales, yet never satisfactorily solved the problem of whether industrial Wales did or did not form part of the *gwerin*, just as, though emphatically not a racist, he would have been at a loss to accommodate the increasingly visible Muslim and Hindu communities of South Wales into his vision.*

By contrast, the Marxist or *marxisant* historians of the south Wales coalfields, themselves self-conscious heirs of the radical traditions of the town of Merthyr Tydfil ('cradle of radicals and Welsh Historians')† and of the Monmouthshire valleys, had no trouble accommodating the collier, the puddler and the ironstone-miner into their world-view. The WEA, founded in 1903, with its strong links to the Trade Union movement and to the Labour Party,‡ furnished the apostolic succession from the chapels and debating societies of the 19th-century iron and coal communities to the scholarly activists of the South Wales Miners' Library, to the Welsh Labour History Society and to its journal *Llafur* ('Labour'). The compelling and wayward Professor Gwyn Alf Williams (1925-95) drank at the same spring as the English scholars Richard Cobb and E.P. Thompson, but Antonio Gramsci, Fidel Castro and Ché Guevara also flavoured the heady brew he dispensed at the University of York and later (from 1974) at Cardiff. His bravura and over-stated performances on television placed the industrial history and social turmoil of the valleys, and in particular Merthyr, at the forefront of debate on contemporary Welsh politics and identity. Not all his goals were achieved; his Cardiff Research Unit on the industrial history of South Wales was founded on the boast that South Wales would stretch as far as Amlwch in Anglesey – one of the many promises it never delivered.§

North-west Wales remained largely immune from the intellectual ferment of the south. Given its patchy history of industrialisation and its strongly Welsh-language traditions, it was not surprising that Iorwerth Peate should speak more compellingly to the *gwerin* than Gramsci. One seminal study of North Walian industrial workers which did owe much to wider currents of thought was Merfyn Jones's *The North Wales Quarrymen 1874-1922*, published in 1981.¶ The author (endorsed characteristically by Gwyn Williams as 'the most brilliant, the most trenchant and the most effective of a stunning new generation of Welsh historians') was brought up in a former slate-quarrying district of Gwynedd, and had carried out the initial research as a PhD thesis at Warwick University, becoming a co-director of the Social Sciences Research Council coalfield project at Swansea before moving on to Liverpool University and ultimately to a chair and the university vice-chancellorship at Bangor.

Merfyn Jones's study examines the years from the establishment of the North Wales Quarrymen's Union until its amalgamation with the Transport and General Workers' Union, but concentrates particularly on the traumatic strike in the Penrhyn slate quarries, the largest regionally-based employer, from 1900 to 1903, which ended in victory for the quarries' owner, Lord Penrhyn. As Professor Jones points out:

---

* Owen, T.M., 'Iorwerth Peate a Diwylliant Gwerin', *Trafodion Anrhydeddus Gymdeithas y Cymmrodorion/Transactions of the Honourable Society of Cymmrodorion* new series 5 (1995), pp. 62-79.
† Morgan, K.O., *Times Literary Supplement*, 1 March 1985, p. 220.
‡ Morgan, K.O., *Rebirth of a Nation: Wales 1880-1980* (Oxford: Oxford University Press, 1981), p. 293.
§ Jenkins, G., *The People's Historian Professor Gwyn A. Williams (1925-1995)* (Aberystwyth: Centre for Advanced Welsh and Celtic Studies, 1996), p. 6.
¶ Jones, R.M., *The North Wales Quarrymen 1874-1922* (Cardiff: University of Wales Press, 1981).

The interest of the episode resides in the fact that men with a non-revolutionary and far from clear class-consciousness, were nevertheless able, in a particular place and time, to conduct a struggle which in a very real sense raised fundamental issues of control and power.*

Jones suggests that the failure of the strike led the quarrymen to break the Radical/Liberal consensus as defined by the region's middle class and to move, slowly and with difficulty, to adopt the language of Labour. There is much truth in this argument – in 1922 the secretary of the union became Labour MP for Caernarvonshire – yet Gwynedd did not remain faithful to Labour for long, returning well before the end of the 20th century to a progressive/nationalist identity which found expression in Plaid Cymru. Though the Thatcher-Reagan decade, just opening as the book was published, elsewhere in Wales and beyond forced some spectacular rethinking of the theoretical assumptions on which labour history was based,† the one subsequent book-length study of the strike, written by Dr Jean Lindsay with the co-operation of the Penrhyn family, failed to redraw the picture.‡

6 An iconic figure: Geoff Charles' photograph of the former quarryman William Williams brings out (as it is meant to do) the stoicism and bewilderment of a generation which saw its entire way of life come to an end. Mr Williams contemplates the closure of Dinorwic quarry, where he spent his whole career (courtesy NLW: GC/F2/20).

What both Jones and Lindsay emphasised and reinforced was that the struggle brutally focused issues of control and of cultural identity in a way that spoke to both the nationalist and progressive traditions, both at the beginning of the 20th century and at its end. Whatever else this demonstrates, it made the quarryman an icon of a certain type of Welshness (Figure 6). This has found its expression in many different ways. The English artist Mary Elizabeth Thompson (1896-1981), who made her home in Bethesda, drew the men who worked in the Penrhyn, Dinorwic, Dorothea and Pen yr Orsedd slate quarries and in the stone quarries of Penmaenmawr, bringing out their qualities of strength, craft and intelligence. Though the influence of both Rodin and Meštrović is apparent in her work, her drawings are portraits of individuals, men whom she knew and whose language she learnt.§ Less solemn but equally relevant is Gwenlyn Parry and Rhydderch Jones's television situation comedy broadcast between

---

* *Ibid.*, p. 328.
† Evans, C., *The Labyrinth of Flames: work and social conflict in early industrial Merthyr* (Cardiff: University of Wales Press, 1993), p. 8. It is only right to mention in this context an earlier study by a veteran Marxist and Congregationalist lay-preacher (a not-unusual combination in Wales), Roose-Williams, J., *Quarryman's Champion: the Life and Activities of William John Parry of Coetmor* (Denbigh: Gwasg Gee, 1978). The tone of this study dates it, but it remains a perceptive and important account.
‡ Lindsay, J., *The Great Strike: A History of the Penrhyn Quarry Dispute of 1900-1903* (Newton Abbot: David and Charles, 1987).
§ Anon., *Artist yn y Chwarel/An Artist in the Quarries* (Cardiff: Welsh Arts Council, 1981).

1972 and 1977, *Fo a Fe* ('Him [North Walian] and Him' [South Walian]) about two widowers who live with their grown-up children, a married couple, in Cardiff. The North Walian, played by Guto Roberts, is a former quarryman, Ephraim, a deacon whose idea of a Christmas present is a new copy of *Taith y Pererin* ('Pilgrim's Progress'), living in a Beckettian impasse with Ryan Davies's beer-drinking communist retired coal-miner, Twm Tomos.*

Few Rhondda coal-miners, even retired ones, were Welsh-speakers by the 1970s, but the unique history of the slate industry had been instrumental in preserving Welsh as the language of choice for the majority of the people of north-west Wales. When Gwynedd Council initiated a particularly pro-active programme to support the Welsh language, it was, in a sense, preserving an important part of the industrial heritage of the region, though it was not, of course, undertaken for that reason. Rather, it is true to say that the will to preserve in Gwynedd has been focused on the intangible forms of cultural heritage, above all, on language.

Preservation of industrial artefacts, by contrast, though it has a long pedigree in the region, was for a long time the preoccupation of individuals who had not grown up in the culture. As in England, the story begins with steam locomotives. In 1882, *Fire Queen*, which had drawn slate trains on Assheton Smith's private railway since 1848, escaped scrapping allegedly because its owner's daughter had grown fond of it.[†] Disused locomotives on the Penrhyn Quarry Railway survived the scrap drive of the Second World War only because J.H. Battersby, the quarry's Manx engineer, deliberately mislaid the key to their windowless shed when the requisitioning authorities came round and swore blind that the building was empty.[‡]

It was in north-west Wales that the movement to preserve and operate an entire industrial/technical system first achieved success, when the Talyllyn Railway was taken over by volunteers in 1951. Much of the credit for this achievement belongs to Tom Rolt, who published a thoughtful and perceptive account of the trials of keeping this near-decrepit line alive in the first crucial years as *Railway Adventure*.[§] Though this was the story which provided the inspiration for *The Titfield Thunderbolt*, there were some crucial changes – far from being state-owned, it was the personal property of a local businessman and former county MP Sir Henry Haydn Jones, and the Talyllyn's rescuers were sympathetic outsiders, not community leaders (Figure 7). Since then, railway preservation with volunteer labour has become a significant element of the regional economy and culture. It has also fed directly into the study of industrial archaeology, as many railway enthusiasts also developed an interest in the slate quarries that had brought the railways into being (see chapter 1). In 1970, week-long courses in the recording of industrial sites were established under the tutelage of Dr Michael Lewis. Initially these were based at Coleg Harlech, the workers' college on the shores of Cardigan Bay, before finding a long-term home at Plas Tan y Bwlch, a former land- and quarry-owner's home in the Vale of Ffestiniog that had re-opened as the Snowdonia National Park Study Centre. Plas Tan y Bwlch also became the headquarters of a

---

* As if *Fo a Fe* were not enough, a further *reductio ad absurdum* on the theme of virtuous quarryman is the headline of Tony Curtis' review of Russell Celyn Jones' attempt at a Welsh magical realist novel, *An Interference of Light*, 'Gay Surfer on Acid meets Striking Quarryman' – *Planet* 114 (n.d.), p. 115.
† Boyd, J.I.C., *Narrow Gauge Railways in North Caernarvonshire Volume 3* (Oxford: Oakwood, 1986), p. 68.
‡ Pers. comm., Iorwerth Jones.
§ Rolt, L.T.C., *Railway Adventure* (London: Constable, 1953).

7 Early days on the Talyllyn Railway; at this stage steam locomotives (in this case a standard class 4) were still operating on British Railways' Cambrian coast line (courtesy NLW: GC/R/576/D).

remarkable group of men from the nearby slate-quarry town of Blaenau Ffestiniog who without any formal training set about recording the industrial archaeology of their area and of the region, producing work of an astonishingly high standard.*

However, at institutional and governmental level, attitudes to the industrial past were ambiguous. The slate quarries were perceived as poor employers, so neither local government officers nor the majority of people who lived in what were becoming post-industrial towns and villages had much interest in perpetuating the visible evidence of the past. The collapse of a coal tip at Aberfan in South Wales in 1966, killing over a hundred children, emphasised that the post-industrial landscape was potentially lethal as well as unattractive (Figure 8), and prompted the Welsh Office to spend large sums removing some tips and levelling others. Slate tips are more stable structures than coal tips, yet in some places they were 'landscaped' at considerable expense, producing an environment that was neither natural nor industrial, and attempts were begun, which continue to this day, to find a way of encouraging plant and tree growth on them.

At the same time, a more sympathetic attitude also began to emerge. There had been a few lone voices associated with the University College of North Wales (now UWB), even before the war – Professor A.H. Dodd (1891-1975) had produced the remarkable *The Industrial Revolution in North Wales* in 1931, and his research student

---

* Jones, G.R., *Hafodlas Slate Quarry* (privately published, 1997).

8 Aberfan, South Wales, 1966 – discovering bodies (courtesy Bryn Campbell, NLW Llyfrau ffoto 3850 D).

Dylan Pritchard (1911-50) carried out invaluable research into the slate industry before his early death.* In 1959 the National Museum of Wales appointed D. Morgan Rees (1913-78), a factory inspector who had graduated at Aberystwyth and at Cambridge, as its first keeper of the Department of Industry. He became Keeper-in-Charge of the Welsh Industrial and Maritime Museum at Cardiff in 1977, but regarded the whole of Wales as his parish, lecturing and generally proselytising over the whole country, as well as producing two book-length studies.† He made possible the purchase in 1969 by the National Museum of the remarkable quadrangular engineering workshops of the Dinorwic quarry as a northern outpost, where the slate industry could be interpreted – though this decision also owed much to the advocacy of Douglas Hague (1917-90), an investigator with the Royal Commission on the Ancient and Historical Monuments of Wales from 1948 to 1981. The RCAHMW had begun the recording of the more important industrial sites in the 1960s; its staff have gone on to publish a series of important works on canals, early railways and collieries in South Wales, as well as a major survey of Swansea's copper-smelting landscapes.‡ Cadw appointed a full-time industrial archaeology specialist in 1990. Cadw's hope was that the increasing interest in industrial archaeology shown by the four Welsh archaeological trusts in the light of PPG 15 and 16 would be taken up by the university, but in fact it was a long time before any of the constituent colleges showed any interest in this area. When the archaeology of the modern world did establish a toe-hold it was in the new departments of heritage management.

A significant departure was the publication of the *Register of Landscapes of Outstanding Historic Interest in Wales* by Cadw, ICOMOS UK and the Countryside Council for Wales

---

* Dodd, A.H., *The Industrial Revolution in North Wales* (Cardiff: University of Wales Press, 1933, 1951, 1971, repr.. Wrexham: Bridge Books, 1990).

† These are *Mines, Mills and Furnaces: an introduction to Industrial Archaeology in Wales* (London: HMSO, 1969) and *The Industrial Archaeology of Wales* (Newton Abbot: David and Charles, 1975). See obituary for David Morgan Rees in *AIA Bulletin* 6 2 (1978), p. 4.

‡ Hughes, S., *The Archaeology of the Montgomeryshire Canal* (1989); *The Archaeology of an Early Railway System: the Brecon Forest Tramroads* (1990); (with Brian Malaws *et al.*) *Collieries of Wales* (n.d.); *Copperopolis: Landscapes of the Early Industrial Period in Swansea* (2000) (all published at Aberystwyth by the RCAHMW).

in 1998. Of the 36 landscapes so designated, 15 lay within the north-western quadrant of Wales. In each case industrial sites were included as elements of the historic character, not only in places like Amlwch or Blaenau Ffestiniog where they utterly dominate but also within more varied and largely rural areas such as Penrhyn Llŷn. Other landscapes elsewhere in Wales on the *Register* that were largely industrial included Merthyr Tydfil and Blaenavon. As the foreword made clear, landscapes of outstanding historic significance were not necessarily also landscapes of scenic beauty:

> Some indeed are ugly, sharp-edged and intensive with painful memories, but nevertheless landscapes whose loss would be a form of cultural cleansing.*

A later *Register of Landscapes of Special Historic Interest in Wales*, published in 2001, included such notable former industrial areas as the Clydach Gorge and the Rhondda.†

The *Register* anticipated the European Landscape Convention's emphasis on landscape as an essential of participatory democracy and of sustainable development, and as essential to tourism. The *Registers* were advisory and non-statutory, but the inclusion of places such as Merthyr and Blaenau Ffestiniog represented a change in perception of the historic environment. The seal was set with the nomination of the Blaenavon industrial landscape in South Wales for World Heritage status, granted by TICCIH in December 2000. As such, Blaenavon joined the existing Welsh World Heritage Sites including the castles of Edward I, and the dozen or so industrial sites world-wide, including the Ironbridge Gorge in Shropshire. A blighted and desperately impoverished area of Wales now began to reap the indirect benefits of its citation, and neighbouring towns which had demolished much of their historic industrial infrastructure and housing now regretted the course they had taken. All over Wales, an important lesson began to sink in.

2.6 Summary and Conclusion

Industrial archaeology, at least in its functional interpretation (the study of the material evidence of industrial sites), has a strong and informed hobby-following, both in Wales and beyond. It is also recognised within professional archaeological units and contracting organisations. Whereas it has established a precarious foot-hold in universities in England and elsewhere in the English-speaking world, it has made very little progress in the University of Wales, any more than any archaeology of a later period than the medieval. The situation in the universities is complicated by the current debate on the nature of the archaeology of the recent past, yet the fact that the debate is taking place at all is encouraging, and the establishment of courses in heritage management offers the opportunity for further dialogue within academe.

Just as industrialisation and social change took very different regional and national forms, it is also clear that attitudes to the industrial and to the recent past vary considerably within different cultural groups. Industrial archaeology as it is understood in Wales and perhaps particularly in north-west Wales is the product of social and

---

* Cadw, ICOMOS UK and the Countryside Council for Wales, *Register of Landscapes of Outstanding Historic Significance in Wales* (Cardiff, 1998), p. ix.
† *Register of Landscapes of Special Historic Interest in Wales* (Cardiff, 2001).

intellectual forces that are recognisably different from those which have moulded the discipline elsewhere in the world, even from those in neighbouring England – or perhaps especially from England, given the tendency of smaller national groups to define themselves in opposition to a dominant culture. It is not surprising that historical understanding should be influenced by the distinct form that industrialisation has taken within different social and cultural groupings, nor that factors such as language and religion should play a part. Gwynedd provides the opportunity for a regional study with the potential to examine many of the assumptions that underlie archaeological approaches to the recent past.

Chapter 3

TOPOGRAPHICAL, CULTURAL AND ECONOMIC CONTEXT

3.1 Topography

The topography of Gwynedd – the north-west quadrant of Wales – contains a considerable variety of landscape, yet forms a distinct area, markedly different from its neighbouring regions. Taking the Conwy valley and its tributaries as the eastern boundary, the lands beyond are characterised by gently rolling hills and areas of moorland as well as the rich agricultural valleys of the Clwyd and the headwaters of the Dee. To the south-east and east, the Dyfi valley forms a natural boundary; beyond, the Severn gathers on the slopes of Plynlimon.* Its northern coast forms part of Liverpool Bay, its west coast, Cardigan Bay; the east coast of Ireland lies barely 100km away (Map 1).

Anglesey itself, an island separated from the mainland of Wales by the narrow but turbulent Menai Strait, has been since Prehistoric times one of the great granaries of Wales, a rich agricultural landscape which earned it the name *Mam Cymru*, 'the Mother of Wales'. It also contained commercially viable mineral deposits – copper ore on Mynydd Parys, coal in the marshy inlet between Llangefni and Malltraeth, and limestone, the so-called 'Anglesey marble', along its south-eastern coast. Its western shore was exposed to the prevailing winds, but along its northern and eastern coasts vessels could be loaded and unloaded with comparative ease. Holyhead became the packet harbour for Ireland, and the little harbour at Cemaes, now given over to pleasure- and fishing-vessels, was reckoned by the Medieval *Trioedd Ynys Prydein* ('Triads of the Isle of Britain') as one of the three principal ports of the Island of Britain.† At Amlwch in the late 18th century the narrow creek became crammed with vessels exporting copper ore from Parys to the smelters of Swansea and South Lancashire, and Traeth Coch, where once Vikings had established themselves, became the entrepôt for the island's limited coal exports, as well as the landing place for consumer goods from Liverpool.

The topography of the Gwynedd mainland, the Edwardian counties of Caernarvonshire and Merioneth, is dominated by the Snowdonian massif and the Carneddau in the north, by the Rhinogydd and by Cader Idris in the south. Much of the land is poor, and only suitable for sheep grazing, with very little of it under tillage crops, yet here and there – in the Conwy valley, on the Arfon coastal plain and in Penrhyn Llŷn – are areas where beef and dairy cattle are also raised. The mountains

---

* The total area thus represented is 3,979km² (397,900 hectares, 1,536 square miles).
† Bromwich, R., *Trioedd Ynys Prydein: The Triads of the Isle of Britain* (Cardiff: University of Wales Press, 2006), p. 255.

Map 1 Topography

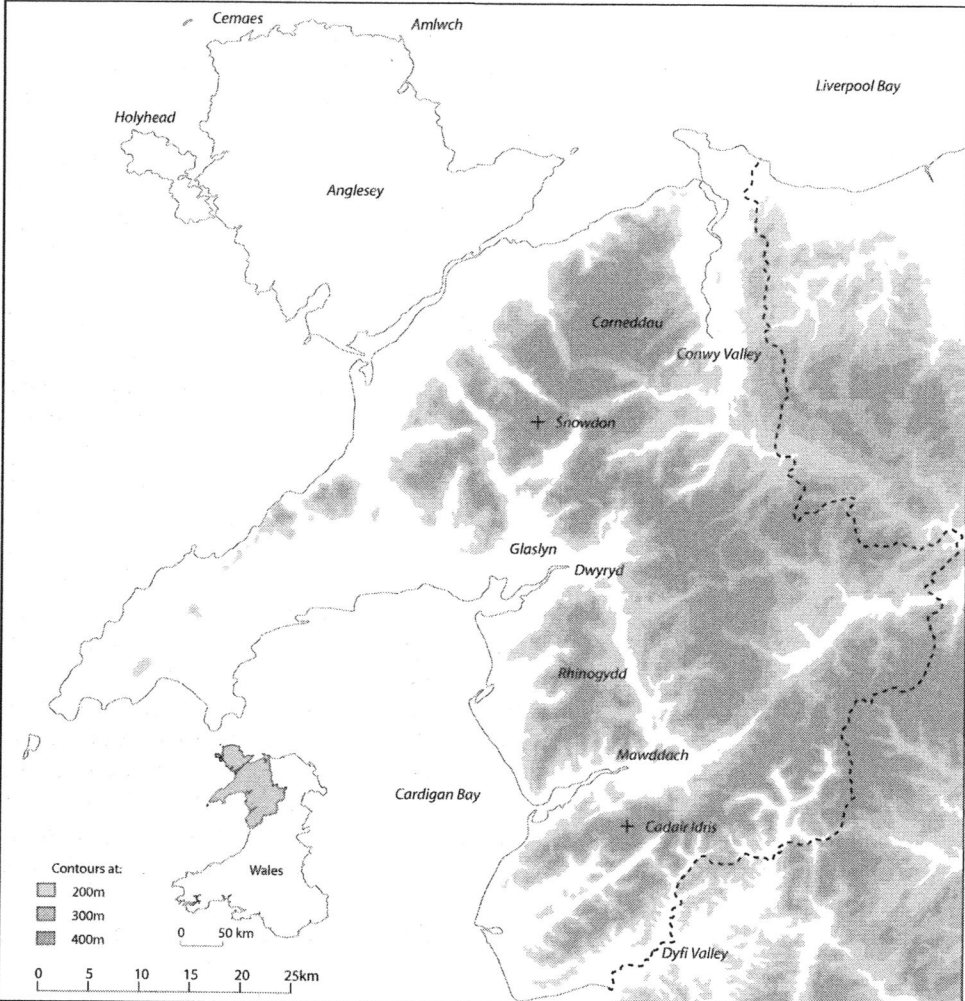

are rich in minerals, and the heartlands can be accessed by a number of tidal rivers and estuaries – the Conwy, the longest tidal river in Wales, the Glaslyn, until it was enclosed by a sea-wall between 1808 and 1813, the Dwyryd and the Mawddach.

3.2 Cultural Context

3.2.1 Pre-modern history

The record of continuous human occupation in the region begins after the last ice-age. Anglesey was an established centre of the Druidic religion until the arrival of Suetonius Paulinus in AD 60, when the legions laid waste their sacred groves – where these were, no-one knows. Otherwise the Roman occupation left native structures comparatively undisturbed. *Romanitas* remained an important concept to the successor dynasties which established themselves as the rulers of *Uenedos* (= Gwynedd) after the collapse of imperial authority, but more long-lasting in its effects were the adoption of Christianity by the sixth century and the change, at much the same time, in the inflected British language spoken from before the Roman occupation to a form of speech recognisable as Welsh. This forms one of the Celtic language group, and is closely related to Breton and to Cornish, as well as having a more distant relationship to Irish, the Gaelic of Scotland and the Manx language. It is spoken by the majority of the population of Gwynedd. It has official status in both local and national government, and an extensive literature.

Gwynedd's dynasties maintained a precarious independence from alien rule until well into the Anglo-Norman period, at a time when other parts of Wales were falling under the sway of the marcher lords. Though traditionally Gwynedd has been taken to mean the *pura Wallia* of the north-west, it fluctuated in size and shape with the successes and reversals of its princes. Its emergence as the dominant force in Welsh politics in the 13th century reflects the state-building of its last native rulers, who sponsored an emerging feudal society and were alive to continental influences.* The Cistercians were established at Cymer Abbey in 1198-9 under the patronage of Maredudd ap Cynan, and at Aberconwy shortly before. Gruffudd ap Cynan 'made Gwynedd glisten with lime-washed churches', and Llywelyn Fawr founded proto-towns, though it was only with the conquest by Edward I in the 1290s that boroughs came to be established on any scale. These were substantial walled *bastide* settlements and castles such as the Plantagenets had already established in Gascony, and which Edward also set about building elsewhere in Wales. This ambitious project, realised over the space of 12 years, cost him ten times his annual income, and was financed by Tuscan bankers. The intention was that the burgesses of these new settlements were to civilise a wild region and introduce a money economy. It has meant that north-west Wales has a legacy of Medieval military architecture and defended settlement that is of international significance, but it was to be another 500 years before the towns significantly changed the economy of their hinterlands.

The Edwardian settlement applied the English shrieval system to Gwynedd, which now became the counties of Anglesey, Caernarvonshire and Merioneth. The Laws in Wales Acts of 1535-42 applied to the whole of Wales, and aimed to 'extirpate … the sinister usages and customs of Wales', but provided for a more beneficial relationship between the Welsh elite and central government in London. The administration of the area was effectively handed over to a class of (usually) native Welsh gentry who now became justices of the peace, eight for each county, appointed by the Lord Chancellor of England, initially on the advice of the Lord President of the Council of Wales. These gentry families and their successors ruled Wales until the late 19th century.

The religious settlement of the 16th century was slow to put down roots until after the publication in 1588 (that year of Protestant triumph) of a Welsh translation of the Bible by Dr William Morgan. This single act, more than any other, ensured the survival of the Welsh language, and paved the way for the 18th-century circulating schools, sponsored by the Society for the Promotion of Christian Knowledge. Though their purpose was to ensure basic literacy to read the word of God, they also

---

* Stephenson, D., *The Governance of Gwynedd* (Cardiff: UWP, 1984).

ensured that ordinary Welsh people became literate in their own language before they had any knowledge of English. They in turn made possible the remarkable revival throughout Wales of the 'Old Dissent' (the Baptists and the Congregationalists, who had traditionally enjoyed very little support since their first appearance in the 16th century) and the emergence of the 'New Dissent' (the Wesleyans and the Calvinistic Methodists, the latter the only uniquely Welsh denomination). Between the late 18th century and the middle of the 19th the great majority of the population of Wales as a whole changed their allegiance from church to chapel, from the reformed Anglican (Episcopal) communion to the radical Protestantism of the dissenting congregations.

The causes of the rise of the chapels are still a matter of debate; their growth was common to rural and industrial areas, and to all parts of Wales, though the north-west was from early days a great nursery of preachers, from strongholds such as Llangefni in Anglesey and Bala in Merioneth. Dissent grew to be a particularly formidable political and social force in Wales; it ensured that until well into the 20th century all Welsh men and women, Anglicans and Catholics as well as those who followed other faiths or none, grew up in the shadow of the chapel. The legacy of the chapels remains controversial, yet there is no doubt that their positive contributions to Welsh life include a strong democratic tradition and an encouragement to learning.

Partly in the wake of the revitalised religious life of Wales came a remarkable cultural revival – or perhaps it would be truer to say, a whole series of cultural revivals. Welsh poetry had been influenced by some of the themes and motifs of the continental renaissance, but retained many of its traditional forms, including a dedication to intricate internal rhyming and assonance. Though many of the gentry still sponsored a bard into the 18th century, whose function was, much as it probably had been in the Iron Age, to compose praise songs and to celebrate family events, a new generation of poets began to emerge, less dependent on the goodwill of the patricians, many of whom were now unable or unwilling to speak Welsh. Some of these were in areas of Wales from which the language has since largely retreated, such as the Vale of Glamorgan, where *Iolo Morgannwg*, Edward Williams (1747-1826) held sway, or around the ironworks of Merthyr and Dowlais and the neighbouring market town of Abergavenny, under the influence of the remarkable Lady Charlotte Guest (1812-95). The Morris brothers from Anglesey led a literary renaissance which was felt in Gwynedd, particularly around the village of Llanystumdwy, where later David Lloyd George grew up, and along the Gwyrfai valley. Some members of these groups were churchmen, some were sympathetic to the Evangelical movement and to Methodism; some even flirted with Jacobinism. Tavern get-togethers called *eisteddfodau* (literally 'sittings') increasingly led to adjudicated competitions, and to the distinctive village-based literary culture which marks the life of Welsh-speaking Wales in the Modern period. Prose was also encouraged – mainly historical, religious or critical; fiction in Welsh barely emerged before the last decade of the 19th century, other than the improving moral tales which appeared in denominational magazines and other explicitly religious publications.

The literary awakening and the rise of religious dissent reflected a gulf between patricians and plebeians which continued to widen and deepen in the 19th century. Initially the chapels were quietist in their politics, and revolutionary teachings made next to no impact in Gwynedd. Sympathy for the French Revolution withered away when it became clear that this was no anti-papal shift among the governing classes such as the Glorious Revolution had been in England, and which any loyal Protestant could therefore in good conscience support. The Methodists were sometimes explicitly Tory in their sympathies. When in 1839 the Chartists of Monmouthshire had marched on the town of Newport in South Wales, no-one was quicker to condemn the rising than the leader of Anglesey Methodism, the Rev. John Elias of Llangefni, whose detractors called him 'the Pope'. Much more far-reaching in its effect was the reaction to a government report published in 1842 on the state of school education in Wales, which caused great offence amongst Welsh speakers and chapel-goers by equating the language and religious dissent with immorality and ignorance. Thereafter and for many years, the Welsh were increasingly anxious to cast themselves as, and to be seen to be, a moral community. From the 1850s the chapels increasingly and publicly called for temperance or total abstinence from alcohol, and the ethic of respectability took powerful hold in Wales. The arrival of working-class consumer choice in the comparatively prosperous years of the 1870s increased the temptation for young colliers and quarrymen and their wives to deck themselves out in cheap finery, but it also made it possible for this new aristocracy of the working class to embody the virtues of the Gladstonian democracy, with their comfortable well-appointed homes and hire-purchase pianos. The chapels ultimately found their voice as radical and campaigning organisations, supporting the Anti-Corn Law League and the Liberation Society.

By this stage the wealthy landowning families were already beginning their long retreat from political power, and indeed from wealth and land-ownership. The election of 1868 sent shock-waves around Wales, as for the first time families which had represented the area in parliament for generations found themselves under pressure from forces they barely understood. Welsh political life had with some exceptions been dominated by the Tories for as long as England had been dominated by the Whigs – effectively since 1688. Now Whigs were mutating into Liberals, and were moving into the ascendant. True, their candidates and MPs were initially themselves landed gentlemen, even though some were hardly 'old money' – men such as David Williams (1799-1869), a solicitor from the remote parish of Llanfihangel Bellacheth, who became rich enough to buy the Deudraeth estate and to send his son to Eton, and who served as MP for Merioneth in 1868-9. His successor was Samuel Holland (1803-92), an English-born quarry-tenant from Blaenau Ffestiniog and a Unitarian. He in turn was followed by Tom Ellis (1859-99), a Methodist tenant-farmer's son from near Bala, a graduate of the new University College at Aberystwyth and of New College, Oxford. The Caernarvon Boroughs constituency was represented from 1890 to 1945 by the Liberal David Lloyd George (1863-1945), Prime Minister of the United Kingdom from 1916 to 1922, one of the towering figures of modern British politics. He had been brought up in the village of Llanystumdwy, and learnt his skills as a lawyer in the harbour town of Porthmadog and the quarry town of Blaenau Ffestiniog. Anglesey similarly aligned itself with the Liberals from 1868 onwards, and in all the constituencies of the area represented in this volume the overall pattern is the same – the Tory/Conservative domination coming to an end in 1868, and thereafter the Liberal high noon until the 20th century and the dominance of Labour, followed by the successes of Plaid Cymru ('the Party of Wales') from the 1970s onwards. Even so, the Conservatives managed some sort of fighting retreat; they briefly recaptured Lloyd George's old constituency in 1945 before it was abolished a few years later and, with the influx of English retirees changing the island's demographic patterns, they were able win back Anglesey in 1979 and to hold on to it until 1987.*

The late 20th century saw constitutional and administrative change in Wales unmatched since 1535-42. Local government reform in 1972 saw the restoration of the historic name Gwynedd for an area approximately corresponding to the historic counties of Caernarvonshire, Anglesey and Merioneth, though in 1996 the boundaries were redrawn again and Anglesey (or Ynys Môn, to give it its Welsh name) became a separate county. In 1998 the people of Wales voted, by the narrowest of majorities, for an assembly, ultimately established at Cardiff, which gave them, for the first time in their history, a measure of self-government, within a broader United Kingdom and European Union framework.

3.3 Economic Context

3.3.1 Pre-modern industry

Industrial activity has a long pedigree within the area. Much the earliest site is the axe-quarry and factory at Mynydd Rhiw in Penrhyn Llŷn, where as early as the Mesolithic period a series of shallow pits were worked, each one being backfilled after it had grown too deep. On a much larger scale was the late Stone-Age axe factory at Penmaenmawr, dubbed 'a Sheffield of the Stone Age'.† In the Bronze Age, copper was worked from substantial underground chambers at Mynydd Parys in Anglesey and the Great Orme, part of a production area that included a number of sites in mid-Wales, in south-west Ireland, Bradda Head in the Isle of Man and two isolated sites in England – Alderley Edge in Cheshire and Ecton Hill in Staffordshire.‡ Further evidence continues to turn up at the two Gwynedd sites, and it is possible that other Bronze-Age sites may be conclusively identified, yet there is much that remains uncertain – for instance, no smelting site has yet been identified. If anything, less is known about industry in later Prehistory. Characteristic of the very late Bronze Age and early Iron Age is the occupation of enclosed or unenclosed hill-top settlements, several of which have turned up evidence of smelting – of iron at Bryn y Castell and Crawcwellt, possibly of copper at Ty Mawr on Holy Island. The copper is likely to have come from one or other of the sites worked in earlier times, but the origin of the iron ore is unknown.

The Romans actively prospected for, and worked, mineral ores elsewhere in Wales. At Dolaucothi in the south-west, evidence for complex hushing systems and waterwheel pumping systems has survived. In the north-west, evidence is strong but only circumstantial. Copper-ore 'cakes' (plano-convex ingots) have been discovered in sufficient number on Anglesey to make it highly likely that the Parys mines were

---

* Jones, B., *Etholiadau'r Ganrif* (Y Lolfa, 1999).

† Bradley, R. and Edmonds, M., *Interpreting the Axe Trade – production and exchange in Neolithic Britain* (Cambridge, 1993).

‡ The most useful summary of the evidence so far published is Simon Timberlake's 'Archaeological and Circumstantial Evidence for Early Mining in Wales' in Ford, T. D. and Willies, L., *Mining Before Powder* (Peak District Mines Historical Society Bulletin vol. 12 3, Historical Metallurgy Society Special Publication), pp. 133-43. Unless otherwise acknowledged, this paragraph and the following two are based on this paper.

Map 2 Industry and settlement pre-1700

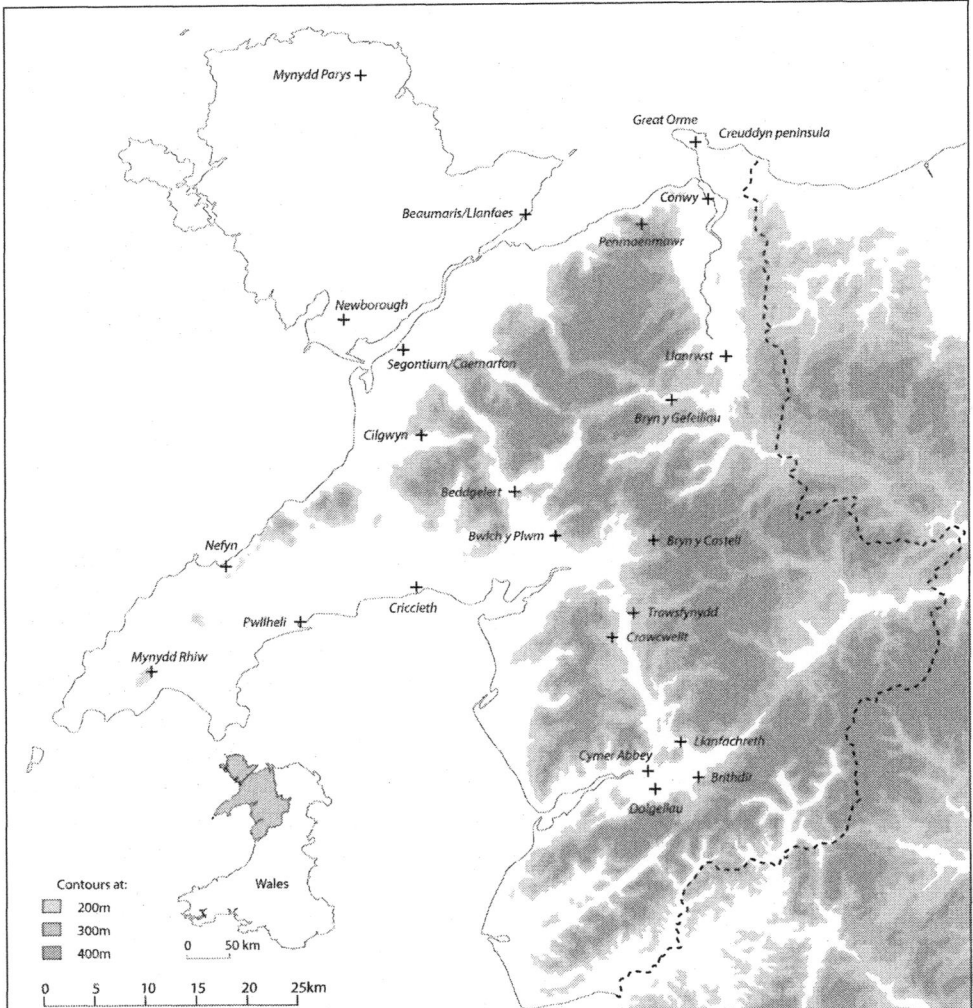

exploited in the Roman period, and it is probable that the Great Orme mines were as well. It is not clear whether these workings were under Imperial or legionary control or whether they represent a native response to Roman demand, but the configuration of the fort at *Segontium* (Caernarfon) suggests an increased emphasis on economic rather than purely military activities in the early third century AD.[*] Two lead smelting hearths have been identified in a building of the first-second century AD outside the fortlet at Brithdir in Merioneth, probably processing ore from a nearby outcrop, but a number of other possible Roman lead-mine sites have been suggested, such as Bwlch y Plwm (mountain pass of the lead), where the Roman road is presumed to have crossed the estuary of the Traeth mawr, and at Cae Mawr near Capel Curig, near the Roman fort

---

[*] Nash-Williams, V.E., *The Roman Frontier in Wales* (Cardiff: University of Wales Press, 1969 – second edition, revised Michael G. Jarrett), pp. 62-3.

of Bryn y Gefeliau (hill of the smithies). Sawn slate blocks have been identified in the Mithraeum at Segontium, confirming that the slate industry dates to the Roman period.*

It is likely that organised mineral extraction and any other forms of industrial activity largely ceased in the immediate post-Roman period and for several centuries thereafter. Archaeological evidence suggests that high-status buildings from before the Anglo-Norman conquest were likely to be slated rather than thatched, perhaps with slate from the Cilgwyn quarry on the Moel Tryfan commons,† and the monastic orders may have revived the fortunes of the area's metalliferous mines. It is tempting to suggest that the Augustinian canons of Beddgelert profited from the copper ores in the hills that surrounded their church. Furthermore, though Beddgelert now lies many miles inland, until the early 19th century it lay much nearer the sea, which then reached Aberglaslyn, so export would have been a comparatively simple matter. Similarly, Llywelyn the Great's charter to the Cistercians at Cymer Abbey, at the tidal head of the Mawddach, allowed it to take 'stones of any kind, metals and treasures' and they were certainly strategically placed to take advantage of the rich deposits of copper on their lands, as well as to ship them out. The abbey had a forge at Trawsfynydd, in the hands of the Crown in 1393, and possibly another at Llanfachreth.‡ The Cistercians, and later the Anglo-Norman invader, helped spread the technology of water-power.§ Extraordinary though it seems in view of the abundant discoveries of water-driven corn-mills dating to the seventh century AD in Ireland,¶ there is no demonstrable evidence for powered milling in north-west Wales before the 13th century, and certainly no explicit reference to water-driven milling in medieval Welsh law.** What is certain is that, in the immediate aftermath of the Conquest, water-mills were established with great rapidity in and around the *bastide* towns, and that their use certainly spread to the countryside within a generation. An outcrop on Anglesey proved an excellent millstone quarry, and in 1303 the area's first windmill was erected, at Newborough on Anglesey.

3.3.2 Urban development

The native settlements which grew up outside the Roman forts soon withered, though the church of St Peblig (Publicius) adjacent to the walls of Segontium (Caernarfon) suggests some sort of continuity into the early Christian period. Otherwise, it is not until the state-building of the last rulers of Gwynedd that anything resembling a town can be recognised, and even so little is known about the process by which these native vills were transformed into urban centres. When Giraldus Cambrensis rode through Gwynedd with Archbishop Baldwin to preach the crusade in 1198, he

---

* Boon, G.C., 'A Temple of Mithras at Caernarvon – Segontium', *Archaeologia Cambrensis* 109 (1960), pp. 141-2, 150, 157, 170 and 171.

† From the author's own experience of digging at the site of the royal *llys* (palace) at Rhosyr in south-west Anglesey, where roofing slates from a Cambrian vein were discovered.

‡ Williams, D.H., *The Welsh Cistercians* (Gracewing, Leominster: 2001), p. 269.

§ The possession of mills except for their own use was initially abjured by the White Monks. An existing mill was granted to Aberconwy at some stage between 1188 and 1199 – see Hays, Rh.W., *A History of the Abbey of Aberconway* (Cardiff: University of Wales Press, 1957), pp. 18, 21. The corn lands of Penrhyn Llŷn supported two dozen crown mills in the 14th century – if the technology was a new one, it had taken root very quickly. See Wiliam, E.,'The Corn Mills of Llŷn in the 14th Century', *Melin* 2 (1986), pp. 26-31.

¶ Rynne, C., *Technological change in Anglo-Norman Munster* (Barryscourt Trust and Cork County Council, 1998); Bielenberg, A. (ed.), *Irish Flour Milling: A History 600-2000* (Dublin: Lilliput, 2003).

** Jenkins, D., *Hywel Dda: The Law* (Llandysul: Gomer, 1990), pp. 45, 113, 156, 194.

noted no borough towns, though it was not long before they appeared. Llanrwst and Dolgellau were both established just above the effective tidal head of long estuarine rivers (the Conwy and the Mawddach respectively), whereas Nefyn evolved as a fishing community around a royal *llys* (palace) on the northern coast of Penrhyn Llŷn and Criccieth was established on Cardigan Bay. These four expanded in the years after the Anglo-Norman conquest. Only Llanfaes on the coast of Anglesey disappeared, swept away to make room for Edward I's bastide town of Beaumaris.

The construction of the King's works – the great string of castles and boroughs stretching around the coast from Flint to Aberystwyth, and inland – represented a substantial industrial undertaking in its own right. In terms of its cost to the exchequer, no subsequent government-sponsored project in Wales has ever come near it, and no other buildings in Wales articulate so formidably the meaning of imperial power. If Cornwall was the first frontier to be closed, Wales was to be the first Anglo-Norman colony. Thousands of workmen were impressed from most counties of England, and the works themselves were to the design of the Savoyard Master James of St George. Welshmen occasionally figure among the ranks of workmen, and some local resources were used – timber and lead from the Conwy valley, limestone from Anglesey.

The introduction of a money economy and of urban living ensured that life would never be entirely the same again after the Conquest, even though the pace of change was to be very slow for a long time. The burgesses of the new towns – 'the lawyers of Caernarfon, the merchants of Beaumaris and the gentlemen of Conway', as Sir John Wynn of Gwydir put it[*] – were the embodiments of moveable wealth, and might in time have evolved commercial relations with towns in England, Ireland and beyond, and hence gained access to venture capital. This much happened in the Edwardian town of Denbigh, in north-east Wales, where in the 16th century the Clough and Myddleton families rose to considerable wealth through international trade links. But Denbigh lay in the lush Vale of Clwyd, where a rich surplus enabled prosperous landowners to send their sons to university or to the counting houses of London and Antwerp. Conwy and Pwllheli both gently stagnated over the centuries, and Harlech, Criccieth and Bala nearly passed out of existence. Only Beaumaris, with its rich agricultural hinterland and the patronage of the powerful local Bulkeley family, and Caernarfon, with its small but growing export trade in slate, developed beyond their Medieval walls before the Industrial period. Even so, an early 18th-century visitor who knew Bristol or Liverpool would have seen here only a sleepy backwater where groceries, hides and nails were landed from coastal sloops. Ship-wrighting, which had loomed large in the Medieval economy and was to do so again in the 19th century, was all but unknown.[†] So were 'manufactures', in the sense of goods produced and processed for external markets. Clock-making, that useful index of local consumer demand and technical self-sufficiency, had not yet established itself.[‡] If anything, it was the two of the boroughs founded before the Conquest, Llanrwst and Dolgellau, which prospered most. Llanrwst became a centre of the stocking trade, famous also for the manufacture of harps, and Dolgellau for its woven cloths.[§]

---

[*] Wynn, J., *History of the Gwydir Family and Memoirs* (Llandysul: Gomer Press, 1990), p. 49.
[†] Thomas, D., *Hen Longau Sir Gaernarfon* (Caernarfon: Caernarvonshire Historical Society, 1952).
[‡] From 1745, at Llanrwst, as an enclave of the clock-making industry of Lancashire and Cheshire – Brown, C. and M., *The Clockmakers of Llanrwst* (Wrexham: Bridge Books, 1993), pp. 217-8, 262-3.
[§] Soulsby, I., *The Towns of Medieval Wales* (Chichester: Phillimore, 1983), *passim*.

3.3.3 Landed estates and economic development

From the Act of Union until well into the Industrial period, the main instigators of economic change and of industrial development were the great estates and their owners. Yet even here, growth was sluggish before the 18th century. The crown had acquired extensive tracts of land through the conquest in the 13th century and the dissolution of the monasteries in the 16th, but made very little or no attempt to develop their mineral resources. The Welsh families who formed the bulk of landowners at the time of the Tudor settlement of the 1530s have left their mark in the form of the Renaissance architecture of Plas Mawr in Conwy, a town-house built between 1576 and 1580 by the courtier and diplomat Sir Robert Wynne, perhaps the defining monument of its period in the area, and of Plas Berw in Anglesey, built in 1615. Their legacy is also to be found in distinctive structures like the bridge over the Conwy at Llanrwst, decorated with the Stuart arms and the Prince of Wales' feathers (Figure 9), or – a very late example – the Wynn chapel at Gwydir Uchaf of 1673. The Wynn family of Gwydir, near Llanrwst, were almost alone in developing mineral resources, leasing out the lead mines on their estate from 1607 until about 1666.

9 Llanrwst bridge.

Although farming may well have benefited from the more peaceful conditions of the 16th century, there is little sign that it was a particularly dynamic sector. The farmer was increasingly coming under the control of the landlord by this time, but he was at least preserved from the exactions of the English manorial system, and generally held his farm for a term of three lives. Stuart farming in Gwynedd has been aptly described as 'basically traditional and unimproved ... nevertheless, as sophisticated as the times demanded'.* Mixed farming predominated, and the more prosperous farmers ensured that they were self-sufficient in all that they needed. Despite the region's very acidic soil, the use of fertilisers was limited – shell-sand off the fish-weirs around the mouth of the Ogwen river, marl from Anglesey, possibly some lime. Dung from cow-houses or from pinfolding cattle in fields was also used. Livestock would be sent to upland pastures during the summer, but increasingly these *hafodydd* ('summer dwellings') were being enclosed as personal property rather than as common waste, and became separate holdings in their own right. Transhumance appears to have declined even before the end of the 17th century, though it persists in very limited form to this day. Farmers' tools were varied and specialised. Wheeled carts, for instance, were a rarity outside Anglesey, though one is recorded on the Creuddyn peninsula as early as 1564; it was to be the end of the 18th century before they penetrated some of the upland parishes.†

---

* Williams, G.H., 'Farming in Stuart Caernarvonshire', *TCHS* 42 (1981), pp. 49-79. Unless otherwise acknowledged, information in this and the following paragraph is based on this article.
† Owen, T.M., 'Y Drol Gyntaf', *Medel* 3 (1986), pp. 21-6.

Wheeled ploughs and the newer oblong harrow were used before the end of the 17th century.

The money-spinner was rearing cattle for the English markets. The trade had gone on since the Medieval period, but grew after 1666, when an act was passed against the importation of cattle from Ireland. Adam Smith observed that 'The mountains of Scotland, Wales and Northumberland indeed are not capable of much improvement, and seem destined by nature to be the breeding grounds for Great Britain.'* Archbishop Williams called cattle-droving 'the Spanish fleet of Wales, which brings hither the little gold and silver we have', though remarkably little of the capital thus accumulated seems to have been spent in Wales. Because landed families tended to tie up capital in new houses or in litigation, the drovers were as a rule the only men in Gwynedd who could produce ready cash. However, their memorials are the banking systems of London and its dairying industry rather than investment in their own native areas.†

A number of coincident factors may have limited the influence, at least in the short term, that the landed families might have brought to bear. Several families fell foul of the political changes of the 17th century, such as Owen of Clennenau, Nannau of Nannau and the Bulkeleys of Baron Hill (who compounded their offences by Jacobite sympathies). Many others intermarried with English and Anglo-Irish dynasties at this time, and some of the great houses ceased to be family homes as a result. Gwydir itself became in 1678 an outpost of a Lincolnshire estate following the heiress' marriage in Westminster Abbey to Robert Bertie, 4th Earl of Lindsay.‡ Alliances with wealthy families who lived outside Wales were eventually to provide the economy of Gwynedd with a much-needed boost, but at the time it encouraged nobody to see a house where for generations bards had been entertained and the poor relieved, become merely a lodging for the steward and his kindred after its owners had gone to live elsewhere.

Another setback was the decision of most of the Quaker community of the town of Dolgellau and its surrounding area to emigrate to Pennsylvania in the late 17th century. The Quaker message had found a receptive soil here, where the Anglican gentry had little control, but the harsh political climate of the Restoration drove them away. This deprived the area of many of its potential leaders and removed their link with the network of businessmen and bankers that was already beginning to develop the iron industry of the English midlands and the Wrexham area.

3.4 Summary

It is probable that what little industrial activity there was by the early 18th century lay mostly in the hands of local partnerships, working slate, stone, coal, lead and copper on their own account, unmolested by the titular landlords and selling their ores and minerals around the Irish sea. The overall picture is of a backward society of bucolic squires and tight-fisted farmers, lagging far behind even its neighbouring regions – Cardiganshire with its lead mines, north-east Wales with its long tradition of iron-working around Wrexham. Machines of any sort were practically unknown, other than water- or wind-mills for grinding corn or fulling cloth.

---

* Smith, A., *The Wealth of Nations*, bk IV chapter 2, para. 18 (London: Methuen, 1904).
† Dodd, A.H., *A History of Caernarvonshire* (Wrexham: Bridge Books, 1990), p. 92.
‡ Other instances are the Wynns of Ynysmaengwyn, the Owens of Talybolion, the Wynns of Gwydir and the Williams family of Cochwillan – see *DWB*.

This was the situation in Gwynedd at the beginning of the 18th century at the same time as Atlantic trade and the leading sectors of iron, coal and textiles were transforming England, Scotland, Ulster and indeed north-east and south Wales into a recognisably modern industrial society.

Chapter 4

INDUSTRIAL ARCHAEOLOGY OF GWYNEDD

This chapter examines the industrial archaeology of Gwynedd, following what constitutes the broadly accepted understanding of its scope as a discipline and as a category. It therefore includes 'functional' sites and their distribution systems, and non-functional types of historic environment that are nonetheless associated with them. These are considered on a sector-by-sector basis, beginning with the slate industry, which is not only the most distinctive and best-known of the region's historic industries but is also the most telling in the way that it has come to be understood.

This approach seems the most logical, but it is important to bear in mind that it runs the risk of imposing a set of artificial distinctions on surviving archaeology. As industries grow, they often reinforce each other – this is the concept of 'take-off' familiar to economic historians. In addition, although the archaeological environment of (for instance) a slate quarry will be very different from that of an agricultural area, often the same, or closely-related, social processes will be at work. The Ogwen valley, for instance, is a classic 'improver's' landscape in that patrician investment and patrician control is very clear indeed in several different productive and distributive sectors – in farming, in mineral extraction, in roads, railways and ports – and, for that matter in the provision of communal buildings and housing. To consider these separately runs the risk of underplaying the extraordinary level of change which will become apparent to the reader within this particular area from the 1770s onwards. Similarly, the Glaslyn area, also under close patrician control, saw tremendous changes in terms of water-control systems, housing and infrastructural provision, from around 1800, with the important and interesting distinction that whereas these were unsuccessful for the landowner within his own lifetime, they laid the foundations for developments which continue to this day and which extend well beyond the immediate area – the growth of the slate quarries at Blaenau Ffestiniog in the 19th century, the building, or re-building, of what will become Britain's longest narrow-gauge railway in the twenty-first.

Cost-effective transport systems represent another way in which industrial systems reinforce each other. Developments such as the Holyhead road and the Chester to Holyhead railway in particular need to be seen as themselves 'patrons' in and industrialising landscape. There can be little doubt, for instance, that had Porth Dinllaen on the northern coast of Penrhyn Llŷn been chosen in preference to Holyhead as the packet port for Ireland, the southern part of Gwynedd would have taken off to a much greater extent and the northern coastal strip and Anglesey would have languished – especially if Brunel's proposed broad-gauge railway from the English midlands had been built. Understanding the relationship between different sectors is crucial to understanding the dynamic of industrialisation in this region as any other.

4.1 Extractive Industries

4.1.1 Quarrying for Slate

The slate industry of Gwynedd was for many years the major industrial provider of roofing materials across a world market.

Probably few distinctive regionally-based industries have had the benefit of the level of research that has been carried out into the Welsh slate industry – not only by archaeologists but also by historians, and sociologists. As **2.6** has suggested, even in the 19th century its past and present were a subject of great interest to contemporaries, and particularly from 1970 onwards individual quarry sites have been surveyed by interest groups. Several synthetic histories and gazetteers have been published. Its importance in Welsh and Gwynedd history has been emphasised by the media, and the landscape impact of the quarries by the inclusion of some of the industry's major centres in the *Register of Landscapes of Outstanding Historic Interest*.[*]

For this reason, and also because the archaeology of the industry world-wide is distinctive – it bears, for instance, little relation to the historic environments of stone-quarrying[†] – it is important to emphasise that Gwynedd was, and is, by no means the only area where slate has been won. At the beginning of the 20th century Gwynedd produced about three quarters of British output and one half of the world's output. There were workings near Llangollen and Glynceiriog in north-east Wales, in Pembrokeshire, in the English Lake District, in Scotland, and in Ireland, where the most important quarries are situated on Valentia island in County Kerry and on the banks of the Shannon. Deposits have been worked in the Ardennes, at Trélazé near Angers at the mouth of the Loire, in Norway, Germany, India and the USA. Spain and China are now the leading producers of roofing slate in the world market.

Though slate has been quarried at more than 400 locations in Gwynedd, the region has been dominated by five main areas – Dyffryn Ogwen, where in the 18th century the great Penrhyn quarry reaped the benefit of re-investment from its owner's West Indian sugar plantations; Llanberis, Nantlle-Moel Tryfan (where quarrying dates to the Medieval period), Ffestiniog and what might for convenience's sake be called southern Gwynedd, at Talyllyn, Corris and Dinas Mawddwy. There were also smaller 'outlier' groups of quarries north of Porthmadog, in the Conwy valley and its tributaries, as well as in various places in Gwynedd (see map 1). Four quarries are now (2006) operational in Gwynedd, three run by McAlpine Welsh Slate – Penrhyn itself (SH 620 650), Ffestiniog (the former Oakeley quarry – SH 694 470) and Graig Ddu (SH 724 454), and a fourth, Llechwedd (SH 700 470), by J.W. Greaves Welsh Slate (Map 3).

Slate is basically a metamorphosed compacted mud with fissile properties. Its colour and its composition vary considerably, even within a small quarry, but broadly speaking the Cambrian veins of Dyffryn Ogwen, Llanberis and Nantlle-Moel Tryfan tend to be purple in colour, the Ordovician veins of Ffestiniog and southern Gwynedd

---

[*] See Lindsay, J., *A History of the North Wales Slate Industry* (Newton Abbot: David and Charles, 1974), Richards, A.J., *A Gazetteer of the Welsh Slate Industry* (Capel Garmon: Gwasg Carreg Gwalch, 1991), Williams, M.C., *The Slate Industry* (Princes Risborough: Shire Publications 1991). For the sociology of labour conflict in the industry see Jones, R.M., *The North Wales Quarrymen 1874-1922* (Cardiff: University of Wales Press, 1981), Lindsay, J., *The Great Strike: A History of the Penrhyn Quarry Dispute of 1900-1903* (Newton Abbot: David and Charles, 1987).

[†] See Stanier, P., *Quarries of England and Wales* (Truro: Twelveheads Press, 1995).

grey, and softer. In some areas, such as southern Gwynedd and the outliers of the Conwy valley, the grain is coarse, and fewer roofing slates can be made from one block, with the result that these quarries tended to concentrate more on producing slabs for architectural work, urinals, switchboards, and vats for breweries. It is, however, not the quality of the stone so much as the angle of the vein which dictates the method of extraction, which varies from area to area. Between 1800 and 1825 Penrhyn quarry, where the vein is near-vertical, came to be worked as a series of uniform galleries, 18m (60ft) high, a practice followed at its only slightly smaller neighbour, Dinorwic, in the Llanberis area (SH 595 603 – Figure 15). The Glynrhonwy quarries, also in Llanberis (SH 560 605 C) and the Nantlle-Moel Tryfan group of quarries (SH 500 530 C) were worked as pits with few intermediate levels (Figure 14). In Ffestiniog, the vein dips; until the early years of the 19th century these could also be worked as open quarries

Map 3 Principal slate quarries

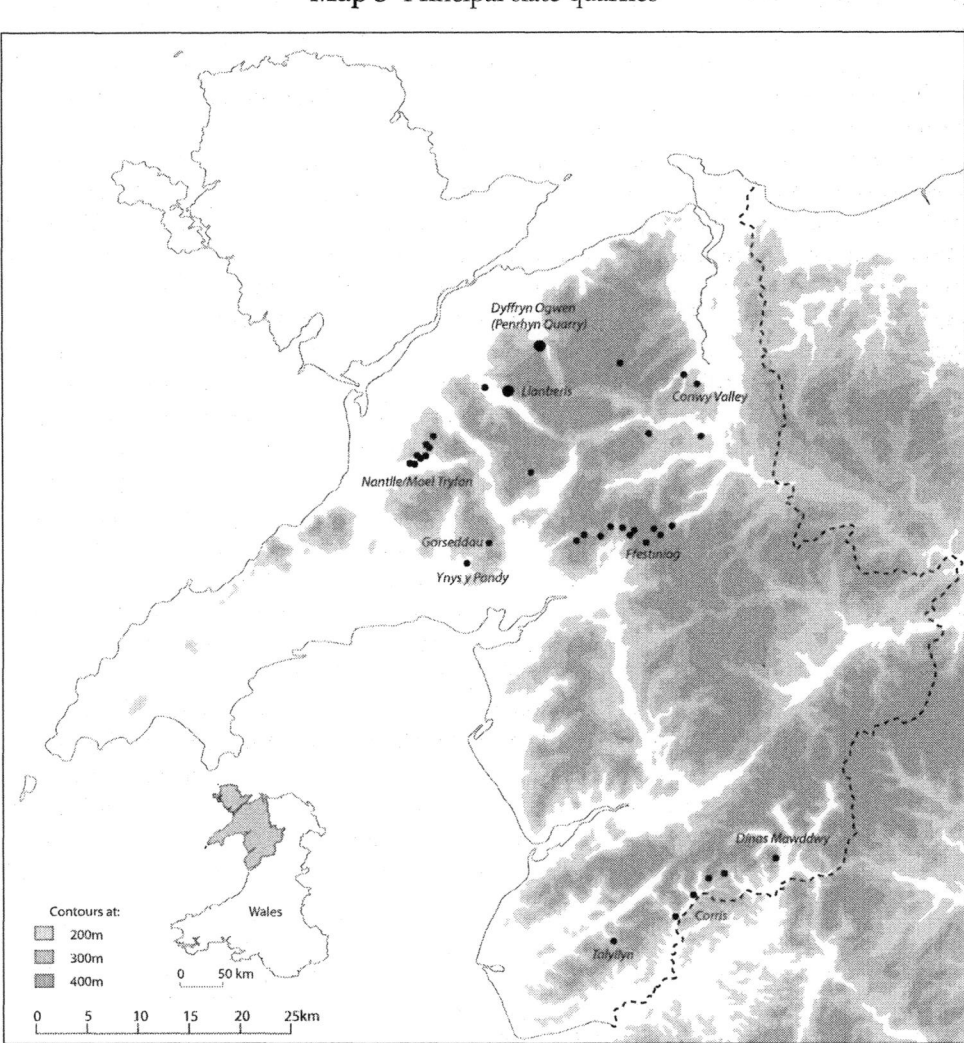

10 An aerial view of Penrhyn quarry in the 1940s (Crown Copyright CUCAP BQ-2, 20-07-1948).

but from the 1820s onwards, in order to follow the vein underground, they had to be opened as mines, though they are still conventionally referred to as quarries (Figure 16). The arrival of powerful earth-moving machinery in the 1960s made it possible to remove large amounts of overburden, with the result that the remaining Ffestiniog operations reverted to open quarrying, and underground operations ceased in the early 1990s. At Corris (SH 745 090 C), geology mostly left no alternative but to seek the rock underground, in large bottle-shaped chambers, a system which lasted until the closure of the final quarry in 2003.

Just as there were considerable variations in methods of extraction, so there was considerable variety of scale. The smallest quarry, one that had barely made the transition from a trial to commercial production, will be no more than a single cutting in a hillside. One or two of these survived as working units until the 1990s. A giant like Penrhyn quarry, for many years the largest slate quarry in the world, now (2006) covers 225 hectares (556 acres); at the end of the 19th century it employed 2,750 men, producing 110,368 tons of slate a year (Figure 10).*

---

* CRO: XPQ/997, p. 68. At a rough calculation, the quarries of the four major slate-quarrying areas of Gwynedd cover a total of 24.5 km^2 – the inclusion of outliers would perhaps take the overall figure into the region of 30km^2. These figures have been derived from various audits of the historic landscape carried out by the present author and by the Gwynedd Archaeological Trust.

11 A 'landscaped' quarry environment at Allt Ddu, Dinorwic.

The scale of even comparatively small workings and the absence of any reason, for the most part, to fill in extraction areas or to move tips has meant that many quarry landscapes have survived largely intact, and it is in the working quarries that most archaeology is lost, though this has been mitigated by detailed assessments. Cilgwyn quarry in Nantlle (SH 500 540) has been largely back-filled by tipping household waste and the archaeology of some other pit and underground quarries is obscured by flooding. Some 'landscaping' has taken place on quarries in Llanberis, Nantlle and Corris, in which significant sums of money were expended on bulldozing piles of slate rubble to create an environment that is neither one thing nor the other (Figure 11), and more recently the Welsh Assembly's commitment to renewable sources and to sustainable development has led to a re-examination of slate waste as possible hardcore. At Penrhyn quarry, the owners, in partnership with the University of Wales, Bangor, encourage wildlife habitats on disused tips as part of a programme of greening post-industrial landscapes, and elsewhere a number of quarries have become part of a forestry plantation. For the most part, however, disused slate quarries are robust sites in which evidence of former working practices survives.

A working face, whether surface or underground, will typically show the half-channel of a drill into which black powder was packed to blow slabs off the parent rock without shattering workable material. It is rare to come across a quarry with no archaeological evidence of the use of drills, where the rock was presumably crow-barred away, and the skilled eye can distinguish between the hole formed by the hand-held drill (the 'jumper', found with variations in stone and hardrock mines and quarries throughout the world) and those formed by power drills. The gunpowder itself would be kept in a magazine, either on- or off-site, typically a stoutly-built shed surrounded by baffle walls (Figure 12). Underground workings are more likely to contain iron-work such as rails and wagons, sometimes the remains of haulage equipment, but exploration can be difficult and dangerous.*

---

* Lewis M.J.T. and Denton, J., *Rhosydd Slate Quarry* (Shrewsbury: Cottage Press, 1974) gives a good indication of the sort of feature that survives in an underground working.

Early mines were worked as large caverns supported by pillars of rock, a method long considered unsafe and only to be seen in a couple of places where operations came to an end very early on – at Pen y Ffridd (SH 776 612) and Clogwyn y Fuwch (SH 759 618), both Conwy valley outliers. From the later 19th century the practice was to extract the slate in honeycombed chambers, though the walls between them are still called 'pillars'.

12 A powder magazine at Hafodlas quarry, Bettws y Coed, with its protective walls and mortared slab roof.

Mines relied on access tunnels, driven by specialist workmen, to the underground chambers. At Ffestiniog these are often driven underneath the 'hard', commercially useless rock, with the result that many are near-triangular in section. Double-track roadways are uncommon, though where locomotives were used underground a passing loop might be provided. Drainage adits are cut in much the same way. In three quarries (Maenofferen in the Ffestiniog area [SH 714 465], Cwm Machno on its periphery [SH 750 471] and Abercwmeiddaw in Corris [SH 746 089]) levels have been cut with a Hunter boring machine, a device that involved a drum with renewable tip cutting points.*

Pumping of pits and mines took many different forms. Water-wheel pits survive in abundance. Pump-engines driven by water-pressure were a common feature of metalliferous mines but were rarely encountered in the slate industry. Penrhyn quarry had two, built by Easton and Amos in 1859 and 1872.† They were similar in design, strongly-built machines on a triangular frame, each with three cylinders

13 One of these Easton and Amos water-pressure engines survives underground at Penrhyn quarry (courtesy Gwynedd Archives Service: CRO XS/1353/41).

14 (right) A pit working – Dorothea in the Nantlle group (Crown Copyright: 93-cs-1125).

---

*   At Maenofferen, two of the bores are 2110mm, a third is a twin bore each of 1600mm. At Cwm Machno the bore is 2040mm, and a third twin bore at Abercwmeiddaw quarry (SH 746 089) is inaccessible.
†   CRO: XPQ/997 erroneously ascribes one to the Caernarfon firm of DeWinton.

15 The gallery system at Dinorwic quarry (Crown Copyright: AP-2005-2951).

16 Underground working – honeycomb chambers partially untopped at Blaenau Ffestiniog (Crown Copyright: 94-cs-0720).

mounted on the lowest part of the hypotenuse operating bucket pumps. Their purpose was to raise water from the lower reaches of the quarry to the point where water could be handled by the drainage adit, and they were powered by a leat from the Ogwen river. One of these engines remains *in situ* (Figure 13); the other was raised to the surface a number of years ago in the hope that it might be conserved and interpreted, but the components have since been mislaid. The most spectacular pumping system is the Cornish engine at Dorothea quarry (SH 4974 5312, SAM) in the Nantlle area, discussed below.

Loading of rock was generally by hand, or with the assistance of a portable wooden tripod crane, hand-powered in the early days, latterly operated by compressed air. Penrhyn quarry operated a number of 'American Devil' steam excavators from the 1920s. By the early 1960s two of these – possibly the whole complement – had been dumped by the road into the quarry from Mynydd Llandygái, by which time more modern machines and dumper trucks were making their mark. In underground quarries, rail-mounted loaders were increasingly used from the 1950s for rubble.

Though the quality of the slate and the methods of working vary from area to area, all quarries have in common the fact that the vast majority of rock extracted – well over 90 per cent – is unusable, and has to be tipped. This not only called for effective internal transport to avoid bottlenecks but also created what are often the most apparent landscape feature of the industry, the distinctive pattern of the tips, which often hide the working face and processing areas. The tips themselves are surprisingly eloquent features, where different types of rock provide clues as to how the quarry has evolved (Figure 17). Particularly in Nantlle, these are sometimes covered with the remains of small roofless shelters erected during the great depression by quarrymen who found that by reworking rock that had been thrown away in the industry's heyday they could produce small slates for damp-coursing or for roofing. These are unobtrusive features, for the very good reason that the men who worked in them might also be drawing unemployment benefit.

As quarries grew, internal movement broadly fell into four categories – movement of good blocks to the processing area; movement of unworkable rock to the tips; movement of processing waste to a tip; movement of processed slate to a marshalling area. Only the tiniest of quarries could do this all on one level, and each of these movements could well involve a considerable height difference – at Dinorwic quarry, for instance 500m separated the top levels from the marshalling yard where trains were made up to take the slate to the port; at Oakeley quarry in Ffestiniog the processing area lay 300m above the lowest levels of the mine. The tipping of rubble was especially problematic; where unworkable rock was raised from a pit or a mine, there was often no room for it to be dumped near the processing area, and it had to be raised to a still higher level for tipping.

The systems for moving the rock within the quarries from the early 19th century to the late 20th generally involved railed vehicles, usually to a gauge of around 0.6m (1ft 11½in), though 0.813m (3 ft) and 1.067m (3 ft 6 in) were not unknown, especially where large slabs had to be moved.* Even a small quarry like Diffwys in Ffestiniog

---

* The oft-quoted gauge of 1 ft 11⅝ in as the 'standard' for Gwynedd's quarry railways equals 0.6m, yet seems to have little basis in fact. The Festiniog Railway's gauge is actually 0.597 (1 ft 11½ in), and the variations of a few inches around this gauge derive from a convention, natural with double-flanged rolling stock, of measuring the rail from the centre. Small variations in gauge crept in according to the width of the rails themselves, though with the poor standard of quarry track and the 'threepenny bit' curves, an official gauge only mattered when ordering locomotives.

17 An aerial view of slate tipping at Alexandra (Cors y Bryniau) quarry, showing the several layers of slate rubble from different periods of working (Crown Copyright: 99-cs-2025).

(SH 712 463) might have 8km (5 miles) of track and a large undertaking like Penrhyn about 80km (50 miles).* Blocks of slate for sawing and splitting were moved on flat wagons, though in some quarries the blocks were broken into pallet-sized pieces and transported in three-sided iron-bodied wagons such as were also used to tip rubble. Finished slates were generally moved in the familiar crate wagons, or sometimes in box wagons, especially where there was likely to be back-traffic in coal or provisions, and slabs would be moved either on flats or on trestles. Other than on the iron-bodied wagons and for components such as drawbars, wheel-sets and couplings, wood was the

---

* Boyd J.I.C., *The Penrhyn Quarry Railways* (Oxford: Oakwood, 1985), p. 79; DRO: ZDK/43.

18 (left) Trackwork at Maenofferen quarry in 1976 showing stub points.

19 (above) *Chaloner*, the only remaining DeWinton locomotive capable of steaming, operates on the Leighton Buzzard Railway.

material of choice, as it flexed better on bad track. There is archaeological evidence of cast-iron plateways in a number of locations, as well as cast-iron edge rails at Penrhyn and Dinorwic, but otherwise track components were nearly always wrought-iron or steel.* However, local idioms prevailed, and pre-assembled narrow gauge trackwork such as was produced by firms like Hudson of Leeds was never common. As many internal quarry wagons ran on double-flanged wheels loose on their axles, conventional points were impossible, so stub points or even simpler types were used, as well as wagon turntables (Figure 18). Rail and other track parts survive in abundance. Rails are often used as lintels or as fencing materials, and stone sleepers are incorporated into walling, or as at Gorseddau (SH 573 453), still *in situ*.

Hand-tramming and horse-haulage were the most common means of locomotion on level sections. Locomotives were only ever used at the largest quarries. The earliest were built by DeWinton's Union ironworks in Caernarfon from the late 1860s, launch engines and vertical boilers in a rail frame, some of which remained in use until the 1950s and survived to be preserved (Figure 19). Another popular type was produced by the Hunslet Engine Company of Leeds, a compact 0-4-0 saddle-tank design. Fifty-one such locomotives were constructed to the same basic design between 1870 and 1932, of which the majority went to Gwynedd slate and stone quarries. Thirty-nine survive, in Wales, England, the USA, Canada and even Puerto Rico, partly because so many lasted until the modernisation of the largest quarries in the 1960s, and partly

---

* To provide references for all these different types of track lies beyond the scope of this study; some of the early material is summarised in Lewis, M.J.T., 'Bar to Fish-Belly: The Evolution of the Cast-Iron Edge Rail' in *Early Railways 2* (London: Newcomen Society, 2003) pp. 102-17.

20 *Vaenol* (later *Jerry M*) was one of the larger Hunslet-built locomotives, and was bought new for Dinorwic quarry in 1895. Other Hunslet locomotives for the Gwynedd slate industry were typically cabless and less powerful.

21 An overhead wire locomotive at Llechwedd quarry, built using parts of a redundant steam engine.

because of the very successful nature and attractive appearance of the design, which has made it possible for them to operate on heritage railways (Figure 20).* Some second-hand steam locomotives to standard designs by Bagnall's of Stafford, Andrew Barclay of Kilmarnock, Avonside of Bristol and Kerr Stuart of Stoke on Trent were also to be found. From 1935 onwards Ruston Hornsby petrol engines with mechanical transmission were introduced, preferred by the quarries to other internal combustion designs because they could be driven whilst walking alongside them, much like a horse, allowing the driver to change points. Electric locomotives were also used; in 1904 Moses Kellow of Croesor quarry (SH 657 457) built his own overhead-wire electric locomotive with parts supplied by Kolben of Prague, and in 1927 and 1930 Llechwedd

---

* Thomas, C., *Quarry Hunslets of North Wales* (Oakwood, 2001).

22 Multi-track incline at Maenofferen quarry, 1976.

converted two Bagnall steam locomotives to overhead wire traction, both of which survive as museum pieces at the quarry's tourist operation (Figure 21).*

More important than locomotive haulage in many ways were the inclined planes which were a feature of even quite small quarries. These were first introduced at Penrhyn quarry in 1800-1, and their use spread gradually throughout the industry. There came to be many variations in technology between them, with local peculiarities and vocabulary much in evidence. In some inclines, wagons ran on their own wheels; in others, they were carried on special transporter wagons, running on a broader gauge. At Penrhyn the 1800 workings were originally all above the processing and marshalling area, so the inclines could operate on the counter-balance principle, whereby the descending heavier load pulls up the empty wagons on a parallel track, but by 1810 the quarry had a powered incline for raising the blocks from lower workings, operated by a water-wheel. Up-haulage inclines such as these spread comparatively slowly, but were to be found by 1822 in Nantlle for raising slate rubble from the pit and in the Ffestiniog area and its outliers by the 1840s for raising both workable rock and rubble from a mine. Water-wheels were commonly used, though steam was applied to winding in 1847, and electricity in 1906. Water-balance systems are first recorded in 1832, whereby the load is raised by the weight of a railed water-tank, which is filled at the top of the incline and emptied at its foot.† The Ffestiniog quarries evolved a distinctive form of multi-

---

* The literature on these locomotives is vast. See Bradley, V.J., *Industrial Locomotives of North Wales* (London: Industrial Railway Society, 1992), *passim*.

† Gwyn, D., 'Hoisting Machinery in the Gwynedd Slate Industry', *Transactions of the Newcomen Society* 71 22 (2000), pp. 190-4.

23 Archive view of the transporter inclines at Vivian quarry; the lowest incline was restored to working order with Heritage Lottery funding by the National Museum of Wales in 1998.

track incline, each track communicating with a different level, and controlled from its own drum running on the one spindle and engaged or disengaged as necessary. The controllers operated the system from a platform above the rails, moving the clutch levers back and forth (Figure 22).

Inclines could be seen in operation until the early 1990s. Because they require considerable earthworks, their remains tend to be the most obvious of the engineered features in a quarry, such as the massive four-track inclines at Dinorwic (SH 5953 5950) which are visible from the road along the west side of the valley, or the inclines which make their way down the edge of slate tips to the railway at Blaenau Ffestiniog. One incline, a 'transporter' type, has been restored to working order, at the Vivian quarry, a department of Dinorwic, now part of the Welsh Slate Museum (Figure 23, SAM). Several other inclines survive relatively intact and partly conserved near the museum.

Water-balances had first appeared not as inclines but as the means to raise vertically through shafts in the 1820s, when they were introduced to the Nantlle area

24 (left) 'Princess May' water-balance shaft head-frame at Penrhyn quarry.

25 (below) Water-wheel (left) operating a ropeway head-frame (right) at Rhos quarry (courtesy Gwynedd Archives Services: CRO XS/1608/6/148).

by two Black Country colliery engineers.* It was at Penrhyn quarry that this system was used to greatest effect, with no fewer than eight double-acting shafts operating on this principle at various times between 1850 and 1965, in which the weight of a full tank under one of the cages pulled up a cage containing a five-ton load. Two of the headgear frames have been preserved by McAlpine's Welsh Slate, and the shafts remain open (Figure 24).† Water balance inclines were extensively used in Blaenau Ffestiniog, though examples could be found in most quarrying areas, and several examples remain at Aberllefenni quarry, where they were used as late as the 1950s (SH 768 103).‡

Ropeways were used in open quarries. No trace is known to exist of any of the early horse-whim systems, recorded from the late 18th century,§ though as late as c.1934 the blacksmith at the impoverished Rhos quarry in Capel Curig (SH 729 564)

---

* Sylwedydd: *Chwarelau Dyffryn Nantlle* (n.d.), p. 21.
† Gwyn, *op. cit.*, pp. 183-204.
‡ Richards, A.J., *Slate Quarrying in Corris* (Llanrwst: Gwasg Carreg Gwalch, 1994), p. 67.
§ Rees, T. and Thomas, J., *Hanes Eglwysi Annibynol Cymru* 3 (Liverpool, 1873), p. 227.

rigged up a ropeway coupled to a second-hand overshot composite water-wheel[*] – archaic in appearance but adequate for the quarry's scale of operations (Figure 25). The immediate successors to these early systems, the chain inclines, have bequeathed a distinctive form of archaeology, in the shape of high slate bastions over the edge of pits. They were first introduced in Cornwall, at Delabole Slate Quarry, by Thomas Avery between 1833 and 1848,[†] and consisted of a chain running from a headframe on the lip of the pit at an angle to a fixed point on the floor of the pit. On this ran a traveller carriage to which a wagon was attached, and which was powered by a winding rope which passed over the headframe to a power-source. By paying this rope out, the carriage could be lowered at the angle of the chain until it reached a stop-block, at which point the winding rope began to travel vertically down to the pit floor where the empty wagon would be unhooked. The process was reversed for a wagon loaded with blocks or rubble, which would be removed at a landing stage underneath the headframe and wheeled to the processing areas or to the tips. Commonly two chains ran parallel to each other, and operated in tandem from the same winding drum, one uphauling while the other one downloaded. They appeared in Nantlle c.1842, powered by water-wheels or steam, and a number of sites are evident. The best surviving example is a water-wheel driven system installed by a Nantlle manager in Bryneglwys quarry in the Talyllyn area around 1862, though even here no machinery and very little timber-work remains (SH 6934 0518, SAM).[‡]

A later system was the blondin ropeway, named after Charles Blondin who walked across Niagara Falls on a tightrope in 1852, which was developed in the Scottish stone quarries in the 1870s. John Fyfe installed a blondin at Kenmay quarry in Aberdeenshire in 1872, but they made comparatively little impact, and as late as 1886 only two other quarries in Aberdeen were using them, assisting derrick cranes. They had a lifting capacity of three tons.[§] In 1896 Henderson's of Aberdeen patented a form of blondin cableway which quickly became popular in Gwynedd and elsewhere and which made use of the newly-available light steel ropes, in place of heavy iron ropes or chains.[¶] There were differences in detail between those used in the granite quarries of Scotland, in Gwynedd slate quarries and at Delabole,[**] but all made use of the same principle, whereby a catenary rope is suspended from towers across a pit, along which a traveller carriage is run, from which depends a vertical haulage rope to which a wagon is attached. Movement of both the traveller and the haulage rope is controlled by an engine on the bank. Their use was not confined to extractive industries, and they were extensively employed on construction work (Figure 26).[††] Llechwedd quarry in Blaenau made use of a more complicated system, similar to the ropeways used in American slate quarries. These involved a mechanism for tipping the wagon to empty its contents, which tends to leave conical piles of rubble rather than the rail-generated

---

[*] CRO: GPJ/126.
[†] Kent, J.M., 'The Delabole Slate Quarry', *Journal of the Royal Institution of Cornwall* new series 5, part 4 (1968), 321.
[‡] Williams, R., 'Hunangofiant Chwarelwr', *Cymru*, 16 90 (1899), pp. 55-9, 18 107 (1900), p. 330; NLW: Ms 8412; Gwyn, *op. cit.*, p. 186.
[§] Donelly, T., 'Structural and Technical Changes in the Aberdeen Granite Quarrying Industry 1830-1880', *IAR* 3 3 (1979), p. 233.
[¶] Jones, G.P., 'The Slate Quarries of the Nantlle Valley', *Stationary Power: The Journal of The Stationary Engine Research Group* 2 (1985), p. 30.
[**] Foster, C. and Cox, S.H., *Ore and Stone Mining* (London, 1910), pp. 432-4.
[††] Henderson, J.M., 'Aerial Suspension Cableways', *Proceedings of the Institution of Civil Engineers* 108 (1904), pp. 186-204.

26 A chain incline and a blondin ropeway at Pen yr Orsedd quarry, c.1910 (courtesy NEI Peebles).

finger-run tip. Pen yr Orsedd quarry in Nantlle (SH 510 538, SAM) preserves the towers and the engine houses with their 1905-7 Bruce Peebles three-phase slip-ring electric motors, operating at 600rpm, and at nearby Blaen y Cae quarry (SH 498 535, SAM) a steam winch engine and the toppled masts of a system built c.1910 survive.

Processing of the blocks to make commercial products was completely unmechanised until the 19th century, and retains to this day an element of craft-skill. A plan of Penrhyn quarry dated 1797 shows 'cabbins', probably the first evidence of the familiar *gwal* ('lair').* This was an open-fronted booth (Figure 27) where two slate-makers worked in partnership with two or more quarrymen on the rock-face. The initial stage of processing, reduction into smaller pallets, if it had not already happened at the rock face, was carried out with a substantial hammer of African oak. The splitting into thin laminae was carried out by hand using a hammer and chisel (as it is to this day), and the trimming of slates into neat rectangles was carried out with a trimming

* CRO: X/M/1311/5.

knife, or sometimes by a hand-operated guillotine with a curved blade like a paper-cutter. The site of *gwaliau* can often be identified by the fine waste generated by the trimming process.

Dedicated mill buildings for the sawing of blocks into architectural slabs first appear at the turn of the 18th and 19th centuries. None of these first-generation mills survives above ground level – Rhyd y Sarn for Ffestiniog (SH 691 423 – by 1802, possibly late 18th-century), nor felin fawr for Penrhyn (SH 615 663, which opened in 1803.* It is known from documentary sources that they were water-powered and typically made use of reciprocating sand-saws, in which wrought-iron strips tensioned in a frame are moved back and forth by a crank and a paste of sand and water is fed into the cuts, the sand acting as the cutting agent. Circular saws are first noted about 1805, the date of death of Suwsanna Pierce whose tombstone in Ffestiniog churchyard is marked with circular striations.† The Gwynedd slate industry seems to be the first recorded area where they are used for stone cutting, though they were only gradually adopted. At Pant yr Ynn in Ffestiniog, Diffwys quarry erected a water-powered mill between 1844 and 1847‡ which later became a school and a woollen mill, and is now, much altered, an artist's studio. It was unusual in being served by carts rather than by rail. The three-storey mill at Ynys y Pandy (SH 5497 4337, SAM) associated with Gorseddau slate quarry, built in 1856-7, is the oldest substan-

27 *Gwaliau* at Foel quarry (courtesy Gwynedd Archaeological Trust).

28 Ynys y Pandy slate mill.

tial unaltered slab mill in existence, but is utterly untypical, in its architectural pretension and its sheer scale (Figure 28). Built, in all probability, by Sir James Brunlees, it appears to be based on a workshop building at Miles Platting in Greater Manchester on the Manchester and Leeds Railway, on which Brunlees had worked in the 1840s.§ It is unusual but not unique in that it was built on several floors – several other mills which produced writ-

---

* CRO: Glynllifon 4736 old, PQ/22/1, entry for June 1803.
† For the late 18th and early 19th centuries, striation marks on slab gravestones provide a convenient way of dating the introduction of new machines, though a few years' leeway in both directions is indicated – sometimes slabs were sawn in advance and kept in stock, sometimes they could only be bought once the family had paid off the funeral costs. NLW: 839C pp. 17-18 (undated but later than 1808) mentions a 'pretty toy of a small rotary saw, worked by the hand, for cutting the school slates' at Penrhyn quarry, which may predate the Ffestiniog saw.
‡ CRO: XBJC X647, DRO: DCH/3/77, 3/84.
§ Marshall, J., *The Lancashire & Yorkshire Railway*, vol. 2 (Newton Abbot: David and Charles, 1970), p. 89.

ing slates as well as slabs were also multi-floor, for reasons that are not now clear.* It is an exceptional survivor on many counts, visually very attractive with its echoes of a ruined abbey, and has been conserved by the Snowdonia National Park.†

The earliest mills for the mechanical processing of roofing slate appear in the mid-19th century, reflecting improvements in stone-processing technology. The Greaves patent saw-table of 1852, which became standard, involved a worm feed which moved the table on to which the block was chained or wedged against a circular saw. A mechanical guillotine to trim the edges of the slate tile was patented in 1850; this operated like a French executioner's machine, except that the blade was activated by a crank.‡ This was largely superseded by a device based on the agricultural chaff cutter, essentially like the blade of a lawn-mower, though, in quarries operating in the

29 Posed archive photograph of slate-splitting and a saw table (from *The Penrhyn Quarry Illustrated*).

Cambrian veins, trimming with the knife was considered preferable on some types of rock (Figure 29).§

It is possible that a small mill of 1845 (SH 8534 1396) at Minllyn quarry, near Dinas Mawddwy, was built for the production of roofing slates as well as slabs, since there are what appear to be traces of chutes for trimming waste in the oldest part of it.¶ Otherwise, the earliest is generally considered to be the mill of *c.*1859 at Diffwys Casson

---

* For instance at Clwt y Bont (SH 571 630), where such a mill survives in use for light industry; see also CRO: XS/1998.
† Lewis, M.J.T., 'New Light on Ty Mawr Ynysypandy', *Industrial Gwynedd* 3 (1998), pp. 34-49.
‡ Patent 13019. See Williams, M.C., 'An Early Mathews Dressing Machine in the Ffestiniog Quarries', *Archaeology in Wales* 25 (1985), pp. 53-4.
§ Patent 2347 of 1860.
¶ *Caernarvon and Denbigh Herald*, 23 August 1845, p. 2 col. c; Gwynedd Archaeological Trust, *Gwynedd Slate Quarries: Appendix 1 – Archaeological and Documentary Data* (report 252, 1998), pp. 87-8.

quarry (SH 7115 4614). In many examples, a vestigial *gwal*, in the form of a private space where the hand-splitting of the block takes place away from the machinery, is often evident within the building. Though this is particularly marked in some early mills such as at Rhos quarry, it survives even in some built in the 20th century – for instance the 'Australia' mill at Dinorwic quarry (SH 600 603) built in 1924 – suggesting that pre-industrial notions of craft and independence died hard.[*] Men bred on farms and who had grown up to think of themselves as free agents may not have taken kindly to working in these buildings, for factories of a sort they undoubtedly were. Layout and organisation varied according to the type of machinery required and topography – some were fed by transverse rail lines, others by a railway running the length of the building, or by a single track feeding a turntable in the middle of the building from which sidings would radiate. Those that concentrated on slab production were the ones that most resembled factories, such as the extensive range of buildings erected at Hafodlas quarry near Betws y Coed (SH 779 562, SAM) in the 1860s. These made use of the Hunter patent circular saw, developed in the freestone quarries of Aberdeen, a fearsome machine which turned at a very slow speed, and which represents an early example of renewable tip tooling.[†]

Hafodlas, a quarry which has been very thoroughly recorded to a high standard by an amateur group from Blaenau Ffestiniog, was unusual in that there was an element of architectural pretension in its mill buildings, though not to the same extent as Ynys y Pandy. Otherwise mills were generally very simple buildings, low-walled and rectangular in plan, their plainness only relieved by the occasional hipped or half-hipped roof, sometimes by a rounded window-head. Building material is nearly always slate rubble, though corrugated iron was occasionally used, such as the 'tin can' mill of *c*.1935 which survives at Llechwedd (SH 7027 4673).[‡] The 1866 slab mills at Penrhyn Quarry's felin fawr were built of an attractive gneiss stone with a pattern of flattened arch doorways;[§] these housed circular saw-tables and planers, powered by a water-wheel set between them, a high backshot iron suspension type, 9.14m (30ft) diameter by 1.6m (5ft 3in) breast. The mills were designed by John and Thomas Francis of Penrhyn quarry, who tried out the design two years earlier at the remote Prince of Wales quarry in Cwm Pennant (SH 5453 4926), one of the comparatively few instances of a distinct style that can be attributed to specific individuals.[¶]

As well as on-site mills, a number of mills operated at remote locations or were only loosely connected to a particular quarry. Only one remains in operation, the Inigo Jones works at Groeslon (SH 4708 5511), the only site where the enamelling kilns found in a number of locations are preserved intact. These were used to create fancy work such as fireplace surrounds.

Documentary sources for mills are generally comprehensive, as quarry managers and tenants were at pains to emphasise in the pages of the *Mining Journal* or a prospectus how well equipped their concern was. Particular types of saw leave a distinct archaeological record – the site of a reciprocating saw is often indicated by

---

[*] Williams, M.C. and Lewis, M.J.T., *Chwareli Gwydir/Gwydir Slate Quarries* (Penrhyndeudraeth: Snowdonia National Park, 1989), p. 10.
[†] Jones, G.R., *Hafodlas Slate Quarry Bettws-y-Coed* (privately published, 1998).
[‡] DRO: Z/DAF/1/58; the penalties for urinating against the wall of this mill were severe – pers. comm., the late Dafydd Price, Dolau Las.
[§] Hughes, H.D., *Hynafiaethau Llanllechid a Llandegai* (Bethesda, 1866), p. 127; CRO XPQ/997, p. 20.
[¶] *Mining Journal*, 31 December 1864, p. 916, 1865, p. 335; CRO: XPQ/921.

a deposit of sand, of a planer by powdered slate, and a Hunter saw by its distinctive H-plan foundation and by the substantial off-cuts with deep striations, as well as by the discarded cutting tips, which resemble a golf tee. Mills were extended and adapted throughout a quarry's working life, though changes were as a rule not great once the 'expansionist' period came to an end around 1877 – in many a quarry a young man starting to learn his craft as a splitter in the 1950s would have been working in an environment that would have been familiar to his great-grandfather. Diamond saws were introduced very gradually from the 1920s and, with the gradual adoption of road vehicles from the 1960s, some old mills had to be rebuilt or replaced. Doorways that were high enough for two men pushing a flat rail wagon could not accommodate a dumper or fork-lift truck, and sometimes floors had to be lowered because lintels could not be raised. At Penrhyn and Dorothea a limited amount of rail traffic persisted for a few years after the rest of the system had been scrapped for this reason. A further consequence of modernisation and the move to road transport was that mills sometimes ceased to be dedicated entirely to their adjacent quarry; the mill at Aberllefenni quarry now saws blocks not only from Ffestiniog but from China, and blocks have been moved by lorry within the McAlpine's empire between Ffestiniog, Penrhyn and Nantlle according to mill capacity.

New types of saw also spelt changes in the layout of mills. Instead of the rows of Greaves-type circular saws, large quick-acting diamond cross-cut saws often took over. Penrhyn, for instance, set up its 12 Wessex/Tysaman saws in second-hand corrugated iron buildings in the 1960s, and conveyor belt handling, computerised sawing and trimming superseded the methods of the 1850s. One process remained obstinately un-mechanised, the splitting of the blocks to produce a roofing tile, despite experiments with machines developed in the French slate quarries at Trélazé.

All but the tiniest quarry and the most ephemeral trial will have a smithy, and the larger undertakings had extensive maintenance facilities which were capable of carrying out heavy repairs. Pen yr Orsedd quarry's erecting shop survives, a corrugated iron structure dating from perhaps the 1890s, and Penrhyn quarry's Felin Fawr site includes a large foundry building and locomotive repair shops, but the largest structure in this category is also the biggest single complex in the slate industry, and the best-known, through having been re-opened as the Welsh Slate Museum (SH 5854 6027, SAM). This is the extraordinary workshops at Gilfach Ddu associated with the Dinorwic quarry, built in 1870 at the point where the 0.6m gauge internal quarry railway met the 1.21m (4 ft) gauge railway to the sea at Port Dinorwic. The plan of this building repeats the quadrangular workshop arrangement which becomes common in the 18th century, and which may well owe its origin to the monastic and collegiate courtyard (Figure 30). As such, it has many parallels; in a Welsh context, perhaps with the stables built for Dowlais ironworks in South Wales in the 1820s, or in more general engineering terms with locations such as the Derby railway works. Operations at Dinorwic quarry were almost sufficient to justify it, but possibly there are reasons other than the purely technical which explain why it came into being. The quarry formed part of the Vaynol estate, owned by Thomas Assheton Smith esq.; in 1866 his near neighbour Colonel Pennant, owner of Penrhyn quarry, was elevated to the peerage. There may be an element of both deliberate showmanship and wounded *amour-propre* in the creation of such a lavish establishment.

30 The Gilfach Ddu workshops of the Dinorwic quarry, now the Welsh Slate Museum (courtesy Gwynedd Archives Service; CRO XS/1057/70).

The power-needs of the industry have been mentioned incidentally at several points. On the whole, Gwynedd's slate quarries used water wherever they could – the major exceptions were the quarries on the Moel Tryfan commons (SH 510 550 C), Cwt y Bugail near Ffestiniog (SH 734 468), where there was insufficient gathering-ground, and Diffwys in Ffestiniog (SH 712 463), where streams were inconveniently situated. Many wheel-pits survive in disused quarries, for the most part erected very near to the point where power needed to be applied – in the gable-wall of a mill, for instance, or in its centre. The use of water power made sound economic and technical sense, given the price of coal and the initial cost of installation, and there were some tasks for which slow-moving water-power was better suited than steam, such as operating bucket pumps. However, water dried up in summer and froze in winter, and in some circumstances it could be denied to a quarry by a commercial rival. Such a case is detailed in the most comprehensive study of the use of water-power in any one group of quarries, a series of papers on the smaller quarries of the Ogwen valley published by John Ll. Williams and David Jenkins in the *Transactions of the Caernarvonshire Historical Society* between 1993 and 1996.* The most detailed archaeological description of a slate-quarry water-power site is to be found in Griff Jones's splendid *Hafodlas Slate Quarry*, which outlines how a quarry with a galaxy of engineering talent on its board made use of an ingenious double water-wheel system to operate the mill and to power an incline.† Wherever possible, mills and pumps were arranged on successive levels so that the tail-race of one wheel could feed the header-tank of the next.

---

* Williams, J.Ll. and Jenkins, D., 'Dwr a Llechi ym Mhlwyf Llanllechid, Bethesda – agweddau ar ddatblygiad diwydiant yn Nyffryn Ogwen', *TCHS* 54 (1993), pp. 29-62; 'Tair Chwarel ym Mhlwyf Llanllechid, Bethesda', *TCHS* 56 (1995), pp. 47-70; Rhan II, *TCHS* 57 (1996), pp. 65-84.
† Jones, G.R., *op. cit.*

Strangely enough, it was at the mighty Penrhyn quarry that the last two wheels continued to turn in industrial service, one operating saws in the Felin Fawr slab mill, the other blowing the foundry until 1965 (Figure 31). The only wheels that remain are untypical, in that each one is a suspension wheel. These are the two felin fawr wheels, neither of which has been restored, in the care of Gwynedd County Council which is adapting the site for light industry, and the huge water-wheel which powered the Dinorwic quarry's workshop complex at Gilfach Ddu, built by DeWinton's Union ironworks at Caernarfon in 1870. Here a pelton supplied by Gunther of Oldham also continues to operate in the former workshops, coupled directly to lineshafting,* one of several 20th-century examples to remain in working order. An early example is known to have been installed in the mill at Hafod y Llan quarry, on the south slopes of Snowdon (SH 613 524), in 1869,† but they only became common

31 This suspension water-wheel powered the foundry blower at Penrhyn quarry.

with the development of electrical power from the 1890s onwards. Some quarries installed their own power-stations, most notably Croesor quarry, under the energetic and innovative management of Moses Kellow, a pioneer of alternating current supply.‡ In Ffestiniog Llechwedd quarry maintains, though does not at the moment use, a 1905 hydro-power station to generate direct current, believed to the oldest functional industrial power-house where electricity is generated from turbines in the United Kingdom.§ This contains two Gilbert Gilkes peltons each coupled to a Thomson and Phillips d.c. generator, all dating from 1904-5 (Figure 32). Current plans involve making the building accessible to the public as part of the 'Quarry Tours' attractions. Llechwedd also maintains a power-station dating from 1911 at their Maenofferen quarry, which now contains a Gilbert Gilkes pelton of 1927, coupled to a British Thompson Houston d.c. generator.¶ Penrhyn

32 The hydro-station of 1904-6 at Llechwedd quarry (courtesy Gwynedd Archaeological Trust).

---

* Gwyn, D., *Gwynedd Slate Quarries: Appendix 1 – Archaeological and Documentary Data* (Gwynedd Archaeological Trust Report 252), *passim*.
† CRO: BJC/X391.
‡ Kellow, M., *Application of Hydro-Electric Power to Slate Mining* (London, 1907).
§ No comprehensive gazetteer of such structures and machinery has been carried out.
¶ Gwyn, D., *op. cit.*, *passim*.

33 The 1904-6 Cornish engine at Dorothea quarry. Since the photograph was taken the sheer-legs have collapsed and the pump-rod has been cut. Beyond the engine are two of the bastions for the chain inclines.

quarry preserves a Gilbert Gilkes 1929 Francis-type turbine, which formerly powered a vertical cylinder compressor of 1918 but which has been disused for some time.

Stationary steam engines were not used extensively. Penrhyn and Dinorwic made practically no use at all of steam power other than locomotives, though their smaller neighbouring quarries did – in at least one case this reflects the major landowner's refusal to allow a commercial rival access to water supplies.* It was in Nantlle and Ffestiniog, where pumping and winding required a strong power source, that steam was most widely used.† Again, the surviving stationary steam engines are untypical of the industry. Apart from some fragmentary remains here and there, three are in existence more or less complete. The most unusual of these is a boiler and boiler-mounted single-cylinder engine at Cwt y Bugail quarry which once formed part of an Aveling 2-speed chain-driven road locomotive of between 1863-8. These remains were removed in 2004 by a group of enthusiasts who intended that they might be

---

* Williams, J.Ll. and Jenkins, D.A., 'Tair Chwarel', pp. 47-70, 57 (1996), pp. 65-84, 'Rhai Nodiadau Ychwanegol ar Chwarel Bryn Hafod y Wern', *TCHS* 56 (1995), pp. 87-107.

† See Jones, G.P., 'The Slate Quarries of the Nantlle Valley', *Stationary Power* 2 (1985), pp. 47-73 for an informed analysis of the role of steam power in one of the major quarry districts. For the first steam engine in Blaenau, see Jones, O., *Cymru: Hanesyddol, Parthedigol, a Bywgraphyddol* (London, Glasgow and Edinburgh, 1875), p. 552.

'combined' with those of a traction-type tram locomotive by Aveling which ended up as a compressed air engine at a Tunstall coal mine.*

The second is the 68-inch cylinder 10-inch stroke Cornish beam engine by Holman's of Camborne, installed to operate two force pumps in a 155-yard shaft at Dorothea quarry (SH 500 532 SAM) in Nantlle in 1904-6, and operational until the 1950s, which survives with its two Lancashire boilers, the only complete beam engine complex in Wales, and the first industrial Scheduled Ancient Monument in Wales (Figure 33). Conservation of this feature has been held up whilst ownership issues are resolved; the pump rod has at least been cut to allow the piston to sink down in the cylinder. Iconic monument though it is, beam engines were few in the slate industry. Only one other Gwynedd example has been archaeologically identified, at Coedmadog quarry in Nantlle, where it only operated from 1863-4 to 1884-5.† In the late 18th century a Newcomen engine was installed to pump out one of the pits by the Marble and Slate Company of Netherlorn at Easdale quarries to which a windmill was later added,‡ and a Cornish engine house survives in the Killaloe group of slate quarries in County Tipperary, Ireland. A substantial beam engine house for winding at Prince of Wales slate quarry in the Trebarwith valley in Cornwall was conserved in 1976.§

The third is a wall engine built by Mather of Manchester from Pen y Bryn quarry in Nantlle (SH 504 538 SAM), where it powered a mill, possibly bought second-hand, now dismantled and kept at the Welsh Slate Museum. The single-cylinder Caernarfon-built horizontal engine which powered the estate workshops at Glynllifon (see pp. 98-102, 109) is typical of the smaller engines that would have powered mills at one time.

Internal combustion plant was to be found latterly in a great many quarries. Some of these were makeshift but no doubt effective, such as the Austin 7 jacked off its back wheels which for a while operated an aerial ropeway system in a Nantlle quarry. Lorry engines sometimes powered saw-tables. Self-propelling i.c. units were also common – petrol locomotives, often by Ruston Hornsby of Lincoln, or road tractors, which might also be put to shunting rail wagons. From the 1930s onwards, excavators, dumper trucks, lorries and bulldozers began slowly to supersede the rail-based movement of material within the quarries.

Lengthy mechanical power-transfer systems are not common, with two exceptions. At Pen y Bryn in Nantlle the pillars for an extensive flat-rod system survive, radiating from two water-wheels at SH 5041 5352 to pump three pits. At Rhiwbach quarry (SH 740 462 SAM), an outlier of the Ffestiniog group, a dilapidated engine-house and square-plan stack date from a re-orientation of the quarry carried out in 1862-3, which led the engineer to power as much as possible from the one central steam engine. Since the first stage of this journey out of the quarry premises unusually involved an incline uphill, unlike the normal situation in other quarries where counterbalance inclines could take the finished product downhill,¶ a 20-inch single-cylinder horizontal

---

* Lewis, M.J.T., *Blaen y Cwm and Cwt y Bugail Slate Quarries* (Gwernaffield: Adit, 2003), pp. 64-5, http://www.oldglory.co.uk/archive/12May04/ft.1.htm, accessed 23 May 2006.
† Jones, G.P., 'The Slate Quarries of the Nantlle Valley', *Stationary Power* 2 (1985), p. 36.
‡ Breadalbane muniments, Scottish Record Office GD112/18. See Tucker, D.G., 'The Slate Quarries of Easdale, Argyllshire, Scotland', *Post-Medieval Archaeology* 10 (1976) pp. 118-30, Nicholson, C., 'Easdale Island, Argyll', *IAR* 5 2 (Spring 1981), pp. 163-4.
§ Stanier, P., *Quarries of England and Wales: an historic photographic record* (Truro: Twelveheads Press, 1995), plate 25.
¶ For the railway, see *Y Faner* 12 Mehefin 1861, and CRO: Ffestiniog Railway archives 000449, 027017, 032018, C.E.S. Ms 000175.

34 An aerial view of Rhiwbach quarry showing the central engine house and the mill, the shaft-head and the inclines which it operated (Crown Copyright: 94-cs-0714).

engine built by the Haigh foundry of Wigan operating 6ft diameter winding drums was installed at the incline foot.* From here it hauled wagons of finished slate up the exit incline, by means of a return sheave at its summit, operated a shaft to underground workings, and turned machinery in the mill (Figure 34). In its use of a central steam engine to perform several tasks, it invites comparison with Delabole slate quarry in Cornwall, where an engine installed in 1865 drove two haulage systems, a pump through flatrods and possibly powered saws as well.† Wire-rope drives were used in some locations, though they were rarely popular, as the ropes often failed to grip the wheels they were supposed to be turning, particularly in the morning dew. The remains of one survive at Pen yr Orsedd quarry (SAM). Compressor houses are a feature of some quarries, driven by electricity at Dinorwic (SH 5986 6053) and by a water-wheel at Rhos (SAM).‡

Wind-power was used to pump in the Nantlle quarries from 1806 onwards, operating both small-scale timber structures and substantial stone towers.§ No traces are known to survive.

---

* Jones, G.R., *Rhiwbach Slate Quarry* (privately published, 2005); for information concerning *injan fawr*, I am indebted to the late Ifan Owen Roberts.
† Kent, J.M., *op. cit.*, pp. 317-23, plate 3.
‡ The Dinorwic compressor house, which probably dates from the mechanisation of this part of the quarry in the 1920s, preserves some of its machinery – a Tilghman's two-cylinder compressor and an Ingersoll Rand single-cylinder horizontal compressor.
§ UWB: Porth yr Aur 27514, 27937, 27037, 27059, 27087 and 29479.

Service structures are common. Office buildings range from the tiny to the substantial; several had belfries, a reminder of the difficulties of imposing managerial initiative and time-discipline on a workforce more accustomed to working as and when it saw fit.* Penrhyn and Dinorwic quarries had on-site hospitals, strategically located so that visitors to the quarry or to the area would see them. The Pernhyn hospital (SH 6247 6582) opened its doors in 1842, and the Dinorwic building was erected in 1860 (SH 5831 6072) replacing an earlier hospital dating from the 1830s, long covered by slate rubble. The Oakeley estate quarries at Blaenau had the advantage of a hospital in Blaenau Ffestiniog from 1848 (SH 6963 4635) – also built in a commanding position but regrettably over an un-drained bog.† All three buildings are variations on the same basic pattern – a central unit and radiating wings containing the wards. The Penrhyn hospital is a ruin, the Dinorwic one a heritage centre, and the Oakeley hospital a private house (Figure 35). In addition Pen yr Orsedd quarry had a small building generally referred to as the 'hospital' (SAM), in reality more of a first-aid post.

35 The former Oakeley hospital at Blaenau Ffestiniog, now a private house.

The provision of accommodation within or near the quarry premises was considered one of the distinguishing features of the industry, though they seem never to have been found in Dyffryn Ogwen. Though they were referred to as 'barracks' (in Welsh, *barics*), they were very far removed either from military barracks or from the comfortable arrangements which might be found in a German mine. Where individual buildings can be identified from census records, it is often clear that particularly in the expansionist years of the late 1860s and early 1870s people were often living in the most cramped conditions. Typically the architecture of a barracks was little different from a vernacular

36 Barracks at Pen y Bryn quarry (courtesy Gwynedd Archaeological Trust).

---

* It is clear that until well into the 19th century quarrymen largely pleased themselves what hours they worked. At a time before the chapels had had a chance to drum sabbatarian principles into them, it would be common to find much of the workforce in the quarries on Sundays and days traditionally regarded as holidays such as Christmas day and Ascension day – CRO: XPQ/977.

† Davies, E., *The North Wales Quarry Hospitals and the Health and Welfare of the Quarrymen* (Caernarfon: Gwynedd Archives Service, 2003), pp. 57, 70, 89-90.

row, sometimes of two-storey 'industrial' housing (see *4.6.1*, pp. 182-95). There are exceptions. At Cwm Eigiau quarry in the Conwy valley (SH 699 636) a very dilapidated building appears to owe something to the Flintshire origins of its first tenants around 1827, and at Pen y Bryn in Nantlle a row of four cottages appears to incorporate the remains of a sub-Medieval dwelling (SH 5026 5340, SAM – Figure 36). At Glanrafon quarry is the only known Gwynedd example of a dual row (SH 5775 5409), a type of industrial building found in England and parts of South Wales, built into a hillside with entry to the lower-floor dwellings on one side and to the upper-floor dwellings on the other. Most bizarre of all is a row at Hendre Ddu quarry in Cwm Pennant (SH 5195 4454) in which, though it is dilapidated, the doors appear to have been very high and there appear to have been no windows at all. Possibly some sort of fanlight was incorporated above the door. Often these buildings are situated in the working area of the quarry – at Prince of Wales (SH 549 498) a row of cubicle-like dwellings faces a row of *gwaliau* – but sometimes the location of quarry houses represents a compromise between nearness to the workplace and nearness to civilisation (eg at Cwmorthin – SH 6783 4598), particularly when entire families were likely to inhabit them.* Only at Rhiwbach quarry was provision made for the children in the form of a school.†

Barrack buildings have been conserved at a number of locations. At Dinorwic, the *dre' newydd* ('new town') or Anglesey barracks (SH 5895 6022, SAM), built between 1869 and 1873 and condemned as unfit for human habitation in 1937, have been conserved by the Welsh Slate Museum,‡ whereas in the village of Nantlle an off-site barracks (SH 5080 5336) has been turned into business units by the Welsh Development Agency. A row of houses built in perhaps the late 1840s for the men who looked after a steam winder on the Oakeley quarry site was conserved by the Gloddfa Ganol Slate Mine Mountain Tourist Centre but was earmarked for demolition when the quarry was taken over by McAlpines (SH 6925 4692).§

Houses for managers and senior workers were often provided on site or nearby; Glan y Bala, the Dinorwic manager's house (SH 5865 6019), overlooks the main quarry yard. Elsewhere, managers' houses were often sheltered by a grove of trees (*eg* SH 5611 4515).

Enough has been said already to suggest that there were strong cultural and technical continuities between slate quarries in Gwynedd and elsewhere in the world. The slate industry was one of the areas in which Gwynedd was far more of an initiating than a recipient culture, and its influence was felt throughout the world. Some innovations came from outside Wales. The stepped gallery system was introduced at Penrhyn between 1800 and 1825 by James Greenfield, of whose background little is known. At Talysarn quarry in Nantlle a below-ground water-wheel pit seems to have operated a colliery-type tunnel rope-haulage system which may have been one of the 'excellent engines' introduced there by Benjamin Smith, a colliery engineer from the Black Country who had worked in Canada, and who also introduced the water-balance.¶

---

* Isherwood, G., *Cwmorthin Slate Quarry* (Gwernaffield: Adit, 1982), pp. 13, 18.
† Jones, G.R., *Rhiwbach*.
‡ CRO: Vaynol 4194, X/DQ/3168.
§ The origins of this row of dwellings are obscure, since it seems that the climb to the quarry appeared too much for the census takers.
¶ Sylwedydd, *op. cit.*, p. 21.

Delabole quarry in Cornwall, whence came the chain incline, also provided the Welsh slate industry with one of its most remarkable geniuses, Moses Kellow (1862-1943), manager of the Park and Croesor quarry, a pioneer of alternating current electrical power.* More often, however, Gwynedd quarries initiated and others followed, as Welsh workmen and managers went to quarries in Ireland and to quarries in the Lake District and to Cornwall. The Lake District quarries, for instance, gradually adopted the Welsh way of splitting slates instead of their traditional 'riving hammer', though at Burlington quarry at least the 'riving shed' was a much more substantial affair than a Welsh *gwal*.† So far, only one study has explicitly been carried out of technology transfer beyond Wales, to Valentia island in County Kerry, which had Welsh managers, beginning with one John Jones in 1827. The present author was struck to see, in the Valentia museum, track-work of a distinctively Welsh type bearing the stamp of a Cork foundry, though it was only later that he came across a reference in a Welsh context to a John Jones living at Pen y Cae in the Nantlle district, doubly blessed in his own estimation because he could speak English and had managed a slate quarry in Ireland. Welsh-language tombstones survive in the slate-quarrying areas of Ballachulish in Scotland, of County Tipperary in Ireland and of the United States. Evidently, within the Atlantic isles and beyond, slate quarrying formed a homogenous technical culture characterised by the movement of managers and workmen, even though individual items might be resourced or designed locally.‡

Cultural continuity is perhaps strongest between the slate industry of Gwynedd and that of the United States, which was largely initiated and for many years sustained by Welshmen – though like the Welsh foremen of the Pennsylvania anthracite coalfields, they soon found themselves managing men from Ireland, Italy and the Austro-Hungarian empire. American slate quarries used some of the technology familiar from Wales such as the horse-whim to operate ropeways and the chain incline, though steam-powered derricks were also common. Buildings tended to be timber constructions, despite the availability of slate rubble. American slate mills were more likely to be separate undertakings from the quarries than in Gwynedd.§

Gwynedd's slate quarries were major producers in an industry which roofed the world, certainly for much of the 19th and 20th centuries – an industry which, moreover, displaced many traditional materials in favour of a much more uniform product. The craft of the Gwynedd quarryman spelt the end for the primacy of the thatcher, and for the tiler who fixed such distinctive regional products as Derbyshire's Kerridge flags. It created a remarkable industry, by no means moribund even now, which has evolved some unusually impressive industrial landscapes, and which has had a profound social and cultural impact on the region, on Wales and on the wider world.

---

* Kellow, M., 'Autobiography of the late Ex-Alderman Moses Kellow', *The Quarry Managers' Journal*, January 1944-December 1945.

† Geddes, R.S., *Burlington Blue-Grey: A History of the Slate Quarries, Kirkby-in-Furness* (privately published, 1975), p. 65.

‡ Gwyn, D., 'Valentia Slate Slab Quarry', *Cuman Seandáloichta is Staire Chiarrai/Journal of the Kerry Archaeological and Historical Society* 24 (1995 for 1991), pp. 40-57; 'A Welsh Quarryman in County Tipperary: Further Light on Griffith Parry', *North Munster Antiquarian Journal/Irisleabhar Ársaíochta Tuadh-Mhumhan* 43 (2003), pp. 105-9.

§ Roberts, G.R., *New Lives in the Valley: Slate Quarries and Quarry Villages in North Wales, New York and Vermont, 1850-1920* (New Hampshire: New Hampshire printers, 1998); Jones R.M. and Lovecy, J., 'Slate Workers in Wales, France and the United States: A Comparative Study', *Industrial Gwynedd* 3 (1998), pp. 8-16.

4.1.2 Quarrying for stone

Though various types of stone have been quarried in Gwynedd, the industry has not had the benefit of the same level of documentary field-work or archival research as the slate industry. The larger quarries represent significant industrial landscapes in their own right.

Stone has been quarried not only to produce building stone and constructional material but also to be made into street-setts, millstones, hones for sharpening tools, railway ballast and road chippings. Limestone has been worked to produce a water-resistant building material for docks and harbours, for steelworks flux and to be turned into the so-called 'Anglesey marble'. The largest workings are to be found in the granites along the coast between Llanfairfechan and Conwy, around Clynnog,

Map 4 Stone quarries

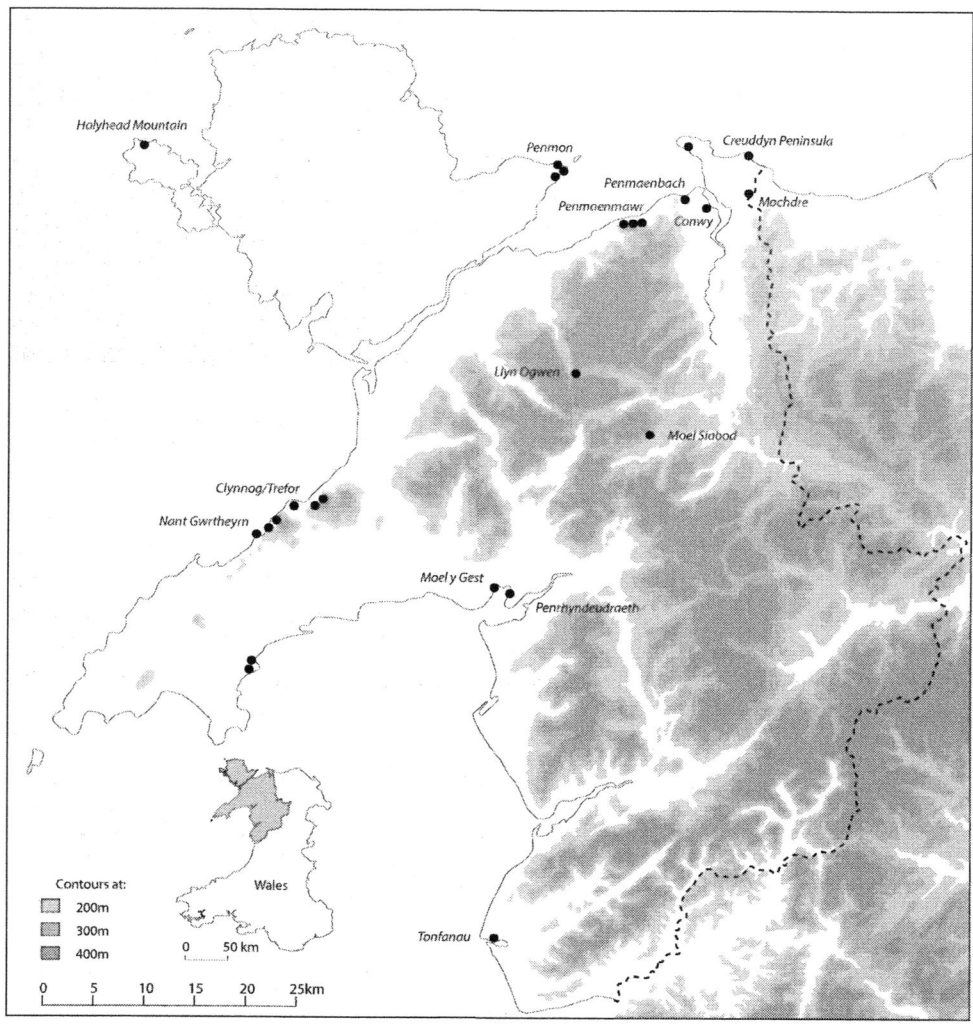

Trefor and Nant Gwrtheyrn on the northern coast of Eifionydd, and at locations along the coast of Cardigan Bay; in the carboniferous limestone of the Creuddyn peninsula and the east coast of Anglesey; and in the recrystallised sandstone of Holyhead mountain (Map 4).

Quarries vary in size from small diggings intended to provide road-mending stone or building material for a single house, to massive undertakings covering many acres. Much the biggest are the quarries which make up the Penmaenmawr group, still in active production (SH 694 755; 700 755; 716 754 – Figure 37), which work a rock originally exploited in the Neolithic period for stone axes. A Prehistoric quarrying area remains evident here to the east of the present workings (SH 717 749).* The sites of Medieval quarries are evident to the south-east of Conwy (SH 7779 7728).†

Methods of extraction in the larger quarries tend to create a stepped or galleried working

37 An aerial view of part of the Penmaenmawr complex in the 1950s showing inclines, crushers and conveyor belt systems. The site has since been extensively landscaped, leaving only the clock visible towards the bottom of the photograph.

face in a sloping hillside, similar to those used in open slate quarries, a common working practice world-wide. There is no evidence of underground working of stone, nor of pit quarries where blocks were raised by crane, though rail-mounted cranes were used in some locations, as were Ruston Bucyrus steam shovels. The Holyhead breakwater quarries made early use of electrically-controlled blasting, and of dynamite.‡ The quarries at Penmon provided the stone for the two Menai bridges.§

Internal transport depended on narrow-gauge railways from the 19th century until the late 20th; there is no recorded use of, for instance, 'blondin' aerial ropeway systems such as were extensively used in the freestone quarries of Aberdeen systems, and in

---

* Williams, J.Ll., '"A Kind of Sheffield of the Stone Age" – Samuel Hazzledine Warren's excavations of a Neolithic Axe Factory on the Graiglwyd, Penmaenmawr, 1919-1921', *TCHS* 59 (1998), pp. 7-34.

† Neaverson, E., *Medieval Castles in North Wales: A Study of Sites, Water Supply and Building Stone* (London: Hodder and Stoughton, University Press of Liverpool, 1947), p. 45; UWB: Bangor ms 2383, 'MAP of Brin y Gynnog and Ty Porth Ucha' by A. Bowdler, 1776, parcel 4b.

‡ Hayter, H., 'Holyhead New Harbour', *Minutes of the Proceedings of the Institute of Civil Engineers* 44 (1875-6), pp. 98-105, 113-16.

§ Greenly, H., *The Geology of Anglesey* (London: HMSO, 1919), p. 853.

the Gwynedd slate industry (*4.1.1*, pp. 42-69). The technology of the railway systems varied very considerably, not only from site to site but within the same quarry, as successive lessees gave up and removed their equipment. Very few early systems are noted; William Madocks' quarries for the construction of the cob on the Traeth Mawr used, bizarrely, plate-rails at the Caernarvonshire end and oval section edge-rails at the Merioneth end.* Otherwise, both documentary and material evidence points to railway systems only becoming common in the 1860s and 1870s as quarries moved into the export market. Often these were to the conventional industrial gauge of 0.6m (2ft), as in the granite quarries around Trefor (SH 365 460) and at Tonfanau (SH 572 033). At Penmaenmawr, at neighbouring Penmaenbach (SH 755 780) and at Dinmor Park on Penmon (SH 633 815), these were for the most part to 0.914m (3ft) gauge, though Penmaenmawr also operated a stretch of 1.435m (4ft 8½in) gauge track on an upper level, as did Dinorben limestone quarry (SH 583 820). Insofar as evidence survives, all of these tended to use wooden-framed wagons with wooden sides, either open along one side for the transport of setts, or completely enclosed. Side-tippers were generally used to tip waste. Many were built by the Britannia Foundry in Porthmadog, and there is comparatively little evidence for the standard products of industrial railway firms such as Hudson. A large concern like Penmaenmawr had specialised wagons for gunpowder and diesel fuel, flats for repair work, tool wagons, mobile chutes and man-riders for inclines.† A number of these survived on site until recent years.

The provision of locomotives tended to follow a familiar progression, starting with the products of DeWinton's Union Ironworks in the 1870s through standard industrial 0-4-0 tanks broadly similar to those used in the slate industry, to Motor Rail, Hunslet and Ruston Hornsby internal combustion units. There were many exceptions – in 1927 the Little Orme limestone quarry (SH 819 823) replaced its fairly youthful fleet of 'Brazil' type Kerr Stuart saddle-tanks with Sentinel geared steam locomotives. Trefor quarry briefly ran a 4-6-0 locomotive. Other anomalies were an ex-Lancashire and Yorkshire 'pug' saddle-tank on the standard gauge at Penmaenmawr, and an ex-Metropolitan Railway 4-4-0 which shunted the confined sidings at Penmaenbach. Remarkably, compared with the survival of many slate quarry steam locomotives, very few of these have been preserved, reflecting the earlier demise of the steam on stone quarry systems (1930s at Trefor, 1942/3 at Penmaenmawr).

As in the slate quarries, inclines were more important than locomotives for internal movement. Those at Penmaenmawr have been the subject of detailed survey. This system, which included no fewer than 62 inclines, operated from 1834 to 1965, and forms one of the most spectacular features of the quarrying landscape for anyone travelling along the A55 coast road. The majority were self-acting counterbalances, though seven were powered for all or part of their existence. Their formations, mostly double track, sometimes with a common centre rail, required some substantial embankments, and the drum houses (*brêc* ['brake'] in local parlance), though they were similar in conception to those in the slate quarries, were much more soundly built

---

* Plate-rails recovered from Britannia bridge (Porthmadog) in author's possession; edge rails recovered from Boston Lodge in possession of Dr M.J.T. Lewis.
† See Boyd, J.I.C., *Narrow Gauge Railways in North Caernarvonshire Volume 3* (Oxford: Oakwood Press, 1986), plates CXXVI-CXLVII, pp. 162-73; *Narrow Gauge Railways in North Caernarvonshire* (Oakwood, 1981), pp. 255-73; Down, C.G., 'Narrow Gauge Wagons: Penmaenmawr Quarries', *Industrial Railway Record* 64 (February 1976), pp. 174-7; 'Narrow Gauge Wagons: The Britannia Foundry', *Industrial Railway Record* 92 (March 1982), pp. 401-7.

38 Inclines at Penmaenmawr (Crown Copyright: 985001-53).

(Figure 38). Dressed stone was used, as was concrete. An unusual feature of the two parallel inclines serving the Penmarian quay (see below) was that when hoppers were installed in 1904 wagons had to be capable of being diverted onto a gantry at the level of the hopper, which was considerably above the quay level. In order to make this possible, moveable sections of track were installed, one on each incline, hinged at the upper end so they could serve either level.* Penmaenmawr had by far the most extensive incline system of any of Gwynedd's stone quarries but they were to be found in most of the large and medium-sized workings. Though they were also a feature of many stone workings throughout the Atlantic isles, substantial and well-engineered systems such as these are rarely found outside Gwynedd.

Provision for processing the rock depended on the product being prepared for sale. None of Gwynedd's granite quarries sought to enter the market for dressed and sawn stone, so there was none of the paraphernalia and dust of a cutting yard such as would have been found in many an English or Scottish undertaking, with saw frames,

---

* Hindley, P.G., 'The Penmaenmawr Quarry Inclines', *Industrial Railway Record* 86 (September 1980), pp. 173-94.

39 Penmon quarry from the air showing the kiln (left) and the crusher (right) (courtesy Gwynedd Archaeological Trust).

polishers, and lathes for turning columns. Machines such as the Hunter saws, with their renewable tip blades, though they had been devised in the freestone quarries of Aberdeen, in Gwynedd were only to be found in the slate industry. Substantial sawing plant was installed in only one location, the Penmon Park quarries (SH 637 817 and 628 805), which marketed limestone as 'Anglesey marble', suitable for monumental work, table tops and mantelpieces. They were equipped around 1875 with processing plant comprising six frame-saws, polishing machines and gantry cranes, all steam-powered, and the following year an elaborate two-storey mill building was completed to house them.* This structure is more reminiscent of a writing-slate mill than of the open cutting-yards typical of most British stone quarries, where the air could blow away unhealthy dust.† So far as is known, the only other stone quarries which used saws were the very small outfits that produced hone-stones for sharpening tools. Near Llyn Ogwen by the side of the Telford road is a single quarry face visible as a slot in the hillside (SH 649 603). Its products were recognised in the 18th century, but the quarry only mechanised in the mid-19th; the building adjacent to it which now serves mountaineers was a water-powered mill for sawing the blocks.‡ The dilapidated remains of a mill built in 1869-70 to serve the tiny hone quarry at Melynllyn survive, complete with part of the drive mechanism and a crank to operate the frame-saw (SH 7062 6561). The saw itself survived until recently in a mill serving a quarry on

---

* UWB mss S6494; PRO: BT311 5098 34326 and date-stone in mill building.

† Stanier, P., *Quarries of England and Wales: an historic photographic record* (Truro: Twelveheads Press, 1995), pp. 45-6, 79.

‡ Davies, I.E., 'The Manufacture of Honestones in Gwynedd', *TCHS* 37 (1976), p. 82. The mill was photographed in 1858 by the Crimean war photographer Roger Fenton. His photograph is reproduced in Bartram, M., *The Pre-Raphaelite Camera: Aspects of Victorian Photographs* (London: Weidenfeld and Nicolson, 1985), fig. 50.

the slopes of Moel Siabod (SH 724 543), whither it was moved in 1908,* extremely battered by the demolition or collapse of the mill built around it but recognisable by the spread of sand.

It was the market for setts – the shaped stone blocks used to pave a road surface – which originally called the Penmaenmawr and Trefor groups of quarries into being. Sett-making was never mechanised, and the stones were hammered into shape by skilled workmen operating in a three-sided stone-built shed, not unlike a slate quarry *gwal*, built either in rows or facing away from each other, presumably to minimise the danger of chipped stone hitting fellow-workers. Some *setsmyn* ('sett-makers') wore specially-made glasses to protect their eyes.

The market for setts declined markedly in the early 20th century but many quarries remained in business because of a growing call for crushed stone for macadamised road surfaces and for railway ballast, which called for crushing mills. The first crushing mill was erected in 1888-9 at Braichllwyd in the Penmaenmawr complex, followed by other mills nearby at Penmaen in 1893 and Penmarian in 1902. Outside Penmaenmawr, crushers were erected at the Nant Gwrtheyrn quarries (SH 3480 4503, 3457 4450 and 3382 4385) and at Trefor. Another crushing mill was erected at the Flagstaff limestone quarry at Penmon (SH 636 807). A two-storey building to house the machinery survives on the site, and is marked on the 1889 ordnance survey. The crusher is believed to have been provided by Caernarfon's Union Ironworks (see pp. 135-7), and to have included an 'elevator', a wheel with buckets which scooped up the crushed stone (Figure 39).†

Flagstaff quarry on Penmon also has a large double kiln, built between 1889 and 1919,‡ which was filled by means of an incline plane. Despite its size, it is firmly in the tradition of 19th-century kiln-building, and there is no evidence here or elsewhere in Gwynedd for the later generation of lime kilns, such as the Robinson or the Hoffmann designs, in a quarry context. Kilns are also associated with the limestone pits at Lledwigan on Anglesey, as well as at a number of smaller sites. The Lledwigan kilns are sited in a prominent location along the edge of the Malltraeth marsh, and can be seen from the A5 road (SH 4537 7359 and 4597 7393) (Figure 40). They were functioning by 1880, and the more northerly was unusual in that it was served by a siding from the standard-gauge Anglesey Central Railway.§

40 Limestone kiln at Lledwigan.

Because most quarries lay within easy reach of the sea, and developed fairly late in the 19th century, there was little need to develop overland transport systems. There does not seem to be

---

* *North Wales Weekly News*, 9 October 1908; Williams, M.C. and Lewis, M.J.T., *Gwydir Slate Quarries/Chwareli Gwydir* (Penrhyndeudraeth: Snowdonia National Park Study Centre, 1989), p. 9.

† Abbott, R., 'Chronicles of a Caernarvonshire Ironworks', *TCHS* 27 (1956), p. 92 and Anglesey 25-inch ordnance survey XV 6 of 1889. The crusher is not shown on UWB mss S6494, dated 1874.

‡ Anglesey 25-inch survey XV 6 of 1889 and 1919.

§ UWB: Baron Hill 7450, booklet, *Descriptive Particulars, Plan and Illustrations of the Anglesea [sic] Diamondhard Stone, Concrete and Hydraulic Lime Works*, published 1904, but includes correspondence dating to 1880.

41 The ropeway base is apparent on the floor of Mochdre quarry.

the network of industrial roads associated with stone quarries as there is with the slate industry. A few short rail systems were built from quarry to sea or to a public railway. Trefor quarry's railway was 1.85km long (SH 3644 4619-3757 4745), Nanhoron and Vaenol quarries' railway 1.07km long (SH 3294 4160-3212 4222). Setts from Moel y Gest (SH 555 390) had to travel 2.87km, partly over a quarry-owned railway, partly over the Croesor and Festiniog railways, to reach a hopper in Porthmadog harbour.* In terms of gauge and equipment, they were generally compatible with the quarries' internal systems, though Tonfanau quarry's connection to the Cambrian system was built to 0.6m (2ft) gauge and later rebuilt as a standard-gauge siding (933m – SH 5713 0329-636 0367). The Garth Shale Company at Mochdre (SH 820 787) installed an aerial ropeway system around 1913 to give connection to the main line railway; remains of the upper sheave housing survive (Figure 41). Finally, road haulage and conveyor belt systems took over in the remaining quarries from the 1950s onwards; at Trefor and at Penmaenmawr the courses of the inclines made a convenient bed for the conveyors. One completely anomalous system in regional terms is described at greater length in *4.5.2* and *4.5.3*; this is the railway serving the Holyhead breakwater quarries, laid to Brunel's broad (2.140m – 7ft 0¼in) gauge in 1847/8.

Remarkably little survives of shipping installations. The quays and piers serving the Penmaenmawr and Penmaenbach quarries have all been scrapped, in one case as recently as 1984. A more recent casualty was the pier serving the Dinmor quarry on Penmon, blown up by the Army in the mid-1990s (SH 6337 8155), before anything other than a very brief photographic record could be made. The Trevor quarry's stone-built breakwater (SH 376 474), completed in 1883, survives. This was equipped with bins fed by a conveyor belt from railway level. Substantial remains of quays and bins also survive at Nant Gwrtheyrn, and concrete bins remain at Llanbedrog. Exchange sidings with main line railways were few, and their sites have been largely destroyed – for instance, much of the interchange yard at Penmaenmawr station, originally laid out *c.*1888, was altered by the construction of the A55 expressway. It was here that a tiny section of the 0.914m gauge survived until 1986, used to collect material that had come adrift from the chutes.† However, the Penmaenmawr quarries continue to export

---

* Clayton, D., 'A North Wales Locomotive Mystery', *Industrial Railway Record* 126 (September 1991), pp. 310-18.
† Anderson, V.R. and Fox, G.K, *An Historical Survey of the Chester to Holyhead Railway* (Poole: Oxford Publishing Company, 1984), plate 201, figure 91 and text; Bradley V.J., *Industrial Locomotives of North Wales* (London: Industrial Railway Society, 1992), pp. 354-5.

by rail as well as by road. At present (2006) new loading chutes fed from the conveyor belts operating on the former incline are used to load bogie stone wagons (Figure 42). Rail ballast is hauled to a stock-pile at Basford Hall yard, Crewe, by a Freightliner Class 66 locomotive.*

The larger quarries had extensive dedicated workshop facilities. Those at Penmaenmawr survive, out of use, together with locomotive sheds in the quarry itself. Service buildings such as these tend to be very thoroughly constructed and to make good use of the quarry's own produce, either as building stone or in concrete.

Settlement associated with stone quarrying is described in 4.6.1 and 4.6.4; suffice it to say here that the sudden development of the industry within the region particularly in the 1870s created a need for worker housing, which was met by the construction of totally new settlements to serve the Trefor quarry and the Nant Gwrtheyrn workings, as well as the expansion of existing settlements at Penmaenmawr.

42 Loading chutes at Penmaenmawr station.

In terms of archaeological study, stone quarrying in Gwynedd has been the poor relation, when set alongside both metalliferous mining and slate quarrying. Though there is undoubtedly considerable variety in the stone-quarrying landscapes of the region, and though there is reason to believe that the larger quarries represent nationally-important sites, insufficient is yet known about the industrial archaeology of stone quarrying throughout the Atlantic isles to place it within context. Some of their products contributed particularly to the distinctive character of the industrial period within the region, such as the limestone which went to build the 'pyramids' of the Menai bridge. On the other hand, minerals from Gwynedd also went to create the distinctive environment of the industrial-era city in England and elsewhere, at a time when building and constructional stone increasingly formed part of an international market, and regional styles began to be effaced.

---

* http://www.page27.co.uk/nwales/swgoods.htm, accessed 4 April 2005.

4.1.3 Metalliferous mining

Mining for lead, copper and gold has a long history in Gwynedd, and has bequeathed extensive archaeological landscapes.

Gwynedd was an important producer of lead, copper, iron-ore, arsenic and even gold at various points from the late 18th century onwards, though the roots of the industry go back into Prehistory. Whilst it never consistently achieved the scale of the Cornish mining industry, nor its landscape impact, the extraction of these minerals is evident in the landscape in several parts of the region. The workings along the ridge of Mynydd Parys (Parys Mountain) in Anglesey, once the most productive copper mine in the world, dominate north-eastern Anglesey, and form one of the most dazzling industrial sites perhaps in the world, particularly when the sun brings out their vivid colours (SH 440 903, Figure 43). Its extensive precipitation lakes cover almost as great an area as the surface workings themselves (Figure 45). Between Trefriw and Capel Curig in the Gwydir ore-field the hillsides are dotted with lead mines, which in their hey-day were sunk in open moorlands but which are now surrounded by forestry. By the 20th century this was one of the most productive lead fields in the United Kingdom, as the mines of the Pennines and mid-Wales went into decline. Copper was extensively worked on the slopes of Snowdon, and hill-walkers now make use of the miners' track from Pen y Pass to the summit, passing the remains of the Britannia mine. Between Dolgellau and Barmouth, copper and gold mines scar the upper slopes of Foel Ispri, though most of Merionethshire's once extensive mines are hidden away in the remote side-valleys around Glasdir and above Bontddu and Taicynhaeaf. Often little survives other than adit mouths and grassed tips.* Elsewhere, smaller ore-fields and mines are evident (Map 5).

Their archaeology forms part of an international culture, even though distinctive forms might be evident. In continental Europe, German miners had been the acknowledged leaders since the Medieval period, and had made their way to Peru, Keswick and Arkhangel in the 16th century, and to the Urals in the 17th. Though there is evidence, so far fragmentary, for Prehistoric, Roman and Medieval mining in Gwynedd, its mines only developed on a significant scale in the 18th century, at a time when Cornish influence was becoming strong. Though the German miner took with him technology such as the force pump, the rod-engine, the railway and the battery stamp, the Cornishman called into being the high-pressure steam engine and the circular buddle. It is partly because of the international nature of mining archaeology, and the abundant technical literature of mining, that the broad typology is already known and understood, and the archaeology of a regional mining area can be placed within this broader context. The knowledge-base also reflects the fascination which mines have always exerted; the thrill of exploring underground attracts nascent industrial archaeologists as well as pot-holers and cavers, and increased leisure and car-ownership, in Britain at least, since the 1950s encouraged many people to visit mining fields in remote areas and to develop their interest. Individual enthusiasts such as Geraint Madoc-Jones of Denbigh, a machinery merchant, began to take photographs

---

* Morrison, T.A., *Goldmining in Western Merioneth* (Llandysul: Gomerian Press for Merionethshire Historical and Record Society, 1975).

Map 5 Metalliferous mines

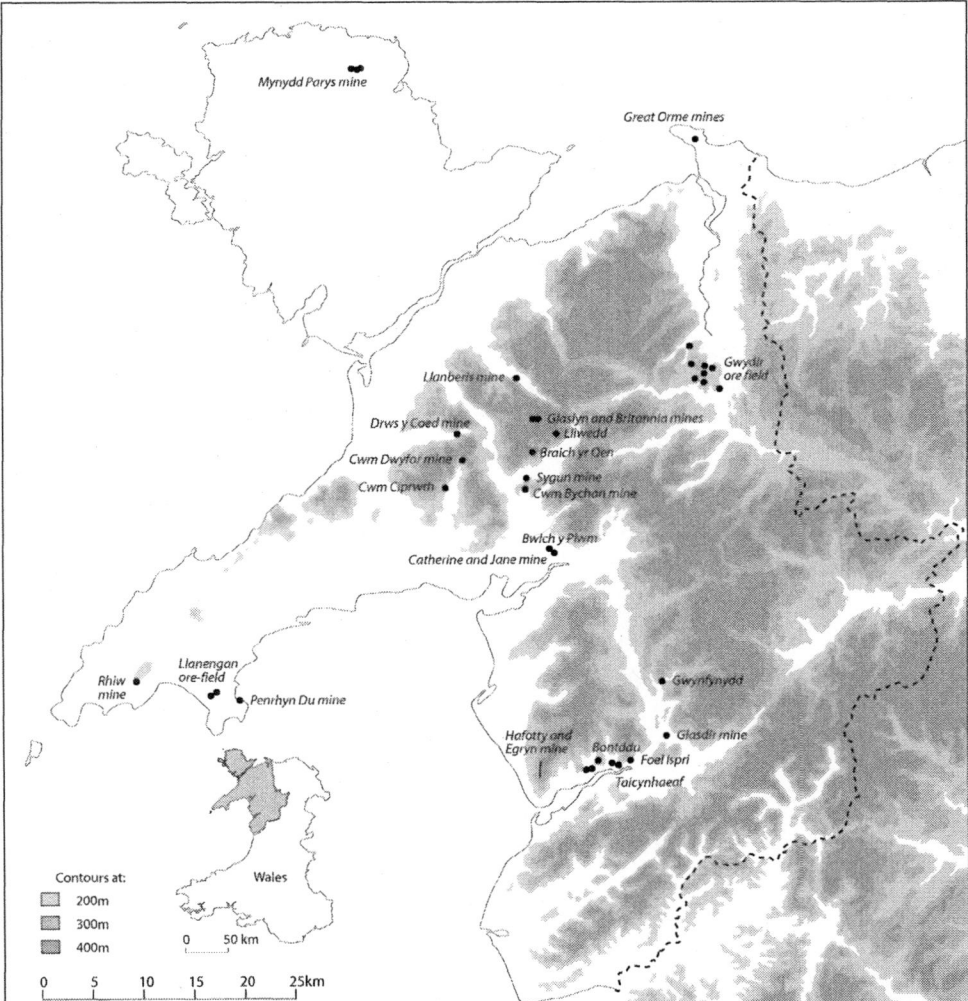

of Gwynedd mines in the 1950s. Rydal, a boarding school in Colwyn Bay, proved something of a nursery of industrial archaeologists as well as of mining engineers through the activities of its Tellurian Society, which made a habit of exploring the Gwydir mines. Other factors which brought the archaeology of mining to prominence were safety issues relating to dilapidated buildings and to pollution, and the broader environmental concerns voiced when mines were proposed for re-opening.

An important breakthrough came in the late 1970s, when a chance discovery led to the identification of extensive ancient workings on the Great Orme (SH 771 831). Investigations by Oliver Davies sponsored by the British Academy in the 1940s had suggested a Roman date, but collected charcoal was dated 2940 ±80BP (HAR-4845) 1410-920cal BC – the Orme, it was clear, was an important Bronze-Age site. This encouraged the establishment of specialist archaeological groups which went on to confirm other Bronze-Age mining sites in the south-west of Ireland, the Isle of Man, Alderley Edge in Cheshire and Ecton Hill in Staffordshire, as well as at Llancynfelin, Cwmystwyth and Nant yr Eira in mid-Wales and at Parys in Gwynedd. Individuals and groups have also gone on to study the archaeological evidence for Iron Age, Roman and Medieval mining and ore-processing within the region and within Wales as a whole. What emerged was fragmentary and circumstantial – though there were Iron-Age smelting sites at Bryn Castell and Crawcwellt, there was no evidence of the mines which supplied them. The distribution of copper ingots strongly suggested, but could not confirm, that the Romans worked Parys, and though lead-smelting hearths have been identified and excavated at Brithdir, there again is no evidence of the mines which supplied them. Even across Wales as a whole, only the gold mine at Dolaucothi in the south-west and the lead mine at Llanymynech in Powys, the great hill which straddles the border between England and Wales, have provided unequivocal evidence of Roman mining. By the second millenium AD, documentary evidence becomes available, in the form of monastic charters with rights of mine and of the mining laws which governed north-east Wales. Archaeology again identifies evidence of processing rather than mining – excavations in Coed y Brenin in Gwynedd have confirmed ten bloomery sites, several of which are associated with slag heaps of between 100 and 400 tonnes (see pp. 123-4).*

Whilst the archaeology of mining pre-1700 may be of only limited significance to understanding later mining within Gwynedd, these discoveries emphasise the long story of mining and the possibility that material evidence could confirm a continuity of extraction. Lead and copper were the staples of the regional mining economy. Lead mines were opened, or revived, in two areas in the 17th century – in the Gwydir ore-field on the western bank of the Conwy valley, and around Llanengan on Penrhyn Llŷn.† The established centres for lead-ore processing lay in north-east Wales, where in 1703-4 the London Lead Company had constructed a smelter at Gadlys on the Dee estuary, and it was to here that the ore was shipped.‡ Copper mining seems to have been revived later, in the 1760s, unless this reflects more detailed documentation rather than an increased scale of working. Certainly, the Vaynol estate re-opened its mines at Drws y Coed (SH 543 533 C) and at Llanberis (SH 599 586 C) in 1768, the year in which the great discovery of low-grade but easily accessible copper ore was made at Parys.§ The Vaynol mines enjoyed limited success into the 19th century but Parys became astonishingly profitable for a few years, and dominated the world copper industry. Ores from Parys, and the other copper mines in Gwynedd, were shipped to the smelters at Swansea, one of the major early metal-processing centres in western Europe, and to Ravenhead and Stanley in Lancashire. Another important industrial landscape outside Gwynedd associated with Parys is the Greenfield valley in north-

---

* Crew, P., 'Excavations at Llwyn Du, 2001-2002: Woodland management and charcoal processing at a late 14th century ironworks' (unpublished interim report, September 2002).

† Bennett, J. and Vernon, R.W., *Mines of the Gwydyr Forest Part 1 Llanrwst Mine and its Neighbours* (Cuddington: Gwydyr Mines publications, 1989), pp. 6-7; *Metal Mines of Llanengan* (Warrington: Gwydyr Mines publications, 2002), p. 1.

‡ Ellis, B., *The History of Halkyn Mountain* (Halkyn: Helygain, 1998), pp. 24-5.

§ 2 March was for years afterwards kept as the anniversary of the discovery. The archive of the Swansea copper smelters does suggest that Parys moved into the export market around this time – NLW: Ms 1510B, entry for 4 October 1769. For Llanberis, see Crew, P., 'The Copper Mines of Llanberis and Clogwyn Goch', *TCHS* 37 (1976), pp. 58-79.

43 The Great Opencast, Parys copper mines, with the pump-windmill in the background.

east Wales, where the Holywell stream powered mills that transformed the cake copper from the Lancashire smelters into sheets and bolts.*

Parys is unusual in that from the late 18th century it was effectively worked as an open quarry (Figure 43, SAM), following a collapse, like the Stora Koparberg in Sweden. It is not always clear to what extent at Parys the practice of open-casting derives from a policy of deliberately collapsing large tunnel workings and multiple shafts driven into a near-horizontal ore body, but the earliest paintings of the site, dated to 1790, already show open pits which became in time the Great Opencast and Hillside Opencast, which now dominate the landscape. The scale of work here appealed to artists influenced by the fashionable notions of the 'sublime' and paintings constitute an important form of evidence for this site.† Traces of earlier arrangements perhaps survive here and there, as in an open cavern known as *gwaith Robin Ellis* ('Robin Ellis' work') at SH 4432 9037.‡

Parys was not the only place where ore was extracted in an open-cast – iron-ore was worked in this way on a small scale near Abersoch (SH 301 271) in the Llanengan field, but there was extensive deep-mining at Parys as well. As the vein became too deep to be followed profitably in open workings by the early 19th century, shafts were

---

* For Swansea, see Hughes, S., *Copperopolis* (Aberystwyth: RCAHMW, 2000). Ironbridge Gorge in the English west Midlands has traditionally been described as the cradle of the industrial revolution, yet it is worth stressing that the Swansea smelters were working on a significant scale and were erecting substantial industrial buildings from the end of the 17th century. For the Greenfield valley and the Parys commercial empire, see Harris, J.R., *The Copper King: Thomas Williams of Llanidan* (Ashbourne: Landmark Publishing, 2003).

† Lord, P., *Industrial Society* (Cardiff: University of Wales Press, 1998), pp. 22-8.

‡ For Parys, see Hope, B.D., *A Curious Place: An Industrial History of Amlwch (1550-1950)* (Wrexham: Bridge Books, 1994), a study which also analyses the host of subsidiary industries which the mines called into being, from ship-building to fertilizers to tobacco.

sunk by the newly-arrived Cornish managers along the north-western perimeter of the mountain to reach the deeper parts of the vein. All the shafts were capped and identified with concrete pillars in the late 20th century, though access underground is possible at several points to the higher levels. In some parts of the mine, Bronze-Age hammer-stones have been recovered from contexts adjacent to where compressed-air piping, wooden pump rods and wheel barrows have also been found. Wooden ladders survive, as do stone-cut footways descending into deeper levels, still flooded.

Narrow adits, stopes and winzes such as these are found throughout the metalliferous mines of Gwynedd wherever mine explorers and industrial archaeologists have been able to venture underground. Artefacts such as tools, chutes and windlasses are occasionally discovered, as well as the pumping and transport equipment described below, and exploration confirms that underground archaeology is typical of conventional small-scale underground metalliferous mining. Workings are supported with timber, sometimes by steel girders. Only at the Parc lead mine in the Gwydyr area (SH 787 600 C), re-opened by Johannesburg Consolidated Investment in 1948, with its concrete adit portal and its well-laid roadway secured with rock-bolting and steel arches, was there anything reminiscent of large-scale modern mining techniques. As an offshoot of a technically-advanced South African concern, Parc made use of methods which were not found elsewhere in Gwynedd, though JCI applied them also at Abbeytown in Ireland and at Matlock in Derbyshire – these included diamond drilling and moveable chutes in the stoping. Parc was for many years after its closure a favoured site for underground exploration, but timbers have rotted and earth movement has led to collapse in the stopes, and much of the mine is now inaccessible.* The Sygun copper mine at Beddgelert (SH 605 488) has been open to the public since 1986, and makes it possible to see the scale of underground operations of a typical Gwynedd mine, medium-sized by regional standards.

Several other methods of extraction deserve mention. Gwynedd is rich in manganese, widely used in the production of bleach and glass, but also a component in hardening steel, and hence vital to the production of armaments. The only deep manganese mine in Britain is situated on Mynydd Rhiw on Penrhyn Llŷn (SH 223 281 C), which was extensively worked in the period 1904-8 and in both world wars, though little trace of the shaft work is evident now. Nearby at Porth Ysgo, in a narrow river valley in a rocky bay (SH 211 266), black piles of manganese still lie near the mouths of the adits.† The manganese workings of Ardudwy are the most remarkable, in that the ore appears as an outcrop extending over many miles, and mines are typically a long scar over the hillsides with minimal underground workings, and banks of spoil on the downslope side (eg SH 6188 1992 – 6170 1799 – Figure 44).

An unusual method of extraction was practised at the Parys mines from the late 18th century, whereby water that had percolated through the tips and the upper workings was allowed to react with scrap metal in an extensive series of shallow

---

* Bennett, J. and Vernon, R.W., *Mines of the Gwydyr Forest Part 3: Parc Mine, Llanrwst and Adjacent Setts* (Knutsford: Gwydyr Mines Publications, 1991), pp. 84-137.
† Griffith, M., 'Manganese Mining at Rhiw in Llŷn between 1827 and 1945', *TCHS* 50 (1989), pp. 41-65.

44 An aerial view of the Egryn and Hafotty manganese mines (Crown Copyright: Royal Commission on the Ancient and Historic Monuments of Wales; 93-cs-1003).

45 Parys mine – precipitation pits with sulphur kilns and sublimation chambers visible towards the top of the photograph (Crown Copyright: 94-cs-1196).

ponds to produce a copper-rich sludge, which was then dried out in furnaces. The extensive 'chequer-board' pattern of the ponds, which were sub-divided into smaller self-contained sections regulated by gates, allowed the water to stand for as long as was necessary. Once the precipitate had been removed, the water was released into large reservoirs, several hectares in extent, where it deposited yellow ochre, used as a gas-purifying material and as a component in paints. The cupriferous water as it flowed into the ponds was the colour of port wine; by the time it entered the sea, it was yellow, and the tinge was noticeable some way into the sea (Figure 45, SAM).[*] This method long outlasted commercial mining, and was continued on a small scale until 1958.[†] It is not unique to Parys, and was practised on a very small scale at Drws y Coed and at Llanberis copper mine, as well as at Avoca in County Wicklow and at Hern Grundt in Hungary. One method that does not seem to have been practised in Gwynedd was hushing, the removal of top-soil by releasing water over it. In several locations a limited amount of copper ore was obtained from turf, which was burnt in open air stone grates and sold to the Swansea smelters (SH 747 256).[‡]

The archaeology of ore-processing throughout Gwynedd reflects the range of methods available to mine captains from the late 18th century to the early 20th – from hand-based techniques to mechanical processing to chemical systems. Mynydd Parys relied until well into the 19th century on its *coparledis* ('copper ladies'), 'showy and picturesque girls', who smashed the rock with small hammers, and who at least latterly carried on their avocation in open-sided shelters with corrugated-iron roofs.

---

[*] *The Mining Journal*, 1878, p.943.
[†] Pers. comm., Bryan Hope.
[‡] Richards, A.J., *Fragments of Mine and Mill in Wales* (Llanrwst: Gwasg Carreg Gwalch, 2002), p. 121.

These women were famous for their Jim Crow hats, the rings they wore to protect their fingers from the hammers and the handkerchiefs over their faces to protect them from the dust, and had their sisters in the 'bal-maidens' of the Cornish tin and copper mines. However, all that remains of the shelters are some flat cobbled areas, traditionally identified as the scenes of their labours (*eg* SH 4437 9057). More survives at Drws y Coed copper mine in the Nantlle valley, where tiny shelters each enclose a stone bucking anvil at the mouth of the Fron Felen levels, above the road (SH 544 534). Nearby, on the valley floor, is a stone-built structure built to house water-powered stamps, dating from 1768 (SH 5441 5346 – Figure 46).* Devices such as these were used by the Romans at Dolaucothi gold mine in south-west Wales, and had become a common feature of Cornish tin-mines from the 15th century at least, reaching the mid-Wales ore-fields by the 17th century.† Drws y Coed may have the oldest known stamp-mill to survive in Wales, and though it is not clear how it functioned, it was clearly unusual in that it was stone-built. Stamps are normally constructed of timber or of iron, and tend only to be recognisable archaeologically by their distinct waste. A half-size reconstructed stamp battery, designed by the mining historian David Bick, has been reconstructed at the Sygun mine. At the remote Lliwedd mine, on the southern slopes of Snowdon (SH 6340 5302, SAM), there survive the shrouds of a water-wheel and the fluted rollers for a rotary crusher (Figure 47). This is the only location identified where crushing machinery survives, but the stone housing for crushers survives at a number of locations, such as Hafna in the Gwydyr ore-field (SH 7805 6013, SAM).

46 Stamp mill of 1768 at Drws y Coed copper mine.

47 Lliwedd mine – the crusher-house and surviving ironwork.

Washing floors were constructed at Llandudno for the Great Orme mines, one of which survives adapted as a model yacht pond, presided over by a statue of the white rabbit from *Alice in Wonderland* (SH 7710 8205). It drains the Penmorfa adit, which flows out of the mine past the house built by Henry Liddell, the Dean of Christ Church, Oxford from 1855 to 1891, Alice's father, which has suggested to at least one historian that it may have provided the inspiration for the story.‡ Parys made use of a

---

* CRO: Vaynol 5047 p.8, p.10 and p.20 refer to the construction of a stamp-mill, and the wooden axle.
† Lewis, M.J.T., *Millstone and Hammer: The Origins of Water Power* (Hull; The University of Hull, 1997), pp. 106-10; Gerrard, S., 'The Medieval and Early Modern Cornish Stamping Mill', *LAR* 12 1 (Autumn 1989), pp. 9-19; Thorburn, J.A., 'Stone Mining Tools and the Field Evidence for Early Mining in Wales' in Crew, P. and Crew, S. (eds), *Early Mining in the British Isles* (Maentwrog: Plas Tan y Bwlch, 1990), p. 45.
‡ Williams, C.J., *Metal Mines of North Wales: a collection of pictures* (Wrexham; Bridge Books, 1997), fig. 91 caption.

system of sulphur kilns, which are now evident as vivid discolouration of the ground – often a pink or dull red – and a crater which might be anything up to 17m long and 6m across, where the ore was piled and roasted. In some cases there run parallel to the long axis of the crater two parallel stone walls, typically 16m long, 1m across and 0.8m high (*eg* SH 4472 9036, SAM). These are sublimation chambers, in which the sulphur was condensed to a powder, having been conducted thither in flues from the ore-pile,

48 This letter-head engraving and some maps constitute the main evidence for the smelters at Porth Amlwch. The site is now a housing estate.

in order to be sold to the chemical industry (Figure 45). The extensive 18th-century smelters once situated at Porth Amlwch, and, probably, on the mountain as well, have left no trace beyond the occasional slag run (Figure 48).

More sophisticated processing arrangements are evident at Hafna, in the Gwydir ore field, at Sygun and at Glasdir in Merioneth (SH 7388 2255). Hafna, a site which benefited from considerable investment from the 1860s to the early years of the 20th century, remains in essence a gravity-feed processing plant but with remains of flotation systems as well as mechanical crushing and a smelter. At Glasdir, Alexander Elmore of Leeds first successfully applied the flotation method, now widespread in world mining, which involves the attraction of sulphide ores to a film of grease, a method which he later applied at Sygun, near Beddgelert. At both mines, the stone stepped bases for the plant survive, those at Glasdir forming part of an extraordinary and complicated site once covered with timber and corrugated iron buildings (Figure 49).*

The substantial stone-built mill erected by the Welsh Crown Spelter Company near Llyn Geirionydd in the Gwydir ore-field in 1900-1 (SH 7650 6215), included a stone-breaker, Cornish rolls, trammels, jigs and a Wilfley tables, and stands in an area of extensive tailings.† More commonly, buildings were made of timber or of corrugated iron, and have largely disappeared, though often the foundations are impressive enough in their own right.

Smelting of the ores mined in Gwynedd continued to be carried out mostly outside the region, a tendency confirmed by the move from charcoal to coke as fuel (see pp. 124-5). The Parys mines built smelters both on the mountain and at the port, of which

---

* Bick, D., *The Old Copper Mines of Snowdonia* (Newent: the Pound House, 1985), pp. 64-8.
† Bennett, J. and Vernon, R.W., *Mines of the Gwydyr Forest Part 6: Pandora and Other Mines in North West Gwydyr* (Knutsford: Gwydyr Mines Publications, 1995), pp. 61-4, 107.

49 An archive view of the mill at Glasdir mine. Only the stepped stone bases now survive (courtesy Gwynedd Archives: DRO ZS/53/34).

nothing has so far been identified archaeologically. Those at the harbour now lie under the site of a housing estate. Not only were ores from Parys smelted here, but so were ores from the Nantlle Valley and from the Great Orme, and operations seem to have continued into the 1860s. A stated objective of the Anglesey Central Railway was to bring coal from the pits around Pentre Berw to the smelters but the initiative was too late to benefit either the railway or the mines. Otherwise, smelting was carried out at very few Gwynedd mines, and only on a very small scale. A map of Penrhyn Du lead mine dated 1777 shows a 'smelting house' near the sea-shore at SH 322 264, of which no above-ground trace has been identified, and the tenants of the Britannia mine in the 1850s made great play of the fact that peat could be used to fuel the smelting process on this exceptionally remote site (SH 617 548).*

Movement of ore within mines and to processing plants was carried out by a variety of means. Horses and carts were used in the open workings at Mynydd Parys, where roadways are still evident and hold the eye in much the same way as the slate quarry incline systems do. A number of mines are situated on or near what would have been the sea coast at one time, particularly around the Traeth Mawr estuary, and would have been able to export in a small coastal vessel. Boats were used in and around the Llanberis and Snowdon lakes in the 18th and early 19th centuries, and a painting survives of the simple wooden chutes used to load them.† Some anomalous systems were constructed in which different phases are evident, such as Braich yr Oen (SH 6162 5170), on the slopes of Snowdon, where a plateway incline, built before 1841, connected the adit with a cobbing floor, whence carts or sledges made their

---

* CRO: Vaynol 4056, Bick, *op. cit.*, p. 80.
† McElvogue, D., 'The Forgotten ways; evidence for water-borne transport in Nant Peris, Gwynedd', *Industrial Gwynedd* 4 (1999), pp. 5-15.

50 Ty Gwyn tramming level, Llandudno with wooden railway system (courtesy the Great Orme Exploration Society).

way down to a crushing mill on the valley floor (SH 6216 5201). At some stage, part of the road was by-passed in favour of barrow-ways, ore-slides and a strange stone-block railway on a steep but curved alignment.* Generally, for internal transport, narrow-gauge edge railways were used from the 1790s, when they are first recorded in an adit of a Llanberis copper mine, to the end of mining in Gwynedd 200 years later.† The early phase of this technology is exemplified by the Ty Gwyn tramming level (SH 7803 8278) which served a copper mine at Llandudno, so near the surface that the roots from the Promenade gardens grow into the tunnel. Here, not only does a length of wooden railway survive (Figure 50), to an approximate gauge of 0.549m (1ft 10in) but so do pump rods, and even the imprint of miners' boots in a patch of mud. The last phase is represented by the surviving 0.6m gauge system at Gwynfynydd gold mine (SH 7373 2808), with its battery electric locomotive and standard 'off the peg' steel wagons. Locomotives were only ever used at five locations – as well as at Gwynfynydd, they were also to be found at work in the deep mine at Parys, at Clogau gold mine (SH 668 195), the Parc lead mine and the Willoughby lead mine (SH 767 602 C), which was also unusual in that a 2.7km railway connected the mine to an aerial ropeway into the mill building.‡ Very few mines had, or could ever have required, their own railways to connect them to navigable water or to other transport routes. Those that did are discussed in *4.5.2*, though as an instance of how commercial optimism ran away with promoters' ideas, one of the least productive of the mechanised mines in Gwynedd, the Cwmdwyfor mine in Cwm Pennant (SH 541 505), was served by one of the longest railway systems, the Gorsedda Junction and Portmadoc Railways, to which it contributed no more than several wagon-loads throughout its entire life – far less than the traffic required to build even its 1.89km (1.175m) branch line. An aerial ropeway built by White's of Widnes after the First World War survives partly intact at Cwm Bychan (SH 6042 4764 – 5977 4626), ostensibly to provide the mine with access to a processing plant near the newly-constructed Welsh Highland Railway, though the barely-developed and archaic form of the workings themselves strongly suggests that this enterprise was fraudulent and that management hoped that the state-of-the-art processing and transport system would discourage shareholders from exploring too near the mine itself. The ropeway has been conserved by the National Trust, as owners of the land (Figure 51). Fragmentary remains of another such system survive in the Rhiw manganese mine, including the base for the return mechanism and the boiler for

---

* Bick, D., *op. cit.,* pp. 69-74.
† Bingley, W., *North Wales, including its Scenery, Antiquities, Customs etc* (London, 1804), i 231.
‡ Bradley, V.J., *Industrial Locomotives of North Wales* (London: Industrial Railway Society, 1992), entries C16, G26, P10, P12 and W8.

51 Ropeway at Cwm Bychan.

the steam engine that powered it, though here the purpose was to connect the mine with a jetty on Porth Neigwl. The trace also survives of a 3km long, 0.914m (3') gauge railway which connected the mines on Mynydd Rhiw to a wharf at Porth Ysgo.*

Shaft-winding was commonly practised, though mechanical winding was extremely rare. Horse-whim circles survive at a number of locations, such as at Parys (example at SH 4473 9069) and above Bontddu. Early photographs of the Parys mines show a steam winder in a corrugated iron shed associated with a wooden head-frame typical of the mid-19th century. The Morris shaft at Parys (SH 4338 9030), on which sinking began in 1988, was wound from a tall steel head-frame which forms a distinctive landscape feature although the haulage ropes were cut pending a change in the international price of zinc.†

Pumping machinery survives in only a few locations, though buildings for pump-engines are a little more numerous. The 20m-high stone pump-windmill tower at Parys, erected in 1878 (SH 4432 9051, SAM), is unique within the region, perhaps the UK.‡ At Cwm Ciprwth copper mine (SH 526 478) a water-wheel by Dingey and Sons of Truro (which also did duty for winding), a flat rod system and a pump shaft survived in poor condition into the 1990s, when the Snowdonia National Park archaeologist, Peter Crew, initiated a programme of conservation (Figure 52). Features such as these were typical of the arrangements at most Gwynedd mines, and their sites can be traced at many locations. The Great Orme mines installed what was probably the longest rod-system in the area, stretching across the peninsula from the pumps at SH 7705

---

* Williams, W., *Muyngloddio ym Mhen Llŷn/The Llŷn Peninsula Mines* (Llanrwst: Gwasg Carreg Gwalch, 1995).
† Pers. comm., Ian Cuthbertson, mine manager.
‡ Cockshutt, E., 'The Parys and Mona Copper Mines', *TAAS* 1960, p. 18. There had been earlier windmills on Parys – see UWB: Mona Mine 3040.

52 Conserved water-wheel, winding equipment and rod-engine at Cwm Ciprwth.

8318 to a primitive bucket-engine at SH 7637 8306, later replaced by a water-pressure engine a little lower down the hill. The course can be traced for much of the route, marked as shallow pits at 6m intervals in which the rocking A-frames were situated.* Rod-engines survive underground at Llanrwst mine, at Ty Gwyn (SH 7803 8278) and at Catherine and Jane Consols near Penrhyndeudraeth (SH 631 411 C). No water-pressure engines are known to survive, though it is possible that examples remain undiscovered.†

Engine houses are few, but some remarkably early examples survive – a reverse of the situation in Cornwall, where well over 100 houses survive, but none older than 1826.‡ It is now clear that a beam-engine house at Penrhyn Du lead mine on Penrhyn Llŷn (SH 3225 2624 – Figure 53) is in essence a structure of 1779 built to house a Boulton and Watt reciprocating engine.§ This may be the oldest beam-engine house in Wales, if not the UK. The Pearl shaft engine-house at Parys (SH 4476 9079, SAM), dating from 1819,

53 Boulton and Watt engine house of 1779 at Penrhyn Du.

---

* Williams, C.J., *Great Orme Mines* (Northern Mine Research Society, 1995), pp. 33-5, 49.
† Water-pressure engines are commonly found underground in metalliferous mines, often at the drainage level, where they operated pumps drawing water up from lower levels.
‡ David Bick lists three beam-engine houses in Gwynedd metal mines, out of a Welsh total of 39 – see Bick, D.E., 'The Beam-Engine House in Wales', *IAR* 12 1 (Autumn 1989), pp. 84-93.
§ See Birmingham City Library, Boulton and Watt agreements box 27/4, and Hills, R. and Gwyn, D., 'Three Engines at Penrhyn Du, 1760-1780', *Transactions of the Newcomen Society* 75 1 (2005), pp. 17-36.

possibly the oldest Cornish engine-house in Wales, was conserved by Cadw with the advice of the Amlwch Industrial Heritage Trust and the Welsh Mines Preservation Trust in the 1990s, when missing lintels were replaced and new stonework was put in.* Future plans include the rebuilding of the round-plan stack, blown down in a gale in 1987. Mynydd Parys lacked the gathering ground for water to turn a prime mover, and made practically no use of water-wheels for any purpose. Housing for horizontal steam engines is evident at two locations at Parys, at the foot of the Great Opencast (SH 4407 9027), and near the summit of the mountain, where twisted holding-down bolts mark the site of a substantial machine of 1880 built by the Sandycroft Foundry, possibly a differential compound (SH 4427 9054).† The most spectacular stack within the region is at 'Port Nigel' mine in the Llanengan field, which perhaps dates from the 1870s, built on a hillside above the mine to give a sufficient draught (SH 2949 2673). Though the engine-house associated with it is now known only from an old post-card and other documentary sources, the round-plan stack, built of country rock in its lower part and banded brickwork in the upper part, was conserved in the late 1990s.‡

Two engine-houses were deliberately blown up in the 1960s, one at Catherine and Jane Consols, built in 1860 to house a 24-inch Cornish rotative engine,§ the other at Cyffty in the Gwydir ore field (SH 7725 5890). The engine house at Llanrwst mine nearby (SH 7796 5933), which housed a 25-inch horizontal engine, and the circular plan stack, were conserved, rather crudely, in 1986.¶ This is now the one point in the Gwydir mining field where one chimney can be seen from another, since the stack of the Hafna smelter is visible from this point.

Though there is nothing comparable with the extensive barrack accommodation of the slate industry, workers' housing survives at several mines, and in the case of Drws y Coed, the miners' village lies immediately adjacent to the working areas (see p. 187). At Penrhyn Du mine, a recently-constructed house has been built on the footing of a barrack block, but retains the name, 'Cornish Row' (SH 3233 2647), a reminder of the fact that skilled workers were often drawn from the established Cornish mining areas, and that it was to persuade them to make their way to Wales that such buildings were often constructed. Though mine technology might show Cornish influence, there is nothing to suggest that domestic accommodation reflected west-country idioms.** The manganese mines of Ardudwy, as government-sponsored initiatives, required accommodation for the workforce; the concrete bases of wooden huts survive at one

---

* UWB: Mona Mine 232, 280, 304. The engine was built by the Neath Abbey Ironworks (West Glamorgan Record Office D/D NAI/M10/1-6, 264/1-3), and appears to have been the only Gwynedd contract ever carried out by this well-known firm, which dealt with clients from north-east Wales, England, Ireland, Chile, Calcutta and continental Europe as well as from within south Wales. See Ince, L., *Neath Abbey and the Industrial Revolution* (Stroud: Tempus, 2001). It was replaced, or some of its components were replaced, by products bought from Hocking and Loam of Redruth – see UWB Mona Mine 2025-2039, 2786-7.

† An engine in the Opencast is noted in 1841 (LlRO: W/DC/27, entries for 11-12 January, 6 February, 30 July, 3-5 August, 27 September and 1 October) – early for a horizontal engine. The Sandycroft engine is noted in the *Mining Journal* for 6 November 1880, p. 262, 11 December 1880, p. 1418.

‡ Bennett, J. and Vernon, R., *Metal Mines of Llanengan* (Warrington: Gwydyr Mines publications, 2002), pp. 116-24.

§ Bick, *Copper Mines*, pp. 15-21.

¶ Vernon, R.W., 'Conservation of Mining Sites in the Gwydir Forest Area of the Snowdonia National Park', *IAR* 12 1 (Autumn 1989), pp. 77-83.

** Cornish, Derbyshire and Flintshire miners were to be found in Parys, Llanberis and in Drws y Coed in the 18th century. They married local women, and their legacy survives in the double-barrelled surnames of Amlwch and Llanberis – Rothwell-Hughes, Roose-Williams, Closs-Stephens. Remarkably, French and Belgian miners were employed at the Glaslyn mine for a while in 1852 – see Bick, *Copper Mines*, p. 80.

such site, the only upstanding feature being the remains of a lavatory pan (SH 6509 2655 – 6515 2655).*

As with the slate industry, mineral extraction and heritage have overlapped considerably in Gwynedd. The Gwynfynydd gold mine marketed itself as a tourist attraction in the 1990s, before reverting to limited mining. When operations came to an end in the late 1990s, the site preserved the characteristics of a small Merionethshire mine, with its narrow-gauge tracks snaking into the adit, and a strong-room door said to have come from Dolgellau gaol. At Parys, the management of Anglesey Mining plc have co-operated enthusiastically with the Amlwch Industrial Heritage Trust to ensure a sustainable future for the historic mining landscapes. Individual enthusiasts and professional archaeologists have also been able to ensure the consolidation and interpretation of important mining features, particularly in the Gwydyr minng field.

4.1.4 Mining for coal

The Anglesey coal-field is small and contains few upstanding buildings, but preserves the surface remains of late Medieval mining as well as of later periods.

Mining for coal has traditionally been regarded as one of the 'leading sectors' of British industrialisation, and the collier as 'the archetypal proletarian'.† Throughout Britain, its origins can be traced back to the Medieval period, but the industry grew steadily from the 16th century onwards as coal became increasingly used as a domestic fuel and for a growing variety of technical functions. The demands of the coal industry led to technical innovations such as the adoption of the railway, from 1604 onwards, and of the steam engine.

The bulk of Welsh coal reserves are to be found in south-east Wales, though important mines were to be found near Wrexham and Ruabon near the English border in north-east Wales. Apart from some unsuccessful trials in mainland Gwynedd, the only coal mines in our area were to be found in Anglesey.‡

Here, the seams of coal constitute a syncline longitudinally bisected by a boundary fault known as the Malltraeth marsh or Cors Ddygái. In the Medieval period this was a long arm of the sea that extended from the present village of Malltraeth to near Llangefni, a distance of 16km (10 miles), but it was beginning to silt up even before a major water-control system was constructed in the late 18th century (p. 176). The coal seams run in the same general direction – north-east to south-west – but cross from one side of the inlet to the other and become progressively deeper towards the sea. The earliest evident workings are situated where they were shallowest, at the north-east, whereas the most recent are at the south-west, and in one case actually appear to extend under the sea-bed (Map 6).§ The earliest reference to coal-mining dates from 1441, and thereafter for the next few centuries there are several scattered references

---

* Gwynedd Archaeological Trust, *Gwynedd Metalliferous Mines* (for Cadw, 1998: Report 291).
† Harrison, R. (ed.), *Independent Collier: the coal miner as archetypal proletarian reconsidered* (New York: St. Martin's Press, 1978).
‡ There is an excellent summary history of the Anglesey coal-field in Bassett, T.M. and James, G., 'Coalmining in Anglesey', *TAAS* 1969-70, pp. 137-63.
§ Greenly, E., *Geology of Anglesey* vol. 2 (Memoir of the Geological Survey, 1919) p. 812; Williams, E.A., *Hanes Môn yn y Bedwaredd Ganrif ar Bymtheg* (Eisteddfod Gadeiriol Môn, 1927), p. 38.

Map 6 Coal mining area

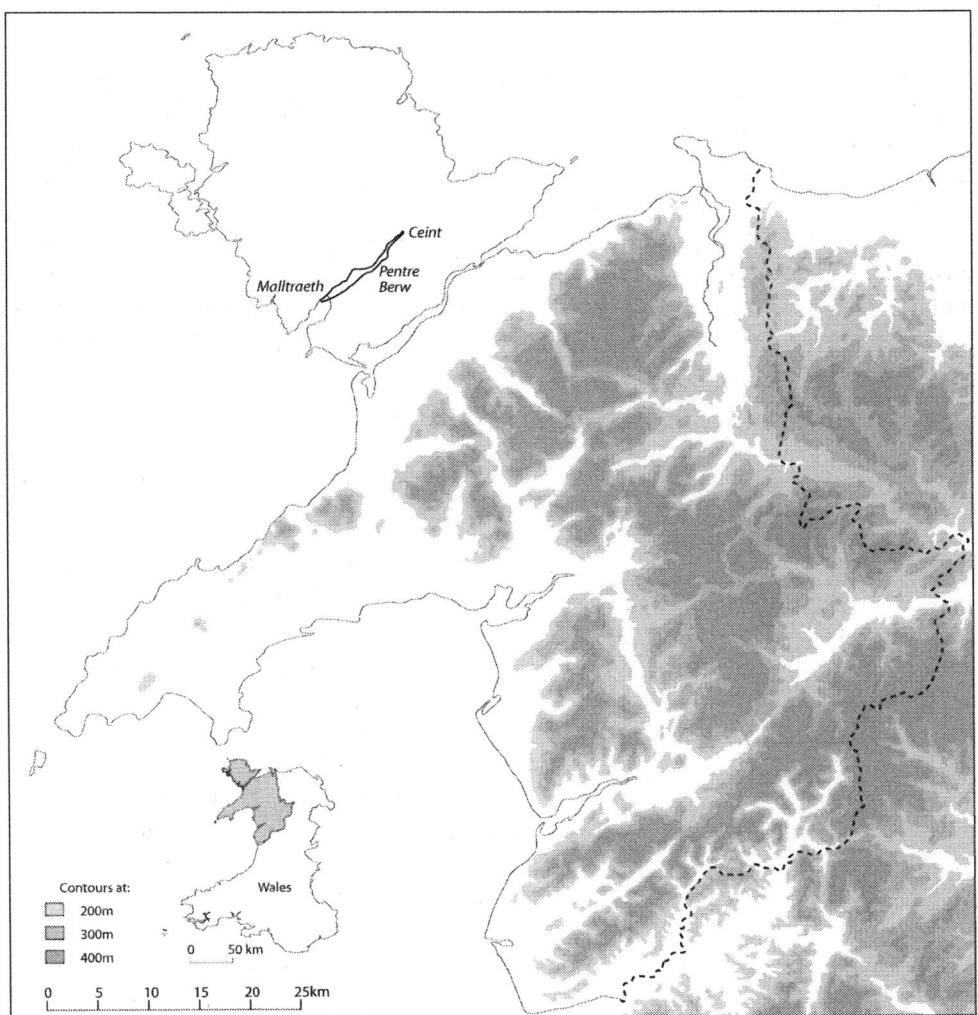

to mining. One document specifies that 'no pitt shall be dug in a cornfield, without warning the tenant before the corn is sown', suggesting minimal capitalisation and seasonal work. In 1610 some of the low-lying shafts were flooded as part of a quarrel between two local magnates.

By the early 18th century the area's landowners were becoming more actively involved. Penrhyn Mawr (SH 468 728) was actively exploited by Sir Nicholas Bayly, owner of the Penrhyn Du lead mines on Penrhyn Llŷn as well as of the Parys copper mines (p. 81) elsewhere on Anglesey and collieries in Staffordshire. With the drainage of the marsh, the seams towards Malltraeth could also be worked. Lessees, consultants and miners, sometimes local men, sometimes from further afield, including quite a number from the Ruabon area, tried to make a success of the pits, but the Anglesey coal-field never seriously broke into the export market and most of its produce went

54 Medieval and later coal-mining at Tyddyn Mawr (Crown Copyright: Royal Commission on the Ancient and Historic Monuments of Wales: 995015-5).

to local hearths and local industries such as lime-burning. The end came just before the First World War when the last handful of men gave up.*

Because the mines are very low-lying, it is likely that they all have long flooded and there can be little hope of recovering archaeological evidence of the underground workings themselves. Surface features give us some idea what form they might have taken. Near the north-eastern limit of the Anglesey coal-field various trenches and mounds are evident (SH 475 736, Figure 54). The prominent trench in Fig. 54 corresponds with where one of the seams outcropped on the surface and may therefore represent the site of a shallow open digging. Nearby (towards the bottom of the Figure) are several doughnut-shaped mounds, no more than 4m high, which correspond to where the deeper seams of coal lie. These are likely to be the upcasts of shallow shafts which would have been wound by horse-gin from deeper seams. Archaeologists have too often assumed that shafts such as these are bell-pits – self-contained single workings worked out from the foot of the shaft until the whole excavation threatened to collapse, at which stage another shaft would be sunk nearby. This may be the case here, but it is significant that at the one pre-Modern coal mining site in Britain which has been archaeologically recorded, Coleorton in Leicestershire, active from 1450 to 1600, an extensive surface network of shafts, some as deep as 30m (100'), gave access to interconnected pillar and stall mining.† George Owen's account

---

* Pers. comm., Tomos Roberts, former archivist, UWB.
† Hartley, R.F., 'The Tudor Miners of Coleorton, Leicestershire', *Mining Before Powder* (Peak District Mines Historical Society 12 3, Summer 1994 and Historical Metallurgy Society Special Publication), pp. 91-101.

of work in Pembrokeshire coal-mines, written in 1602-3, records windlass shafts being sunk to a depth of 20 fathoms (36m – 120 ft) and providing work for 11 underground men (three diggers, seven bearers and one filler) as well as six surface workers (four winders and two riddlers).* This suggests that even a peripheral coal-field had moved well beyond the primitive bell pit system by the early 17th century.

Other upcasts nearby are much more substantial, and are probably the result of winding by horse-whim, a technology first recorded in the region at Penrhyn Mawr colliery in 1744.† These upcasts are typically 70m or more apart. Elsewhere, particularly in the central and south-western parts of the coalfield, there is map evidence that identifies some of the largest upcasts as the sites of steam engines. Underground plans from the 19th century show extensive pillar-and-stall working, in which pillars of useable coal are left to support the roof, though some documents specify the 'long way' – longwall mining, a technique now known to have been used as early as 1620 in Leicestershire, in which all the coal is removed and the roof behind supported with stone.‡

The first record of a steam engine in any of the Anglesey collieries is in 1812, though it has left little archaeological trace (SH 4706 7306).§ Penrhyn Mawr colliery, the largest and the most extensively worked, made use of several engines from 1815 onwards, but their sites have been largely obliterated at surface level by the construction of the new A55 in 2000. Plans and other documentation make it possible to reconstruct how surface arrangements might have appeared here in the early years of the 19th century, a scene not dissimilar to one of the best known industrial paintings of this period, an anonymous oil painting now in the Walker Art Gallery in Liverpool.¶ At the nearby Berw Colliery, there survive the chimney and part of the housing for a pumping and winding engine installed in the 1840s (SH 463 725, Figure 55).** Local legend recalls a night of torrential rain in the 1860s when all the Berw miners were summoned to the *Collier's Arms* in Pentre Berw and given their orders to man the pumps, but the black waters overwhelmed the mine and flooded the workings.††

The near-demise of the British coal industry in the later years of the 20th century led to the sudden obliteration of many important mining sites, though as a rule archaeological recording took place before the demolition contractors moved in. However, in most cases,

55 Berw colliery.

---

* Owen, G. (ed. Miles, D.), *Description of Pembrokeshire* (Llandyssul: Gomer Press, 1994), pp. 91-3.
† UWB: Plas Newydd mss IV 8484.
‡ Hartley, *op. cit.*, p. 94.
§ UWB: Plas Newydd 5vi 1204, Bangor mss 118a.
¶ Walker Art Gallery, Liverpool, *Pit-head of a Coal-Mine with Steam Winding gear*, oil on canvas 95 x 135, artist unknown.
** Williams, E., *The Day Before Yesterday* (Beaumaris, 1988), p. 138; UWB: Boston mss 137-8.
†† Pers. comm., John Pritchard, Pentre Berw.

more recent working had long obliterated traces of workings from the Medieval or early Industrial periods. The Anglesey coalfield is not unique in British terms in that it preserves evidence of coal-mining from, probably, the 17th century into the 19th, but it is one of very few.

4.1.5 Agriculture in the industrial period

The archaeology of agriculture within Gwynedd reflects the sector's growth in the industrial period of the 18th, 19th and 20th centuries. Whilst 'high farming' never had the same impact as in England, the material evidence confirms that land-use and farming methods went through profound changes in this period. Farming remains the dominant activity within the historic landscape, though continued changes now pose significant conservation problems for historic agricultural structures.

The 18th century onwards in Gwynedd not only saw unprecedented development in industry as traditionally understood but also in agriculture, with active elite sponsorship of improvement. In the fullness of time, this habit of patrician control was to give the emergent radicals of the late Victorian period some of their most powerful weapons in the war they declared on 'landlordism', a war which the most able of them, David Lloyd George, took to Westminster, where he laid an axe to the roots of landed power over the United Kingdom as a whole. Understanding farming practice and patterns of land-ownership in Gwynedd may therefore inform the study of a crucial turning point in both Welsh and British history – but to what extent, and in what way, can agriculture be regarded as part of the archaeology of the industrial period? By convention, agriculture has not come within the remit of industrial archaeology, and its material remains, insofar as they are studied within an archaeological framework at all, have been regarded as the province of the student of vernacular building or of the post-Medievalist.*

A preliminary answer must be that agriculture and industry closely affect each other, and that their archaeology might be expected to reflect this. In Gwynedd the relationship was particularly close. Industrialisation was driven by the great estates rather than the burgess towns, yet the estates' focus was primarily rural; the same individuals who oversaw the fortunes of mines and quarries, whether at first hand or as lessors, were also managing the rural economy. At the other end of the social scale, very often the same people were working the land as were blasting for copper, lead or slate, alternating between the land and the quarry or mine on a seasonal or daily basis. Industrial-era transport links could also service farms. A horse-drawn railway that took minerals to harbour could also bring back lime for slaking fields; its steam-powered replacement meant that away-wintering sheep could be sent to another county rather than to a lowland pasture in the same valley. Today, motorways ensure that small Gwynedd lambs find a ready market in southern Europe. Finally, the park and the estate might themselves require industrial infrastructure and call for engineering skills.

---

* As early as 1996, Barrie Trinder remarked that 'It is philosophically indefensible to omit agriculture from archaeological studies of recent centuries. Its exclusion can be partly justified on pragmatic grounds, shortage of space, the author's ignorance and lack of coherent published works. A more coherent argument might be that agricultural buildings evolve over a long period, and that barns, dairies, ploughs and wagons of recent centuries are better seen in an extended agricultural context than in a broader chronological setting' – *The Industrial Archaeology of Shropshire* (Phillimore: Chichester, 1996), p. 213.

The problem in providing specific answers for Gwynedd is that material evidence is often either lacking or unacknowledged. Changes in stock or herd sizes are not always reflected in the archaeological evidence, and humdrum but important changes such as field drainage systems are easily destroyed and frequently go unnoticed during assessments. Paper sources, on the other hand, abound, and provide a starting point; land-holding is the most documented form of social relationship, even if it tends to focus on the activities of the elite. The 'spirit of improvement' took hold at a time of widespread literacy and inspired much sharpening of quills even in remote Llŷn *plasdai* and chilly Merioneth rectories. Just as Jane Austen satirised the English 'improver' in *Mansfield Park*, Twm o'r Nant pricked the pretensions of his Welsh counterpart in *Pedair Colofn Gwladwriaeth*,* with less subtlety but quite equal literary panache. The Llangefni, Caernarfon, Dolgellau and university archives are full of estate correspondence and maps, of travellers' accounts and topographical studies, of reports of the Board of Agriculture and of the county societies.† Enclosure records allow the spirit to be given a local habitation and a name; between 1802 and 1870, 2,737.6 hectares (6,765 acres) of Anglesey, 19,750.3 hectares (48,805 acres) of Merioneth and 15,730 hectares (38,870 acres) of Caernarvonshire were subject to parliamentary enclosure, to which must be added an extra 6,883.6 estimated hectares (17,010 acres) in Caernarvonshire.‡ Appendix 1 makes clear just how much of Gwynedd lay in patrician hands once this process was complete and before the agricultural depression set in. Nearly a third of Caernarvonshire was owned by four men, all peers of the realm; 33 men between them (an additional 10 *great landowners* and 19 *squires*) owned around three-quarters of the county. Only in Merioneth were smaller proprietors (*squires*, and the *greater* and *lesser yeomen*) in the ascendant. Even allowing for the tendency of documentary sources to give more emphasis to the activities of the wealthy and the powerful, there is no doubt that, at a crucial time, agriculture in Gwynedd was explicitly directed and controlled by a regional patrician elite.

Yet 'lordship' within the rural economy of Gwynedd has undergone significant changes in the period from 1700, reflecting major changes in the agricultural sector. In 1700 the Atlantic isles were largely self-sufficient in the matter of foodstuffs. On the eve of war in 1938, the United Kingdom imported 70 per cent by value of the food it required.§ By the late 20th century, even less was home-produced; agribusinesses, often remote corporations, had taken over much farming, and membership of the European Union had led to changes in the way that agriculture was co-ordinated and in the crops that were grown.

The very incomplete picture of agriculture in Gwynedd at the beginning of our period shows a variety of practices from estate to estate – some traditionalist and conservative, others, particularly those that were coming under 'remote control' from larger English estates, more dynamic and in the words of one historian already 'overtly

---

* Edwards, T. ('Twm o'r Nant'), *Pedair Colofn Gwladwriaeth* ('Four Pillars of the State') (Caerfyrddin: Jonathan Harris, 1810).

† The Merioneth Agricultural Society was established in 1801, followed by Caernarvonshire in 1807 and Anglesey in 1808; see Dodd, A.H., *The Industrial Revolution in North Wales* (Wrexham: Bridge Books, 1990), pp. 39-40.

‡ The first Welsh parliamentary enclosure was of the Dee estuary in 1752, but only 13 took place before 1790 and over half took place after 1840 – a century later than the core area of the English midlands. Chapman, C., *A Guide to Parliamentary Enclosures in Wales* (Cardiff: University of Wales Press, 1992).

§ Short, B., Watkins, C., Foot, W., and Kinsman, P., *The National Farm Survey of 1941–1943: State Surveillance and the Countryside in England and Wales in the Second World War* (Wallingford and New York: CABI, 2000), p. 19.

capitalist' in their management of resources.* These are the ones which emerge as the classic estate-controlled landscapes which take shape in the late 18th century. Their heyday lasted only about a hundred years, until agricultural depression and political pressure for tenants' rights began to tell. There is also evidence in the 19th century for an increasingly entrepreneurial attitude amongst tenants and smaller proprietors, some of whom ran farms in Gwynedd whilst at the same time managing holdings in Wisconsin† – quite apart from the many who emigrated permanently to Australia, New Zealand and the USA.

Although estates in Gwynedd were being broken up from as early as 1887, elite patronage of a very different sort soon becomes apparent, when central and local government and academia began to assume responsibility for the training and education of agriculturalists rather than landowners or their stewards. This reflected developments that were taking place particularly in the USA, with the establishment of the 'land grant colleges' after the civil war, and in Canada and Denmark, as well as home-grown initiatives such as the creation of dedicated agricultural colleges. After two false starts, the University College of North Wales took a lease on Tanyfynwent farm at Aber from Lord Penrhyn in 1910 and invested substantially in it (SH 6516 7272). Caernarvonshire County Council established a farm institute at Madryn on Penrhyn Llŷn (SH 2850 3627) in 1912‡ and purchased Glynllifon park, house and home farm (SH 4584 5554) in 1954 to establish an agricultural college.§ Gwynedd even provides an example of a completely abortive form of rural management, in the experimental nationalisation of the Glanllyn estate (SH 8893 3210) in Merioneth when the Wynnstay estate was obliged to pay estate death duties in the 1950s. This was the so-called 'Dol Hendre' scheme – the land was later sold to the farmers. The social ownership of land had been under discussion at governmental level since the early years of the 20th century, with Gwynedd-bred radicals such as Lloyd George particularly vocal, but the nationalisation of a complete estate as a going concern was a rare event outside the former German Democratic Republic. The Town and Country Planning Act of 1947 and the establishment of the Snowdonia National Park in 1951 did, however, strengthen the role of central and local government. The National Park, like others in the United Kingdom, did not set out to create, or recreate, a wilderness but to sustain a working environment as well as to manage a public open space. More recently the European Union has significantly changed the appearance of the farming landscape both by making grants available to erect new farm buildings and by subsidies. It is important to emphasise that these changes are not uniform throughout the area; some estates remain in being, in the hands of families who have lived in the *plas* for hundreds of years, or in the stewardship of the National Trust, or run by professional managers, and in many ways the continuities within Gwynedd's agricultural sector are more striking than the changes.

How can we best set out to analyse the archaeology of the rural economy in Gwynedd? In that the *plas* is its traditional centre and the point from which for the

---

* Williams, G.H., 'Estate Management in Dyffryn Conwy, *c.*1685', *Transactions of the Honourable Society of Cymmrodorion*, 1979, pp. 31-74.
† Pers. comm., Einion Tomos, UWB archivist.
‡ Williams, J.G., *The University College of North Wales: Foundations 1884-1927* (Cardiff: University of Wales Press, 1985), pp. 165-75.
§ Cadw/ICOMOS UK, *Conwy Gwynedd & The Isle of Anglesey: Register of Landscapes, Parks and Gardens of Special Historic Interest in Wales: Part 1 Parks and Gardens* (Cardiff, Cadw, 1998), p. 210.

Map 7 Agriculture

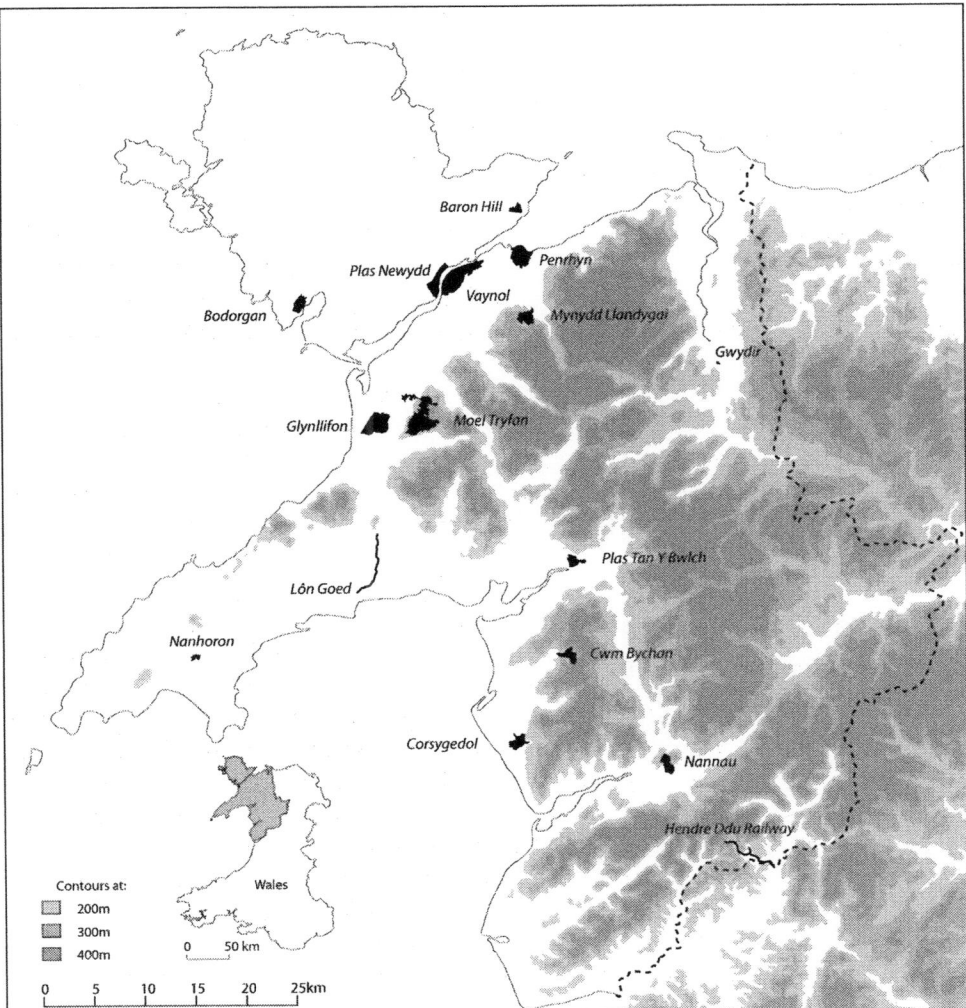

greater part of the last three hundred years it was governed, it seems sensible to start here, before moving out to the farming landscapes, and beyond them to the bleak moorlands.

The locations of Gwynedd's parks sometimes hint at ancient tenurial systems and strategic imperatives – smaller ones often stand guard over fords, such as Nanhoron, or control access to mountain pastures, such as Cwm Bychan. Plas Tan y Bwlch, Gwydir and Nannau are situated near the head of tidal waters, and the largest parks, Penrhyn, Baron Hill, Plas Newydd and Vaynol, are all situated along the Menai Strait. These last might be anything up to 4.5km² in area (Map 7).*

---

* Vaynol = 4.5km², Penrhyn = 3.158km², Glynllifon = approximately 4km²; information from Gwynedd Archaeological Trust.

56 Penrhyn estate map of 1768, showing productive land which was later subsumed into the park (courtesy of UWB: Penrhyn Castle mss, S2205.

Tellingly, these extensive ornamental landscapes were often once productive land. Leigh's 1768 map of the Penrhyn estate identifies field names around the medieval house that make it clear they were not for ornament – *Park y Moch* ('pig enclosure'), *Bryndillad* ('clothes hill', presumably where the laundresses hung out linen) and *Cae'r Efail* ('smithy field') (Figure 56). By the time of Richard Williams' 1804 survey, this house had been subsumed by an exercise in Gothic (the gigantic neo-Norman castle still lay some years in the future), and the whole is now surrounded by an ornamental parkland. The labour of servants and retainers had now become invisible, and industry banished to the park's periphery. However, even the quarry railroad could be subsumed into the ornamental landscape, as runs of wagons passed under the markedly 'polite' architecture of the Marchogion incline drumhouse (SH 593 719 – see p. 157) to make their way across the backdrop of the estate agent's water-garden at Lime Grove. The same process is repeated elsewhere, such as at Glynllifon (SH 45 55 C), where late Medieval pack-horse bridges and mills became part of a new enclosed park in the 1820s, or Bodnant (SH 8000 7234), where a Victorian industrialist's garden includes an ornamental mill on the site of an 18th-century blast-furnace (p. 124).*

Some areas within or near the park remained functional. The extent of provision varied greatly, according to the resources (and perhaps the self-image) of the landowner. The smallest *plasdy* might have only a laundry or a brew-house or a smithy in its vicinity, though these categories conceal considerable variations of scale. The Penrhyn laundry served the needs of the estate as a whole, including the London town house; linen would be sent up by train to be washed in the cleaner water of Wales and hung from lines supported on slate pillars to dry in its purer air.† Several parks – Vaynol, Tan y Bwlch, Penrhyn, Plas Newydd, Dolmelynllyn – had dairies, ornamental as much as

---

* *Register of Landscapes, Parks and Gardens*, p. 58.
† Pers. comm., Marian Gwyn, National Trust. Other laundries are recorded or survive at, or associated with, Bodorgan, Garreglwyd and Plas Tan y Bwlch – *Register of Landscapes, Parks and Gardens*, pp. 5, 11, 275-6.

productive, often decked out with ceramic tiles. Tan y Bwlch preserves an octagonal buttery (SH 6579 4063); Vaynol's gothic dairy (SH 5376 6956) was built as late as 1911.* They represented a break from the farming methods of the 16th and 17th centuries, when milk and cheese production took place in the upland summer pastures,† though a shadow of this arrangement persisted on the Penrhyn estate. The first Lord Penrhyn not only built an ornamental cow-shed with Doric colonnades in the park (which has long vanished) but also the dairy in the grounds, which survives, as does the (later) dairy pantry in the castle itself where ice-creams could be produced from ice kept in one of the towers. So does the part-gothic, part-classical dairy farm at Pen isa'r Nant, six miles away, with its slate slab shelving, even though the fountain no longer plays in the courtyard (SH 6308 6507, Figure 57).‡

57 Pen isa'r Nant, the Penrhyn estate's ornamental farm.

Some service facilities were manifestly 'industrial' in scale and conception. Bodorgan (SH 3859 6737), Glynllifon and (inevitably) Penrhyn had their own gasworks, though it is only at Glynllifon that any evidence survives, in the form of retort bases as well as of the plans produced by DeWinton's Union ironworks in Caernarfon. In the 1880s William Edward Oakeley at Plas Tan y Bwlch created two artificial lakes to form a wilderness garden and in 1896 installed a hydro-electric plant to light the *plas*, and power the flour mill, timber saw mill and a smithy, each one an exercise in 'estate vernacular' (plant at SH 6581 4079).§

The only estate workshop complex to remain largely intact is at Glynllifon (SH 455 554). This includes on the one site a timber mill, smithy, carpenters' shop, office, and a stone-cutting table, powered by an 1855 horizontal steam engine built in Caernarfon.

---

*   *Register of Landscapes, Parks and Gardens*, pp. 35, 191, 304.
†   Williams, G.H., 'Farming in Stuart Caernarvonshire', *TCHS* 42 (1981), p. 59.
‡   National Trust, *Penrhyn Castle* (London: The National Trust, 1991), p. 17.
§   *Register of Landscapes, Parks and Gardens*, pp. 275-9.

58 Glynllifon estate workshops.

Nearby is a timber saw-mill powered by a water-wheel and a hydro-electricity station (Figure 58).

The creation of the park landscape and its immediate environs also sponsored engineering skills in an indirect way. It is hard to imagine that Penrhyn castle was built without the assistance of a railway to move the blocks of Penmon limestone from the port through the park. The impressive but much decayed block of limekilns at Port Penrhyn is believed to have been used to prepare mortar for the castle, having originally functioned as flint kilns (SH 5931 7269).* The fine iron bridge of 1821 cast at the Penydarren Ironworks in south Wales which crosses the Ogwen river on the park's periphery (SH 6106 7214) illustrates the estate's tendency to buy in from outside, whereas the water-control system on the stream at Glynllifon is the work of John y Gôf ('John the blacksmith', John Hughes, 1766/7-1845), a local man and proficient engineer, a slate-quarry manager.† A background in managing ornamental landscapes could also lead to managing industrial projects – John Williams, who had worked under Humphry Repton as a gardener for the Marquess of Anglesey at Plas Newydd, became Madocks' site-manager and executive engineer at Traeth Mawr.‡ Madocks' own efforts to turn the Traeth into a landscape that was both productive and aesthetically pleasing serve as a reminder that the distinction between the private park and the estate as a whole was not always one which landowners chose to make.

The comparative size and provision of the larger Gwynedd parks reflected the extent rather than the quality of their owners' land-holdings. Even by Welsh standards, farming land in Gwynedd is mostly poor, and farms tend to be small.§ The better corn-

---

* Boyd, J.I.C., *Narrow Gauge Railways in North Caernarvonshire Volume 2 The Penrhyn Quarry Railways* (Oxford; Oakwood, 1985), p. 65.

† CRO: XD2A/1586, Gwyn, D., 'From Blacksmith to Engineer: Artisan Technology in North Wales in the Early Nineteenth Century', *Llafur* 7 (1999), pp. 51-65.

‡ *Register of Landscapes, Parks and Gardens*, pp. 34-42; Beazley, E., *Madocks and the Wonder of Wales* (Aberystwyth: P&Q, 1985), pp. 78, 192-7.

§ In 1997 it was calculated that 0.1% of Gwynedd land was grade 1 (the best) compared to the figure for Wales as a whole which is 0.2%), 0.1% was grade 2 (Wales 2.3%); 8.4% was grade 3 (Wales 17.5%); and 65.4% was grade 5 (the poorest – Wales 35.3%). Rough grazing predominates (47.2%, compared to 20% of Wales as a whole), as do cattle and sheep farms (91.2% – Wales 70.1%) – http://hen.gwynedd.gov.uk/adrannau/economaidd/ffeithiau/agriculture, accessed 21 November 2004.

growing lands are to be found on Anglesey and the Arfon plain, and it is no surprise that some of the earliest substantial surviving agricultural buildings in Gwynedd are to be found here. The great corn-barn of 1605 associated with the old hall at Vaynol (SH 5376 6965) measures 42.7m by 9.14m (140' by 30') and is perhaps the oldest intact purpose-built agricultural building within the area (Figure 59). Only slightly smaller is the barn at Henblas (SH 4227 7254) on Anglesey, dating from 1733, which still measures 30.5m by 8.2m (100' by 27') and is roofed in ten bays. More surprising is the barn of 1685 at Corsygedol (SH 6002 2318), which illustrates the need to grow corn even in the unfavourable conditions of upland Merioneth, an area that would now only be considered suitable for grazing. Each of these follows the distinctive pattern, with opposed doorways and ventilation slits; it was in places like these, as well as in many smaller and later barns, that the farm labourers worked on the threshing floor in the months after the harvest whilst the breeze winnowed the grain. Corn barns were typically given an architectural emphasis which other farm buildings were not, as the symbol as well as the storehouse of the surplus. Even so, it is significant that none of these matches the storage capacity of the great aisled barns of the south-east of England, and the majority of Gwynedd barns were no more than three bays wide.*

These early barns do not appear to have formed part of a planned farmstead. Where early farm complexes survive, such as at Gerddibluog in Merioneth (SH 6193 3085), there is little sense of a planned environment; here the free-standing farmhouse of 1667 faces the *tyddyn y traean* (dower house), and looks away from the mill, the cart-shed, the byre, the barn of 1728 and the stable of 1779.† The same is true of Maesygarnedd, not far away (SH 6421 2692), where the house and byre of *c.*1600 are free standing at an approximate right-angle to each other but a lateral extension of the house containing a barn, a hay-barn and a shed erected in the 19th century began to create something of a court-yard feel to the farmstead. These early Gwynedd

59 Vaynol barn (Crown Copyright: NBR AA51/1702 3-566).

---

* RCAHMW *Central*, p. 244; Smith, P., *Houses of the Welsh Countryside* (London: HMSO, 1988), pp. 150-1b, plate 105.
† Smith, *op. cit.*, p. 647.

60 A Merioneth hay-barn showing the distinctive long slabs supporting the roof timbers.

farmsteads have more in common with their counterparts in Ireland, particularly those of the west, than in England, where a courtyard plan is more common.*

The open-sided hay-barn appears to have been introduced in the late 18th century, and is particularly numerous in Gwynedd, perhaps because of the heavy rainfall; those in the northern part of Merioneth typically make use of distinctive long slabs, many of which came from Gelli Grin quarry (SH 640 393 – Figure 60). Another distinctive building, more common on mainland Gwynedd than on Anglesey, is the field-house, a small building for cattle and hay sited away from the main farm complex, because it was easier to store the hay where it was cut than to move it to the homestead.† In the early 20th century the availability of corrugated iron led to the building of large hay-sheds and other structures, and in the 1980s and 1990s European Union grants made possible the erection of standard-issue agricultural buildings, typically of the 'Atcost' type with breeze-block lower walls.

Mechanisation is late and limited, though sufficient to change the character of the region's farms. Even wheeled carts were a rarity until the last decades of the 18th century in some of the upland parishes,‡ and it may be significant that distinctive regional building materials such as the Gelli Grin slabs come to be used around this time. It is only in about 1905 that steam engines and threshing machines began to supersede threshing with flails – later than in England and the American mid-West. Their arrival was an important day in the farm's calendar, as the machinery was invariably peripatetic, the property of an agricultural contractor, and there is no known instance in Gwynedd of a dedicated traction engine shed such as would be found on some large English farms. The engines might in the early days be portables, which would have to be drawn by horses, or tractions which could draw the threshing machine itself. Though no record has come to light of cable-plough engines in Gwynedd, some use

---

* Aalen, F., Whelan, K. and Stout, M., *Atlas of the Irish Rural Landscape* (Cork: Cork University Press, 1997), p. 165.
† Smith, *op. cit.*, pp. 152-3, plate 107b.
‡ Owen, T.M., 'Y Drol Gyntaf', *Medel* 3 (1986), pp. 21-6.

was made of light steam tractors for direct ploughing.* Internal combustion tractors such as the 'International Junior' began to appear after the First World War, and the Fordson in the 1930s. The *ffergi bach* ('little Massey Ferguson') was the tractor of choice for young farmers after the Second World War. Many survive, and restoring them to working order is a popular hobby. The tractors were more economic and more versatile than the steam engines, especially with the introduction of the self-lift plough from 1939 onwards. This change was a gradual one, as some farms made a point of providing work for horse-ploughmen (and for the horses) as long as they were able to work. Reaping machines and reaper-binders were commonly found from around 1910, and were used for the corn harvest until the advent of the combine harvester in the 1950s and '60s, about eighty years after they first appeared in the USA.†

Only two farms in Gwynedd were ever equipped with stationary steam engines, the Penrhyn home farm (SH 5947 7136) and Cremlyn (SH 7520 7714) on the Baron Hill estate on Anglesey. Otherwise small water-wheels or horse-whims did duty, though a few Anglesey farms had tower wind-mills to cut hay or roots or churn butter as well as grind corn.‡ In the 20th century, some farms were equipped with hydro sets. Many of these were built by Richard Edwards of Llanuwchllyn, with castings supplied by the Britannia Foundry in Porthmadog; between 1907 and 1917 he supplied 221 turbines for farm power (and 13 for farm lighting), over an area as far south as Machynlleth and as far east as the English border, to an average horse-power of 3.7.§ A chapter of Thomas Firbanks' *I Bought a Mountain* eloquently describes the problems of setting up such a system on a farm bought from the Penrhyn estate near Capel Curig in the 1930s.¶ Small fixed or portable internal combustion plant was also installed in many farms from the 1920s onwards.** The extension of the electricity supply system to rural areas after the easing of post-war restrictions connected the vast majority of farms to the grid by 1975. One result was an increase in dairy farming, with power for milking machines and separators; another was the substitution of razor-shearing for the traditional hand-shearing.

There is little evidence of dedicated transport routes being sponsored directly by the estates, doubtless in part because landowners dominated the turnpike trusts and could see that their interests were served this way. One exception is the mysterious early 19th-century haulage road, the *lôn goed* in Eifionydd, celebrated in the poetry of R. Williams Parry, which extends for 4.6 miles (7.5km) from Hendre Cennin farm to the turnpike at Afonwen (SH4596 4382-4395 3764). The impact of railways has already been mentioned, but it is worth adding that in a number of places lightly-engineered narrow-gauge railways primarily built for mineral traffic also served farms, such as Sir Edmund Buckley's Hendre Ddu railway, which ran from his standard gauge

---

* *Myfanwy*, a Mann tractor of 1918, supplied new to the Anglesey Farming Co-operative, survives in private ownership. Despite weighing only five tons, it proved a little heavy for direct ploughing – http://www.steam-up.co.uk/dsf2k2/u4748_dsf2k2.htm, accessed 3 June 2006.

† This section draws on various sources, such as Jenkins, J.G., *Life and Tradition in Rural Wales* (London: J.M. Dent and Sons, 1976); for American material, see Bogue, A.G., 'An Agricultural Empire' in *The Oxford History of the American West* (New York and Oxford: Oxford University Press, 1996), pp. 294-6.

‡ The remains of only one survive above ground, Melin y Pant at SH 416 493; others are recorded as Treban-Meurig and Fferam at Pen Carnisiog – see Guise B. and Lees, G., *Windmills of Anglesey* (Builth Wells: Attic Books, 1992), pp. 65, 131.

§ Thomas, D.W., *Hydro-Electricity in North Wales* (Llanrwst: Gwasg Carreg Gwalch, 1997), pp. 5-13.

¶ Firbanks, T., *I Bought a Mountain* (London: Harrap, 1953), pp. 231-42.

** Parry, G., 'Owen Charles Jones, Gosodwr Peiriannau Oel', *Fferm a Thyddyn* 5 (Calan Mai 1990), p. 18.

Mawddwy Railway at Aberangell (SH 8463 0999) into the hills, sending off sidings into farmyards and timber mills as well as to the slate quarries.*

Enough has been said to suggest that 'high farming' (the high-input, high-output agriculture associated with the mid-19th century) is conspicuous by its absence, even though the majority of surviving farm complexes date from the classic period when it was practised. Very often, even dates are unknown, and a precise typology is certainly lacking, but it appears that few of the farm buildings constructed even on the great estates are particularly large compared with their equivalents in the 'highland zone' of England or even upland areas of South Wales, and are mostly much later in date.† Substantial planned complexes are represented by the home farms at Penrhyn (SH 5950 7130) and Plas Newydd (SH 5140 6910) and in a few other locations. Sometimes a farm within easy reach of the house was specially favoured, such as Ty'n y Hendre on the Penrhyn estate (SH 6227 7114), which follows an enclosed courtyard pattern, set with an ornamental pattern of cobbles. Smaller examples are very numerous. Around Ysbyty Ifan, the well-constructed farm buildings, such as Hendre Isaf (SH 8547 5118), appear to post-date the purchase of the estate from the Mostyn family to form part of the Penrhyn estate in 1866. On Sir Edmund Buckley's former estate at Dinas Mawddwy, there survives an experimental pre-stressed concrete farm yard complex (SH 8629 1491).‡

Farmhouses tell a similar story of late development and only moderate investment. Though few pre-1700 farmhouses survive – far fewer than are to be found in the Vale of Clwyd and the Vale of Glamorgan, or in the hinterland of Oswestry – those that do are typically two-unit gable-chimney stone houses with a first floor. Built of stones obtained locally, and slated, this type first appears in the 1560s.§ Even in an area such as Blaenau Ffestiniog, where slate outcropped and could have been worked easily, a slate-roofed house was unusual in the 16th century, but a thatched roof had become a rarity over most of Gwynedd by the 19th. Double-fronted farmhouses of the 18th or 19th century tend to preserve the same basic shape as their precursors of the 16th century, and distinct sub-regional and local patterns survive well after 1700, such as the pattern of pointed dormers which adorn many farmhouses particularly in Merioneth. Only rarely is there any attempt to build to Georgian proportions, and there is little of the sort of detailing that would be found on houses of the wealthier agricultural areas of England or of the Irish midlands.

There is little evidence for the cottages of labourers and the very poor within the farming landscape before the beginning of the 19th century. Traditionally, labourers lived in the farmhouse, a practice which continued for many years in some parts of Gwynedd, but from the 1780s onwards there are increasingly frequent references in the accounts both of gentlemen-travellers and statisticians to the wretched habitations of the rural poor. This may reflect the greater availability of literary sources, but it

---

* Cozens, L., Kidner, R.W. and Poole, B., *The Mawddwy, Van and Kerry Branches* (Usk: Oakwood Press, 2004), pp. 79-108.

† Barnwell, P.S. and Giles, C., *English Farmsteads 1750-1914* (Royal Commission on the Ancient and Historic Monuments of England, 1997), Hughes, S., *The Archaeology of an Early Railway System: The Brecon Forest Tramroads* (Aberystwyth: Royal Commission on the Ancient and Historic Monuments of Wales, 1990), pp. 184-9.

‡ Lord Sudely was experimenting with un-reinforced concrete farm buildings, school and mansion at Gregynog in mid-Wales at much the same time; see Alfrey, J., 'Rural Building in Nineteenth-century North Wales; The Role of the Great Estates', *Archaeologia Cambrensis* 107 (2001 for 1998), p. 206.

§ Smith, *op. cit.*, pp. 172-5, 434-7.

may also indicate a change in living patterns, perhaps as pressure on land became such that labourers could no longer expect to become tenants, and married men were anxious to have their own house, even if it were only built of, and roofed with, sods. Not surprisingly, none of these has survived, though their sites may well underlie later dwellings. The only study that has so far attempted to deal with the homes of those below the tenant-farmer class in the period 1700 onwards in Gwynedd, at Mynytho on Penrhyn Llŷn, identified cottage-sites that are recorded in the parish papers early in the 18th century but without excavation there can be no certainty that any surviving remains are that early; surviving structures may have been built on the site of cruder dwellings still. Even some of the dwellings that are late 18th- or early 19th-century in date are still remarkably primitive – Pen Cae may have been built of stone, but it was no more than a rectangle 8.5m by 4m, with two doors, one tiny window and no proper hearth, only some fire-blackened stones in one corner of the single room.*

Estates only started sponsoring the building of new or replacement farmhouses or cottages from the end of the 18th century – unless one can count a remarkable settlement at Ardda in the Conwy valley, probably built in the late 17th or early 18th century, where the similarity in the single-celled dwellings and their associated field house and enclosure suggests that they are planned (SH 765 661 C).† These are ruined and roofless, though many of the later examples survive and are still inhabited. Here, very traditional forms are perpetuated but sometimes in a self-conscious, almost exaggerated, way. The Gwydir, Nannau and Penrhyn estates in particular at various times constructed dwellings in which local vernacular idioms are combined with fanciful or winsome details (see p. 188).‡ Where these were cottages for labourers rather than farmhouses, they are typically *crog-lofftydd*, a type of two-unit dwelling with a loft over one of the rooms. This evolves in the early years of the 19th century from the un-lofted cottage and shares a common ancestor in the medieval hall-house with the two-unit farmhouse, but it is remarkable that a type of dwelling elsewhere built by quarrymen on the commons (see below) should also have been adopted enthusiastically by the estates. These are discussed more at length in *4.6.1*, pp. 182-95. Only Penrhyn flirted with a radical departure from traditional norms, with proposals, apparently unrealised, for classical farmhouses. The Newborough estate built a number of central chimney houses with a pyramidal roof designed to accommodate a family in each quarter, to a plan which originates with gentry dwellings of the 16th century (*eg* at SH 4511 5588).

Perhaps the most dramatic evidence of the changes in farming practice within Gwynedd is not the farmhouses and courtyards but the enclosures of the 19th century. Their scale has already been indicated but it is their long straight stone walls marching across the horizon, often starting from a straggling boundary that might represent a settlement of the Elizabethan period, that seem above all else to symbolise and confirm patrician power. These were certainly the most controversial of the changes in the agricultural landscape made in the 19th century, and left a legacy of bitterness which provided Liberalism with its radical edge. Where roads led from the enclosed

---

* Wiliam, E., 'The Vernacular Architecture of a Welsh Rural Commnuity, 1700-1900: The Houses of Mynytho', *TCHS* 36 (1975), pp. 173-93.
† RCAHMW, *East*, pp. 205-7. I am grateful to Andrew Davidson of the Gwynedd Archaeological Trust for the suggestion that these might represent an early planned settlement.
‡ Alfrey, *op. cit.*, pp. 199-216.

61 Multi-cellular sheepfold in the Anafon valley (Crown Copyright: Royal Commission on the Ancient and Historic Monuments of Wales: 94-CS-1112).

areas on to the unenclosed mountains, often a gate marked the boundary, sometimes with a gate-keeper's house nearby (*eg* SH 5052 5735). Even the unenclosed mountains are very far from featureless landscapes; they often contain sites such as turbaries for domestic fuel, pillow mounds for farming rabbits, mineral workings or the large multi-cellular sheepfolds which are a feature of the Snowdonian uplands (Figure 61).[*]

Some enclosures were carried out in order to create dual-economy settlements – typically a *tyddyn* (smallholding) incapable of supporting a family by itself but providing them with butter, eggs, bacon and buttermilk, either for their own use or for sale.[†] These are often associated with the slate quarries of Arfon, where workers well into the 20th century lived in a semi-rural, semi-industrial environment. Some are estate developments, such as the rigid linear pattern of allotments on Mynydd Llandygái in the Ogwen valley, laid out by Penrhyn stewards. Others, such as on Moel Tryfan, were created by the quarrymen and their families themselves on the commons, without legal sanction but with the tacit approval of parish authorities, and are constituted by a jigsaw of geometrically-shaped enclosures of a few acres, with a pig-sty, and sometimes an outbuilding large enough for one animal. Very few – generally those of more than 10 hectares (25 acres) – have even a barn and cow-house, and very often the pattern is the same one of lateral extension found on some of the farms.[‡] On both these examples, the dwellings are vernacular in inspiration, with the important difference that those on Mynydd Llandygái are all to the same uniform *crog-lofft* design whereas those on Moel Tryfan are more roughly built, more varied in design and are more likely to have been adapted and altered (see pp. 182, 188 and 216).

---

[*] Johnston, F., 'The Archaeological and Agricultural Significance of the Multicellular Sheepfolds of Snowdonia' (B.A. thesis, University of Manchester, 1998).
[†] Roberts, K., *Y Lôn Wen* (Denbigh: Gwasg Gee, 1960), p. 29.
[‡] Alfrey, J., 'A New Look at Conservation Values', *Heritage in Wales* 12 (1999), pp. 13-17.

In terms of archaeological survival, the story is a different one from place to place. The patrician landscape of house and park has on the whole fared well. The National Trust manages both Plas Newydd and Penrhyn Castle. At Maentwrog, Plas Tan y Bwlch has become the Snowdonia National Park's Environmental Studies Centre, and the home farm has been taken over by a pottery. At Glynllifon, despite uncertainty as to the future of the house itself, the park is open to the public and the estate workshops have been conserved. The steam engine was restored to working order by the steeplejack and television personality Fred Dibnah (1938-2004) and the workshops are variously given over to interpretation and to the work of craftspersons such as the weaver Cefyn Burgess, the blacksmith Ann-Catrin Evans and the clock-maker Paul Beckett. Vaynol has become a buildings conservation school, and an internationally-recognised concert venue. Others remain family homes, and some are still the centres of landed estates, such as Bodorgan, Baron Hill and Nanhoron.

On the other hand, historic farming landscapes within Gwynedd now face the likelihood of greater changes than at any time within the period of this study – perhaps since the Black Death. This reflects a broader uncertainty as to the future of the food industry within a globalised economy, but the shift in emphasis from production to conservation-based stewardship is particularly evident within the area, beginning with the establishment of the Snowdonia National Park in 1951. The National Trust owns large swathes of land, including the former Penrhyn lands in the Carneddau and around Ysbyty Ifan, as well as former Nannau land in the Dyfi forest. The Trust has consciously assumed much of the role of the individually-owned estates that preceded its stewardship, and has developed specific conservation policies for historic buildings and field-boundaries. Both the Trust and the Park employ archaeologists and conservation experts. However, in Gwynedd as a whole, as elsewhere in the Atlantic isles, the general collapse of the economy of the great estates, from the 1880s onwards, did not necessarily liberate the former tenant farmer, who frequently had to pay back a substantial bank-loan over many years, and who lost the support of the estate's resources when times were bad.

Many farms have ceased to exist as independent units. Upland settlements that might have been first established on the waste in the 16th century were abandoned in the 20th, or reverted to being the upland pasture of a lowland holding. Pastoral transhumance is still practised in some areas. Elsewhere, a tendency to farm amalgamation and to the employment of contractors, though not as marked as elsewhere in Wales and in England, does mean that field boundaries are removed and buildings decay. Corn barns are now used as stores, whilst a lorry carrying imported foodstuffs unloads in the yard. The comparative weakness of the regional housing market in the late 20th century has meant that there has been comparatively little pressure to turn them into dwellings, the 'barn conversions' of the south-east of England which excited much satirical comment in the 1980s.[*] Diversification has meant that some other buildings have found a new use, which might be anything from holiday lets or riding schools to car-body repair workshops, though changes are difficult to quantify in the absence of detailed survey. Many farmers are determined to continue, but holdings are now often insufficient to support a family, and a dual economy is no longer confined to the

---

[*] Though see Monmouthshire County Council: *Addasu Adeiladau Fferm Hanesyddol yng Nghmyru/Converting Historic Farm Buildings in Wales* (Cardiff, 2004).

quarrymen's *tyddynod*. Teaching, or working for the council, provides the certainty of a regular monthly income.*

Although some aspects of the archaeology of agriculture within Gwynedd have been studied in some detail – primarily the *plas* itself and the opposite end of the social spectrum, the cottages of the near-landless labourer and the small-holder – much work remains to be carried out. Partly because agriculture is seen as a non-industrial activity and because there is no developed school of historical archaeology in Britain as there is in the USA, it tends to be ignored by archaeologists in Wales once it has reached the 18th century, despite the fact that farming remained the dominant economic activity in both England and Wales until the mid-19th century.† Even where building recording has been carried out, it has not always been related to changes in field-systems, and work has concentrated on earlier, more obviously 'vernacular' structures. Tir-gofal, the all-Wales agri-environment plan introduced in 1999, has meant that archaeological surveys have been carried out on some of the farms signing up to the scheme but there is no sign as yet that the evidence has been systematically analysed.

An important preliminary study of two tightly-defined areas within Gwynedd, Llanbedr y Cennin in the Conwy valley and Llanaber in Merioneth, has outlined a methodology which combines place-name analysis with palaeo-botanic evidence to map the ebb and flow of settlement since prehistoric times. This study recommends creating a typology of boundary types as a priority, combined with soil studies.‡ Such an approach has much to commend it, and has the potential to furnish the detailed evidence of agricultural change over time, potentially well into the post-1700 period. Yet an equally important priority must be to identify through base-line research what survives in the way of farm buildings and even very recent field patterns.

4.1.6 Forestry and the timber trade

Gwynedd's forests have been commercially exploited since the Medieval period but the sector assumed considerable importance in the 20th century with state management of commercial woodlands. Both native and imported timber played an important part in the regional economy and have influenced the built environment, engineering and the ship-wrighting industry of Gwynedd.

Forestry tends to be regarded by archaeologists as one of the factors that threatens the material evidence for the past rather than as primarily a form of historic environment in its own right. Partly for this reason and partly because Gwynedd was one of the least well forested areas of Wales,§ evidence of the commercial management and exploitation of its woodlands is small-scale and is often unacknowledged and

---

* See Brayshay, M. and Williams, A., 'North Snowdonia: an upland landscape under pressure' in Whyte, I.D. and Winchester, A.J. (eds), *Society, Landscape and Environment in Upland Britain* (Society for Landscape Studies supplementary series 2, 2004), pp. 125-39.

† As an example the only index entry for 'Agriculture' in Briggs, C.S., *Towards a Research Agenda for Welsh Archaeology* (BAR British Series 343, 2003) is 'agriculture, Medieval 133'.

‡ Hooke, D., 'Place-names and vegetation History as a key to Understanding Settlement in the Conwy Valley' in *Landscape and Settlement in Medieval Wales* (Oxford: Oxbow Monograph 81, 1997), pp. 79-95. Despite its title, this paper also considers historical land-use in Llanaber, Merioneth.

§ In 1924 in Anglesey 1.2% of the total area was wooded, in Caernarvonshire 3.6%, and in Merioneth 4.5%, compared to a Welsh average of 5%. The proportions of uneconomic woodland were also high – see Linnard, W., *Welsh Woods and Forests: A History* (Llandysul: Gomer Press, 2000), p. 182.

unrecorded.* Even so, it has formed a significant element in the regional economy from the Medieval period to the present day, and the research of Dr William Linnard in particular provides an overall Welsh historical context.

The earliest evidence of the management of woodlands in Gwynedd is documentary. In 1739 we first hear of the felling of woods in the parishes along the Afon Dwyryd – Llandecwyn, Maentwrog, Ffestiniog and Llanfrothen.† Thereafter, documentary references indicate an active process of woodland management in coastal or estuarine Merioneth, in the Conwy valley and on the great Arfon estates and on Baron Hill.‡ From the late 18th century onwards, many Gwynedd landowners, in common with their class elsewhere in Wales and in England, began ambitious programmes of planting, William Oakeley of Tan y Bwlch even going to the extent of spelling out his initials in trees on the hillside opposite the *plas*, where they can still be made out amongst later growth (SH 659 399). The Penrhyn estate planted 600,000 trees between 1780 and 1797, John Maurice Jones 1,700,000 from 1804 to 1810, and the Glynllifon estate over 3,700,000 between 1815 and 1827 (including many outside Gwynedd).§ The dense broadleaved Glynllifon woodlands at Fachwen near Llanberis, now the Padarn Country Park (SH 583 608 C), and above Dolgarrog (SH 769 667 C) may represent work of this period.

From the 1890s, the state began to take a more active interest in forestry, with rather greater success than in the case of farming (see p. 98) – Britain was by then importing vast amounts of timber from North America and continental Europe. In 1899 the Crown purchased a Merioneth sheepwalk for planting, and between 1902 and 1907 the University College of North Wales's course in Forestry evolved into a full school.¶ Both the 1909 budget and the outbreak of war in 1914 resulted in an extension of state control, leading to the establishment of the Forestry Commission in 1919. An experimental 25-acre plantation was established by the University at Corsygedol during the war, and long-term plantations by the Forestry Commission began at Gwydyr in 1920 and at Coed y Brenin in 1923.** In the late 1930s the Snowdonia National Forest Park was established, based on Gwydyr Forest (Map 8). The Forestry Commission escaped wholesale privatisation in the 1980s, and became the responsibility of the Welsh Assembly in 1999.

The uses to which timber was put were various. Charcoal was the main industrial fossil fuel until well into the 18th century, and was distilled in many Gwynedd forests from the Medieval period certainly into the 1880s, perhaps for longer – some authorities believed that it produced better charcoal than the use of cast-iron retorts at fixed sites, introduced in the early 19th century. The place-name Cwm y Glo (SH 550 628 C

---

* As an example, the Gwynedd Historic Environment Record contained no post-Medieval woodland features at all in February 2005.
† UWB: Maenan 419.
‡ See Thomas, C., 'The Corsygedol Estate in an Age of Improvement', *JMHRS* 6 (1971), pp. 303-10; Matts, R.S., *A Century of Timber Management at Baron Hill, Anglesey, 1734-1835* (Diploma dissertation, UWB, 1977); CRO: Glynllifon papers.
§ Linnard, *op. cit.*, p. 152.
¶ Williams, J.G., *The University College of North Wales: Foundations 1884-1927* (Cardiff: University of Wales Press, 1985), pp. 173-5.
** The principal forests managed by the Commission are Gwydir (8045 hectares – 20,112 acres), Deudraeth (995 hectares – 2,460 acres), Coed y Brenin (6301 hectares – 15,600 acres), Penllyn (3,100 hectares – 7,800 acres), Dyfi and Dyfi Corris (7,770 hectares – 19,170 acres, of which only part lie within Gwynedd) – areas as identified in Forestry Commission Booklet 28, *Gwydyr Forest in Snowdonia: A History* (London: HMSO, 1971) and Forestry Commission Guide, *Cambrian Forests* (London: HMSO, 1975).

Map 8 Forestry

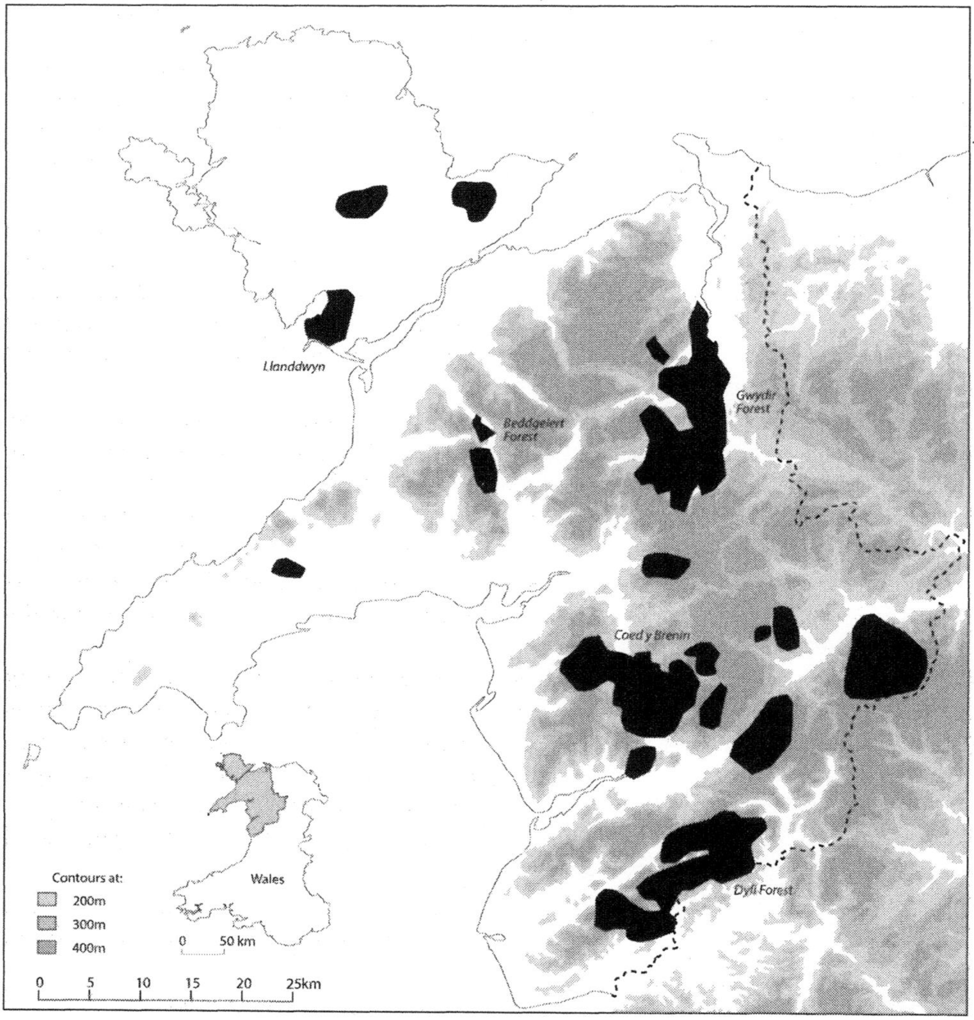

— modern Welsh 'valley of the coal') indicates charcoal burning, not coal seams (which did not deter a group of entrepreneurs from sinking a shaft there in the 19th century) and it is possible that this may have been to smelt the copper mined at Llanberis, at the other end of the two long lakes, Llyn Padarn and Llyn Peris. Gloddaeth (SH 803 806 C) also preserves the *glo*-element.[*] Timber was burnt for charcoal near where it was cut, as charcoal is easier to move than wood. Typically, hardwood billets were closely staked on a level floor of earth and ashes to form a conical or domed mound perhaps about 5-12m in diameter and 2.7m high with a central vent for firing,[†] though no post-Medieval charcoal platforms have so far been identified in the region. Neither of

---

[*] Linnard, *op. cit.*, p. 94.
[†] Jenkins, J.G., *Life and Tradition in Rural Wales* (London: J.M. Dent and Sons, 1976), pp. 79-80.

Gwynedd's two iron furnaces that were in blast in the early 18th century ever worked long enough to denude local forests (pp. 124-5).*

Another small-scale industry of which little is known is clog-making; a painting of an itinerant clog-makers' camp at Rhostryfan showing the beehive stack of clog-soles and the simple tent to shelter the workmen is confirmed by photographic evidence from elsewhere in Wales. This work was generally carried out by Lancashire people who either settled locally or moved from plantation to plantation before sending the soles to a North of England factory.†

Probably most timber felled locally before 1700 was used for building and construction purposes. Timbers from the Conwy valley were used in the building of Caernarfon castle.‡ There are records of oak trees being felled in the same area in the late 17th century for export to Liverpool, most of it unsawn as spars and poles, some sawn or cloven to produce laths, pegs, staves for buckets, barrels and churns and cartwheel spokes.§

The revival of ship-building from the 1820s onwards created a need for a variety of hardwoods. It is unlikely that much Gwynedd timber went into warship construction, a trade which in any case declined with the wooden man o' war from mid-century onwards, but wooden sailing ships continued to be built at Amlwch until 1897 and Porthmadog until 1913.¶ The preparation of pit props represented an important part of the output of Gwynedd's state-managed forests until the 1960s, though other needs assumed importance from time to time – ladder-poles for the fire service during the Blitz for example.**

There is little evidence of methods of harvesting the timber crop and moving it through the forest. Horses were used as late as the 1960s though the first tractors had appeared in 1941. Perhaps because of the steepness of the slopes, little use was made of lightly-laid rail systems, such as operated elsewhere in Wales.†† Wire ropeways were introduced at Gwydyr in the 1940s and spread to other North Wales forests. Bulldozers, and engineered haulage roads (to a maximum gradient of 1/10) appeared in the early 1950s.‡‡

---

* Linnard, *op. cit.*, pp. 83-5; Riden, R., *A Gazetteer of Charcoal-fired Blast Furnaces in Great Britain in use since 1600* (Cardiff: Merton Priory Press, 1993), pp. 68-9.

† Linnard, *op. cit.*, p. 175; Jenkins, *op. cit.*, plate 110, pp. 77-9.

‡ Taylor, A.J., *The Welsh Castles of Edward I* (London and Ronceverte: Hambledon Press, 1986), p. 96.

§ Williams, G.H., 'Estate Management in Dyffryn Conwy, c.1685', *Transactions of the Honourable Society of Cymmrodorion*, 1979, p. 76.

¶ Hope, B.D., *A Curious Place: An Industrial History of Amlwch (1550-1950)* (Wrexham; Bridge Books, 1994), p. 154; Hughes, E. and Eames, A., *Porthmadog Ships* (Caernarfon: Gwynedd Archives Service, 1975), p. 89; Greenhill, B., *The Evolution of the Wooden Ship* (London: Batsford, 1988), pp. 182-92 describes the timber used in the making of the *MA James*, one of the last Porthmadog vessels. The framing, deck beams and heavy timbers at bow and stern were made of English (*sic*) oak, the keel of American elm, the keelson of greenheart, the lower planking of American elm, English elm and pitchpine, the upper planking of greenheart and English oak, the topsides and sheer startes of English oak, greenheart and pitchpine, the deck of New England white pine, the beam shelf and clamp of English oak and greenheart. The registered tonnage was 97 tons, her cargo capacity over 200 tons. She measured 27.4m (90') long by 6.7m (22') in the beam.

** Forestry Commission Booklet 28, *Gwydyr Forest in Snowdonia* (London: HMSO, 1971), p. 58.

†† The only significant exception was around Rhyd Ddu, where Thomas Parry, timber merchant of Mold, operated an extensive system in the forests between Beddgelert and Rhyd Ddu, apparently in conjunction with the Canadian Forestry Corps, from around 1914 to around 1920. Lines in the forest were worked by winch, horse, and gravity, and a DeWinton locomotive took the logs to a saw-mill in Rhyd Ddu. See Bradley, V.J., *Industrial Locomotives of North Wales* (London: Industrial Railway Society, 1992), p. 385.

‡‡ Forestry Commission Booklet 28, pp. 59, 65, 67-9.

Off-site powered sawing may date back to the late 18th century. It is possible, though unconfirmed, that the water-powered industrial mill at Rhyd y Sarn (SH 6910 4229), just beyond the tidal reach of the Dwyryd, which is believed to have been a slate mill, may have had an earlier history, perhaps stretching back to the 1770s, as a timber saw-mill, which would make it the earliest in Wales.* Otherwise, circular timber saws from the 19th and 20th centuries survive on a number of farms and estates, though no saw-pit is recorded anywhere within the area. Large-scale timber processing plant is rare. The ship-wrighting towns tended to have them – the ruins of Paynter's water-driven saw-mill at Porth Amlwch survive (SH 4490 9327), and Porthmadog had a steam-driven timber saw-mill with rail access (SH 5706 3396). Timber warehouses survive in re-use at Menai Bridge (SH 5576 7192), though the Caernarfon timber-merchants' yard at SH 4781 6298 is the last survivor of Gwynedd's quayside yards. The record office is sited next door, on what used to be the timber pond. Baltic pine was regularly imported from the early 19th century, New World pine from a little later.† The availability of comparatively inexpensive long straight timbers not only influenced the design and building of Gwynedd's distinctive sailing ships but also made possible the region's distinctive built heritage. Roof trusses of pine went into both chapels and slate mills, as well as into structures such as the Welsh Slate Company's viaduct at Rhiwbryfdir (SH 6964 4678; see *4.1.1* [pp. 42-69] and front cover).‡

Of the by-products of timber, bark was sent to tanneries not only in the region but also in Ireland.§ Tanning is the process of converting animal hides and skins into leather, first by soaking them for a few weeks in milk of lime, then by soaking them for anything up to a year either in a pit or a tank in a liquid containing tannin, obtained from bark. This notoriously pungent process attracted other trades that offended both the senses and morality, so they were often the first casualty of redevelopment, but the documentary and map evidence suggests that in Gwynedd they were generally very small undertakings.¶ An exception was Tremadoc tannery which took over the substantial loom-house of the woollen mill (see pp. 121-2). Some lasted into the 20th century, but the trade had been in decline for many years by then and little survives.

Forestry workers were provided with their own accommodation. In 1927 bungalow settlements were established in the Gwydyr forest, some of them soon to be inhabited by former coal-miners and their families under the Distressed Areas Scheme, though later foresters' houses were clustered timber-built Alpine chalets in which senior workers' status was recognised by a larger size of house and garden (examples at SH 7904 5694).** As new plantings were carried out, families had to forsake upland farms for social housing in the villages.

---

* The suggestion has been made by Dr Michael Lewis on a close reading of the parish registers, on the basis of PRO LRRO 5/32, Hawarden Record Office D/NH/990 and on the evidence of Williams, G.J., *Hanes Plwyf Ffestiniog* (Wrexham, 1882), p. 232.

† For the Baltic trade, see Schama, S., *Landscape and Memory* (London: Fontana, 1996), pp. 23-36.

‡ Archaeologically, New World pine and Baltic pine may be distinguished by the fact that the former is often marked up in Arabic or Latin numerals, whilst the latter is often identified by symbols whose meaning is not yet understood. The present author believes that these are Yiddish.

§ Lewis, M.J.T., *Sails on the Dwyryd* (Maentwrog: Plas Tan y Bwlch, 1989), pp. 21-2.

¶ For those of Caernarfon, see UWB: Porth yr Aur mss 14461e; Evans, K., 'A Survey of Caernarvon, 1770-1840 Part 1A', *TCHS* 32 (1971), pp. 43, 69; Lloyd, L., *The Port of Caernarfon, 1793-1800* (privately published, 1989), pp. 149-50. One was situated at SH 488 616, and appears to have been a more substantial site. For parallels, see Royal Commission on the Ancient and Historical Monuments of Scotland, *Monuments of Industry* (HMSO, 1986), p. 19.

** Forestry Commission Booklet 28, pp. 32-3, plate 1.

The archaeology of managed woodland and of the timber trade in Gwynedd is neither extensive nor particularly complex, and offers little that is unique to the region. It has, however, had a significant impact on the landscape, and illustrates the changing role of the state in industry in the 20th century.

4.1.7 Brick-making and ceramics

Brick-making has bequeathed several visually spectacular sites in Gwynedd, and is still carried out near Caernarfon.

Though Gwynedd is manifestly a 'stone' region, there has been some limited use of brick since the 17th century, when Bodwrda in Penrhyn Llŷn (SH 8195 2762) was extended by Hugh Bodwrda around 1621. No other substantial brick-built dwelling was to be erected until Penrhyn castle (SH 6026 7191) in the early 19th century – brick is used in the inner walls, and Anglesey limestone on the outside.*

* RCAHMW, *Caernarvonshire (West)*, pp. 3-5.

62 Holyhead brickworks (Crown Copyright: 995061-51A).

Next to nothing is known about the early phase of brick-making within the region, though there are documentary and cartographic references to small-scale brick-pits from the mid-19th century, in Traeth Dulas in Anglesey, and in the Conwy valley. Later, more developed, sites from the main Industrial period are to be found on Anglesey and in Arfon; though they neither have the long history nor the scale of their counterparts in north-east Wales or the main brick-making areas of England and Scotland, they are archaeologically important and visually impressive.

The remains of four significant brick-making sites survive on Anglesey. Two have been conserved and interpreted, at Holyhead and Cemaes. At Holyhead the brickworks opened in the former breakwater quarry has been consolidated as part of a country park (SH 226 832 – Figure 62). At Cemaes not only does the quay built to export bricks survive, so does the course of the narrow-gauge railway which connected it to the Hoffmann kiln (SH 374 931), consolidated by Anglesey Council. This is a form of multi-chamber continuous kiln (in other words, one which can be kept continuously at work), devised by a German scientist, which evolved between 1859 and 1884 from an annular (ring-plan) design into an elliptical or sub-rectangular plan arranged around a central flue, as in this example. This appears to have been one of two such kilns in Gwynedd, as another is marked on a brickworks at Llandudno Junction, a site that has been completely landscaped.

The other sites have not been conserved. One is at Porth Llanlleiana (SH 388 951), a remote coastal location, where bricks were made from the china clay deposits in the hillside nearby and fired in the now ruined stone buildings nearby before being shipped out from the bay. The buildings, which include a remote chimney, were badly damaged by fire in 1920.

The third site poses a significant management problem. This is the spectacular coastal brickworks and quarrying complex at Porth Wen (SH 402 946 SAM – Figure 63), dominated by its two tall chimneys. Although it produced some ordinary red house bricks and some roofing tiles, its main output was yellow clay bricks which could be used as lining in furnaces and kilns because of the high alumina content of the quartzite rocks above the site. A brickworks of some description was in existence here in 1893,[*] but the extensive buildings which survive today were built early in the 20th century and functioned until just before the Second World War, when most of the useful equipment and machinery in the brickworks was removed for use in the main Caernarfon brickworks.[†]

Porth Wen illustrates the constituent processes of brick-making. The quartzite was worked in several quarry faces above the works. The incline from the quarries survives in good condition; it led to a breaker near a china clay pit, whence crushed rock was sent down a slide. Immediately adjacent are moulding and brick-making buildings, and a large multi-storeyed drying shed. Machinery was driven by a steam engine, of which some parts survive. Further north is a warehouse and engineering complex. The three surviving round 'downdraught' kilns, which replaced earlier 'beehive kilns', were designed to contain and control the firing process. This destroyed the initial plasticity of the clay and led to shrinkage, greatly increasing the mechanical strength and weather resistance of the bricks. Completed bricks could be loaded directly into

---

[*] *Y Clorianydd*, 26 Hydref 1893.
[†] LlRO: WM/628/1-11, papers concerning Porthwen and Cemaes brickworks.

63 Porth Wen brickworks.

vessels from the quay on which the kilns were built. Porthwen is a scheduled ancient monument but suffers from severe coastal erosion, and the larger buildings on the site are steadily disintegrating.*

A later form of continuous process, the gas-fired car tunnel-kiln, is used at Caernarfon brickworks (SH 4886 6149). Pits were opened here in the 19th century and grew to a considerable size. The present operation dates from the late 1960s.

The production of ceramics within Gwynedd has never moved beyond the *atelier* stage, though several primary sites and industrial-scale processing sites are known. A quartz quarry was identified by Walter Davies at Tyddyn y Gaib in the Conwy valley but has left no identifiable trace. In the Lledr valley a quartz working complete with a barrow-way and a chute was identified during the improvements to the A470 road at SH 7659 5410. At Port Penrhyn an impressive bank of kilns, kidney-shape in plan, survives (SH 5930 7269). These were converted to lime production in 1829, possibly in order to build Penrhyn castle, but initially formed part of a complex which included a mill to grind flint obtained from the chert of local limestone and from Ireland brought in by sea.†

---

* LlRO: WSH/5/14 – photograph of Porthwen brickworks.
† Boyd, J.I.C., *Narrow Gauge Railways in North Caernarvonshire volume 2 The Penrhyn Quarry Railways* (Headington: Oakwood Press, 1985), pp. 8-9, 65.

4.2 Processing Industries

4.2.1 Textiles

Textile processing is an industry which became of lesser importance in Gwynedd from the early 19th century onwards, faced with pressures from the north of England.

In Britain as a whole textiles exemplify the shift from domestic production to factory production which many have considered to be the defining characteristic of the Industrial Revolution. After the early primacy of East Anglia and the West Country, the industry came to dominate the economies of Yorkshire, Cheshire, Derbyshire and Paisley in Scotland. New Lanark, Styal, the Derwent valley and Saltaire in their different ways all symbolise this new industrial order, not only in their four-square mills but also in their radical social experimentation. Above everywhere else, it was Lancashire which embodied the spirit of the age; it was here that cotton production, against all the odds, took a raw material from India and North America, processed it on the banks of the Tame or the Irwell, then sold it on all over the world.* The human society thereby formed gave rise to the first inter-urban main-line railway and led Engels to pen *The Condition of the Working Class in England*. The weavers' cottages of Manchester and the Pennines, with their long-light windows, remain as witness to the trauma which forced once-independent workers to choose between starvation and the tyranny of the machine, and the great urban mills and warehouses have more recently become symbols of renewal and regeneration.

By contrast, the processing of raw wool into cloth and blankets which constituted the textile industry of Gwynedd is a story of decline, not growth, in the Industrial and Modern period, from a brief period of development in the late 18th and early 19th centuries. It had already bequeathed the English language one of its few words of Welsh origin, 'flannel', from

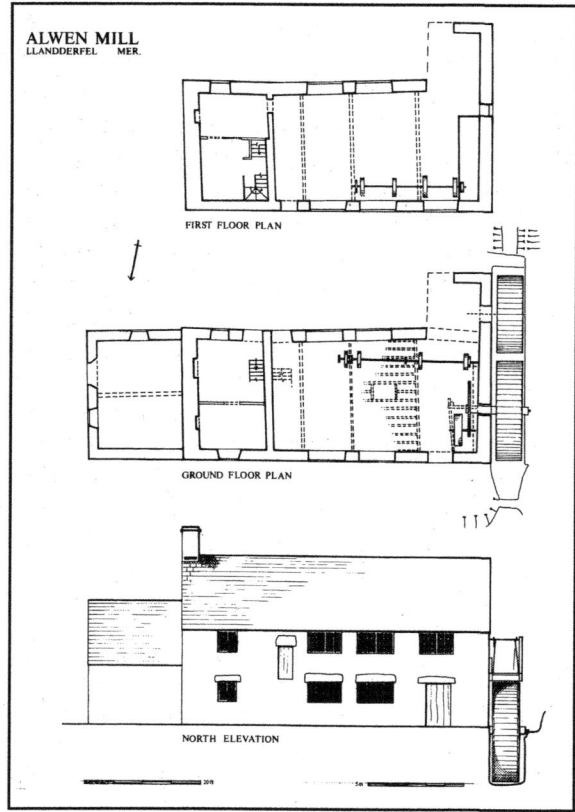

64 Woollen mill at Llandderfel (Crown Copyright).

---

* For the world-wide significance of the textile industry and its role in the growing divergence of living standards between Asia and Europe, see Broadberry, S. and Gupta, B., *Cotton Textiles and the Great Divergence: Lancashire, India and Shifting Competitive Advantage* (London: discussion paper 5183, Centre for Economic Policy Research, 2005).

gwlannen ('wool'), the soft loosely woven fabric transported from north and mid-Wales to Drapers' Hall in Shrewsbury, which from 1565 to the mid-18th century claimed and exercised a monopoly of the trade. By the 20th century the industry was a shadow of its former self. A report commissioned in 1927 paints an extraordinary picture of an industry in which, throughout Wales, tiny rural factories (the woollen mill was generally *y ffatri* in Welsh, rarely *y felin*, 'the mill', sometimes a *pandy* from the fulling mill which had preceded it) might be run by octogenarians, and explicitly describes much of its machinery as worthy of the interest of the National Museum (Figure 64).* As it happened, the first building acquired for re-erection at St Ffagan's (see p. 21) was a woollen mill from Brecknockshire. Even after the Second World War, a few small rural factories remained in being. Elsewhere, in A.H. Dodd's words, the traveller might 'stumble across a rusty heap of textile machinery – hopelessly antiquated, but once the pride of some humble millowner and the fruit of all his savings – buried under the debris of a derelict mill-roof, or lying neglected in a field, not even worth the expense of removal.'†

Dodd himself and J. Geraint Jenkins at the Museum of Welsh Life researched documentary sources, and a few studies of individual sites have been published. From these it is clear in broad outline that the fulling mill became established in Gwynedd in the 16th century, if not earlier, and that from the late 18th century, possibly as a consequence of Shrewsbury's loss of the monopoly, the other processes involved in the production of wool were gradually incorporated on the one site. The overall picture is of a technically conservative industry. In Wales, spinning with distaff and spindle was displaced by the spinning wheel only very gradually, between the 14th century and the 19th, just as the spinning wheel itself lasted into the 20th century, even though the jenny could wind twenty or more threads simultaneously. Power looms were also late coming into Wales. Even though steam pressing equipment was available from the 1860s, well into the 20th century, cloth or blankets would in some places still be screwed down in a press and warmed by a fire – which had to be made of peat. Newspaper reports and advertisements and estate papers give some indication of when and where particular machines were introduced into Gwynedd. The jenny and the carding engine, for instance, arrived by 1803 (at Twll y Bwbach, near Dolgellau). Though there was said to be some resistance to mechanisation, there is no record of machine-breaking or other forms of violent protest. Though hand-looms were installed in factories from 1805, and became common in the 1820s, the powered loom was only to be found from the 1880s, at Dolgellau, Bala, Blaenau Ffestiniog and Llandderfel. One place, Llanegryn near Tywyn, was still using handlooms in 1938 (Map 9).

Mechanisation therefore was small-scale and limited; places like Llanrwst and Ysbyty Ifan never progressed beyond a domestic knitting industry, though they did market their products across the western world. Much of Anglesey is better suited to the plough than to sheep-raising, though Llangefni and Llannerch y Medd were centres of hand-loom weaving; it was the poorer lands of Caernarvonshire and, in particular, Merioneth which formed the centres of woollen production. At Dolgellau there grew up from about 1800 a concentration of factories, often on the site of *pandai*, or of

---

* Crankshaw, W.P., *Report on a Survey of the Welsh Textile Industry made on Behalf of the University of Wales* (Cardiff: University of Wales Press, 1927).
† Dodd, A.H., *The Industrial Revolution in North Wales* (Wrexham: Bridge Books, rep. 1990 of 1971 edition by UWP), pp. 278-9.

Map 9 Textiles

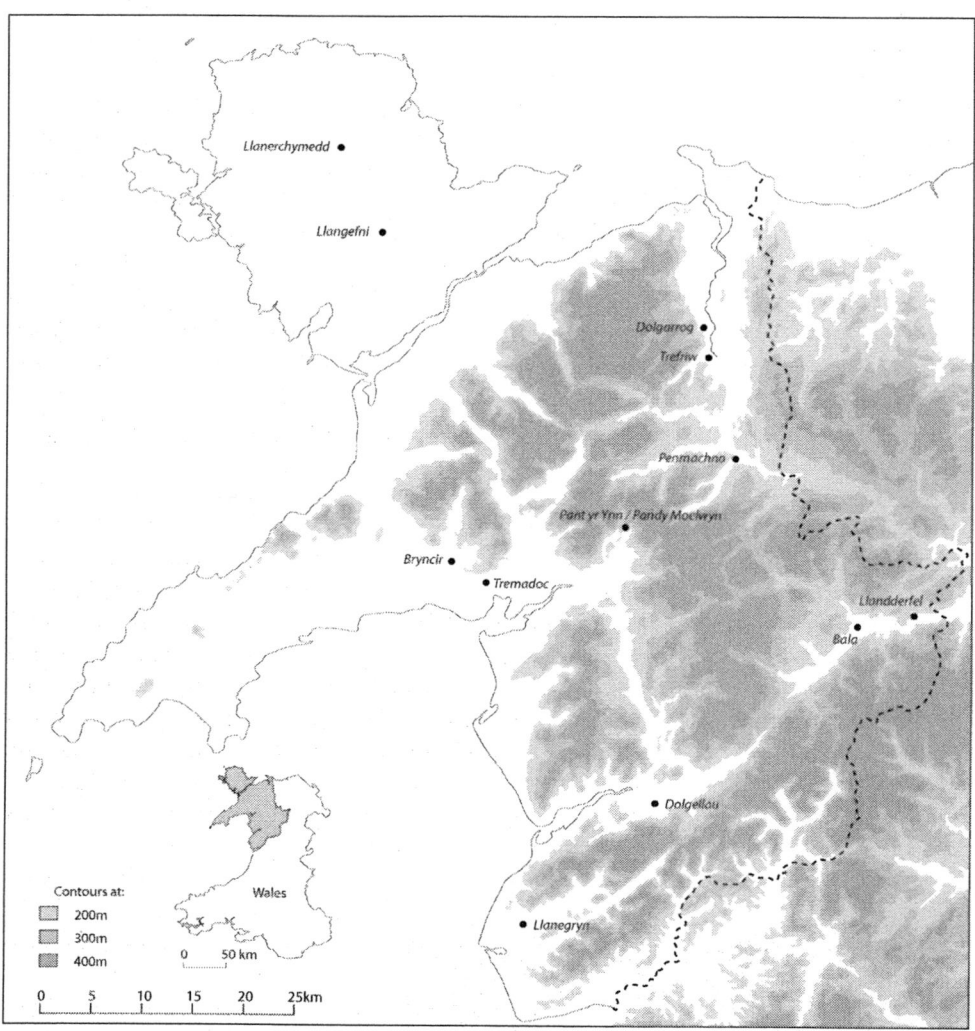

corn mills, powered by the Aran, a stream flowing off Cader Idris. Yet even here, the main business was, or came to be from about the 1820s, processing wool for the farming population of the surrounding countryside – unlike the woollen industry of the Severn valley, around Newtown and Llanidloes, which rashly attempted to compete with the manufacturers of Lancashire and Yorkshire on their own terms. Gwynedd, in common with most other areas of Wales, actually saw the trade contract to its own locality, when other regional industries were opening up to a world economy, and in contrast to the times, only a generation earlier, when stockings and woollens had been exported from the Mawddach or the Conwy to the Americas.

Yet, remarkably, little is known about it in archaeological terms; no overview has been attempted and the overall resource remains unquantified, despite the best efforts of, for instance, the RCAHMW. The fact that *Pandy* should be such a common placename element throughout Wales is telling, but it is clear from valuations and from paintings that pre-19th-century fulling mills were small affairs and, though some sites have been recorded, so far no excavation has been carried out. In many cases *pandai* have become private houses. Even the archaeology of the larger, more mechanised mills has proved to be very vulnerable; Dolgellau's mills fell into disuse in the course of the 20th century, but in several cases the buildings survived for many years and were only demolished very recently. *Ffatri Fawr* (SH 7294 1725) was pulled down as recently as 2003, leaving only the wheel pit. This was the only textile site in Gwynedd to have had a steam engine, as an auxiliary to water power. Near at hand, the massive lower walls of *Ffatri Neint* are now bisected by a public footpath (SH 7302 1706), and one gable end survives of *Ffatri Idris* (SH 7306 1703), surprisingly built, or rebuilt, partly out of brick.* Otherwise practically all that is left of this once-important local industry are the warehouses which are a feature of several of the town's back streets, and possibly also some of the large houses with which Dolgellau seems surprisingly well-endowed.

It may be that the development of small-scale woollen mills around Dolgellau reflects not only the availability locally of fleeces and water-supply but also the traditions of independence and freedom from patrician control that had such marked effect on the area (see 3 Context). Elsewhere in Gwynedd, however, mills were sponsored by landowners, such as *Ffatri Dolgarrog* (SH 7739 6625) erected adjacent to a *pandy* that was fulling cloth there as early as 1575 – if not indeed from when the white monks of Maenan owned the land. It was built by Lord Newborough around 1803 for a Mr Pritchard, who had been his Captain of Militia; the plans show the 'Present Factory', a proposed adjacent spinning room integral with a two-storey dwelling, and a 'Fewel' (fuel) room as well as a stable with sleeping accommodation above.† In that the Dolgarrog factory is a site where there is continuity of use from the 16th century to the 20th, it might repay archaeological investigation.

Without a doubt, the most remarkable of the patrician-sponsored textile mills in Gwynedd is the one built by Madocks at Tremadoc (SH 5644 4030 – Figure 65). It is far larger than anything that had been attempted before in the region, and was not to be equalled in size for perhaps ninety years. The main surviving structure is rectangular in plan, built on the break of slope at the edge of what would at the time still have been the Glaslyn estuary. It is five storeys in height (together

65 Madocks' loom-house.

---

* Lower down, at SH 7297 1751, on a site now engulfed by the town of Dolgellau itself, is a dwelling which was once associated with the building show in plate 55 of Jenkins, J.G., *The Welsh Woollen Industry* (Cardiff: National Museum of Wales, 1969) identified as 'Weavers' house'. It may in fact have been part of a corn mill.
† NLW: Wynnstay 100/30, 100/27, Glynllifon 84 fol. 78r; CRO: XD2A/1554, XD2A/337, XD2/63112.

with an attic floor) on the estuary side, three storeys high on the slope side, and is distinguished by the Regency architectural touches which were the hallmark of Madocks' style. Tradition records that this was the loom-house, and that the other processes were carried out in a smaller but architecturally similar building immediately to the east, long demolished. This certainly seems to have been where the water-wheel was situated and there is no surviving evidence of a power-transfer system from one to the other, though Madocks apparently contemplated powering the looms by water. Interestingly, the building lacks the distinctive longlights of a loom-house.[*] The whole complex was erected from about 1804 to 1807,[†] but did not function for long. It prompted one of the most bizarre and colourful episodes of Madocks' ownership of the Tremadoc estate, when one of the partners, Colonel Gwilym Lloyd Wardle, was accused of supplying cloth to Napoleon I's army.[‡] The surviving building operated as a tannery from the 1830s to the Second World War. In the 20th century the site has also been home to a laundry, a fellmonger (seller of animal skins), and a car-breaking business.[§] It is now the focus of conservation attempts.

A mill at Trefriw (SH 7798 6305) remains in production with facilities for visitors to follow the processes and to see the turbines in action. A spinning mule functions here, together with a couple of looms. Situated where the Afon Crafnant drops down the escarpment to reach the alluvial plain of the Conwy valley, the mill is the only survivor of a group of industries which once functioned here. The mill near Penmachno (SH 8063 5285), built in 1839 and completely rebuilt in 1895 with turbines instead of a waterwheel, closed down in the mid-1960s. It limped on as a shop with some demonstration machinery but on final closure all its machinery was removed. A jacquard loom went to the National Museum of Wales' outpost at Drefach Felindre in the Teifi valley, Carmarthenshire, where the Welsh woollen industry is interpreted.

Two other textile sites have a semi-heritage function. Pandy Moelwyn at Tan y Grisiau (SH 6905 4550) is the only fulling mill in Wales to retain its fulling stocks. Its owner hopes to open it as an attraction but so far his plans have come to nothing. Pant yr Ynn 1.8km (1.14 miles) away at Bethania (SH 7087 45328) is the home of the artist Falcon Hildred, who specialises in industrial scenes, and who has preserved many of the internal arrangements and the 7.296m (24ft) overshot waterwheel. Pant yr Ynn was built initially as a slate-slab mill around 1846 for Diffwys quarry, and had become a woollen mill by perhaps the 1870s or 1880s, closing in 1964.[¶] Brynkir [sic] Woollen Factory at SH 5285 4235 was converted from a corn mill around 1850; the water-wheel remains but the machinery is now turned by electricity generated by a turbine. One spinning mule is used. It carries out its own beaming and weaving, but the cloth is sent for finishing to Galashiels in Scotland.

---

[*] Beazley, E., *Madocks and the Wonder of Wales* (Aberystwyth: P&Q, 1985), p. 105.
[†] CRO: XM/10036, XM/10370/1-2, X/Poole1371/1-2; NLW: Rumsey Williams 355.
[‡] This whole episode formed part of a growing Whig, radical and popular criticism of 'old corruption'. The accusation against Wardle probably had no foundation at all, but formed a useful scare at a time when Wardle was accusing the Duke of York, as Commander in Chief, of corruption in army contracts (and secured the Duke's resignation, a remarkable achievement for a back-bencher.) Much of the public interest in the case revolved around the character of Mary Anne Clarke, the Duke's mistress, and her *demi-monde*. See *DWB* and *DNB* for Wardle and *DNB* for Frederick, Duke of York and Albany, second son of George III, army officer and bishop of Osnabrück, and for Mary Anne Clarke.
[§] Pers. comm., Frances Voelker, Cyfeillion Cadw Tremadoc and David Jones, site-owner.
[¶] CRO: BJC/647, DRO: DCH/3/77, 84; NLW John Thomas CC66; census for parish of Ffestiniog 1881.

Some smaller enterprises also deserve mention. In Pen y Groes (SH 4743 5295) there survive the dilapidated remains of a powered workshop erected during the 1914-18 war to produce socks, still with fragments of pulley and line-shafting in the roof-timbers. A similar venture was established in Blaenau Ffestiniog in the market hall.*

Note: textile technology
Willowing is the process of opening out the fibre before carding (qv), and involves passing the cloth through two rollers, one fluted, one plain, into a larger roller (about 0.6m [24in]) in diameter) covered with metal teeth, on which it is mixed and whence it is ejected. *Carding* is the disentanglement, cleaning and intermixing of fibres to produce a continuous web or sliver, and was carried out with hand-held cards with teeth or staples until the advent of roller carding engines. The *slubbing billy* is a machine with spindles mounted on a travelling carriage which draws out the loose cardings. *Spinning* draws out and twists the carded slivers into a strong yarn, able to bear strain and friction. Spinning with distaff and spindle was displaced by the spinning wheel, which itself was displaced by the spinning jenny (credited to James Hargreaves in 1769), and by the mule (credited to Samuel Crompton in 1770). A *twisting machine* imparts a three-ply twist to yarn that is to be made into blankets. The threads are then *woven* on a loom, the essentials of which are the same whether it is power-driven or hand-operated. Jacquard weaving is used to create a pattern in the woven material; a jacquard loom is controlled by a series of punched cards, each perforation of which controls the action of one warp thread for the passage of one pick. The next stage involves *scouring*, at one time a process which involved immersion in a wash tub in a substance one part urine to three parts warm water, but which could later be carried out mechanically in a trough containing an alkaline solution. The newly-woven cloth is then *fulled*, in a set of stocks (a fulling mill) in which it is pounded in an alkaline liquor, thereby thickening the fabric. The nap is raised by hand-teaseling, or by a gig mill, and the wool is sheared. Cloth was *dried* on tenter frames, until spin-drying or hydro-extractor machines became a possibility. Finally cloth is *pressed*, either by being screwed down in a press and warmed by a peat fire or (from the 1860s) by steam equipment.

4.2.2 Metal processing

There is archaeological evidence for metal-processing in Gwynedd in the Medieval period, in the 18th century and again in the 20th, and the production and rolling of aluminium is a significant element in the regional economy.

The processing of metallic ore into a commercially useful product is one of the few areas of the industrial archaeology of Gwynedd where there are some evident links between the archaeology of the later Medieval period and the period of the present study, from 1700 onwards. Ten bloomery sites have been identified in the northern part of Coed y Brenin, the lands to the north of the tidal limit of the Mawddach, which historical records, excavation and radio-carbon slag-analysis confirmed were exploited in the late 14th century. One, at Llwyn Du (SH 7240 2780), was surveyed

---

* Jones, E., *Stiniog* (Caernarfon: Gwasg Gwynedd, 1988), p. 25.

and partly excavated in 1997 and 2001, yielding evidence for a large furnace with clay superstructure and a refining hearth within a 15m by 4.5m building, a tank made from sloping stones sealed with clay, perhaps for temporary storage of hot charcoal, and the remains of structural timbers.

Neither field evidence nor documentation suggests that other iron sites from this period are likely to be discovered, though it is possible that evidence will emerge for the smelting of iron, lead and copper in the vicinity of other Gwynedd mines where work may have gone on in the later Medieval period. As it is, however, the story resumes with the first recorded blast furnaces, charcoal-fired and water-blown, within Gwynedd. One was constructed at Dol y Clochydd (SH 734 219) in the late 16th century, again in Coed y Brenin.* The second was erected by Abraham Darby I, and others of the Quaker ironworking fraternity not far away, at Dolgun to the east of Dolgellau (SH 751 187) in 1717. It was blown out in 1734. Darby had already succeeded in using coke instead of charcoal to smelt iron in his blast furnace at Coalbrookdale.

The earliest blast furnaces were developed in Sweden and Germany in the 12th century, and spread to northern France and the Low Countries around the end of the 15th. They were introduced to the heavily-wooded areas of south-east England in the 1490s. They required substantial investment. Because of their size compared with a bloomery, and because they remained in blast for months at a time, they needed sufficient supplies of iron ore and charcoal, as well as a dependable water supply to operate the bellows, and an organised workforce, a state of affairs which Dolgun exemplifies well. The farm on which it was built was the home of the first effective yearly meeting of the Society of Friends in Wales, and the centre of a network of local Quaker families with access to timber resources and iron ore on their freeholds. The furnace structure partly survives, having been consolidated by the Snowdonia National Park in the 1980s, with the pit for the wheel which operated the bellows.† A related site within this part of Gwynedd for which only artistic and scanty documentary evidence survives is a water-driven forge observed by Paul Sandby in the 1770s, which is likely to have been situated on the Afon Cwm Mynach (approx. SH 689 193), a tributary of the Mawddach.‡

A later blast-furnace, again charcoal-fired and water-blown, has left no above-ground remains; this was at Eglwysbach in the Conwy valley, built about 1748-50 and abandoned by the early 1770s. As with Dolgun, there were abundant supplies of timber available locally, but the ore that it smelted was Furness haematite.§ It was situated in what is now Bodnant gardens, though its exact location is unknown – possibly on the site of the later ornamental corn-mill (SH 79- 72-). 'Furnace' survives as the name of a nearby farm. In all probability, it resembled the slightly later Dyfi furnace in Cardiganshire (SN 685 951), now conserved and interpreted by Cadw. Both

---

*   Crew, P. and Williams, M.C., 'Dol y Clochydd', *Archaeology in Wales* 24 (1984), pp. 25, 83 (1985), pp. 54-5 and 26 (1986), p. 68.

†   Williams, J.G.: 'The Quakers of Merioneth During the Seventeenth Century' *JMHRS* 8 2-3 (1978-9), pp. 122-56; Riden, P., *A Gazetteer of Charcoal-fired Blast Furnaces in Great Britain in use since 1660* (Cardiff: Merton Priory Press, 1993), pp. 68-9; Thomas, B., 'Iron-making in Dolgellau', *JMHRS* 9 (1981-4), pp. 474-5.

‡   Sandby, P., 'The Iron Forge between Dolgelli and Barmouth in Merioneth Shire', *XII Views in North Wales* (London: 1776): Plate 6 (etching and aquatint printed in brown ink 21.2 x 29.7cm). The estimate of location is based partly on the topography of the original and partly on the Llanelltyd parish census of 1851, which lists a dwelling 'Forge' between Penbryn Melyn and Tai Newyddion (PRO: Llanelltyd parish 1851 census, HO107/2511 Folio 409).

§   Riden, *op. cit.*, pp. 68-9 quotes one source as stating that Dolgun went over to smelting Furness ore from 1720.

Egwlysbach and Dyfi were in the hands of the Kendall family, dissenting entrepreneurs who also ran furnaces in Shropshire, Yorkshire, Furness and Cheshire before making the transition from charcoal to coke production by building the Beaufort Furnace in Ebbw Vale in 1779, thereby setting the south Wales iron industry on its path to greatness.*

Thereafter, little attempt seems to have been made within Gwynedd to process metal ores until the 20th century. As *4.1.3.* outlines, some very small-scale lead smelters were operated within the lead mines of the Conwy valley and at Penrhyn Du, and Mynydd Parys had a more ambitious smelting plant at Porth Amlwch, but there is no evidence for the production of pig-iron in Gwynedd, still less of rolling mills. Despite the area's abundant mineral reserves and capacity for power-generation, the lack of coal prevented it from growing, though the loss of the Quaker community to Dolgellau was probably an important factor as well. In this respect, the area played practically no part in the expansion of the iron industry in the classic Industrial period.

It is only in the 20th century, with the potential for electricity to smelt aluminium, that metal processing once again figures in the regional economy, though this time it assumed considerable importance and placed the area in the forefront of technical development internationally. The discovery of an electrochemical process for the reduction of aluminium in 1887, and the development of dynamos with industrial potential and of turbine technology made the industrial production of this metal a commercial proposition, but it consumed electricity at a very high rate – 18,000 kilowatt hours per ton of aluminium. Aluminium reduction plants were therefore established where water-resources lend themselves to the establishment of power plant, rather than near supplies of raw materials – bauxite, from which alumina is extracted electrolytically, is mined in Provence, in Ghana and in western Australia, and cryolite, a component in the reduction process, in Greenland and Iceland. One consequence is that the archaeology of aluminium plants tends to be associated with dedicated transport infrastructure as well as with extensive power systems. In 1896 a large-scale hydro-electric power station had been commissioned at Foyers in Invernesshire for the British Aluminium Company, which in 1901 set up a similar establishment at Kinlochleven. At Dolgarrog in the Conwy valley, quite literally in the shadow of the Carneddau, a plant was established in 1907 by the Aluminium Corporation Ltd, an organisation with links to Vickers Sons and Maxim Ltd, the armaments manufacturers, Argyll Motors and Bruce Peebles Ltd, a company then at the forefront of electrical technology. Alumina was extracted from bauxite at Hebburn-on-Tyne, and the calcined alumina was sent to Dolgarrog for reduction. A factory to manufacture carbon anodes, initially established on the opposite bank of the Tyne at Wallsend, was moved to Dolgarrog in 1912.

As it was, by the time of the Second World War, cheaper aluminium coming in from Canada spelt the end for the reduction process at Dolgarrog, with the result that the reduction works and the carbon factory were demolished. The factory had had a rolling mill since 1915, and now continues in business as a specialist rolling plant.

---

* Dinn, J., 'Dyfi Furnace Excavations 1982-87', *Post-Medieval Archaeology* 22 (1988), pp. 111-42. Dinn suggests (p. 133) that Dyfi, Eglwysbach and Craleckan in Argyll were all built by the same design and labour force. For the Kendall family, see *DNB*. Confusingly, Dyfi furnace is sometimes referred to as 'Eglwysfach'. Eglwysbach was built to take advantage of competitively-priced charcoal at a location to which haematite could be easily delivered.

However, though the redundant structures were demolished and their sites re-used, a remarkable amount survives from its early 20th-century infrastructure, including much of the original water-catchment system. The mass concrete gravity dam which increased the capacity of Llyn Eigiau survives, including the breach at SH 7235 6535 which in 1925 caused the deaths of 16 people in Dolgarrog. Concrete contour leats from the Afon Porth Llwyd at Trasbwll (SH 7427 6653) and from the Afon Ddu at SH 7512 6472 meet at a penstock at SH 7634 6686, where a length of the original pipeline of 1907 survives. This was made up of steel sections, lap-welded in the lower part, and with Kimberley joints in the upper, 0.914m (36in) internal diameter, supported on concrete blocks.* The system has been altered and upgraded ever since, particularly in the 1920s when it was adapted for public supply, but it constitutes a remarkable industrial landscape (see also p. 143 – Figure 66).

66 The Dolgarrog aluminium works showing the canal (left), the railway and the two power-stations to the right of the carbon factory chimney – the original 1907 station and the 1924 public supply station.

Aluminium smelting was revived within Gwynedd with the establishment of Anglesey Aluminium at Holyhead in 1971, the result of lobbying by Cledwyn Hughes (1916-2001), the island's MP from 1951 to 1979. Whereas the rationale for Dolgarrog was hydro-power, at Holyhead it was nuclear energy, from the Wylfa power station. The plant now requires 12 per cent of all the electrical power consumed in Wales and the smelter produces in excess of 143,000 tonnes of pure aluminium annually. It is jointly owned by Rio Tinto (51 per cent) and Kaiser Aluminium and Chemical Corporation (49 per cent) and is managed by Comalco, a wholly-owned subsidiary of Rio Tinto. Bauxite ore is mined at Weipa in the Western Cape in Australia and refined at Portoscuso in Sardinia as well as in Jamaica and Ireland; alumina and calcined coke

---

* *The Electrical Review*, 6 November 1908, pp. 803-11.

(generally sourced from the North East of England or India) are off-loaded at a jetty at Holyhead and moved by underground conveyor to their storage facilities at the main plant (SH 265 810). Liquid pitch, delivered by road, is mixed with the coke, and then formed to make anodes for the electrolytic cells. These are baked to make them electrically conductive and to give them mechanical strength, and assembled for later electrical connection to the cell when delivered to the cell rooms. Cathodes are purchased externally, with electrical connections cast on site for installation in the cells. In the cell rooms 316 reduction cells produce approximately 400 tonnes of aluminium per day. The anodes are consumed as the alumina is reduced to molten metal, and are replaced to schedule, and the metal is periodically tapped for casting into primary products. Some is cast into 500kg moulds, and the rest is allocated to two direct chill-casting pits that cast extrusion billet or rolling ingot. Finished products are sent away by rail, making the plant one of only two industrial users (along with Penmaenmawr quarry – see *4.1.2*) within Gwynedd of the Chester to Holyhead railway which has a siding connection.

The plant itself is unobtrusively located near the A5 on Holy island, though the smelter chimney is a prominent feature and, along with the Wylfa nuclear power station that feeds it with electricity and the harbour at Holyhead that receives its raw materials, it constitutes an impressive industrial landscape, on a larger scale than Dolgarrog. Even so, its place within an international system of operation and patterns of ownership and risk-management, and its all-important power requirements, perpetuate on a global level the management problems and capital risks which led Abraham Darby and the Kendall family to Dolgun and to Eglwysbach in the 18th century.

4.2.3 The food industry

Archaeological study of Gwynedd's food industry has benefited from the work of 'folk-life' scholars but later developments have been comparatively neglected.

The food industry generally has been very patchily studied by archaeologists, and Gwynedd is no exception. However, the small rural corn mill, as the single most numerous and important monument-type within this category (as well as perhaps the oldest), has been extensively recorded; in Gwynedd, and in Wales as a whole, this is due in no small part to the 'folk-life' focus of the National Museum of Wales and the valuable work of the journal *Melin* ('mill'). The corollary of this is that later developments have been comparatively neglected, as the industry's scale became global in the 19th century.[*]

Mills – machines for grinding cereal crops so that they may become a food source – have been powered variously by water, by wind and by heat engines. As Chapter 3 notes, the water-mill seems to have arrived in Gwynedd perhaps no earlier than the 12th century, and the horizontal mill was unknown in the region, at least in post-Medieval

---

[*] As an example, Watts, M., *The Archaeology of Mills and Milling* (Stroud: Tempus, 2002) only examines mills built up to the 18th century.

times.* Tide mills functioned at several locations – the earliest known reference seems to be from 1524, to a mill at Tre'r Gof in Anglesey. A *felin heli* ('salt mill', signifying a tide mill) is recorded adjacent to Conwy castle and another one has given its name to a settlement on the mainland side of the Menai straits.† So far only those of Anglesey have benefited from any detailed study, which confirms that they were mainly very small structures using 2m diameter wheels to operate a single pair of stones but that they made effective use of a large tidal range and in one case continued to operate into the late 19th century.‡

Otherwise, no water-mill sites from the period 1400 to 1700 have been excavated, but documentary evidence occasionally provides some hints as to how they were constructed and rebuilt. Surviving water-mills are nearly always of 19th-century construction, even where there is documentary evidence of a much older mill on the site. Very many buildings survive, often with parts of the machinery intact, though the only one to have been conserved is Felin Isaf at SH 8028 7496.

A specification for a post-windmill at Newborough in Anglesey dated 1303 is one of the earliest known in Britain,§ though the evidence is sketchy for later Medieval wind-mills. Perhaps as a result of a series of particularly dry summers in the mid-18th century, construction seems to have resumed around 1735 and went on for about a hundred years, giving Anglesey the highest concentration in Wales. A published gazetteer and history identifies the visible remains of 28 wind-corn mills in the island, all of them tower mills, of which one also had an integral water-wheel. Melin Llynon, originally built at a cost of £529 11s. in 1775-6 (SH 341 852), was restored by Anglesey Council in 1986.¶ The 1826 mill at Trearddur Bay (SH 266 788) was the last operational windmill in Wales when it ceased milling in 1938.**

Surviving tower mills are found in some places on the mainland – several on the Creuddyn peninsula, where the earliest example may date from the early 17th century, a few on Penrhyn Llŷn, none, so far as is known, in the old county of Merioneth.††

Corn-grinding in Gwynedd barely developed beyond the small-scale water- or wind-powered mill serving the immediate locality. Only at Porthmadog is there material evidence of a more ambitious set-up, in the shape of a complex in the 'industrial zone' to the north-east of the town at SH 5689 3895 (see p. 219). The older part, a three-storey structure with an attic, contains a date-stone which reads *R(ichard) G(riffith)*

---

* Lewis Morris (1701-65), born and bred in Anglesey, who was very well informed indeed in technical matters, was clearly unaware of the technology when he saw one at Douglas in the Isle of Man – NLW: Add. Ms 67a, p. 183.
† Williams, R., *The History and Antiquities of Aberconwy* (Denbigh: Thomas Gee, 1835), p. 81.
‡ Davidson, A., 'Tidal mills on Anglesey', *Melin* 16 (2000), pp. 29-50.
§ Salmon, J., 'Erection of a Windmill at Newborough (Anglesey) in 1303', *Archaeologia Cambrensis* 105 2 (December 1940), pp. 250-2.
¶ UWB Porth yr Aur 23188.
** Guise, B. and Lees, G., *Windmills of Anglesey* (Painscastle: Attic Books, 1992). Three other windmills are identified which had a non-agricultural function – pumping out Parys mine, grinding paints at Amlwch and powering a sawmill at Holyhead. The second and third of these worked in conjunction with a steam engine.
†† On Creuddyn, Hen Dwr, also known as Melin Gloddaith (SH 8040 8115), is probably the 'windie milne' built by Sir Roger Mostyn between 1617 and 1642 (Dibble, K., *Nant-y-Gamar* [privately published, no date]), and nearby Glanwydden windmill (SH 8169 8047) preserves a lintel marked 'SRM/068/1704' – presumably 'Sir Roger Mostyn ? 1704'. Of those in Penrhyn Llŷn and Eifionydd, the remains of a tower mill survive at SH 3060 3209, working in 1809-1811 (Hyde-Hall, E., *A Description of Caernarvonshire* [Caernarfon: Caernarvonshire Historical Society, 1956], p. 290), Melin Lleiniau in Llanbedrog parish (SH 3202 3190) is marked on the 1838 tithe map (piece 321), Melin Dwylan (SH 2975 2758) is described as 'newly built' in the *Caernarvon and Denbigh Herald* for 7 April 1832, and a wind-mill at Nefyn (SH 307- 405-) is attested in 1795 (Pritchard, O., *Hanes Methodistiaid Calfinaidd Nefyn 1757-1926* [Pwllheli, n.d.] p. 28. It appears on the tithe map of 1838-40 as piece 650.

B(uilde)r {*AD 1862*} with an internal timber framework which re-uses the masts of ships for vertical support. An adjacent structure of 1871 is to the same basic pattern but is five storeys high plus attic, with internal cast-iron columns. The bases for a drive axle from the steam engine survive internally.[*]

The likelihood is that the earlier part was built for traditional millstones, albeit powered by steam rather than water, but the second building was designed for roller milling. Harder American wheats were increasingly being imported, especially during bad harvests in the 1870s and 1880s, but were unsuitable for millstones, with the result that millers in the Atlantic isles were forced to look at the new technologies that were evolving not only in the mid-West, but also in Budapest, the centre for milling for the Danubian plain. To begin with, rollers, first porcelain then iron or steel, only took over certain jobs, such as breaking the outer coatings of bran; then they came to be used to treat middlings (hard particles) which had been produced by millstones. By the late 19th century complete roller systems, with purifiers to sort the flour, became available. Mills such as these, often architecturally prominent buildings, tended to be constructed near transport links and achieved economies of throughput and scale that put the smaller mills out of business. The Porthmadog mill, with its rail access to the harbour and to the national railway network, was well-placed to mill imported wheat, especially as many Porthmadog ships often had to return home in ballast.[†] Interestingly, surviving charter-party agreements indicate that the mill was processing grain from Derry.[‡]

Other large-scale mills do not survive above ground level. The roller mill built by Heinrich Simon (1835-99), one of the most prolific mill engineers of the late 19th century, for Thomas 'Palestina' Lewis in Bangor's Dean Street has been demolished, as have the Holyhead Steam Mills and the Festiniog Flour and Corn Mill.[§] Just as the roller mills put the traditional rural mills out of business, they themselves succumbed to the 20th century's concentration of flour-milling in progressively fewer and ever-larger firms. By the 1960s Rank Hovis McDougall and Spillers utterly dominated the industry. Today, flour continues to arrive by road for Gwynedd bakers, but these are now few and far between.[¶]

Rural mills also ground barley, wheat, oats and maize to produce animal feed, a process that went on until after 1945, when they were superseded by factories on Merseyside and at Maesbury in Shropshire.[**]

Farm dairying is discussed in *4.1.5* but milk-processing also came to be mechanised away from the farms. Three mechanised creameries were established within Gwynedd,

---

[*] CRO: XM/1388/222/16. The site was working into the 1960s; it is now a café, shop, art gallery and a children's play area. I am grateful to Ms Susan Weldon-Booth, the Managing Director, for information and for the opportunity to see what remains internally.

[†] The mill is identified as a 'steam roller mill' owned by M. and J. Roberts in the 1886 *Postal Directory for Caernarvonshire and Anglesey* (New Brighton: 1886), p. 378.

[‡] Hughes, E. and Eames, A., *Porthmadog Ships* (Caernarfon: Gwynedd Archives service, 1975), pp. 338-9.

[§] See *The Miller*, January 1890 (Lewis' nickname arose from his magic lantern slides of his trips to the Holy Land); *Sutton's Directory of North Wales* (Manchester: 1889), p. 33; Owain, S. ab, 'Hen Felinau Plwyf Ffestiniog (2)', *Rhamant Bro* 24 (Gaeaf 2005), pp. 26-7, *Baner ac Amserau Cymru* 21 Hydref 1885. The Ffestiniog mill was powered by a 25hp steam engine, a turbine and an overshot water-wheel, and contained ten pairs of stones, five silk reels, 6m (20ft) long and three silk reels, 3m (10ft) long, three purifiers, three cleaning machines worked from upright shafts, one washer and driver.

[¶] For a study with some interesting points of comparison with Gwynedd, see Bielenberg, A. (ed.), *Irish Flour Milling: A History 600-2000* (Dublin: Lilliput, 2003). Ireland, as a major corn-growing country, invested early on in large scale multi-storey mills.

[**] Trinder, B., *The Industrial Archaeology of Shropshire* (Chichester: Phillimore, 1996), p. 32.

as well as one just outside the border at Mochdre, a development that did much to rescue farming, providing farmers with one reliable and regularly-paid cheque. Rhyd y Main between Bala and Dolgellau (SH 8316 2450) functioned from 1940 to 1966, and is now home to a 'classic cars' business.* Llangefni creamery, as Caws Glanbia (SH 4579 7486 – Figure 67), now employs 175 people in a modern factory producing mozzarella cheese for pizzas, in association with a factory in Northern Ireland, part of an Irish corporation which is now Europe's largest food-processing company.

67 Glanbia cheese factory at Llangefni, formerly the creamery, alongside the track of the former Anglesey Central Railway.

The modernised South Caernarfon Creamery at Rhyd y Gwystl in Eifionydd (SH 405 391) is Wales' only farmer-owned dairy co-operative. It began with 63 producer-members, from whom churns of milk were collected daily, and now has nearly 200 members and its own fleet of road tankers. When the Milk Marketing Board was abolished in 1994, SCC decided to purchase milk directly from its members. A cheese factory functioned at Abergwyngregyn and has been recorded by the Royal Commission.

Breweries were to be found in Caernarfon, Bangor, Llanfairfechan, Conwy, Llandudno, Pwllheli, Dolgellau, even Trefriw, but a developed brewing industry was, needless to say, inhibited by the remorseless campaign waged against alcoholic beverages by the chapels and their political tribunes, such as the young Lloyd George, who thundered against the 'unholy trinity' of squire, bishop and brewer. There is little evidence within the region for malting (the process by which barley germinates after being soaked in water), which seems to have been carried out mainly on farms rather than on dedicated sites, though a *rhes maltsters* ('maltsters' row)' in the village of Bontnewydd (SH 4825 5983), where a pub called *The Maltster's Arms* once stood, shows that this was not always the case. A small brewery survives, little altered on the outside, in Dolgellau at SH 7283 1762. A much larger establishment was the brewery at Porth Amlwch, now demolished above ground level. Amlwch also supported a small-scale tobacco industry, which ran to a *felin snisin* ('sneezing mill') to produce snuff – again no visible trace remains.† The only distillery of any consequence was at Frongoch, north

---

* Williams, G., 'Ffatri Laeth Rhydymain', *Llen y Llannau* (1997), pp. 31-49 describes operations here. Milk brought in to the creamery was poured into a tank and pasteurised by being heated suddenly. A separator removed the cream to make butter; skim was sold to pig farms. Power was supplied by a Blackstone twin turbine and three oil engines. DRO: Z/DCL/351 states that in 1948 1,504,574 gallons were received by the creamery.

† Hope, B.D., *A Curious Place: An Industrial History of Amlwch (1550-1950)* (Wrexham: Bridge Books, 1994, pp. 69-74, 92-7. One of the delights of Hope's study is the advertisement for Amlwch tobacco on the back cover, which proclaims *Os am fwynhad, smokiwch Baco'r Werin* ('For pleasure, smoke the People's Tobacco') over a photograph of a bearded and distinctly elderly artisan with a pipe in his hand. The 'Marlborough man' of 1960s cigarette advertising had curious antecedents.

of Bala (SH 903 393 C), an abortive undertaking of which little or nothing remains above ground level other than houses for its office workers but which achieved an unexpected fame when prisoners from the Irish uprising of 1916 were held there.* Conversely, the manufacture of soft drinks received every encouragement, and small factories existed in a number of settlements such as Caernarfon, Bangor, Porthmadog and Llandudno. Specialist foodstuffs such as sauces and pickles were produced in the resort towns.†

Slaughterhouses are found in many small villages, often easily identifiable by the survival of gruesome internal fittings such as hooks to which the animals were tied, and gutters to drain the blood. Abattoirs operate at Llangefni (SH 4611 7512) and Llanrwst (SH 7983 6202). An early 20th-century slaughter-complex survives in re-use near Llandudno station (SH 7837 8182), whilst a building which currently serves as the café at Seiont Nurseries (SH 5056 6281) functioned as a black-pudding factory during one of its several incarnations. Grampian Prepared Meats, a subsidiary of the Grampian Country Food Group of Aberdeen, a trans-national company which is currently (2006) Britain's largest producer of chickens, operates several chicken farms on Anglesey, where they were first established in the 1950s. The factory, situated on the Llangefni industrial estate, processes 410,000 chickens a week; 10 'growing sites' and a hatchery are operated elsewhere in the island.‡

Traditionally, most animals were transported live to English markets, and made the journey on their own legs until the railways came. The drovers (*porthmyn*) remain romantic figures and many old trackways are still pointed out as the routes they took to the English smithfields. Nevertheless, as agents of – quite literally – capital rather than as managers of land, they are otherwise hard to trace in the archaeological record, and a well-manured field might sometimes be the only evidence of their existence in Wales. One such near Dinas Mawddwy in the south-eastern extremity of Gwynedd is traditionally identified as where cattle were shoed for droving to Birmingham or London; symbolically it lies near the track-bed of Sir Edmund Buckley's Mawddwy railway, itself disused since 1951.§ The market at Bryncir (SH 4799 4452) has survived the closure of the Caernarfon to Afonwen railway; this was where cattle from Penrhyn Llŷn were sold and loaded onto trains. At Holyhead station the extensive lairage facilities for sheep and cattle which had arrived by ship survived until the 1990s.

The storage and distribution of foodstuffs away from the farm has left comparatively little trace. Tithe-barns survive as place-names rather than as archaeological entities and, though there are accounts of corn riots at Caernarfon in 1800 and 1801 and at Amlwch in 1817, there is no account of where the corn was kept before it was loaded on board ship.¶ The playwright Twm o'r Nant speaks of grain being kept *hyd Lofftydd ac mewn Cistie* ('up lofts and in chests'), and it is interesting that the 18th-century balladeers speak of both export and import.** Grain came to be imported to Eifionydd about

---

* Legend has it that Albert Edward, Prince of Wales, after trying a nip of Bala whisky, tactfully remarked that there would always be a crate of it in the royal cellars. For the distillery, see Ebenezer, L., *Fron-Goch and the birth of the IRA* (Llanrwst: Gwasg Carreg Gwalch, 2006).
† Price, E.,'The Smaller Industries in the XIX Century' in *Atlas of Caernarvonshire* (Caernarfon: Gwynedd Rural Council, 1976), pp. 176-9.
‡ 'Chicken Supreme', *The Manufacturer*, December 2005.
§ Cozens, L., Kidner, R.W. and Poole, B., *The Mawddwy, Van and Kerry Branches* (Usk: Oakwood Press, 2004), p. 69.
¶ Rowlands, J., *Copper Mountain* (Llangefni: Anglesey Antiquarian Society, 1981), p. 116.
** Parry, J.G., 'Terfysgoedd Ŷd yng Ngogledd Cymru 1740-58', *TCHS* 39 (1978), pp. 74-107.

1800; at Ty Gwyn y Gamlas, at the mouth of the Traeth Bach, the entrepôt for Harlech and doubtless for much of Ardudwy, is a substantial warehouse (SH 5994 3550), apparently shown on a painting of 1827 (Figure 68). This may have been erected by Richard Jones of Ty Cerig nearby (1756-1825) or Robert Prichard (1790-1875), farmers and merchants who probably for the most part imported rather than exported grain.* The warehouse on the quay at Porthmadog (SH 5686 3834) was in existence by 1845.† The former bonded warehouse on Caernarfon quay (SH 4793 6259), now a night-club, stored wines and spirits rather than grain.‡ Within the town itself is a yellow-brick warehouse of mid-19th-century date (SH 4784 6278), and Caernarfon's substantial self-proclaimed 'Working Men's Conservative Club' (SH 4778 6282) is said to have begun life as a warehouse. At Pwllheli wheat was imported and barley, oats, cheese, butter and bacon were exported from the Napoleonic period onwards,§ yet there is no evidence or record of a warehouse in this period.

68 Warehouse at Ty Gwyn y Gamlas.

Similarly with buying and selling; at Llanerchymedd in Anglesey the unusual width of a particular street is the only sign of its once-famous horse fair. In some places, dedicated buildings survive. The typical late medieval pattern, such as is found in mid- and north-east Wales, in England and the east coast of the USA, in which an administrative house is built over an arcaded market space, is often called a town hall. It is represented by three, late, examples. Tremadoc's of 1807-8 is unusual in forming part of a peripheral development around the market square rather than being free-standing (and in that the arcade could be converted into a theatre).¶ Dolgellau's (SH 7284 1784) was built as late as 1870, with a reading room above the arcade.** One at Bala (SH 9261 3597 – Figure 69), dating from 1815, and once the centre of county administration, is in poor condition.†† Llanrwst's market place had a building of some description as early as 1661, replaced by an early 19th-century structure, itself a casualty of the need to find car-parking space in 1964 (SH 7982 6167).‡‡ Covered markets survive at

---

* Lewis, M.J.T., *Sails on the Dwyryd* (Maentwrog: Snowdonia National Park Study Centre, 1989), p. 61.
† CRO: X/Plans/HR.
‡ Lloyd, L., *The Port of Caernarfon, 1793-1900* (privately published, 1989), p. 52.
§ Lloyd, L., *Pwllheli: The Port and Mart of Llŷn* (privately published 1991), pp. 148, 156.
¶ Beazley, E., *Madocks and the Wonder of Wales* (Aberystwyth: P&Q, 1985), pp. 87-95.
** Schmiechen, J. and Carls, K., *The British Market Hall* (New Haven and London: Yale University Press, 1999), p. 263.
†† DRO: QS/0/1, p. 476, p. 489, p. 506, p. 512, p. 517, p. 524, pp. 528-9. The builder was Owen Owen of Llawrcillan.
‡‡ Bezant Lowe, W., *The Heart of Northern Wales* (privately published, 1927), p. 292.

Caernarfon (SH 4783 6282 – 1832), at Holyhead (SH 2461 8255 – 1855, the latter constructed at the expense of Stanley of Penrhos, the principal local landowner, with its distinctive Jacobean frontage) and at Bangor (SH 5818 7209, 1818), now a branch of W.H. Smith's.* Many towns acquired these features as local magnates attempted 'to regulate the boisterous world of the market',† and they came increasingly to sell products other than food and to incorporate a wider variety of public rooms (see pp. 203-4).

69 Market hall at Bala.

In Gwynedd as elsewhere, the food industry is now dominated by agro-businesses that function on a world scale, and local produce jostles for shelf-space with coffee from Colombia and oranges from Israel in a supermarket that could with very little change be in Cape Town or Ottawa. Whilst this may be a worrying state of affairs on several levels, it is wrong to regard globalisation and the loss of local distinctiveness as purely a function of the late 20th century. The Gwynedd farm-wife who in the reign of George IV took her corn to the mill to be ground participated in a local economy; her great-grand-daughter who in the 1890s sat down with her quarryman-husband to a supper of tinned meat and white bread did not necessarily eat more healthily, but had undoubtedly already entered a global economy. Food supply was the first industry to function internationally. The import of sugar from the West Indies to Britain in the 18th century influenced industries as diverse as ceramics and publishing; its system of capital accumulation made possible the spectacular growth of the slate quarries of the Ogwen valley (p. 42). The following century saw the near-demise of the ancient system whereby farmers sold their produce at the urban market in favour of selling at the gate to intermediaries. This has meant profound changes for both producer and consumer, and it is also changing the historic environment worldwide.

Note: mill technology

A *horizontal mill* (the so-called 'Norse mill') involves a horizontal water-wheel operating a single set of stones without gearing. A *tide mill* is operated by means of tide-water released from a reservoir at low tide.

---

* A granary for grain and covered stalls for meat had been built on Glanrafon in Bangor in 1804 ; the present W.H. Smith's may be in essence a much larger building erected in 1818; see Jones, P.E., *Bangor 1883-1983: A Study in Municipal Government* (Cardiff: University of Wales Press, 1986), p. 9 and *North Wales Gazette* 21 May 1818.

† Schmiechen and Carls, *op. cit.*; Trinder, B., '18th and 19th-Century Market Town Industry: An analytical model', *IAR* 24 (November 2002), p. 78.

4.3 Ancillary Industries

4.3.1 Foundries, ironworks, engineering

Industrialisation called into being several specialist engineering complexes within Gwynedd.

Typically, industries with a strong regional character tended to call into being their own ancillary manufacturing and engineering processes. Lancashire textiles, for instance, relied on regionally-based firms to provide them with machinery, whereas the mines of Cornwall not only called for the engineering genius of individuals such as Richard Trevithick but gave rise to such well-known organisations as Harvey's of Hayle and Holman Brothers of Camborne. Much the same process can be identified within Gwynedd, even though the area was dependent on outside suppliers in the early years of industrialisation, and tended to revert to them in the latter phase of industrialisation.

Broadly speaking, it is possible to identify three phases in the technical capacity of the region. The first begins with the introduction of industrial technologies in the early 18th century, and is characterised by the use of timber, brass and wrought iron as structural materials, as well as by the importation of both machines and knowledge. Understanding of this period and its technical capacity derives largely from documentary sources, but is sometimes augmented by the material record. The surviving engine house at Penrhyn Du mine (p. 90), for example, is in essence the design drawn up by Boulton and Watt. Their archive also preserves Jonathan Hornblower's complaints at having to erect an engine in a part of the world which had no capacity whatsoever to make such a thing possible, neither technical know-how nor a decent inn. As well as the products of Boulton and Watt, engines from Fawcett and Preston and Neath Abbey Ironworks were to be found in Gwynedd, but the area did not, so far as is known, produce its own steam engines until at least the mid-19th century.* It is not possible to tell how the Drws y Coed copper miners put together their stamp mill in 1768 – the inspiration might have been Cornish but whence the ironwork came is not clear (p. 85).

This first period perhaps lasts into the 1820s, when the archives of mines and quarries make it clear that, although items such as rails, wagons and incline machinery were still being purchased from outside, Gwynedd managers and engineers were acquiring some skill in making technical choices from amongst the options available to them.†

The second phase is defined by the characteristic industrial technology of the foundry and the steam engine, and by local or regional supply. The archaeology of this period, from the 1820s to the end of the 19th century, is characterised by the (limited) survival of buildings, a considerable volume of documentary sources, and the survival of artefacts, and suggests not only the increasing technical capacity of the

---

* See Gwyn, D., 'An Early High-Pressure Steam Engine at Cloddfa'r Coed', *TCHS* 63 (2002), pp. 26-43, for early steam engines in Caernarvonshire. For Anglesey, see Bennett, J.S and Williams, C.J., 'Pearl Shaft Engine House, Mona Mine, Parys Mountain', *TAAS* (2000) pp. 40-42 and Birmingham Reference Library Boulton and Watt 6/6/85, folio 150, portfolio 656, folios 133-8, *Caernarvon and Denbigh Herald* 10 February 1838, *North Wales Chronicle* 7 December 1847. For Merioneth, see *Carnarvon and Denbigh Herald* 23 August 1845 and Jones, O., *Cymru: Hanesyddol, Parthedigol, a Bywgraphyddol* (London, Glasgow and Edinburgh: 1875) p. 552.

† Gwyn, D., 'From Blacksmith to Engineer: Artisan Technology in North Wales in the Early Nineteenth Century', *Llafur* 7 (1999) pp. 51-65.

region but also a cross-sectoral cultural trust amongst the small local elite and amongst a largely monoglot workforce.* The strong survival of the Welsh language in the slate communities is testament not only to the very literate culture of the quarrymen but also to the regional self-sufficiency of the industry in this period. The problems that workmen and even managers might have found dealing in an unfamiliar tongue were further reasons for maintaining a local supply-base.

Some large industrial undertakings went on to establish their own facilities in this second phase period – Boston Lodge on the Festiniog Railway (p. 157) and the Marine Yard at Holyhead (pp. 173-4), and even the smallest slate quarry or copper mine would have had a smithy where tools could be sharpened or wagon components forged. However, the increasing trend for Gwynedd's industries was wherever possible to buy machinery from a growing number of specialist local manufacturers. Small-scale workshops begin to appear around 1815 when John Hughes (see p. 102) and John Edwards (1782-1834) opened for business in Pen y Groes (SH 4694 5319), producing water-wheels, castings, track components, pumps and horse-whims for the quarries not only of nearby Nantlle but also of Llanberis and Blaenau Ffestiniog.† Foundries first appear at Bangor and Menai Bridge when the Telford road was under construction,‡ suggesting that this was a significant 'capacity-building' process within Gwynedd. Two other foundries were similarly established on the periphery of industrial areas, Valley Foundry near Holyhead, now the site of a filling station (SH 2852 7982), and Tanygrisiau, with its large water-wheel to provide the blast, which appears as the background to several early photographs of the Festiniog Railway (SH 6829 4494).

Porthmadog, with its hinterland of mine and quarry and with its harbour and ship-wrighting yards, was home to three important foundries. Owen, Isaac and Owen's Vulcan foundry (also known as the Union Ironworks) closed in 1914 and has left little trace (SH 569 390). The Glaslyn Foundry's buildings (SH 570 388) lasted long enough to be recorded by the RCAHMW in 1988, by then an untidy sprawl of 19th-century stone buildings and 20th-century corrugated iron.§ The curious two-storey stone schoolroom with its belfry survived to be incorporated into a supermarket. The most famous was the Britannia Foundry (SH 572 384), not least because its fine double-fronted machine shop and erecting shop appeared as the background to photographs of locomotives and trains on the Festiniog Railway from the 1880s. In 1972, after being effectively disused for 14 years, it was demolished to make way for an undistinguished Inland Revenue building.¶

The most complete survivor of these establishments was also perhaps the most remarkable in terms of what it produced. DeWinton's Union Ironworks at Caernarfon (SH 481 625) had no connection with the similarly-named establishment at Porthmadog. It evolved out of earlier and smaller-scale establishments on the slate

---

* For the outlook and way of life of the region's middle class in the 19th century, see Wood, D. and Field, V., *The Vincent Family Diary: Gentry Life in Victorian Bangor* (privately published, 2002).

† Gwyn, D., *op. cit.*

‡ Gwyn, D., '"Ignorant of all science": Technology transfer and peripheral culture, the case of Gwynedd, 1750-1850', *From Industrial Revolution to Consumer revolution: international perspectives on the archaeology of industrialisation* (The International Committee for the Conservation of the Industrial Heritage, 2001 for 2000), pp 39-45. See also CRO: XM/10414/5 (Caernarfon foundries), and Vaynol 6194, also *North Wales Gazette* 25 March 1819 and 1 April 1819.

§ NMR: NA/CA/89/93.

¶ Down, C.G., 'The Britannia Foundry, Portmadoc', (Festiniog Railway) *Heritage Group Journal* 56 (Winter 1998-9), pp. 5-25.

quay, and owed its origin to a lease of 1848 to an already-established ironfounder, Owen Thomas. Jeffreys Parry deWinton joined him as a partner in 1852, and the firm was operational in one guise or another until 1902. It is perhaps best known for the small vertical-boiler locomotives it produced, but these were only a small part of their output, and a fairly short-lived line. The Union Ironworks also built water-wheels, stationary and marine steam engines, slate saw tables, crushers for copper mines, rolling stock, gas-plant. It mainly supplied the Gwynedd area, though it occasionally tendered for contracts further afield, and a mark of the regard in which it was held was that Liverpool-built vessels intended for the Odessa grain trade would be sailed to Caernarfon to have DeWinton engines fitted. Much of the works survives. The impressive brick-built erecting shop which perhaps dates from the 1870s is in re-use as a plumber's warehouse, much altered but well cared-for. Other buildings include a foundry, carpenters' shop, boiler shop, pattern shop, a fitting shop and a once-handsome office building.* These have been allowed to deteriorate, even the ones that remain in use, despite their proximity to the new Welsh Highland Railway, which has turned this part of the town into a tourist focus (Figure 70).

70 DeWinton's Union ironworks, Caernarfon with the castle in the background.

The last survivor of this Victorian tradition was the tiny Brunswick Ironworks near the Harbour Trust offices on the Caernarfon slate quay (SH 4793 6259). This establishment, which at various times had made the gallows for the county gaol, the gates of Merton College, Oxford and the coffin of the Unknown Warrior, ingloriously ended its working life in 2004 repairing condom dispensers for Caernarfon pubs. It had become a remarkable time-capsule, preserving even the pegs in the office where reps had once hung their bowler hats, but arguments that it should be retained predictably fell on deaf ears. The business was relocated to the Peblig industrial estate, and has

---

* Ex info. Dr G.P. Jones, and A. and D. Fisher, whose research on the history of the Union Ironworks and its predecessors will be published by the Oakwood Press in the near future. See also CRO: XD/15 (Harbour Trust plans) and XD2 (Newborough leases), Abbott., R.A.S., *Vertical Boiler Locomotives and Railmotors Built in Great Britain* (Oxford: Oakwood Press, 1989), pp. 164-71, and Lloyd, L., *De Winton's of Caernarfon 1854-1892* (Harlech: privately published, 1994). The sale catalogue of 1903 gives some idea of the firm's range and capacity – UWB: Sale Catalogue 317.

recently (2006) completed the reconstruction of the Brynyfelin bridge for the Welsh Highland Railway.*

The third phase is characterised by the increased use of steel as a main structural material, and by a reversion to outside supply, with the result that, in terms of archaeological evidence, material remains are those of machines rather than the buildings which produced them.

Needless to say, even when nearby workshops could meet most of the engineering requirements of regional industry, they still had to compete for contracts with outside suppliers. This is well illustrated by the supply of machinery to Gwynedd's quarries. Although DeWinton was probably producing the earliest versions of his vertical boiler devices from around 1869, Dinorwic quarry only ever had one, bought in 1877. The first of the distinctive 0-4-0 saddle-tanks from Hunslet of Leeds, of which the quarry had no fewer than 22, arrived in 1870. Though Penrhyn quarry offered more contracts to DeWinton than did Dinorwic, a sign of the times was that from 1879 their new slate wagons were equipped with steel wheelsets by Hadfields of Sheffield.† The increased use of electrical machinery and of industrial-capacity turbines in the 20th century also helped to move the focus to non-Gwynedd suppliers. So, in one instance, did a decision to remain with stationary steam power. Even had DeWinton's Union ironworks still been in business in 1904, they would have been unable to build a pump-engine sufficiently powerful to drain Dorothea quarry, and the contract went to a long-established supplier in Cornwall (see pp. 64-5).

In terms of public memory, it is the second of these three phases that endures, when the skilled artisan-engineer in his fustian jacket made Gwynedd a prosperous region of the modern world and yet strong in its own identity and its ancient language. The modern threnody for Victorian engineering skills reflects global economic change which has taken manufacturing out of the developed and into the developing world.

4.3.2 Chemicals and explosives

Mineral extraction brought into being an explosives industry and, in the case of the Mynydd Parys copper mines, provided the raw materials. A small-scale chemical industry also existed within Gwynedd.

The needs of Gwynedd's mines and quarries called into being an explosives industry which operated into the late 20th century. Magazines and detonator houses are to be found in many mines and quarries but otherwise the production and distribution of explosives has left comparatively little trace. What does remain is located in three main areas.

Above Bethesda, the remains survive of the two powder magazines operated by William John Parry, a businessman, trade-unionist and polemicist (1842-1927). These (Cilfoden – SH 6283 6725 and Hafoty – SH 3627 6773) are witnesses to the bitter struggle for supremacy in this industrial landscape, dominated by the Penrhyn estate with its huge slate quarry (p. 44) and by the quarrymen's town of Bethesda (p. 217),

---

* Pers. comm., D.J. Williams, manager.
† Boyd, J.I.C., *Narrow Gauge Railways in North Caernarvonshire Volume 2 The Penrhyn Quarry Railway* (Oxford: Oakwood, 1985), pp. 141-3.

and to Parry's own ambiguous role within it, as 'quarryman's champion' and yet also a supplier of explosives to Penrhyn quarry.*

By far the largest of the sites associated with the explosives industry was Cooke's factory at Penrhyndeudraeth, very comprehensively demolished in the 1990s. The origins of the site date back to 1865, when an explosive was manufactured from guncotton, starch and india-rubber at a site adjacent to the Cambrian Railways at SH 620 385. R.T. Cooke bought the site from the Ministry of Munitions in 1922 and sold out to ICI in 1958. By the 1970s it had become a very sophisticated undertaking supplying 90 per cent of the British coal industry's explosives requirements, but with the contraction of mining, work ceased in 1995. Nothing is now apparent of the timber incorporating and mixing mills, nor of the large stone building with its Belfast bow roof. Railways, variously of 0.762m, 0.6m and 0.457m (2ft 6in, 2ft and 1ft 6in) gauge, as well as aerial ropeways, moved materials within the site. Process recording was carried out by the Royal Commission before closure. Other features associated with this site have also vanished in recent years, such as the explosives stores on the Festiniog Railway, near Boston Lodge works, demolished post-1983, where powder was brought by barge from Cooke's to be taken by train to the Blaenau quarries.† Now the only tangible evidence of this industry is the gunpowder wagon on the railway, recently repainted in its former livery of Harvey and Curtis, which forms a component of heritage goods services.

The only explosives site which survives to any degree is the gunpowder works at Tyddyn Gwladys near Gwynfynydd mine, which served the local copper and gold workings. Gold was discovered nearby in 1844 and attracted considerable capital for a few years in the 1860s. The licence for the Tyddyn Gwladys works is dated 1887, and the works was functioning by the following year, part of the commercial empire of the barrister and Liberal MP, William Pritchard Morgan, 'the Welsh gold king'. It saw no use after 1892. The site extends along the west bank of the upper reaches of the Mawddach, here a narrow wooded valley, from SH 735 267 to 735 274. Some of the buildings were shared between the Tyddyn Gwladys gold mine at the southern end and the Gwynfynydd mine at the northern end, and some were turned into miners' barracks when gunpowder ceased to be produced here. Sixteen buildings are identified on the 1:2500 ordnance survey map of 1888; some of these sites are now occupied by 20th-century holiday accommodation but others survive, if only as flattened areas or as dilapidated walls. What was probably the main incorporating mill is situated at the northern end of the site, a stone structure, now roofless, with a water-wheel pit in the north-western gable and six separate chambers, each built over a brick-vaulted drive-shaft. Otherwise, the biggest structure measures 13.3m by 7.0m, the others at most only 8.2m by 4.7m. In two, there is evidence of water-power in buildings that were probably the corning house and a smaller incorporating mill. Others were probably a green charge house, a ripe charge house, and a watch house. Map evidence shows that internal movement was by railway, and an iron rail has been discovered on site; it is possible that wooden rails were used near the danger buildings.‡

---

* Williams, J.Ll., 'Two Powder Magazines in the parish of Llanllechid, Bethesda', *Industrial Gwynedd* 2 (1997), pp. 7-17.
† Anon, 'The Gunpowder Sheds', (Festiniog Railway) *Heritage Magazine* 28 (Winter 1991/2), pp. 10-13.
‡ Crocker, A. and G., 'The Gunpowder Mills at Tyddyn Gwladys, near Dolgellau', *Melin* 12 (1996), pp. 2-25.

What Gwynedd possessed in the way of a chemical industry was located around Porth Amlwch, where it grew up as an offshoot of the work of the Parys mines and their smelters. In 1840 the London chemical engineer Charles Henry Hills established a chemical works at Llam Carw (SH 455 936), near Amlwch port, to produce artificial fertilizers, making use of sulphur as a constituent. Declining output from the mine forced them to depend on imported sulphur, and they seem to have branched out into ore-smelting before operations came to an end at the turn of the 19th and 20th centuries. Little remains beyond some fine clinker and cinder.* In a separate undertaking, iron sulphate from the precipitation pits (pp. 83-4) was deposited as an ochre which was roasted in a furnace before being sent away to be made into a base material for the production of paints. The furnace survives at SH 4382 9137, and operated until 1958. Less remains of the windmill-powered 'St Eilian's Colour Works' at SH 449 913 where only some ruined walls survive. Here the ochre was ground by edge-running stones. For a while, iron oxide from Parys was also sent away for use as a purifier in gasworks.†

In 1951 a substantial plant to extract bromine from sea-water was constructed at Amlwch (SH 446 936) by Associated Ethyl Co. Ltd (later Associated Octel) which had begun life in another copper-smelting and exporting town, Hayle in Cornwall. The plant was served by the 1km-long 'Amlwch Light Railway' which extends from the terminus of the Amlwch to Gaerwen branch line. The works was largely demolished in the early part of 2006, having been out of use for several years.

4.4 Public Utilities

4.4.1 Public water supply

The gathering, storage and piping of water for public supply was increasingly managed from the early years of the 19th century, and became a highly controversial issue in the mid-20th when a dam was erected at Tryweryn to supply Liverpool.

In common with towns and villages throughout the world, many of the earliest of Gwynedd's settlements owe their origins in part to a dependable supply of water. Wells had been pagan places of veneration, and retained much of their significance long into the Christian period. At Penmon Priory (SH 6304 8078) the inner chamber around the holy well was built in 1710; St Cybi's well in Llangybi (SH 427 412) was a traditional place of pilgrimage long before the landowner, Price of Rhiwlas, chose to erect amenities for the sick there in the 18th century following the fashion for the 'cure' in English spa towns. Village wells were sometimes given a lavish surround to serve as drinking fountains as at Llandwrog (SH 4514 5606) or equipped with a decorated hand-pump, as at Llanuwchllyn (SH 8732 3037 – Figure 71), but far more common was the simple stand-pipe and hand-pump. Features such as these not only

---

* The Hills family had been established at Greenwich since 1842 where they produced sulphuric acid, one of several chemical undertakings built on the site of the later Millennium Dome and its associated infrastructure. See Mills, M., *Greenwich Marsh – The 300 years before the dome* (London: Docklands Forum, 1999), pp. 165-9.

† Hope, B.D., *A Curious Place: The Industrial History of Amlwch (1550-1950)*, (Wrexham: Bridge Books, 1994).

71 Ornamental hand-pump, Llanuwchllyn. The casting reads *Cofeb y Cyhoedd am enedigaeth etifedd Wynnstay* ('The people's memorial on the birth of an heir to the Wynnstay estate').

provided the water for domestic washing, laundry and food preparation but also for horse-troughs and road locomotives.

Most of Gwynedd's growing towns depended on sources such as these until the mid-19th century – Amlwch had no fewer than 29 public wells,* as well doubtless as private supplies. They were increasingly liable to contamination, as new houses frequently had either no privies, or access only to facilities shared with a great many other households.† Conwy, for instance, depended entirely on public and private wells until around 1856, when the LNWR created a reservoir at Hofal Wen (SH 7751 7774) to supply their station and to feed locomotives; arrangements were then made both for a limited public supply from the same source and for a fountain in the town square. Systems expanded in the later 19th century, as public awareness grew of the health issues associated with drinking water, and tourists demanded assurance that their annual holiday was not going to be spent in a potential typhoid zone.‡ The Conway and Colwyn Bay Joint Water Supply District went so far as to publish a lavish hard-back of 44 pages and 17 fold-out plates extolling the virtues of their water-supply at Llyn Cowlyd in the Carneddau, complete with plans of the dam, stand-posts, gauge chambers and the distribution system (Figure 72),§ works which were partly effaced and partly drowned by the later water system put in by the Dolgarrog Aluminium Corporation Ltd (see pp. 125-6, 143).

Developments continued to be put into place throughout the 20th century. Dams were completed at Llyn Cefni (SH 442 774) in 1951, Cwm Ystradllyn (SH 562 444) and Llyn Alaw (SH 395 870) in 1966, and an integrated water-supply system was brought into being.¶ Pumping stations were, and are, small-scale installations – there were none of the prestige buildings and substantial machinery such as were to be found in large cities. Recent innovations include a chlorination plant at Dolgarrog (SH 779 667).

A completely different scale of domestic water-supply system is represented by the Tryweryn reservoir (SH 8792 4008), built between 1960 and 1966 by Tarmac Construction Ltd of Wolverhampton to supply Liverpool. Elsewhere in north Wales but outside Gwynedd, several large reservoirs had been built for English cities. Liverpool had been the first, with the Vyrnwy dam (1881-92), in its time the largest reservoir in Europe, and the first large masonry dam in Britain, just over the border

---

* Richards, M., 'Dŵr', in Richards, M. (ed.), *Atlas Môn* (Cyngor Gwlad Môn, 1972), p. 145.
† See for instance Lloyd, L., *The Port of Caernarfon 1793-1800* (privately published, 1989), p. 149.
‡ That this was perceived as a widespread possibility, with potentially disastrous economic consequences, is exemplified by Ibsen's *An Enemy of the People* (1882), where the central character, Dr Thomas Stockmann, a medical practitioner in a Norwegian spa, questions the safety of the town's facilities.
§ Farrington, T.B., *Cowlyd Waterworks* (Conway and Colwyn Bay Joint Water Supply District, 1904).
¶ Richards, *op. cit.*, p. 145.

from Gwynedd. This was followed by Birmingham Corporation in the Elan valley in Radnorshire in 1906, and Birkenhead Corporation's Alwen reservoir, built between 1911 and 1917.

At Tryweryn, water is impounded by an earth dam and passes through a tower which includes an unusual siphon-controlled multi-level draw-off; the siphons are spaced at 6.096m (20') intervals. The dam regulates the water flow in the Afon Tryweryn and, in conjunction with sluices in the river Dee at Bala, ensures a supply of waters to abstractors and to alleviate floods, but it is also equipped with a hydro-station. The controversy surrounding the decision to build the reservoir was central to an emergent sense of national identity in the 1960s, though aesthetic and cultural considerations had been a feature of dam-construction projects since the end of the previous century. The 'Gothic mysteries' of Vyrnwy, where the straining tower resembles a Teutonic fortress, and the 'Birmingham baroque' of the Elan valley complex reflected growing unease about the landscape impact of large-scale public works and a feeling that they should be mitigated by sympathetic design.* The dam at Tryweryn is not a particularly large or innovative structure by comparison with these. Its archaeological significance derives from its cultural meaning; the decision to build it and thereby hand over control of valuable resource to an English corporation, in the process abandoning a small Welsh community, confirmed that Wales could not control its own destiny. Much was made in the media of the village's demolition and for years the slogan *Cofiwch Dryweryn* ('Remember Tryweryn') was to be found daubed on walls and buildings throughout Wales. Tryweryn is by no means unique as a controversial dam project – Manchester Corporation's decision to build a dam in Thirlmere in Cumbria aroused considerable passion at the time. Tryweryn, however, has proved to be a long-standing source of bitterness and a well-spring of modern nationalism.

72 The now dismantled aqueduct over the Conwy river imitated the scale and design of Telford's suspension bridge (from T.B. Farrington, *Cowlyd Waterworks* [1904]).

---

* Hubbard, E., *The Buildings of Wales: Clwyd* (London: Penguin Books, University of Wales Press, 1994), p. 254; Clwyd-Powys Archaeological Trust, *Historic Landscape Characterisation* (unpublished report for Cadw), Elan Valley.

4.4.2 Gas and electricity supply

Little remains of the archaeology of public gas supply in Gwynedd; however, the generation and distribution of electricity for public supply and for industry assumed considerable importance from the early years of the 20th century. Its archaeology includes evidence for important early alternating current systems and extensive water-catchment systems.

The provision of public utilities reflects not only growing technical capacity but also an evolving civic consciousness which was prepared to take a broader view of what constituted local government's responsibilities. Lighting by coal gas had been made a practical possibility by William Murdoch (1754-1839) in 1792 and was beginning to spread even to small market towns in the early decades of the 19th century.* The first recorded public supply of gas in Gwynedd dates from 1833 when Caernarfon gasworks was opened, alongside the course of the railway from the harbour, the better to bring in coal.† Though typically, throughout Britain, gasworks were erected, or relocated, near railway goods yards, few of Gwynedd's gasworks had rail access. Pwllheli was supplied by sea.‡ The basic chronology for gasworks in Gwynedd is known, but very little survived the rationalisation of the industry in state ownership in the 1950s, the arrival of natural gas and the extension of the mains systems. A proposal to preserve Barmouth gasworks came to nothing.§ At Porthmadog some late 19th-century buildings remain at SH 5709 3891. At Dolgellau an attractive stone-built retort-house, with recessed round-headed windows, now in re-use as a cycle shop, survives at SH 7288 1789, and at Bangor the office block remains, having served briefly as the home of the Gwynedd Archaeological Trust (SH 5825 7249).

Electricity has been used experimentally in Gwynedd since the late 1870s for industrial purposes (see *4.1.1*, pp. 42-69) and from slightly later for agriculture (*4.1.5*, pp. 96-110) but it was only with the evolution of practical alternating current systems at the end of the 19th century that it became a practical possibility for widespread distribution. Its history is a complicated one because electricity can be distributed and sold over a wider area to a much greater extent than coal gas could be, with the result that energy became a marketable commodity in its own right. The story of electricity can also be hard to unravel because of the relationship between the various interests involved, which in Gwynedd included aluminium production, railway companies, and local and central government.¶

The Yale Electric Power Company offered the first public supply in Gwynedd in 1902 from its station at Dolwen (SH 6939 4388) near Blaenau Ffestiniog, supplying

---

* There are comparatively few archaeological studies of gas supply. See Hay G.D. and Stell, G.P., *Monuments of Industry* (Edinburgh: Royal Commission on the Ancient and Historical Monuments of Scotland, 1986), pp. 176-80.

† Lloyd, L., *The Port of Caernarfon 1793-1900* (Caernarfon, 1989) pp. 142-74; *North Wales Gazette*, 11 November 1824 p. 3 col. b, 181 November 1824, p. 1 col. e.

‡ Thomas, W.N., *The History of the Gas Industry in Pwllheli* (privately published, Pwllheli, 1976).

§ After Caernarfon, known dates are Holyhead (1850), Llangefni (1855), Llanrwst (1854), Pwllheli (1855), Bethesda (1856), Nantlle vale (1856), Llandudno (1857), Conwy (1859), Porthmadog (1859), Tywyn (1866), Blaenau Ffestiniog (1872), Penmaenmawr (1874), Betws y Coed (1875). Beaumaris gasworks was within the park of Baron Hill, the home of the Bulkeley family, and only gradually came to serve the town. Holywell (1824) and Wrexham (1827) were the only towns elsewhere in north Wales that had an earlier gas supply than Caernarfon. See Jones, R. and Reeve, C.G., *A History of Gas Production in Wales* (Wales Gas Printing Centre, n.d.) and Boyd, J.I.C., *The Talyllyn Railway* (Oxford: Wild Swan, 1988), p. 2.

¶ This sections draws on Gwyn, D. and Jones, E., *Dolgarrog: An Industrial History* (Caernarfon: Gwynedd Archives Service, 1989), Thomas, D., *Hydro-Electricity in North West Wales* (National Power plc, 1997), Electricity Council 1982: *Electricity Supply in the United Kingdom* (London).

not only the quarries but also the town – the first time that a public electricity supply had been generated entirely by water in the United Kingdom.*

In 1906 the North Wales Power and Traction Company commissioned a 2,000kW capacity hydropower station at Cwm Dyli (SH 6532 5396) on the southern flanks of Snowdon to supply three-phase 50Hz electricity to a subsidiary railway company and to the slate industry – a capacity higher than that of many large industrial towns at the time. They also from 1907 supplied the aluminiùm works at Dolgarrog until their own power station was completed (see *4.2.2*, pp. 123-7). Later public-supply power stations were built at Dolgarrog (SH 7700 6759 – 1924) and at Maentwrog (SH 6541 3952 – 1928). These systems continued to operate until the 1980s with remarkably little change.

73 Maentwrog power station.

The power stations survive, and exhibit considerable variation. Dolwen, now a private house, is a manifestly 'industrial' structure. Cwm Dyli's 'arts and crafts' style building shows the environmental awareness of its builders, whereas Maentwrog (Figure 73) and the public Dolgarrog power station reverted to a more functional approach. Maentwrog has a pitched slate roof and a pattern of attic-windowed pediments, perhaps a requirement of the Oakeley estate, which certainly insisted on a screen of trees around it, whereas Dolgarrog is flat-roofed and unadorned. Both have large windows, and doorways for lorry (and at Dolgarrog, rail) access.

74 Pipelines and transmission lines at Dolgarrog.

The dams and pipelines associated with them are typical of evolving engineering practice (Figure 74). Llyn Cowlyd (SH 7377 6334) and Llyn Coedty (SH 7559 6671), which both supply the Dolgarrog system, make use of reinforced concrete core walls with air-face and water-face embankments. The principal dam at the Trawsfynydd reservoir which supplied Maentwrog (SH 6747 3767) was the first large arch dam in Britain, and was followed by examples at Earlston (Dumfries), Tongland (Kirkcudbright) and Monar (Inverness).†

The earliest transmission systems ran on wooden poles, either A or H frame, or light steel frames. A number of distribution pillars from the 1920s survive, far smaller than the ones erected after the nationalisation of the electricity supply industry in 1948.

---

* Earlier public supplies at Keswick in 1890 and Worcester in 1894 were equipped with auxiliary steam engines because of the low head – see Woodward, G., 'Hydro Electricity in North Wales, 1880-1948', *Transactions of the Newcomen Society* 69 2 (1997-98), pp. 205-35.

† Smith, N., *A History of Dams* (Secaucus, New Jersey: Citadel Press, 1972), pp. 232-3, plate 62.

Smaller direct current thermal power stations were built at Bangor, Caernarfon, Llangefni, Menai Bridge, Llanrwst, Holyhead and Llandudno, some of which were associated with refuse destructor plant. Only Llandudno survived until nationalisation.* Their capacity was tiny compared with the main hydro-stations, but they in turn dwarfed some of the more ramshackle attempts at public supply within Gwynedd. An example survives at Ysbyty Ifan (SH 8417 4873), where the National Trust has conserved a water corn-mill built by the Penrhyn estate in the 1860s which was at some stage adapted to provide electricity for the village by the simple expedient of removing one set of stones and replacing it with a generator.†

Nationalisation of the industry did not initially lead to significant capital investment until 1955, when a pumped storage scheme was instituted at Tan y Grisiau (SH 679 444 – Figure 75), commissioned in 1963, consisting of two dams, a mass concrete buttress gravity dam in the mountains and a mass concrete low-level dam connected by four steel pipelines 2.3m internal diameter, powering four vertical shaft reaction turbines coupled to separate 90 MW generators and centrifugal pumps in the same vertical shaft. This was the first pumped storage scheme in the world (whereby energy generated from base-load stations at periods of peak demand is used to pump water to the higher reservoir and reconverted rapidly into electrical power by flowing through turbines at periods of peak demand).

The success of the Tan y Grisiau scheme led to a far larger undertaking at Dinorwic (SH 594 600), commissioned in 1982, and was only exceeded in size by Ludington in the USA, which had been commissioned in 1973. Like Tan y Grisiau, which drowned part of the Festiniog Railway, it affected a major industrial-archaeological landscape of the 19th century, in this case the Dinorwic slate quarry – though here there was something apt about the change, in that the new construction evoked the 'sublime' in its sheer scale, as the quarry had done. Another curious irony in its relationship to the landscape it effaced was that the cable along the shores of Llyn Padarn had to be laid by that time-honoured technology, a narrow-gauge railway, using specially designed rolling stock. The scheme includes 16km of underground tunnels, and required one million tonnes of concrete and 4,500 tonnes of steel. The machine hall is Europe's largest man-made cavern. Adjacent to this lies the main inlet valve chamber housing the plant that regulates the flow of water through the turbines. Dinorwig's reversible pump-turbines are capable of reaching maximum generation in less than 16 seconds. Using off-peak electricity the six units are reversed as pumps to transport water from the lower reservoir back to Marchlyn Mawr.‡

Nuclear power stations were established at Trawsfynydd in 1965 and at Wylfa on Northern Anglesey in 1971. Whereas the early hydro-power stations consciously strove to blend in with their environments, the nuclear stations took the idea of the box-like structure fully into the realms of architectural brutalism. Trawsfynydd, the only Magnox station not built on the coast, ceased to operate in 1994, though Magnox Electric were granted permission in 2003 to leave the radioactive core of the nuclear reactor on site for the next 135 years and to continue to store nuclear waste on site. Wylfa continues to operate at the time of writing. It houses two Magnox nuclear

---

* Woodward, *op. cit.*
† Information from National Trust Dinas estate and personal inspection.
‡ *The Dinorwig power station: papers presented at a major achievement symposium* (London: The Institution of Mechanical Engineers, 1985).

75 Aerial view of the Llyn Ystradau pumped storage scheme (Crown Copyright: Royal Commission on the Ancient and Historic Monuments of Wales 90-cs-188).

reactors, which were built 1963-71, with a combined capacity of 980 MW. It currently has a contract to supply electricity to Anglesey Aluminium Metal at Holyhead until September 2009.* So far only three wind-farms have been erected within Gwynedd, all in northern Anglesey (SH 385 934, 380 928 and 401 927), though several others in neighbouring parts of Wales are visible from within the region.

The modern state's demands for energy have ensured that Gwynedd, despite its peripheral role in the United Kingdom economy, has been at the forefront of the generation and distribution of electricity for much of the 20th century. Despite this, they have not yet been generally recognised as archaeologically significant. Public perception of nuclear power will also make the continued existence in any form of the buildings and infrastructure of the Trawsfynydd and Wylfa stations a deeply contentious issue, and their sheer size poses tremendous logistical problems. At a time when other industries in Gwynedd have become part of the region's identity, nuclear power refuses to be absorbed by an ideology of the aesthetic.

Note: dam construction

Arch dams are built of concrete; in plan they curve in the shape of an arch. They are usually constructed in narrow, steep sided valleys. *Gravity* dams are built of **concrete** or **masonry**, or both; they are so called because gravity holds it down to the ground, stopping the water in the **reservoir** pushing it over. *Buttress* dams are built of **concrete** or **masonry**, supported by buttresses at intervals on the **downstream** side. *Embankment* dams are either **earth-fill** (**compacted** earth) dams or dumped and compacted rock-fill.

---

* LlRO: GB/0221/WDAR, http://news.bbc.co.uk/2/hi/uk_news/wales/north_west/3122269.stm, http://www.publications.parliament.uk/pa/cm200405/cmselect/cmwelaf/329/4031702.htm, accessed 19 March 2005.

4.5 Transport and Communications

4.5.1 Roads

Gwynedd's road system reflects the development of locally-managed turnpike trusts in the 18th and 19th centuries as well as the major government intervention in the form of Telford's Holyhead road between 1815 and 1826 and the improvements carried out from 1930 onwards with the decline in rail traffic.

Gwynedd is one of the few places in the world where a comprehensive archaeological survey has been carried out of an historic roadway. In general, roads and their associated sites – toll-houses, bridges, street furniture, overnight accommodation and catering outlets – form one of the most extensive but also the most neglected archaeological site-types. Within this region, as in many other places in Europe, a modern adopted road with its metalled surface may overlie an 18th-century turnpike, a medieval trackway or a Roman road. Bridges that may date from the late Medieval period, and which were intended for nothing heavier than a harvest cart, regularly carry heavy lorries. The archaeology of roads can tell us much about economic capacity and development.

Thomas Telford famously commented on the poor state of roads in north-west Wales when he began work on the Holyhead road.[*] There was undoubtedly an element of self-glorification here, but the regional road system was certainly primitive into the 18th century at least. Though Caernarfon was served by a carrier from Chester as early as 1637,[†] it is recorded that the carriage of the Lord Lieutenant of Ireland had to be dismantled and carried on horse-back over Bwlch y Ddeufaen, on the old road from Rowen to Abergwyngregyn, a state of affairs which conveys graphically the difficulties of east-west travel until the 18th century. The first man in Gwynedd to own his own coach was Sir Nicholas Bayly of Plas Newydd, after he succeeded to the estate in 1741.[‡]

Most of the trackways in existence by this time were probably adequate for the movement of people and livestock. Much romance attaches to the drovers, who led herds of cattle from Gwynedd (and elsewhere in Wales) to markets in the English midlands and around London (see pp. 39, 131), but their archaeology has not been comprehensively studied. The trade may well have begun in the early Medieval period but undoubtedly grew in the 17th century, until by the early 19th perhaps around 6,000 head of cattle left Anglesey each year, and as many from Penrhyn Llŷn, as well as sheep and geese.[§] Even when the turnpikes had come into being, many drovers avoided them and continued to cross the open mountains. Some of their routes have been incorporated into roads or survive as trackways. Evidence of their function is to be found in upland landscapes – the Migneint, where Ffynnon Eidda (SH 7620 4370) provided water for humans and animals, and Dyffryn Ardudwy, with its drovers' bridges at Pont Fadog (1762) and Pont Ysgethin (SH 6072 2257 and 6345 2355) and the former inn, *Lletty Lloegr* ('England Lodging') with its shoeing station (SH 6064 2265).[¶]

---

[*] Quartermaine, J., Trinder, B. and Turner, R., *Thomas Telford's Holyhead Road: The A5 in north Wales* (CBA Research Report 135, 2003), p. 12. Unless otherwise acknowledged, references to the Telford road are to this volume.
[†] Gerhold, D., *Carriers and Coachmasters: Trade and Travel before the Turnpikes* (Chichester: Phillimore, 2005), p. 16.
[‡] Dodd, A.H., *History of Caernarvonshire 1284-1900* (Wrexham: Bridge Books, 1990), pp. 208-9.
[§] Moore-Colyer, R., *Welsh Cattle Drovers* (Ashbourne: Landmark Publishing, 2002), pp. 58-9, 78-9.
[¶] Godwin, F. and Toulson, S., *The Drovers' Roads of Wales* (London: Whittet Books, 1994 repr.) pp. 79, 98-100. Ffynnon Eidda's surround, with the inscription *Yf a bydd ddiolchgar* ('Drink and be grateful'), dates from 1846.

Wheeled vehicles were a rarity, certainly in upland parishes, until very late – at Ffestiniog they first make their appearance in the 1760s, in Penmachno in 1778, and Llanfrothen probably even later.* The creation of turnpike trusts undoubtedly led to considerable improvement in the area's road networks, though with very limited map evidence it is not always clear where roads were new-build or where they followed existing routes. There is more detailed evidence for bridges in the form of bonds which intending contractors were obliged to put down, which as well as the builders' names often also contain plans (Figure 76). These constitute a potentially very informative type of documentation, which might shed light on regional building styles and individual craftsmen but they have as yet been very little studied. An active landowner or industrial undertaking might construct a road, such as *ffordd y lord* ('the lord's road') built by the first Lord Penrhyn from Bangor to the Penrhyn slate quarry thence to the wilds of Capel Curig in stages between the 1780s and 1803, when it was taken over by the Caernarvonshire Turnpike Trust, or the *lôn felen* ('yellow road' – Figure 77) built in 1788 to connect the Mona copper mine on Mynydd Parys with the port at Amlwch, so named because of the colour of the stones used to construct it, a very rare example of a surviving 18th-century industrial road.†

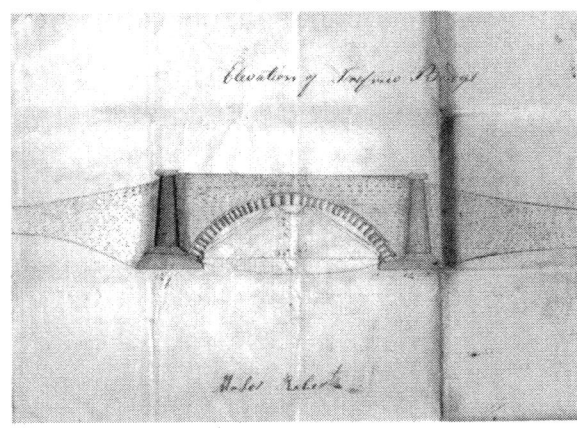

76 A plan drawn up by the mason Moses Roberts of the bridge he proposed to erect at Trefriw in the Conwy valley (courtesy Gwynedd Archives: CRO Plans/B68).

Several early hotels associated with turnpike roads survive, complete or in part. Of the *Penrhyn Arms Hotel* in Bangor (SH 590 725), only a classical portico remains. Some of the original fabric of Lord Penrhyn's *Royal Hotel* at Capel Curig survives in the Plas y Brenin Mountain Centre (SH 717 578).‡ At Maentwrog the substantial *Tan y Bwlch Inn* survives as a pub, the *Oakeley Arms* (SH 660 410). Of a slightly later date are the *Royal Victoria Hotel* in Llanberis (SH 584 596), which now caters

77 The *lôn felen* ('yellow road'), laid in 1788 to connect the Mona mine on Parys mountain to Porth Amlwch. In the background is the 1819 engine house.

---

* Lewis, M.J.T. and Williams, M.C., *Pioneers of Ffestiniog Slate* (Maentwrog: Snowdonia National Park Study Centre, 1987), p. 4.
† UWB: Mona Mine mss, 3040.
‡ Hughes, H.D., *Hynafiaethau Llandegai a Llanllechid* (Bethesda, 1866), p. 125 gives a date of 'around 1791' for work beginning on the *Capel Curig Hotel*.

78 Roads and railways at Penmaenmawr from the period 1930-6 when M.A. Boswell of Wolverhampton was constructing the new road. Near the foot of the bluff runs the Chester to Holyhead railway; above it are the new road then under construction, Telford's road, what may be a temporary contractors' road and a length of railway connecting the main Penmaenmawr group of stone quarries with workings to the east (courtesy Gwynedd Archives Service: CRO XS/1369/1/26).

largely for coach parties, and the *Royal Hotel* (now renamed the 'Royal Celtic') in Caernarfon (SH 481 630).*

The most important road systems in Gwynedd were constructed in 1769-72 and in 1815-26, to provide better access between Dublin and London. They are unusual in that this was a period when central government rarely saw a responsibility to provide transport infrastructure, unlike *ancien régime* France, with its strong absolutist and centralising traditions. Between 1769 and 1772 John Sylvester built a road over the bluff of Penmaenmawr on the north mainland coast, thereby at least diminishing the perils of the coastal journey and doing away with the need to follow the ancient road over Bwlch y Ddeufaen. Sylvester's work was funded by both the London and Dublin governments (Figure 78).

A much more ambitious scheme was the road link from Holyhead through north Wales and ultimately to London, with a spur from Bangor to the east bank of the Conwy river. The driving force was Sir Henry Parnell (1770-1842), Member of Parliament for Queen's County in Ireland, and payment was directly controlled by the Westminster government – the first major civilian state-funded scheme of its type in Wales in modern times, and the harbinger of the very *dirigiste* approach to Irish matters that governments otherwise committed to *laisser-faire* were to take throughout the 19th century. It is arguably the greatest work of Britain's greatest civil engineer (Map 10).

The Welsh section of the road extends from Chirk on the English border to Holyhead in Anglesey, a total length in Wales of 133km (83 miles) and a total length within Gwynedd of 80km (50 miles). In many places Telford improved an existing road, elsewhere he had to build from new. Much of the road remains in use, though it has been partly by-passed by the A55 dual carriageway (see below). Surviving structures

---

* CRO: XD2/15665 refers (1823) to the 'New Inn by Dolbadarn Castle' – this later became the *Royal Victoria Hotel*.

Map 10 Roads

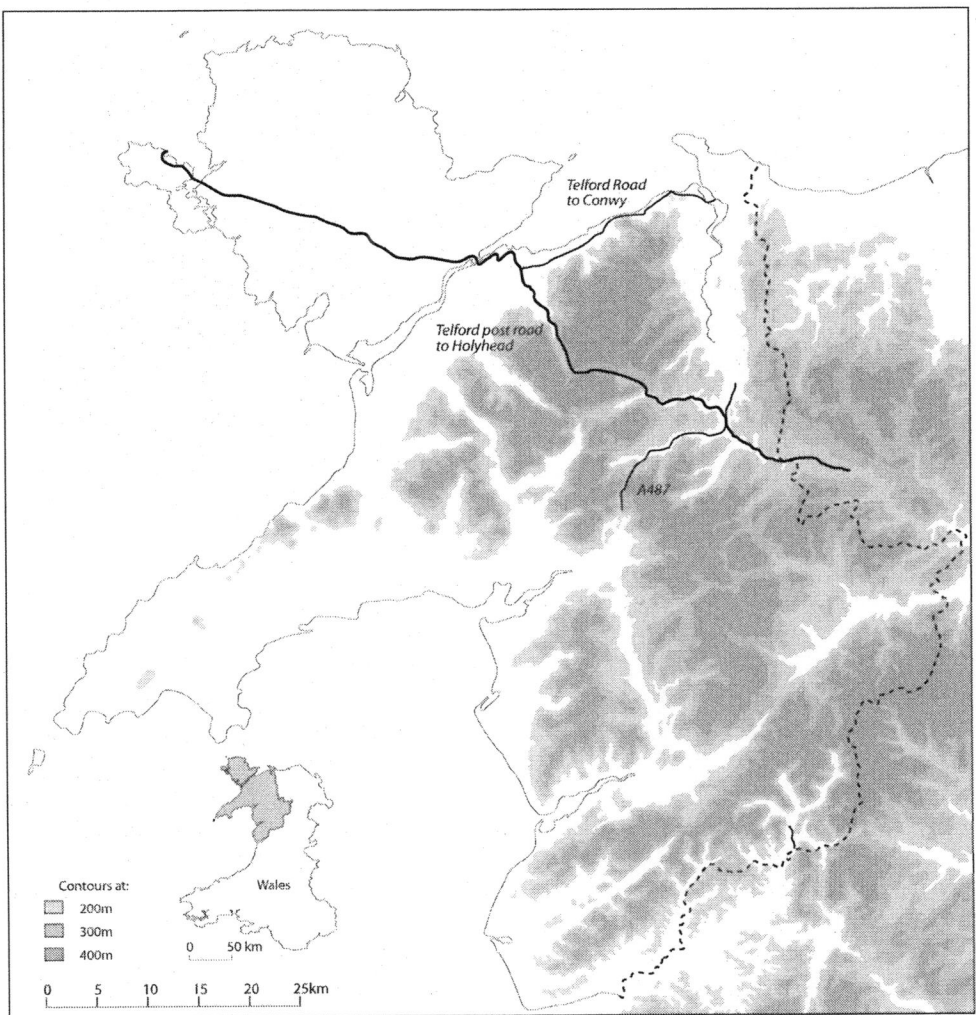

include the distinctive toll-houses at Hendre Isaf, Capel Curig, Bethesda, Lôn Isa, Llanfairpwllgwyngyll, Gwalchmai, Caergeiliog and by the Stanley embankment. There are considerable variations in design. The Lôn Isaf toll-house near Bangor (SH 6021 6938) also incorporates the site of a weigh-bridge (the other is near Corwen in northeast Wales). Only one inn was specifically built as part of the scheme, the *Mona Inn* on Anglesey, constructed 1820-2 (SH 4252 7490 – Figure 79). The accommodation block looks much like a well-appointed Irish farmhouse, whilst the courtyard buildings, which include stables and a carriage house, resemble contemporary model farmsteads. The existing coaching inns at Shrewsbury continued to dominate the coach services, using staging posts at Oswestry, Llangollen, Cernioge and Pentrefoelas (all outside Gwynedd).

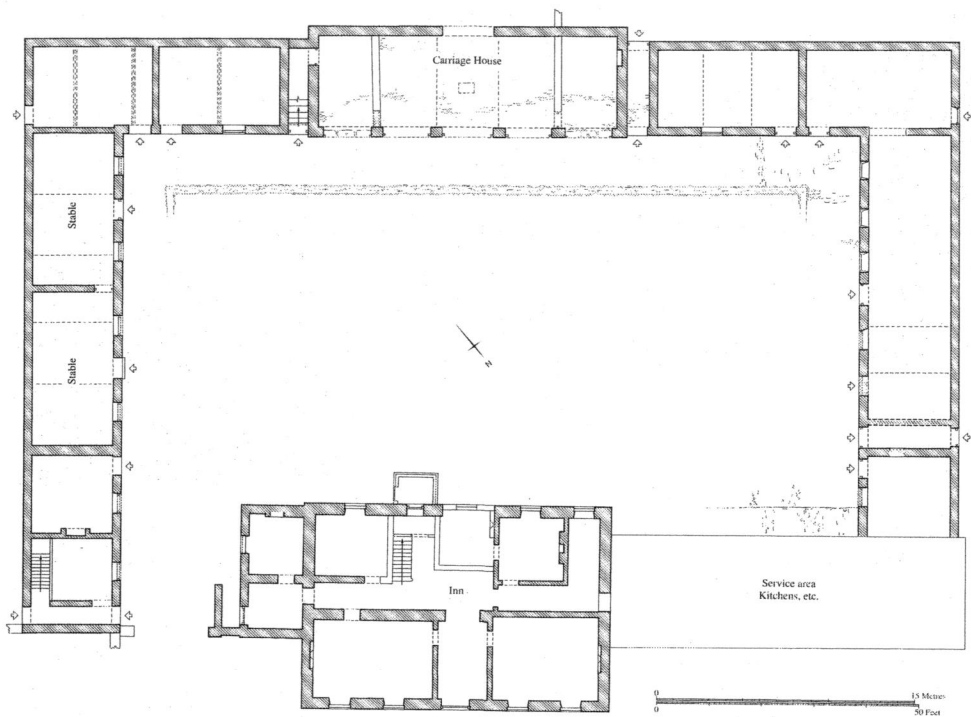

79 *Mona Inn* complex – plan (Crown Copyright: Royal Commission on the Ancient and Historic Monuments of Wales: Figure 7.12 *Thomas Telford's Holyhead Road*).

The civil engineering work of the road is internationally known. The cast-iron Waterloo Bridge at SH 799 557 was completed in 1816 (Figure 80), despite the claim cast into the main rib that it was 'constructed in the same year that the battle of Waterloo was fought'. The castings came from William Hazledine's Plas Kynaston foundry in north-east Wales, and the Waterloo bridge is structurally very similar to two bridges built by Telford in Scotland in 1812 and 1815, the Bonar bridge at the head of the Dornoch Firth and the Craigellachie bridge on the Spey. The bridge spans 32.3m.*

The master-work of the road is undoubtedly the Menai suspension bridge, built between 1819 and 1826 (SH 556 714 – Figure 81). It stands 30.5m above the water, and 176.5m long – longer than any other existing suspension bridge. William Alexander Provis (1792-1870), Telford's resident engineer, was chiefly responsible for its building until his brother John Provis took over. The two towers ('pyramids' as Telford called them) are built of Penmon limestone with hollow interiors subdivided by cross walls. The successive builders were John Straphen and John Wilson. The iron chains were manufactured by William Hazledine at Upton forge near Shrewsbury. Alterations were carried out in 1842, 1893 and 1938-40. The Conwy suspension bridge (SH 784 775) is a much smaller affair, built between 1822 and 1826 in the shadow of Conwy castle.

---

* Cossons, N. and Trinder, B., *The Iron Bridge: Symbol of the Industrial Revolution* (Chichester: Phillimore, 2002), pp. 84, 122.

80 Betws y Coed Waterloo bridge.

81 Menai bridge.

Telford managed to design the bridge in such a way that it appeared as a drawbridge to the castle, an impression enhanced by the castellated towers from which the suspension chains are hung, and dissipated by the construction of the Stephenson railway bridge alongside in 1846-8.

The Stanley embankment (SH 2758 8030 – 2846 7964), built 1823-4, crosses 1180m (1300yds) of tidal sand. A drain arch covers a rock-cut channel to allow tidal waters to pass through the embankment. The railway widened the existing embankment rather than build a new one in 1846-8. The design was Telford's and the contractors were Gill and Hodges, though the signature of William Dargan is appended to one of the plans.* Dargan (1799-1867) is synonymous with the development of Ireland's transport infrastructure. After leaving Anglesey he carried out road construction and maintenance contracts in and around Dublin until in 1831 he obtained the contract for the Dublin and Kingstown Railway. He went on to carry out contracts on the Kilbeggan branch of the Irish Grand Canal, the Ulster Canal and the rail routes from Dublin to Cork, Dublin to Drogheda, Dublin to Wicklow and Mullingar to Galway.†

Dargan successfully made the change to railway contracting. Provis was not so lucky, though he continued to enjoy a high professional reputation. William Owen, an Anglesey farmer who constructed the bed of the Nantlle Railway in 1826-8, may have been a foreman on the road.‡ So, probably, was Thomas Prichard (c.1799-1866), who assisted James Spooner first in building the Festiniog Railway then in running it§ – further evidence that building the road was a 'capacity-building' exercise within Gwynedd (see p. 156). Later roads were more likely to be built, or upgraded, by engineers whose main experience was on railways.¶

---

* PRO: LRRO/1/3032.

† Skempton, A.W., *Bibliographical Dictionary of Civil Engineers in Great Britian and Ireland Volume 1 1500 to 1830* (London: Institution of Civil Engineers, 2002), entry for Dargan.

‡ UWB: Porth yr Aur 30845, 2219/Add. – 2220/Add.

§ Lewis, M.J.T., 'Archery and Spoonerisms: The Creators of the Festiniog Railway', *JMHRS* 13 part 3 (1996), pp. 263-76.

¶ For instance, the Portmadoc and Beaver Pool Turnpike was improved by Thomas Charles Townshend MICE, a contractor on the Hull and Selby Railway, the Bridgwater to Taunton section of the Bristol and Exeter Railway, and the Whitehaven and Furness Railway – Skempton, *op. cit.*, p. 713 (entry for Thomas Townshend, father of T.C. Townshend) and DRO: Z/CD/171.

The road's impact is evident in more subtle ways also. It became something of a symbol of the union of Britain and Ireland, and a memorial to the gallant commanders who defeated Napoleonic France. A traveller setting out from London to Dublin might begin his or her journey at the Marble Arch. In the centre of Shrewsbury it was hard to avoid seeing the Doric column and statue commemorating Viscount Hill. As well as the 'Waterloo' ascription on the Betws y Coed bridge, the main ribs were adorned with castings of a rose, a thistle, a leek and a shamrock, symbolising the unity of the kingdoms in the face of military threat. At Llanfairpwllgwyngyll the road passes between the Marquess of Anglesey's column and the statue of Lord Nelson by the banks of the Menai Strait until finally the ship was boarded in the shadow of Thomas Harrison's Memorial Arch at Holyhead, which commemorated the visit of George IV, a man who, if not actually a hero of Waterloo, eventually persuaded himself that he was.*

82 The distinctive tollhouses form the architectural signature of the Telford road.

The Welsh section of the Holyhead road is unusual in that a comprehensive management programme was drawn up between 1999 and 2003 by Cadw: Welsh Historic Monuments, and an archaeological study of the route published, to date the only one of a major road transport system (Figure 82). The Conwy bridge is managed by the National Trust, whose five-year conservation programme won the Europa Nostra award.

The Telford road represents the last major investment in the local network until 1930-5, when tunnels were built at Penmaenmawr (SH 700 762), avoiding the exposed sections of Telford's work.† The A55 expressway, with its tunnels at Penyclip and Penmaenmawr, and its underwater tunnel at Conwy, was opened in phases from the late 1980s to early in the 21st century.

This and other new roadworks reflect an increased emphasis on the carefully-chosen use of local stones for earthworks and walling to mitigate landscape impact. The widened A470 through the Lledr valley, proclaimed as 'the greenest road in Britain' in 2005, forms part of the major north-south route through Wales; as such it became a symbol of the political will both to ensure good national transport links and to establish environmental standards.‡ In this respect, it echoes the concerns which led to the construction of the rustic castellated railway viaduct alongside it (p. 164).§

---

* Colley, L., *Britons: Forging the Nation 1707-1837* (New Haven and London: Yale University Press, 1992), p. 215.
† Bradley, V.J., *Industrial Locomotives of North Wales* (London: Industrial Railway Society, 1992), p. 366; CRO: XCHS/1369/1/26.
‡ http://news.bbc.co.uk/1/low/wales/4097496.stm, accessed 23 December 2005.
§ Telford was well aware of the way in which his roads and canals could blend into the existing landscape, though conscious theorising about the environmental impact of roads only begins in the 1930s, in Nazi Germany – see Zeller, T.,"'The Landscape's Crown" Landscape, Perceptions and Modernizing Effects of the German Autobahn System, 1934 to 1941', in Nye, D.E. (ed.), *Technologies of Landscape: From Reaping to Recycling* (Amherst, Massachusetts: University of Massachusetts Press, 1999), pp. 218-38.

83 Mid-20th-century garages such as this at Llanuwchllyn are becoming increasingly rare.

Unlike their turnpike predecessors, but like the main-line railways, the new roads have radically altered patterns of growth in existing urban centres, seen to best effect in the retail development to the west of Bangor. They have also created their own distinctive development, as in the nearby complex at Llys y Gwynt, at the intersection of the A55 and the A5, with its Tourist Information Centre, Burger King, Little Chef, Travelodge and Esso Garage, which fulfil the functions once carried out by the coaching stages, though over a much wider area and in a very different form. However, much mid-20th-century infrastructure is already disappearing, such as the familiar flat-roof filling station and 'bus garages (Figure 83).

If the archaeology of roads includes very modern structures, it should also encompass historic vehicles. Persons who interest themselves in such matters have an even worse press and a lowlier public image than railway enthusiasts, yet, as with the railway preservation movement, it is only due to efforts of prescient amateurs that much survives at all. In the context of Gwynedd, no early carts are known to survive. However, a London to Holyhead mail coach, no. 107, built by Williams of Bristol in 1826, which carried six paying passengers, is preserved, one of only two mail coaches surviving in Britain,* as are a considerable number of passenger service motor vehicles ('buses) either built for service in Gwynedd or which have ended up within the area.

Gwynedd's road network reflects a system which after seeing much capital investment in the late 18th and early 19th centuries declined in importance during the railway age, only to come into its own again with the rise of the internal combustion engine. As such, it shares in the experience of the western world generally, though the evidence for a regionally-important class of craftsmen who built stone bridges and roads deserves further study. Where it is unique is in the world-class engineering triumphs of Thomas Telford and his team, and in the role central government played in ensuring the post road was built.

4.5.2 Railways

Not only is the archaeology of railways within Gwynedd extensive, but the area is internationally important on three counts – in the evolution of narrow gauge railways, in the development of railway bridge technology and in the operation of railways as heritage attractions.

Railway archaeology is now a well-established discipline, however unfamiliar such a statement may seem to the many people who interest themselves in railways, and indeed to many archaeologists. It includes the traditional skills of excavation (often

---

* At the Red Stables Working Carriage Museum in Derbyshire; ex info, Working Carriage Museum.

Map 11 Railways (i) – railways built to serve regional needs

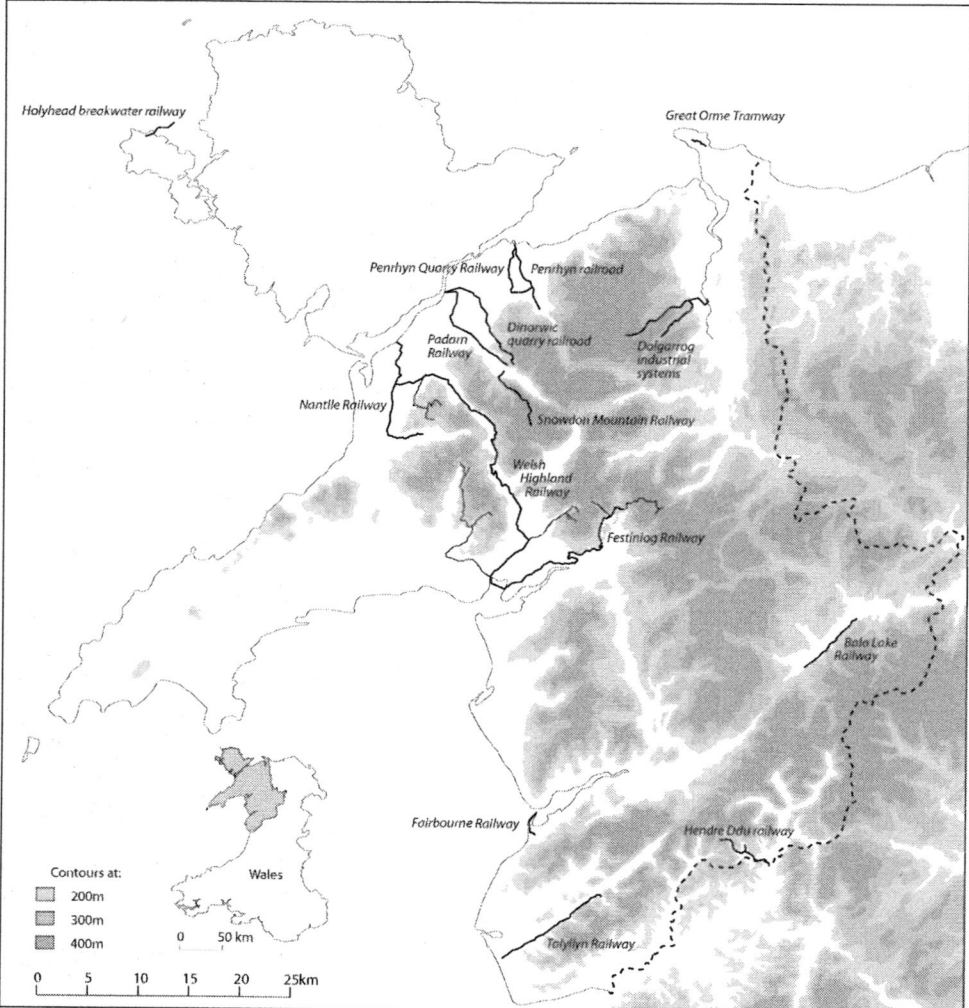

in connection with a long-buried piece of permanent way), buildings archaeology and the archaeology of an item such as an engine or a carriage.* Even so, there is little agreement as to how best to categorise railways for the purposes of a study such as this. They may be defined according to technological evolution as *early* (pre-1780), *hybrid* (1780-1830) and *modern* (1830 onwards). They may be defined by their legal status as *privately owned* or *publicly owned* (either by a public limited company, by the state or by a local authority), which often means as much as another commonly-used distinction, between *industrial railway* (that is, a line that serves the need of one or a group of industrial undertakings) and *public railway*. In practice, these definitions

---

* Morriss, R., *The Archaeology of Railways* (Stroud: Tempus, 1999). See also Hughes, S., *The Archaeology of an Early Railway System: The Brecon Forest Tramroad* (Aberystwyth: RCAHMW, 1990), Laun, J. van, *Early Limestone Railways* (London: The Newcomen Society, 2001) and Bailey, M.R. and Glithero, J.P., *The Engineering and History of* Rocket (London and York: National Railway Museum, 2000) p. 40.

Map 12 Railways (ii) – the national railway network

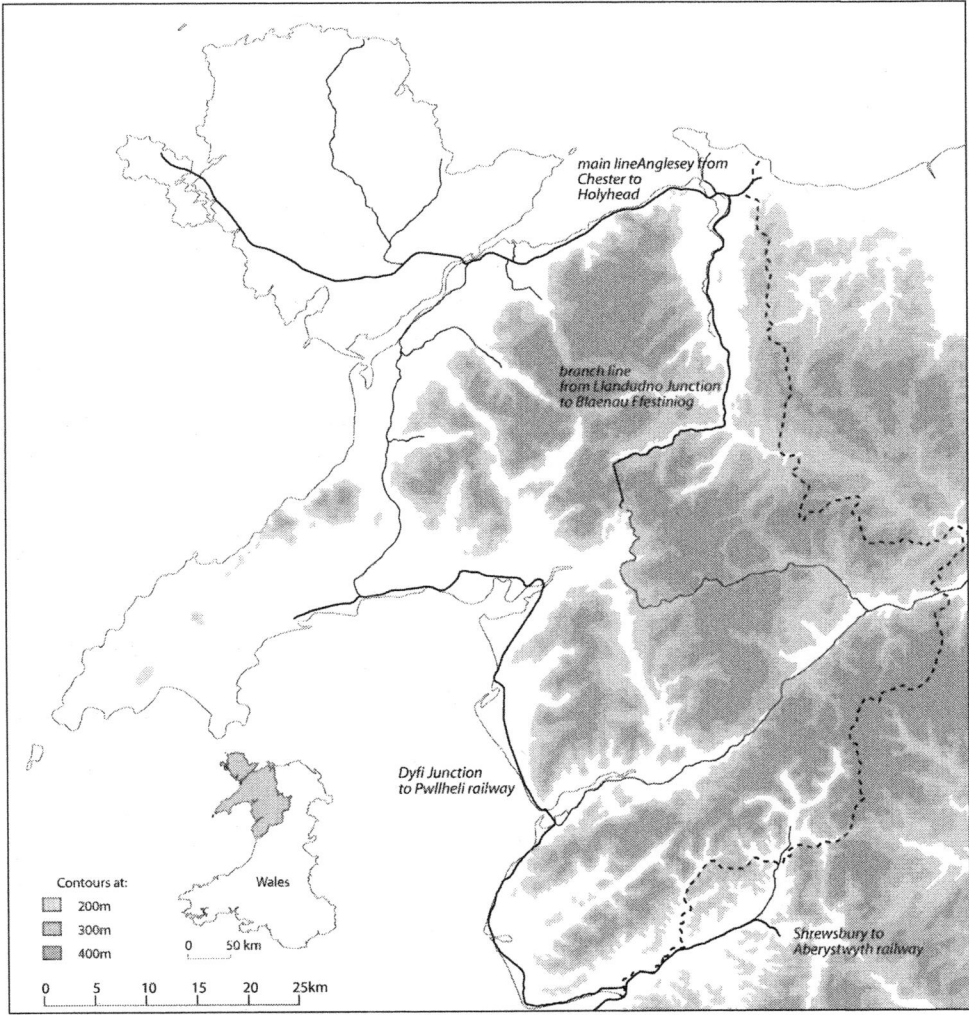

often cross-cut each other. The distinction offered here, between *railways built for local and regional needs* and the *national railway network* also has its problems, in that railways in the first category might serve a world market by bringing slates from a quarry to a harbour, whereas the second category might include a tank-engine and a single carriage rumbling once a day along a bucolic branch line – even though in theory they might connect with the Euston express, this was a far more 'local' service than a run of a hundred slate wagons on its way to the harbour for shipment to Melbourne or Hamburg. But with this reservation, let us examine what these categories might mean in practice (Maps 11 and 12).

Railways first appear in Gwynedd in the context in which they had come to notice more than three hundred years earlier in central Europe and two hundred years earlier in parts of Britain – as haulage systems in mines (see pp. 87-8). However, these and the internal systems in slate quarries are here considered as part of the archaeology of the industries in question, even though they might share many of the technical characteristics of the railways that led from mine or quarry to the port. The 'first generation' of railways built to serve the local and regional economy may be said to be made up by five systems laid between 1800 and 1843; these were the Penrhyn railroad, completed in 1801; the Dinorwic railroad, completed in 1825; the Nantlle Railway of 1828;* the Festiniog Railway of 1836; and the Padarn railway† of 1843. They had much in common with each other, as well as significant differences. All were between 10 and 22km in length. All five connected slate workings with the sea, though the Nantlle also carried a limited amount of copper, lead and other goods as well as passengers. Both the Penrhyn and Dinorwic railroads made use of a distinctive (and impractical) cast-iron oval-section rail, derived from South Wales practice, which was little imitated – the other three lines used wrought-iron rails on stone sleepers. A more lasting legacy was that they were both built to a gauge of approximately 0.6m (2ft), which meant that they could be built with comparatively light earthworks to follow sinuous contour alignments, but could also move sufficient quantities of slate in trains of up to 40 wagons, pulled by two horses.‡ In the quarries themselves, and in the ports, small wagons running on 0.6m gauge tracks could easily manoeuvre into restricted areas. This gauge was adopted by the Festiniog, though the Nantlle was built to 1.067m (3ft 6in) gauge and the Padarn to 1.219m (4ft). Charles Easton Spooner, the engineer of the Festiniog, designed the Padarn so that it made use of a distinctive system of 'piggy-backing' the 0.6m gauge wagons from the internal quarry system onto the larger wagons, a system he may have observed at Dowlais in south Wales whilst serving his apprenticeship with I.K. Brunel on the Taff Vale Railway.§

The fate of these railways was varied and this has affected the way their archaeology survives – the Penrhyn, the Dinorwic and the Nantlle were all superseded by steam-hauled lines in the 19th century, the Padarn lasted until 1961 and the Festiniog still operates in a much-altered guise. A perhaps surprising amount remains of each one. At the most basic level, items such as iron rails and stone sleeper blocks are likely to be re-used in fencing and walls; sometimes lengths of early track are simply buried, to be recovered years later. Track parts such as these constitute valuable archaeological evidence as a typology of such components evolves. Few very early items of rolling stock exist – simple wood-framed wagons saw much abuse, and made a good source of firewood when their lives were over. One remarkable survivor, however, is the locomotive *Fire Queen*, built by a firm of marine engineers for the Padarn railway in 1848, little altered in service and preserved as a museum piece since 1882. *Fire Queen* is the equivalent in locomotive terms of the sealed deposit, and is now the object of intense archaeological scrutiny in the National Trust's Penrhyn Castle Industrial Railway Museum (Figure 84).

Civil engineering also survives to a great extent. Here and there routes have been ploughed out or obliterated by later works, and can only be identified from archive

---

* Gwyn, D., 'Transitional Technology – the Nantlle Railway' in *Early Railways* (London: the Newcomen Society, 2001), pp. 46-62.
† So called by most who knew it, though its official title was the Dinorwic Quarry Railway; its informal title is used here to distinguish it from the Dinorwic railroad, which it replaced.
‡ Boyd, J.I.C., *Narrow Gauge Railways in North Caernarvonshire: Volume 2: The Penrhyn Quarry Railway* (Oxford: Oakwood, 1985), p. 25.
§ CRO: Festiniog Railway collection, uncatalogued.

84 A sealed deposit: *Fire Queen* at Penrhyn Castle Industrial Railway Museum.

maps – the lane which forms one of the two thoroughfares of the village of Clwt y Bont, for instance, is not immediately recognisable as the track-bed of the Dinorwic railroad (SH 5757 6295). Sometimes two parallel stone walls provide the only evidence. The substantial civil engineering features of the Festiniog remain intact for the sufficient reason that they continue to carry trains, far longer and heavier than the ones for which they were intended.

Quite a number of buildings have survived, some in remarkably good condition, such as the Marchogion incline drum-house on the Penrhyn railroad, now a private house (SH 593 719). This is a listed building, but the problems which others face are compounded by a failure of recognition, despite extensive documentary work by scholars such as James Boyd and Michael Lewis, and the studies carried out by organisations such as the RCAHMW. For instance, of the several depots which survive, the passenger road-rail interchange on the Nantlle at Pen y Groes (SH 470 532), now a hardware shop, is listed, but the warehouse at Port Penrhyn (SH 5913 7260), which may be the oldest surviving such building intended for rail access, is not, neither is the remarkable 1843 stable-depot on the Padarn railway at SH 5361 6428 (Figure 85).

85 Stable-depot on the Padarn Railway.

One depot which does survive and is listed but which faces pressure of a different sort is Boston Lodge on the Festiniog Railway (SH 585 378), exceptional in having been the engineering focus for the one railway from the 1830s to the 21st century, and for having served horse, steam and diesel locomotion. In the 1860s and 1870s the Festiniog took the traditions of the unimproved mineral railway into the age of steam traction and passenger carriage, and evolved the use both of a distinctive type of articulated steam locomotive, the Fairlie, and the bogie carriage (Figure 86). Neither was as much of an innovation as was claimed at the time (or indeed since) but the result was that the Festiniog Railway came to be regarded as a prototype that could be

86 Replicated single Fairlie locomotive on the Festiniog Railway.

usefully followed, along with the way in which the Norwegian engineer Carl Abraham Pihl had managed to adapt British railway practice for lightly-built narrow-gauge lines in the mountainous terrain of his native land. By the 1870s political conditions in mainland Europe, the Russian and the British empires and in the United States of America were favourable to the construction of inexpensive secondary lines. As a result, many thousands of miles of railway were built throughout the world to gauges of less than the Stephenson standard – typically, gauges between 0.6m and 1.067m were adopted.* Their effect on the economy of the developing world in the late 19th and early 20th centuries is incalculable, and makes the Festiniog a railway of world significance. In many ways its closest copy outside the Atlantic isles is the Darjeeling-Himalayan Railway, a 0.6m gauge line which climbs from Sukna on the Bengal plain to the Darjeeling hill-station. Some of the preliminary planning for this railway, now a World Heritage Site, was carried out in the Festiniog's offices at Porthmadog (Figure 87).† The example was also followed in Gwynedd, with the building of a number of 'second generation' narrow-gauge railways, using a variant of Festiniog technology but purpose-built for locomotive haulage, such as the 0.686m (2ft 3in) gauge Talyllyn Railway.

The growth of these narrow gauge systems throughout the world rested on two assumptions; firstly, that the costs of building a

87 Cultural borrowing – a train on the Darjeeling Himalayan Railway at Batasia, with the Himalayas in the background; a Gwynedd traction system transplanted to India.

---

* Ransom, J.P.G., *Narrow Gauge Steam: its origins and world-wide development* (Yeovil: Oxford Publishing Company, 1996), 104-11 and Hilton, G.W., *American Narrow Gauge Railroads* (Stanford University Press, 1990).
† Martin, T., *Halfway to Heaven: Darjeeling and its Remarkable Railway* (Chester: Rail Romances, 2000).

narrow-gauge line would be considerably less than the costs of a line built to standard gauge; and secondly, that the costs of incompatibility with other railway systems were small enough to be justified in the light of the initial cost of construction.* Just as the first generation railways were means of transferring goods from rail to ship (and occasionally vice-versa), inter-modal transport links with the growing national network of standard-gauge lines were increasingly important to these second generation lines, such as the ingenious arrangements at Minffordd yard on the Festiniog (SH 5977 3858) or the simpler arrangements where the Talyllyn met the Cambrian Railways (SH 5857 0042).† At the time of writing (2006), the exchange sidings at Pant yr Afon near Blaenau Ffestiniog remain in being (SH 6969 4681), though the site is earmarked for destruction by improvements to the A487 road.

The end of rail-borne slate traffic in Gwynedd in the 1960s meant that mineral and goods handling facilities such as these have been allowed to decay. Even on the railways revived as heritage attractions these sites have been shorn of a purpose and have had to be re-used for other purposes, and it is the paradox of 'railway preservation' that when heritage items are given a new lease of life they become subject to other pressures which compromise their historic integrity. Locomotives, rolling stock, permanent way and buildings have all had to change to accommodate the altered role of these railways; elderly steam locomotives suddenly acquired mechanical lubricators and super-heaters, or were converted from coal to oil firing. If *Fire Queen* in its museum at Penrhyn castle is that exceptionally rare thing, a largely original steam locomotive of the 1840s, the locomotives built in the 1860s for the Festiniog and the Talyllyn probably now contain no original components at all. The historic authenticity of later motive power, such as the world's first Garratt articulated locomotive, has also been compromised by rebuilding to suit the exigencies of the 21st century. Some smaller locomotives now used for demonstration purposes and for special events, such as the Festiniog's *Palmerston* and *Lilla*, have been spared the modernisation process and preserve both the appearance and the general character of a 19th-century locomotive. The Festiniog is also home to the oldest surviving British-built diesel locomotive, a Kerr Stuart design of 1928, which will be restored to original external condition.‡

Arguably, heritage is now part of these railways' archaeology. The Talyllyn was the first railway in the world to be revived by enthusiasts, with a small permanent staff and volunteer input, under the management of Tom Rolt in 1951. His account of the early preservation years on the Talyllyn demonstrates not only an engineer's fondness for antiquated technology but also his sensitive awareness of the railway's cultural dimension, serving a quiet Welsh-speaking community.§ Without a doubt, the Talyllyn was unbelievably rickety by the time Rolt took over, though there was already something self-conscious about it – when a photographer from *Picture Post* came down in the late 1940s a cow was shooed onto the track so that it could be photographed holding up a train.¶ The Festiniog was revived in stages from 1955; always in its own estimation something of a main line, it went on to acquire a reputation for sacrificing

---

* *The Times*, leader, 24 December 1872; Hilton, *op. cit.*, p. 19; Ransom, *op. cit.*, p. 104.
† Hilton, *op. cit.*, pp. 240-71.
‡ Anonymous leaflet, *4415 An Introduction to Britain's oldest diesel locomotive*, n.d. The locomotive in question was sent for trials on the Welsh Highland and the Festiniog and, after a career which later took it to Liverpool, County Tyrone and Mauritius, returned to Gwynedd in 1997.
§ Rolt, L.T.C., *Railway Adventure* (London: Constable, 1953).
¶ Boyd, J.I.C., *The Talyllyn Railway* (Didcot: Wild Swan, 1988), p. 134.

heritage for modernity, until it began to make amends in the 1990s by creating lovingly-crafted replicas of long-lost locomotives and rolling stock. This in part reflects the establishment of the Festiniog Railway Heritage Group in 1984, a body operating largely within the Festiniog Railway Society and which has become the railway's informal conscience on conservation matters. Bizarrely, Boston Lodge works is now the only place left in Britain which still regularly builds railway carriages.

The revival of these lines reflects the extraordinary level of public and juvenile interest in railways, which is by no means unique to Gwynedd. However, it is remarkable that the region is very commonly regarded as the narrow gauge area *par excellence*, an association strengthened through the marketing consortium 'The Great Little Trains of Wales' and through the children's stories of Wilbert Vere Awdry (1911-97), a member of the Talyllyn Railway Society from its inception, and later its Vice-President.*

The paradoxes of preservation have been compounded more recently still by the Festiniog's attempts to rebuild another of the 'second generation' lines, the Welsh Highland Railway, with which it will eventually make an end-on junction. The Welsh Highland's antecedents are complicated in the extreme, but, unlike both the Talyllyn and the Festiniog, it was actually scrapped after it ceased operating, and very little survived beyond the formation and some very ruinous buildings. The revival of this system has included some fanatically detailed restoration work by the railway's own

88 'Last generation' steam traction – a Beyer Garrett locomotive of 1958 takes water at Caernarfon station on the Welsh Highland Railway.

Heritage Group, established in imitation of the Festiniog's, to the extent of excavating the shattered remains of a waiting-room lavatory pan and the installation of an exact replica with the advice of a Staffordshire pottery museum.† However, the locomotives that thunder up and down outside are neither the railway's originals nor replicas, but large articulated steam engines bought second-hand from South Africa, pulling

---

* The Reverend Wilbert Awdry's series of children's books which began with *The Three Railway Engines* in 1945 (*Thomas the Tank Engine* followed a year later) introduced a narrow gauge railway very closely based on the Talyllyn in 1955 (*Four Little Engines*). In 1959 Oliver Postgate and Peter Firmin created the cartoon 'Ivor the Engine', which (or who) hauls trains for the 'Merioneth and Llantisilly Rail Traction Company' in the 'top left-hand corner of Wales'.

† Pers. comm., John Keylock, and Esposito, L., 'At Your Convenience', *Welsh Highland Heritage* 28 (June 2005), p. 2.

modern carriages (Figure 88). These represent the final flowering of the technology bequeathed to the world by the Festiniog in the 1870s, so there is a form of technological continuity here. A similar instance of the parent coming to resemble the child is to be found on the Festiniog itself, where a new section of line had to be built between 1965 and 1979 to regain the upper terminus following the construction of a dam. In order to gain height, the first leg of this new line crosses over itself on a spiral, a form of railway engineering practically unknown in a British context, but widely used on the Festiniog's Indian offspring, the Darjeeling Himalayan Railway.

Whether the Welsh Highland counts as a 'second generation' line at all, or as a 'third generation' tourist line built on the track-bed of an earlier one, it certainly has historical precedent within Gwynedd, since two railways specifically for tourists were constructed, one just before the end of the 19th century, one early in the 20th century, both of them of non-standard design for climbing up a steep gradient. The Snowdon Mountain Railway was opened in 1896 to the design of the Swiss engineer Dr Roman Abt of Lucerne (1850-1933) – its Alpine ambience initially extended even to the 'cuckoo clock' architecture of its wooden station buildings at Llanberis, now alas somewhat muted (Figure 89). The hope of creating something of Switzerland on a Welsh mountain, though this time all modernism and plate-glass, may have inspired Clough Williams-Ellis' 1934 design for the summit station; unfortunately, as built, there can be no more unattractive railway station in a more glorious setting than this.* Though rack railways are extensively used in Switzerland, they were by no means a Swiss invention, since the Middleton Railway in Leeds used such a system from 1811 as did Dowlais ironworks in south Wales from 1832 and the Madison and Indianapolis Railroad in Indiana from 1847.† The first mountain rack railway was Sylvester Marsh's Mount Washington Cog Railway in New Hampshire, completed in 1869. Abt's own first railway ran in the Harz mountains in Braunschweig (Brunswick) in 1886, but it was in the 1890s that they became popular, when Abt systems were built in Colorado, Venezuela, Japan and Sumatra.

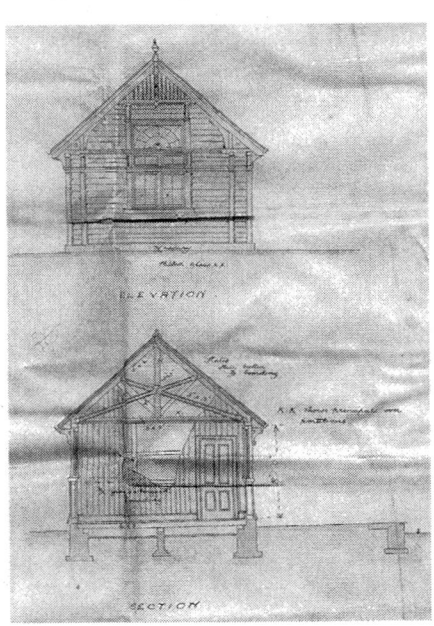

89 Cultural borrowing – Swiss-style station building on the Snowdon Mountain Railway (courtesy Gwynedd Archives: CRO XM/Maps/11274/1).

The other is the Great Orme Tram – officially a 'tramway' on its lower section where it runs along the street, and a 'tramroad' where it runs on its own right of way – which connects the tourist

---

* Haslam, R., *RIBA Drawings Monographs no. 2: Clough Williams-Ellis* (London: Academy Editions, 1996), drawing 54. The station is currently (2006) undergoing demolition so that a more imaginative and appropriate substitute can be built.

† Marshall, D., *A History of Railway Locomotives Down to the Year 1831* (London: Locomotive Publishing Company, 1953); Lewis, M.J.T. and Rattenbury, G., *Merthyr Tydfil Tramroads and their Locomotives* (Oxford: Railway and Canal Historical Society, 2004); *Illustrated Catalogue of Baldwin Locomotives, Burnham, Parry, Williams & Co., Philadelphia* (London: reprint of J. B. Lippincott and Co. edition of 1881, Bishopsgate Press Ltd, 1983), p. 29.

resort of Llandudno with the summit of the Great Orme, the limestone peninsula which juts out into Liverpool Bay. The swivel truck trams are cable-hauled by a central electric motor operating two drums, which on the upper section winds the rope over a return sheave at the summit. Rope-haulage systems were extensively used on railways from the 1770s onwards, and for some time even found a place on main lines, such as the incline from Euston to Camden and on the London and Blackwall Railway. There are many local parallels in the inclines in the slate quarries, but cable-hauled street trams are now only to be found in Llandudno, Lisbon and, most famously, San Francisco. Like the Elevador da Bica at Lisbon, the Great Orme is a stopping cable system, whereas San Francisco is a moving cable system, in which the cars can grip onto the rope.

One or two anomalous lines deserve mention at this stage. At Fairbourne a miniature railway which has gone through several changes of gauge takes passengers through the sand-dunes to the point where the ferry crosses the Mawddach to Barmouth – an example not only of a railway that was built for pleasure but is also in itself a form of mimic or 'frivolous' technology.* The Holyhead breakwater is described on pp. 174-5 but the railway used to build and maintain it is of interest. The contractors, Joseph and Charles Rigby of Westminster, were responsible for Swindon station and locomotive works in Wiltshire for the London and Bristol Railway, later the GWR, to the designs of James Meadows Rendel (1799-1856). Rendel was engineer to both the Holyhead and Portland breakwaters, so it is not surprising that there were close technical parallels between both schemes, nor that they should have made use of the GWR's broad gauge of 2.140m (7ft 0¼in).† There were sound engineering advantages, since broad gauge tipping wagons could carry and drop larger rocks, so the example of Holyhead and Portland was followed by breakwater railways at Port Erin (1864-70), Table Bay Harbour, South Africa (c.1885) and Ponta Delgada, São Miguel in the Azores (late 19th century). The engine sheds at Holyhead, though badly damaged by fire and since rebuilt, are among the oldest industrial locomotive facilities in existence.‡ The remains of a few other contractors' railways are evident elsewhere in Gwynedd, such as in the hills to the west of Dolgarrog, laid to build dams and water-courses. These used typical early 20th-century 'off the shelf' equipment, and were only lightly engineered.§

Enough has been said to indicate the interest and significance of the railways built to serve Gwynedd's own needs; what of the second category, the railways which formed part of the main British rail network? These belong to the period when railway engineering was becoming standardised and as such regional peculiarities are much less marked than in the other systems considered here. At Bangor, Aber, Bodorgan and Valley on the Chester to Holyhead main line, the original station buildings designed by Francis Thompson for the opening survive, together with a slightly later but Thompson-inspired station building at Penmaenmawr – Thompson also carried out work for other railways in which Robert Stephenson was involved, such as the

---

* Coulls, A., 'The Ephemeral Archaeology of the Miniature Railway', *LAR* 25 1 (May 2003), pp. 31-41.
† MacDermott, E.T., *History of the Great Western Railway 1833-1863 volume 1* revised C.R. Clinker, repr. 1989; Jackson, B.L., *Isle of Portland Railways volume 1 The Admiralty and Quarry Railways* (Oakwood Press, 1999), pp. 63-73.
‡ Neale, A., 'Broad Gauge at Holyhead', *Industrial Gwynedd* 2 (1997), pp. 18-25; Manning, I., 'Broad Gauge Rolling Stock at Holyhead Breakwater', *Industrial Gwynedd* 3 (1998), pp. 17-22. Morriss, *op. cit.* mentions the surviving Chalk Farm roundhouse of 1847, the Derby roundhouse, shed and works of 1840 and the Ladybank workshops of the Edinburgh and Northern Railway of *c.*1847, all of which are on public railways – pp. 182-3.
§ Jones, E. and Gwyn, D., *Dolgarrog: An Industrial History* (Caernarfon: Gwynedd Archives Service, 1989), pp. 166-87.

London and Birmingham and the North Midland.* As the Holyhead main line came more firmly under Euston's control, this tendency to uniformity is even more marked; at Holyhead itself, for instance, the handsome curved red-brick train shed with its Euston roof is one of many surviving structures on the former London and North Western Railway to have been authorised, if not necessarily designed, by William Baker, its chief engineer.† The hotel which formed part of this complex has now been demolished. It was one of several on the LNWR, but appears to have been the only railway-owned hotel within Gwynedd.‡ Railwaymen's houses, at 'Abyssinia' in Bangor (SH 572 716), were probably put up from a pattern-book by a local speculative builder under contract to the railway, as they have no clear parallels with housing elsewhere on the system.§ Nearby is the LNWR institute, now a night-club.

However, two structures remain in use on this railway which are of world-class significance, and which focused the eyes of the world on Gwynedd even more than Telford's work had done over twenty years earlier. These are the wrought-iron tubular bridges over the Conwy (SH 785 775) and the Menai Strait (SH 541 710 – Figure 90). Robert Stephenson had developed the cast-iron beam to form a longer span for locations where a masonry arch was not practical, but the collapse of his Dee bridge at Chester under a train in May 1847 discredited cast iron as a structural material. The solution for the Menai Strait and Conwy bridges was rolled and riveted wrought iron such as had come into use for ship-building, and the construction of hollow cellular girders through which the trains would run. Effectively, the bridges would be like the hull of an iron ship. The Conwy bridge was opened in 1848, the Britannia bridge (as the Menai Strait bridge had come to be known) in 1850. They were followed by similar bridges over the Nile at Benha, across the Rosetta branch and the Birket el-Saba waterway in Egypt between 1853 and 1859, and across the Victoria bridge over the St Lawrence in Montreal, completed in 1859 (Figure 91). Revolutionary though their design was, by the late 1850s, wrought-iron had already become an anachronism, and steel was shortly to take over as the dominant structural material.¶

90 Preserved section of tube with the reconstructed Britannia bridge in the background.

---

* Anderson, V.R. and Fox, G.K., *An Historical Survey of the Chester to Holyhead Railway* (Poole: Oxford Publishing Company, 1984); Bailey, M. (ed.), *Robert Stephenson – The Eminent Engineer* (Aldershot: Ashgate, 2003), pp. 243, 284-5.
† Reed, M.C., *The London and North Western Railway* (Penryn: Atlantic Transport Publishers, 1996), p. 76.
‡ The LNWR owned hotels in Fleetwood, Liverpool, Dublin, Greenore (on Carlingford Lough in Ireland) and Euston – Reed, *passim*. Though hotel accommodation formed part of the plans of the promoters of the various railways that amalgamated to become the Cambrian in 1866, their ambitions focused on Borth and Aberystwyth, in Cardiganshire, rather than on Gwynedd.
§ Even large railway companies frequently resorted to outside contractors working to their own designs – for instance, the Lancashire and Yorkshire Railway when Horwich works was being expanded in the early years of the 20th century. I am grateful to Dr Diane Drummond for her observations on the Bangor houses.
¶ Sutherland, J., 'Iron railway bridges', in Bailey, M.R. (ed.), *Robert Stephenson – The Eminent Engineer* (Aldershot: Ashgate, 2003), pp. 301-35.

91 Technical dissemination – Stephenson's tubular bridge across the St Lawrence river in Canada (from J. Hodges, *Construction of the Great Victoria Bridge in Canada* [London: 1860]).

The Britannia bridge was badly damaged by fire in 1970, and was rebuilt incorporating only the masonry work, with a road deck above the rail, the span being carried on steel arches of N-truss spandrel bracing in each half arch. The Conwy bridge remains much as built, and along the length of the line Stephenson-era masonry bridges survive – as does at least one cast-iron bridge, at Bangor station (SH 576 715).

Though the network of secondary and branch lines within Gwynedd has shrunk, two other standard gauge routes still operate. The Dyfi Junction to Pwllheli railway was built in the 1860s as a secondary single-track route and continues to run as a passenger line only. Its route (and that of the Shrewsbury-Aberystwyth line with which it connects) incorporates some of the last remaining wooden railway bridges in Britain. The Dyfi Junction bridge (SN 6943 9790) and the 800m Barmouth viaduct (SH 6229 1503) are partly of steel construction; those at Pensarn (SH 5794 2771), Pont Briwat (SH 6191 3829) and Traeth Mawr (SH 5886 3902) are entirely wooden. The basic structure consists of piers of four or five piles, with a cross-head timber and diagonals. Timber pile bridges such as these were cheap, and had the advantage of a certain amount of 'give' over a boggy river-crossing, but their survival into the 21st century is remarkable.*

The second is the branch line from Llandudno Junction to Blaenau Ffestiniog, which includes two major civil engineering works. Its castellated stone viaduct Pont Gethin (SH 7809 5387) was built by the local contractor Owain Gethin Jones, and designed in response to environmental concerns. Its 3.51km tunnel (SH 6880 5034 – SH 6968 4697) from Blaenau Dolwyddelan to Blaenau Ffestiniog made early use of compressed air for drilling, drawing on the experience of the St Gothard tunnel in Switzerland.† Apart from the miracle of its survival as a working railway, as a consequence of the need to carry nuclear waste from Trawsfynydd by rail and the

---

* Lycett-Smith, R., 'Cambrian Timber Trestle Bridges and Viaducts in 1994: A Photographic Survey', *Historical Model Railway Society Journal* 15 7 (1994-6), pp. 208-17.

† Smith, W., 'Summit-Level Tunnel of the Bettws and Festiniog Railway', *Proceedings of the Institution of Civil Engineers* 59, pp. 150-77.

prospect for moving slate waste, it preserves the character of a Victorian branch line, running on a token system with semaphore signalling at Llanrwst (SH 7940 6238) controlled from a manual signal-box.

One other length of former standard gauge line still operates as a railway, though to narrow gauge. The Bala Lake Railway is an 0.6m (2 ft) gauge steam-operated tourist railway, one of several in the United Kingdom that operate on a standard gauge trackbed.

Otherwise, what the surviving systems have in common with each other and with many railways elsewhere, is that much of the old infrastructure has been lost both through modernisation and through concentration on core services. Nineteenth-century buildings survive on many railway systems world-wide, but their context has been changed. When diesel multiple units replaced steam locomotives and trains of coaches, track arrangements could be simplified; as goods services were lost to the roads, yards could be sold off as retail space, and radio token signalling has meant that many semaphore signals and lever signal boxes have gone. The locomotive shed at Bangor has become a steel stockist's warehouse, and a multiplex cinema has arisen on the site of the Llandudno Junction sheds, where, in the foyer, photographs of locomotives under repair hang on the walls (Figure 92).

Despite the loss, decay or demolition of many historic features, the railway archaeology of Gwynedd is of international significance. The standard gauge network includes iconic features such as the Stephenson bridges, as well as rare surviving examples of humbler forms of technology. The distinctive technology of the region's narrow gauge slate railways came to be adapted in an imperial context all over the world, with far-reaching effect, whilst their revival as heritage attractions has meant

92 The changing context of the national railway network: a 1956 photograph of Llandudno Junction shed, showing two locomotives in steam, including a Stanier Class 5MT, no 44738, with Caprotti valve gear. The site is now a multiplex cinema.

the survival, though also necessarily the adaptation, of much Victorian and early 20th-century infrastructure. It is unlikely, for instance, that a mass of early rolling stock equivalent to Gwynedd's now operates anywhere else in the world, to say nothing of replications and adaptations. The fact that narrow-gauge steam locomotive technology was developed in Gwynedd with such success, and is now being taken forward into the 21st century, increases the archaeological significance of the remains of the earlier horse-worked systems; these can be seen not only as important in their own right, but also as the early stages of a distinctive traction system in which the region has been an initiator rather than a recipient.

Note: terminology
The word *railroad* is used here, as it was used by contemporaries, to signify a pre-locomotive edge railway system using iron rails.

4.5.3 Docks, quays and harbours

Gwynedd's docks, quays and harbour facilities reflect the region's long coastline, its strategic importance as a link between London and Ireland, and its mineral wealth.

The archaeological study of docks, quays and harbours remains in its infancy, in Wales and elsewhere in the world (though an important survey of lighthouses in Wales has been published).[*] They resist easy classification. They are called into being by a variety of factors, of which topographical suitability is only one. Some reflect the economy of their immediate hinterland, others broader commercial, governmental or strategic issues. As inter-modal transport sites, they reflect the changing technology of both sea and land travel, as well as the economic and social forces which brought them into being, or sustained them, in the Modern period. They are prone to the effects of silting and, as easily identifiable strategic sites, many were targeted by the Luftwaffe in the Second World War. It has been suggested by one authority that they can be categorised partly according to size and partly according to function as follows – *major ports*, *mineral ports*, *packet ports*, *minor ports* and *canal ports*. On this basis, most of the ports in Gwynedd can be classed as mineral ports, and all can be classed as minor ports, even Holyhead,[†] one of the principal packet ports which connected Britain with Ireland. There are no canal ports within the region (Map 13).

Although it is probable that the Romans built wharves at Segontium and perhaps at Holyhead, nothing is known to survive of their works. Similarly, it is possible, though equally unproven, that the Cistercian monasteries at Cymer and Maenan had a wharf on the Mawddach and the Conwy respectively. The Edwardian towns at Conwy and Caernarfon had quays and there was a dock at Beaumaris and water-access to Harlech, though the scale of trade may be imagined from the narrow arches through the town

---

[*] For Wales, see Gwyn, D., 'Partnerships and Priorities for the Industrial and Modern Period' in Briggs, C.S. (ed.), *Towards a Research Agenda for Welsh Archaeology* (BAR British Series 343, 2003), p. 184. See also Jarvis, A., 'Introduction: The present state of the History of Ports' in Jarvis, A. (ed.), *Port and Harbour Engineering* (Ashgate, 1998), pp. xiii-xxxiv. For lighthouses, see Hague, D.B., *Lighthouses of Wales* (Aberystwyth: RCAHMW, 1994). In view of the comprehensive nature of this publication, Gwynedd's 10 lighthouses are not considered in the present volume.

[†] Jackson, G., *The History and Archaeology of Ports* (Tadworth, 1983), p. 137.

Map 13 Harbours

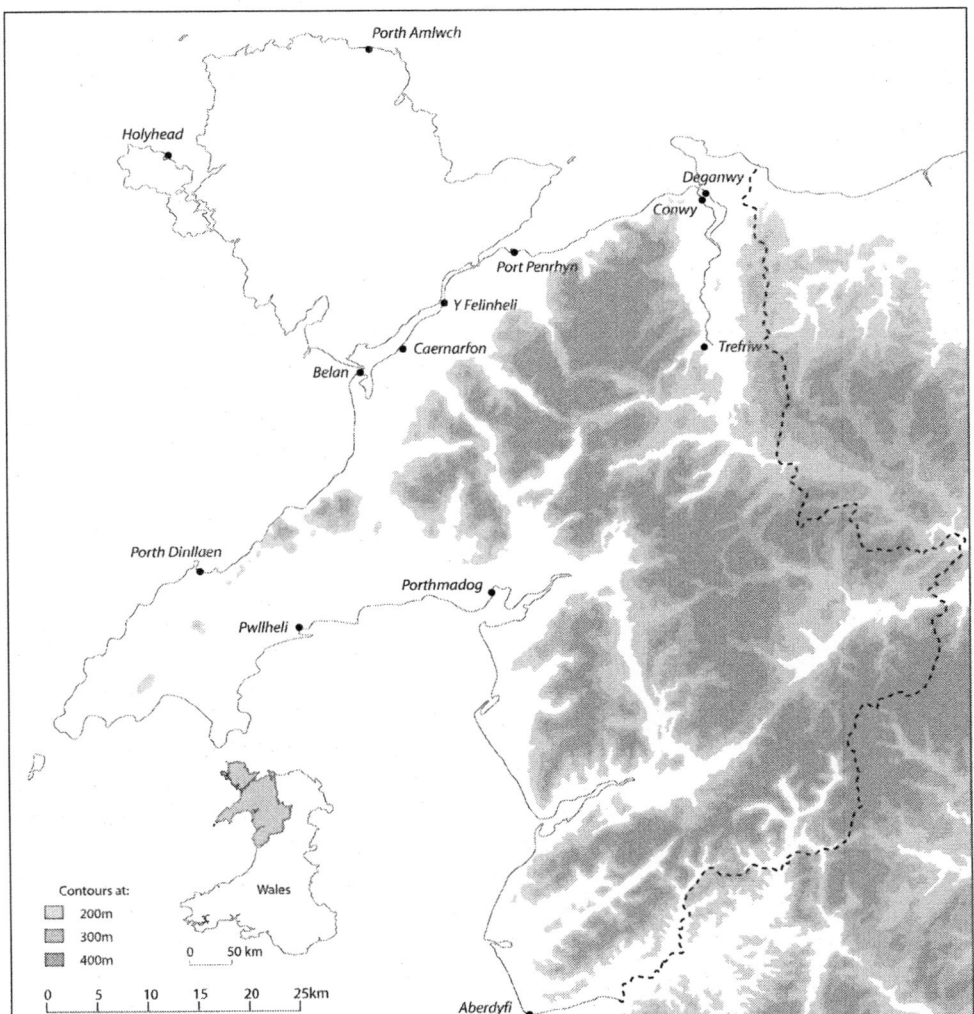

walls connecting the landing place with the market area at Porth yr Aur in Caernarfon (SH 4772 6279) or the lower gate at Conwy (SH 7821 7770).* As with other forms of transport facility, development only began at the turn of the 18th and 19th centuries; as with roads and railways, some docks and harbours came into being to serve local and regional needs – primarily the export of minerals – and others to service broader political and strategic considerations.

Small mineral loading points were found all over Gwynedd, on the sea coast, on tidal rivers, and inland waters, though for a long time they did not necessarily involve built or engineered structures at all. Beaching even of sea-going ships long outlasted the 'proto-industrial' stage, demonstrated by a photograph of Llandudno in 1857

---

* Taylor, A.J., *The Welsh Castles of Edward I* (London and Ronceverte; Hambledon Press, 1986), pp. 51, 72, 88, 109, 111.

which shows single-masted ships lying on their bottoms on the sand for loading from the Ty Gwyn copper mine.*

Engineered quays appear in the late 18th century wherever substantial amounts of mineral needed to be loaded, and were extended piecemeal for as long as the trade expanded – at Porth Amlwch (SH 450 935), y Felinheli (Port Dinorwic – SH 524 677), Port Penrhyn (SH 592 728), Caernarfon (SH 479 626), Porthmadog (SH 570 386). Typically they were constructed of limestone blocks built on piles; the fill might be locally-quarried rubble or it might have arrived as ballast from the Elbe or Pensacola or anywhere in between.† There are many exceptions to this generalisation; the LNWR's quay at Deganwy (SH 782 787), built in 1882 to ship slate from Blaenau Ffestiniog, used spoil from the enlargement of Belmont tunnel at Bangor and made use of projecting timber jetties around its perimeter.‡ At Aberdyfi the Cambrian Railways completed in 1885 a stone wharf and a wooden jetty (SH 614 959).§ Stone quarries on Penrhyn Llŷn and in Eifionydd, at Penmon, Penmaenmawr, Penmaenbach and the Great Orme built jetties and piers of timber, stone or steel, as did the manganese mines at Rhiw (see pp. 82, 88).¶ Those associated with the Penmaenmawr quarries were substantial, but were very thoroughly scrapped when sea-borne distribution came to an end.

Their infrastructure varied according to the mineral that was being loaded. Copper ore required secure storage, as in the 'bins' (walled compounds) which survive at Porth Amlwch, some of them roofed, some of them open. One of these retains its timber chute so that carts on the road above could discharge into it. With a smelter immediately adjacent to the harbour, coal also needed to be delivered in quantity, for which a separate bin

93 Porth Amlwch, showing the copper and coal bins.

---

* Williams, C.J., *Great Orme Mines: British Mining History No. 52* (Keighley: Northern Mine Research monograph, 1995).

† Hughes, H., *Immortal Sails* (Prescot: T. Stephenson and Sons, 1977), p. 59.

‡ Anderson, V.R. and Fox, G.K. *An Historical Survey of the Chester to Holyhead Railway* (Poole: Oxford Publishing Company, 1984), figs 78-9 *et seq*.

§ Boyd, J.I.C., *The Talyllyn Railway* (Didcot: Wild Swan, 1988), pp. 310, 316-21.

¶ Smith, G., 'Aberdaron Bay to the Great Orme', unpublished GAT report, 1995; Griffith, M., 'Manganese Mining at Rhiw in Llŷn between 1827 and 1945', *TCHS* 50 (1989), pp. 41-65.

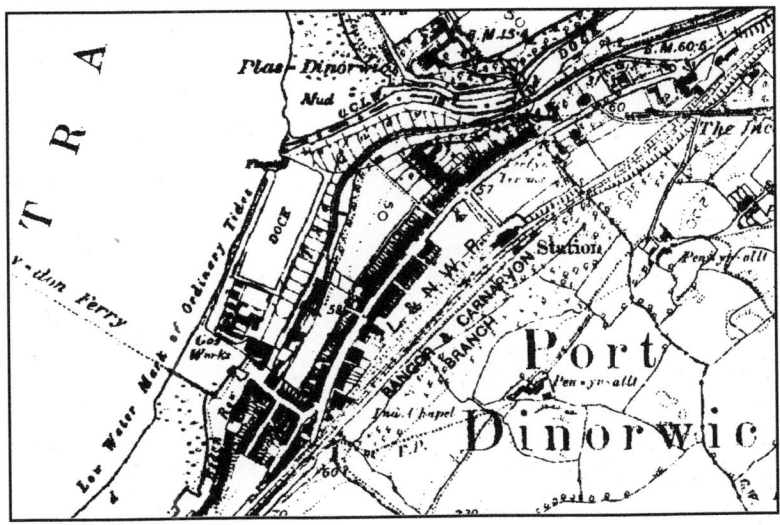

94 Ordnance Survey 25-in/1 mile map showing slate-handling facilities and the criss-cross pattern of narrow gauge railway and turntables at Port Dinorwic/y Felinheli.

was constructed (Figure 93).* At Caernarfon the bins for copper and lead ore were adapted as workshops, a smithy and offices in the 19th century, and their site survives as such to this day. The private stone quarry piers were often equipped with massive stone bins fed by conveyor belt, or, if topography allowed, from railways running across their top† – their scale reflects both a strongly engineered approach to the problem of transferring large quantities of rock into ships' holds and also probably an increasingly international technical culture. 'Coal yards' are marked on early 19th-century maps of Traeth Coch (Red Wharf Bay – SH 530 810), the entrepôt for the Anglesey collieries (*4.1.4*, pp. 92-6), where several houses containing some early building work lie within the trace of walled yards, but it is not clear how these functioned, and they are not associated with any built-up quays. Certainly there was nothing remotely resembling the sophistication of coal-handling systems on the Tyne.‡

The most distinctively regional type of mineral quays were those built to export slate (Figure 94).§ These needed little in the way of specialised equipment, only sometimes a crane for handling slabs, though the Oakeley quarry wharf at Porthmadog included a range of covered sheds for their slate stocks, only one of which survives, as the maritime museum.¶

---

* Hope, B.D., *A Curious Place: An Industrial History of Amlwch (1550-1950)* (Wrexham: Bridge Books, 1994), pp. 98-113.
† Boyd, J.I.C., *Narrow Gauge Railways in North Caernarvonshire vol. 3* (Oxford: Oakwood Press, 1986), pp. 164-6, 197-9, plates CXXVII-CXXXI.
‡ LlRO: WCD 30.
§ Despite there being many slate quarries elsewhere in the Atlantic isles, few had a railway connection to the sea. Delabole quarry in Cornwall used carts to export slate through Tintagel, and Honister quarry mules to reach the sea at Ravenglass. Some quarries such as Abereiddy in Dyfed and others in Scotland and Cornwall were so near the sea that slates could be loaded directly onto vessels from the splitting area. Quarries in north-east Wales connected with canals. Williams, M.C., *The Slate Industry* (Princes Risborough: Shire Publications, 1991); Fairweather, B., *The 300-Year Story of Ballachulish Slate* (Glencoe: Glencoe and North Lorn Folk Museum, n.d), pp. 7, 14; Cameron, A., *Slate from Coniston* (Barrow in Furness; Cumbria Amenity Trust Mining History Society, 1996).
¶ Certain types of slate lose their texture quickly if stored in the open, and the shelter also made it easier for the loaders and clerks to do their work. Slates would be delivered to the quay in wagons containing various sizes and would need to be sorted into loads for ship-board delivery.

95 An early 20th-century view of Port Penrhyn, and (on the right) its harbour office (from *The Penrhyn Quarry Illustrated*).

What many quays had was an office, or offices, sometimes prestigious buildings, sometimes fairly humble affairs. Caernarfon, as a harbour run by a Trust, not only has its own handsome offices of 1842 facing the castle, but also a row of offices once maintained by each of the Nantlle slate quarries, now in re-use for one purpose or another (and under threat of demolition – SH 4790 6260). Quarries were frequently managed from the port rather than from the quarry bank. Port Penrhyn's dignified regency port house of 1832 (SH 5927 7263) bespeaks the confidence of a prosperous concern, and is still the estate office (Figure 95). At Porthmadog, the Oakeley quarry shipping manager's house and office (SH 5696 3847) are now being sympathetically rebuilt, having fallen on hard times, but in the 19th century its lawn and garden furniture had to be fitted in around busy narrow gauge lines.*

The means of access from quarry or mine varied. In a number of locations, smaller quays served to load tidal water vessels which transferred their cargoes to sea-going ships in sheltered bays, purpose-built harbour or sometimes in open water. Lead and slate from Cardiganshire was boated from Derwenlas (outside Gwynedd) to Aberdyfi for re-loading, and slate from Blaenau Ffestiniog was carted down to quays on the Dwyryd, then boated to Ynys Cyngar (SH 554 365), later to Porthmadog. The Dwyryd quays are the only smaller examples within Gwynedd to have had the benefit of detailed archaeological study (Figure 96).† In some cases, small vessels have been identified and recorded. A flat-bottomed keel-less boat of the *bateau* type was raised from Llyn Padarn (SH 565 619) in 1979 where it had sunk with a cargo of slate from

---

* Morris, M., *Porthmadog: Llanw Ddoe/Yesterday's Tide* (Caernarfon: Gwynedd Archives service, n.d.), fig. 33.

† Lewis, M.J.T., *Sails on the Dwyryd* (Maentwrog: Snowdonia National Park Study Centre, 1989).

96 Tyddyn Isa wharf on the Dwyryd.

Dinorwic quarries, sometime after 1788. It measures 6.3m by 2.16m (19ft 9in by 6ft 1in). Its clinker sides (overlapping planks) suggest that it is an intrusive type of design in Gwynedd, where a Nordic-derived system of clinker planking built onto a central frame with keel and internal framing predominates. Such a boat was discovered nearby at SH 581 597, dated by dendrochronology to between 1547 and 1549.[*] In 1988 a vessel was discovered in the saltings of the Traeth Bach at SH 6050 3670, a single-masted hybrid (clinker sides and carvel bottom – planks abutting) measuring 7.92m (26ft) by 2.9m (9ft 6in). A third vessel could be studied only very briefly when it was exposed during the building of the Conwy tunnel; it had sunk with a cargo of slate. The sides were carvel and the bottom was probably flat. Its width was 2.7m (8ft 10in).[†]

This last boat is witness to an active river trade on the Conwy which is attested from documentary sources. The tidal waters of the Conwy penetrated many miles inland but water-transport was hampered for years by a reef known as yr Arw at Tal y Cafn (SH 785 717 approx.), only partly removed by 1810.[‡] Hitherto only rafts or the smallest of boats could make the journey up the river to the tidal head near Trefriw, and most loads had to be landed at a depot near the reef, whence the 'great ships' could go on to Liverpool. Thereafter, ships of up to 100 tons burden could take cargoes of slate and lead all the way from Trefriw.[§]

Some of the earlier quays were built for cart-access and then became rail-connected as they expanded, such as Port Penrhyn, y Felinheli, Caernarfon and Porthmadog.

---

[*] McElvogue, D., 'The Forgotten Ways: evidence for water-borne transport in Nant Peris, Gwynedd', *Industrial Gwynedd* 4 (1999), pp. 5-15. The slate boat is now preserved at the Welsh Slate Museum.
[†] Lewis, *op. cit.*, pp. 87-90.
[‡] Davies, W., *A General View of the Agriculture and Domestic Economy of North Wales* (London: 1810), p. 280.
[§] Williams, G.H., 'Estate Management in Dyffryn Conwy, c.1685', *Transactions of the Honourable Society of Cymmrodorion*, 1979, pp. 65-71; Trefriw wharf books, ex info Dr M.J.T. Lewis.

Porth Amlwch remained the only significant mineral harbour never to enjoy rail access, though it had a short line to carry coal to the smelters. Later quays such as Aberdyfi and Deganwy were purpose-built for rail access. Typically, rails were laid so that wagons could be hand-shunted or moved by capstan, obviating the need to build or enlarge quays so as to accommodate the large-radius curves which standard-gauge lines in particular required, and the weight of locomotives. Narrow gauge railways on the slate ports were often laid in a chequerboard pattern with wagon turntables at the intersections, to allow slate to be stacked in between. At Port Penrhyn and at y Felinheli, facilities were developed to transfer slate not only from narrow gauge wagon to ship but also to the standard gauge. Otherwise, by the late 1830s it was only the quarries and lead mines along the Conwy river and the dwindling band of Blaenau quarries that refused to use the Festiniog Railway that were still having to depend on carts to reach navigable water.

Several towns had public quays, either separate affairs as at Bangor (SH 587 728) or Caernarfon (SH 478 631), in and amongst the mineral-exporting quays as at Porthmadog, or forming the principal business of the harbour, as was the case at Pwllheli (SH 380 350). These and the mineral quays sustained what was for many years in each town a busy, crowded and noisy environment, which their surviving archaeology cannot convey. Buildings that were once sail lofts, ships' chandlers, navigation schools, brothels or insurance offices are now private houses.[*] The entertainment in pubs like the *Australia* or the *Ship on Launch* is wide-screen and digital, not old captains' memories of rounding Cape Horn, or of disturbing a multi-national hangover in Pernambuco harbour with a 'Welsh Sunday' ship-board service.

Much of the noise of a Gwynedd port in the 19th century would have come from ship-building yards. They would also have added a quota of smells – of sawn pitch pine and oak, and of boiling cauldrons of pitch and buckets of Stockholm tar[†] – but they have left remarkably little trace in the archaeological record, not least because the ships constructed there were typically built using hand-tools and a minimum of machinery. Only at Porth Amlwch is there much evidence of how and where the ships were built. Here, ship-builders were able to make the transition from wooden sloops, recorded from 1788, to iron-hulled schooners from 1858, and ultimately to steamships and vessels with auxiliary engines in the early years of the 20th century. A dry dock, slipways and the remains of a water-powered saw-mill survive.[‡]

A completely different type of harbour is represented by Holyhead (SH 250 827) – still perhaps a 'minor' port but on a much larger scale than any of the others, the results of investment by central government agencies and by a major joint-stock company. Holyhead was strategically important. The abolition of the Irish parliament in 1800/01 created a clamour amongst Irish MPs now forced to travel to Westminster, and prompted a government otherwise committed to *laisser-faire* to control a potentially dangerous neighbour by adopting interventionist policies. These included sponsorship of Telford's Holyhead road and of works at Holyhead, carried out by John Rennie and by Telford between 1810 and 1826, at Howth harbour in Ireland and the road from

---

[*] A harbour brothel is said to have operated at Amlwch, where Chinese women received their clients.
[†] Hughes, H., *Immortal Sails* (Prescot: T. Stephenson and Sons, 1977), p. 46.
[‡] Hope, *op. cit.*, pp. 98-154 and *A Commodious Yard: The Story of William Thomas & Sons Shipbuilders of Amlwch 1858-1920* (Wrexham: Bridge Books, 2005), the latter based on a very comprehensive archive for a firm that dealt not only in ship-building and repair but also shipping operation and ship-brokerage as well.

Howth to Dublin. Holyhead itself nearly lost out to Porth Dinllaen on Penrhyn Llŷn, a natural harbour with very little in the way of built features but which formed the goal of several abortive road and railway schemes from the 1770s to the 1840s (SH 277 414).*

Hitherto, Holyhead had been a barely 'engineered' port in any way. Ships were beached below the church and provision for travellers included the *Eagle and Child* hotel. The new work is similar in purpose and execution not only to Howth but also to Dun Laoghaire (Kingstown) in Ireland, and is typical of both Rennie and Telford in its rugged construction and polite conception.† The graving dock and the related engine house form the earliest complex in Britain where the archaeology of steam pumping in a harbour is evident,‡ and the value of these features is enhanced by the comparatively good survival of the engine house, including a fragment of the pump mechanism. The graving dock itself, though it has been filled in, may be an early example of the type; they were possible and necessary in British ports because of the wide tidal range.§

Like Dun Laoghaire (and other established packet ports such as Southampton and Weymouth), Holyhead became a tempting prize once the railway era dawned. The original railway works put in from 1843 have gone. The Y-plan arrangement of platforms on either side of the harbour dates from 1877-80 and offered a rationally-conceived answer to the problems of moving passengers and to some extent animals and goods on and off ships. It formed part of a programme which included more efficient rail and sea transport between Holyhead and Dublin and the building of a new station at the North Wall in Dublin. This was built by the LNWR and conceived as an architectural unity with Holyhead, rather than following Dublin's own tradition of station-building,¶ but the station as a whole followed a very different plan from its Welsh counterpart, whereby the terminus faces onto the harbour front, with a hotel nearby. The complex is now occupied by Iarnród Éireann signals and telegraph department,** whereas Holyhead has been replaced by nondescript modern buildings, apart from one impressive curved train shed (Figure 97 – see p. 163).

In the 1960s equipment was installed for shipping containers, and improvements for loading car ferries came in the 1970s.†† In the 1990s the sidings and overhead crane on the east side of the dock were swept away to provide a new terminal for the catamaran services to Dun Laoghaire and to Dublin.

Just as the smaller mineral ports such as Porthmadog and Amlwch had their own distinctive traditions of ship-wrighting, so Holyhead had the Marine Yard, a handsome set of buildings in stone, one of the most remarkable survivors of a site-type that was once common on the Clyde, the Laggan and the Thames (Figure 98). The earliest

---

  * Dodds, A.H., *The Industrial Revolution in North Wales* (Cardiff: University of Wales press, 1971, repr., Wrexham: Bridge Books, 1990), pp. 113-14. The construction of a Brunel-gauge railway through Merioneth and across Penrhyn Llŷn instead of the standard-gauge Chester to Holyhead main line would have radically altered subsequent industrial patterns in Gwynedd.
  † Royal Commission on the Ancient and Historic Monuments of Scotland, *Monuments of Industry* (RCAHMS, 1986), pp. 216-7.
  ‡ Bick, D.,'Evolution of the Pre-Cornish Beam Engine House', *LAR* 21 2 (November, 1999), pp. 134-5.
  § Jarvis, A., *op. cit.*, p. xviii.
  ¶ Craig, M., *Dublin 1660-1860* (Dublin: Allen Figgis, 1980), pp. 300-1.
  ** Pers. comm., Peter Swift.
  †† Anderson, V.R. and Fox, G.K., *An Historical Survey of the Chester to Holyhead Railway: Track Layouts and Illustrations* (Poole: Oxford Publishing Company, 1984), opp. plate 266.

97 The hotel at Holyhead harbour station, from a 19th-century postcard.

98 The Marine yard at Holyhead.

part appears to date from around 1857 to maintain the six second-hand vessels which the Chester and Holyhead Railway had purchased to operate to Dublin (North Wall). From 1873 the LNWR, as successor to the C&HR, was also operating services to Greenore, on Carlingford Lough, and by 1920 the LNWR was maintaining 16 vessels at Holyhead.[*] The surviving buildings here include a smithy, fitting shop, foundry, erecting shop, fitting shop, offices, paint shop, boiler and engine room, boiler shop, a smithy, saw mill, a boiler shop extension, the site of a chimney, an engine house, and sheds. A sail-makers' and upholsterers' workshop was demolished post-1986. All are now out of use, and their future is uncertain.

An indirectly related development, which profoundly altered the appearance of Holyhead harbour, is the huge breakwater, constructed between 1847 and 1873 to create a 108-hectare (267-acre) harbour of refuge for Liverpool shipping and the packet boats themselves – rendered largely redundant by the adoption of steam power in the Irish sea. A Royal Commission in 1847 discussed the need for a harbour of refuge at Holyhead and at Portland for Channel shipping.[†] The main contractors, Joseph and Charles Rigby of Westminster, were responsible for Swindon station and locomotive works in Wiltshire for the London and Bristol Railway, later the GWR, to the designs of James Meadows Rendel (1799-1856), who became Engineer-in-Chief to the Holyhead scheme until his death in 1856.[‡] Rendel was also engineer to the Portland breakwater, constructed by convict labour between 1849 and 1872, and it is clear that

---

[*] Reed, M.C., *The London and North Western Railway* (Penryn: Atlantic Transport Publishers, 1996), pp. 150-5, 219.
[†] *Royal Commission to Enquire into Harbours of Refuge* (British Parliamentary Papers 1847 411 LXI.1).
[‡] MacDermott, E.T., *History of the Great Western Railway 1833-1863* volume 1 revised C.R. Clinker, repr. 1989.

there were close technical similarities in the construction methods used in both places, including a broad gauge (2.140m – 7ft 0¼in) contractor's railway (see p. 162).*

Breakwaters on this scale can be traced to the massive fortified breakwater at Cherbourg, begun in 1783 but which was many years in the building,† and later examples such at Plymouth from 1811 to shelter the channel fleet.‡ Other continental ports at which substantial breakwaters were constructed include Le Havre and Marseilles.§

One completely anomalous harbour also deserves mention. This is Belan, near the western mouth of the Menai straits, where in either 1703 or 1763 two warehouses were constructed by the Wynn family of nearby Glynllifon, and there are references to 'Abermenai barracks' from 1776. From 1824 to 1827 a fortified extension was built (SH 4403 6095) and a dockyard (SH 4416 6094) was added in about 1845. Belan, like the fort which Thomas Wynn built at Glynllifon, was more than ornamental or ostentatious, though both undoubtedly marked the Wynn family's loyalty to the Hanoverian dynasty and secured their eventual elevation to the peerage. Belan protected the Menai straits from invasion or amphibious raiding parties and also from privateers, and retained a defensive function into the Second World War. The dockyard includes a tidal dock 64m (210ft) long by 12.8m (42ft) wide, to the north of which is a chain furnace and two large stone boat sheds. The longer of these had a railway track from the eastern end of the davits on the side of the dock for handling boats.

In 1977 it opened to visitors, complete with ferry access from Caernarfon, pottery, gift shop, miniature steam railway, pleasure flights from the airport and demonstrations of cannon firing. Initially a success, visitor numbers declined sharply, and it had to be put up for sale. It is now back in private hands. The collection was moved to the Merseyside Maritime Museum, where many of the items are on permanent display, including the restored paddle engines from the yacht *Firefly II*, and the figurehead from the barque *William Turner*.¶

4.5.4 WATER-CONTROL SYSTEMS, FLOOD DEFENCES, CANALS

Though canals in Gwynedd were few and short, two important water-control systems are located within the area.

Water-control systems may be regarded as part of the archaeology of docks, quays and harbours or of enclosure (see *4.1.5*, pp. 96-110).** The two principal examples in Gwynedd were completed in the second decade of the 19th century, though one had been much longer than the other in construction (Map 14).

---

* MacDermott, E.T., *op.cit.*; Jackson, B.L., *Isle of Portland Railways volume 1 The Admiralty and Quarry Railways* (Usk: Oakwood Press, 1999), pp. 63-73.
† *Royal Commission to Enquire into Harbours of Refuge*, pp. 25, 45-8.
‡ Naish, J., 'Joseph Whidbey and the building of the Plymouth Breakwater', *The Mariner's Mirror*, 78 1 (February 1992), pp. 37-56.
§ Kirkpatrick, C.R.S., 'The development of dock and harbour engineering', in Jarvis, A. (ed.), *op. cit.*, pp. 13, 41-3.
¶ Stammers, M., *A Maritime Fortress: The Collections of the Wynn Family at Belan Fort c.1750-1950* (Cardiff: University of Wales Press, 2001), *passim*.
** Jones, E.J., 'The Enclosure Movement in Anglesey (1788-1866)', *TAAA* (1926), pp.31-89, quoting Evans, J., *Topographical and Historical Description of Anglesey* (London, 1810).

Map 14 Water control systems

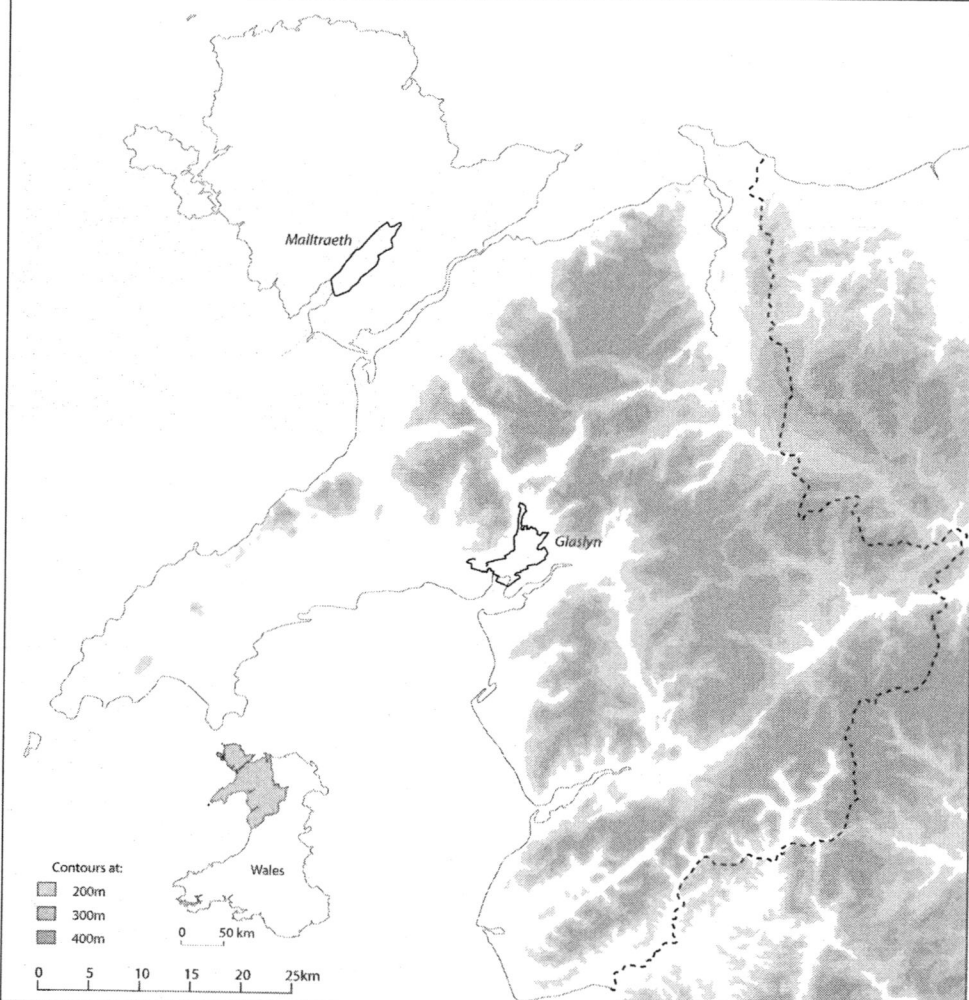

Cob Malltraeth is a 1.62km (1 mile) -long sea-defence constructed at the mouth of the Afon Cefni in south-west Anglesey which enclosed and drained 1,111.7 hectares (2,747 acres) of marsh, already crossed by paths and fords,[*] but which in the Medieval period had been an arm of the sea that had reached as far as the court of Ednyfed Fychan near Llangefni. Local tradition speaks of a ship-wreck near Plas Berw (SH 465 718), over 10km from present-day deep water, as late as the 17th century.[†] To this day, the people of Newborough refer to the people of Malltraeth as *pobl trwy'r Afon*, 'people beyond the river'.[‡]

---

[*] UWB: Bodorgan 1583; see also Jones, G.T., *The Fords of Anglesey* (Bangor: Canolfan Ymchwil Cymru, 1992), pp. 32-9.
[†] Pers. comm., Tomos Roberts, former archivist, UWB.
[‡] Jones, *op. cit.*, p. 34.

99 The sluice bridge at Malltraeth, with the village in the background.

Discussions had been under way since the early 17th century, but it was only in 1781 that a resolution was passed in favour of an embankment, and work began.* Storms badly damaged it on at least two occasions, and it was not until 1811 that the final phase of construction began.†

The landowners involved were Lord Boston, the Earl of Uxbridge, Lord Newborough, Sir Hugh Owen of Bodeon, Sir Hugh Williams and Owen Putland Meyrick of Bodorgan, a group which could afford the services of the most experienced men available. James Golborne (1746-1819) was the leading water-control engineer of his day, and was by then Superintendent General of the Bedford Level, responsible for a water-control system covering 300,000 acres. Of the two original contractors, Jonathan Pinkerton, of Spark Hill, Warwick (d. 1813), was a member of a family that might be regarded as the earliest contracting business in civil engineering, whereas Jonathan Dyson (d. c.1804) was an established engineer, and a Commissioner for the embanking and draining of the Timberland fen.‡ At a later stage, W.A. Provis, then working as Telford's assistant on the post road, prepared an estimate for a sluice gate across the main river, possibly as a replacement for an existing structure, and advised on regrading the banks.§

As constructed, the system consists of a main embankment and a landward catchwater embankment, on which the road runs. The sluice is situated at SH 4078 6868 (Figure 99), over the mouth of the side drain known as the Menai drain or *yr afon fain* ('the narrow river'). The village of Malltraeth grew up on the site of the

---

* UWB: Baron Hill 1695 and 1697-1700; NLW: Carreg-lwyd 957 'An affidavit concerning the Cefni River being dammed'; CRO: X/Poole 1729, resolution concerning embankment, 20 September 1781. An enclosure bill received the royal assent in June 1788 – 28 Geo. III, *c*.71. Later acts are 23 Geo. III *c*.71, 1788, 30 Geo. III *c*.59, 1790 (copy in Bangor mss 35317), 52 Geo. III *c*.132, 1811 (draft in UWB: Bangor mss 13780c), 22 and 23 Vict. Session 1859 (copy in UWB: Bangor mss 24807). The enclosure was awarded in 1821 – PRO: LRRO 1/3019.

† CRO: X/Poole 1749; E.J. Jones, *op. cit.*, p. 37; LlRO: WDAK/2, entry for 25 November 1811; UWB: Porth yr Aur 13771-6.

‡ CRO: X/Poole/1765-6; Skempton, A.W., *Biographical Dictionary of Civil Engineers: Volume 1 1500 to 1830* (London: Institution of Civil Engineers, 2002), relevant entries.

§ LlRO: WDAK/2, entry for 21 April 1820; E.J. Jones, *op. cit.*; UWB: Bangor mss 29495.

workshops and labourers' houses; its industrial origins are preserved in its local name, *y iard* ('the yard') and in *The Joiner's Arms* public house.

The other sea-wall, the cob across the Traeth Mawr, is far better known, partly because the town and harbour of Porthmadog came into being at one end, and partly because the Festiniog Railway now runs across it. The history of its construction, and of its promoter's struggles to develop the area, has been told in compelling detail by Elizabeth Beazley.* Whereas the Malltraeth cob gave a temporary lease of life to the struggling Anglesey coal-mines and improved the cultivation of agricultural land, the Traeth Mawr cob transformed what was literally a rural backwater into a remarkable industrial and urban community.

Like Malltraeth, the Traeth Mawr had been silting up for centuries, though it remained navigable by small craft until the closure of the cob in 1813. All along the former shoreline are features which testify to the way in which this arm of the sea was both a barrier to, and a means of, transport from the earliest times – the Roman bath-house, possibly a *mansio*, at Tremadoc (SH 5573 4013), the early Christian foundations of St Beuno (SH 5412 4028) and at Llanfrothen (SH 6222 4119). The area's mines of lead and copper are now some way from the sea, but at one time they lay within easy reach of at least a boat if not a sea-going ship. Whereas Malltraeth was the work of a group of local landowners and other worthies, Traeth Mawr was the vision of one man, William Alexander Madocks, owner of the Tan yr Allt estate. Madocks had built earlier, lower embankments around Tremadoc, and some of his neighbouring landowners had clearly done the same a little before – at any rate, a plaque in Llanfrothen church pointedly claims that Williams of Plas Brondanw 'was the first to introduce sea-banks into Wales'. The Traeth Mawr embankment, however, is a much more substantial work. Despite being very slightly shorter than Malltraeth at 1.55km/0.959miles, and without the benefit of either the landed wealth or engineering talent associated with Malltraeth, it is a more consciously engineered structure, with prominent quarries at each end. It drains a smaller area.†

Construction methods at both places were broadly similar. Stones and other fill were dropped through a wooden staging to form the embankment, from barrows at Malltraeth, by a railway system at the Traeth Mawr.‡ Time-worn boats were filled with stone and sunk in the breach at the Traeth Mawr; local tradition speaks of the same happening at Malltraeth.

The Traeth Mawr cob was completed in 1813, but went through several phases of development and rebuilding. Originally, the road ran along its top, but was displaced by the Festiniog Railway in 1832-6, and a new, lower-level cob was built on the landward side in 1834. The original sluice bridge was complete in 1809-10 but the sluices were replaced by new ones designed by Jesse Hartley, the Liverpool dock engineer (SH 5708 3848).§ The sockets in the masonry for the timbers survive. By this time, the Afon

---

* Beazley E., *Madocks and the Wonder of Wales* (Aberystwyth: P&Q, 1985).
† Precisely how much area the cob recovered is uncertain, because the extent of previous silting and of earlier embankment construction is unknown. The total area of the Glaslyn estuary upstream of the cob is approximately 2,000 hectares (4,942 acres).
‡ Oddly, the Traeth Mawr cob used a plateway at the Caernarvonshire end, and an edge-railroad of Penrhyn quarry-style oval-section cast-iron rails at the Merionethshire end. LlRO: WDAK/2 (entry for 25 November 1811) confirms that the Malltraeth commissioners required 200 barrow-bodies, as well as deal planks and baulks, scantlings and poles to complete the work – there is no mention of rails.
§ GAT, *Historic Landscape Characterisation: Vale of Ffestiniog* (Report 422, 2003), p. 46.

Glaslyn had fortuitously scoured out a harbour nearby, which had already evolved into a busy ship-building and slate-exporting port. A new embankment was built on the landward side of the sluice bridge in 1851, in the hope of forming an inner harbour and the sluices were removed to a new position in this embankment. The present sluices consist of five steel balanced gates pivoted on a horizontal axis.*

A curious feature associated with the inner harbour, though older than it, is the channel which runs from here towards Tremadoc for a distance of 1.14km (0.707 miles) known as *y cyt* ('the cut', an English dialect word for a canal). It is now much overgrown and it is hard to see it as anything other than a drainage ditch, yet an early map shows it extending half as long again into Tremadoc itself, past a shallow iron-ore digging at Pen Syflog and in the direction of the Llidiart Yspytty ironstone mine. Persistent claims have been made that it carried goods, and that from 1807 it terminated in a part-functional, part-ornamental 'bason'.† A building near here in private hands known as 'the granary' certainly bears a resemblance to known types of canal warehouse (SH 5609 4011).

Though Gwynedd's long navigable rivers were important transport arteries, canals were few and short, and the region's share of the 6,500km or so of canal built in England and Wales is microscopic. A channel which runs from Ty Gwyn y Gamlas to Harlech (SH 5997 3549 – 5824 3148) has been suggested as a Medieval canal on the analogy of Rhuddlan in north-east Wales, where King Edward I's workmen certainly did construct a canal between 1277 and 1280. This is unlikely. Unless the Tremadoc *cyt* is accepted, the only evident canals in Gwynedd are the Cemlyn canal at Maentwrog and the Dolgarrog canal.

The first of these, also known locally as *y cyt*, is a diversion of a natural stream flowing into the Dwyryd near its tidal head, carried out in two stages before 1823, 114m in length to serve a general-purpose wharf, part of the busy river traffic which prevailed here from the mid-18th century for about a hundred years (SH 6602 4020 – 6630 4028).‡ The other was built in 1913-14 to allow barges and steam lighters to reach the aluminium works at Dolgarrog from the Conwy river, and is 638m long (SH 7753 6805 – 7710 6765). It saw use into the late 1920s at least, and is still evident, though much overgrown.§

4.5.5 Telegraphy and wireless

Several significant long-distance communications systems functioned in Gwynedd, including mechanical and visual systems, electric telegraphy and radio communications.

Gwynedd's strategic location on the western periphery of Britain and on the sea-lanes to Liverpool led to the construction of a number of important communications systems, just as it caused the building of major transport links such as the Holyhead road and the Chester to Holyhead railway.

---

* National Rivers Authority report, reproduced in (Festiniog Railway) *Heritage Group Journal* 29 (Spring 1992), pp. 13-16.
† Boyd, J.I.C., *Narrow Gauge Railways in South Caernarvonshire 1* (Oxford: Oakwood Press, 1988), pp. 8-9; Beazley, *op. cit.*, pp. 122-3.
‡ Lewis, M.J.T., *Sails on the Dwyryd* (Penrhyndeudraeth: Snowdonia National Park, 1989), pp. 26-36.
§ Jones, E. and Gwyn, D., *Dolgarrog: An Industrial History* (Caernarfon: Gwynedd Archives Service, 1989), pp. 50-2, 129.

The first of these was the 'visual telegraph', a relay of semaphore stations between Holyhead Mountain and Liverpool built by the Mersey Docks and Harbour Board as a one-mast, three-arm system in 1827, and upgraded to a two-mast, four-arm system in 1841. As originally built, there were 11 stations, of which five lay in Gwynedd – Holyhead (SH 2172 8340), Llanfaethlu (SH 3077 8800), Llaneilian (SH 4783 9219), Puffin Island (SH 6545 8235) and the Great Orme (SH 7668 8336 – Figure 100). In 1839 the station at Llanfaethlu was abandoned in favour of a new one at Cefn Du (SH 3250 8982), 2.5km to the north-east. The distances between them varied from 20.2km (12.5 miles) to 10.1km (6.3 miles). Messages were sent by raising or lowering the semaphore arms in an agreed code, which would be picked up by a staff member looking through a telescope at the next station; he or she would relay the message to a colleague who would operate the levers which would move his or her own semaphores. The system could not operate at night or in fog and, as it ran west to east, was often ineffective at sunrise and sunset when the semaphores would be in line with the sun. A message is said to have been sent along its length in 23 seconds on one occasion.

100 An archive sketch of the visual telegraph station on the Great Orme in 1857 (courtesy Conwy Archive Service: XS/2224/78/28).

The stations typically consisted of a dwelling, square-plan with a central chimney set in a hipped roof, and a signal room. These might be integral with each other or separate. For the most part, the signal room had a semi-circular window in the gable which sighted on the two nearest stations. The ruins of the Llanfaethlu station show a more primitive arrangement, with a two-unit dwelling and an outshot structure to house the signal levers.

The visual telegraph followed several earlier systems designed to alert harbours of shipping movements, including a system installed by the Royal Navy to alert Liverpool of possible enemy attack in 1804, which extended as far as Llaneilian on Anglesey. Each station consisted of a hut and a flagstaff with a diagonal yard-arm. In 1810 one Evans erected a system on Holyhead Mountain to warn the mail coach that the packet was on its way, which may have had three masts and seems to have been a private venture. Faint above-ground traces are visible adjacent to the 1827 signal station.

Each of these systems reflects the evolution of visual communication systems in the 18th century. By 1807 Paris was connected to Brest, Strasbourg, Brussels and Lyon by visual telegraph, and in 1795 the Royal Navy resolved to construct an optical telegraph system using a chain of 13 intermediate signalling stations between the Admiralty in Whitehall and the naval bases at Portsmouth and (from 1806) to Plymouth. The first system depended on the reading of coded messages based on the varying positions of shutters in a frame but between 1816 and 1822 a semaphore which anticipated the

Holyhead system was substituted. It was superseded by the electric telegraph in 1847, but the Liverpool to Holyhead system operated until 1861, the last major example of such a system in use. In the meantime, the semaphore signal principle had found a new use, controlling the movements of trains.*

The electric telegraph was widely adopted in Gwynedd though the region cannot claim any particular novelty in this regard. The first commercial system was Charles Wheatstone and William Cook's system installed on the Great Western Railway between Paddington and West Drayton in 1838. It was rapidly and extensively adopted throughout the United Kingdom and the USA. It is not clear when the first cable was laid between Britain and Ireland, though presumably it formed part of the first attempt to lay the transatlantic cable in 1857. From Killarney the cable was carried on the British Post Office inland network, whence three submarine cables were laid across the Irish sea. Two came ashore in Gwynedd, one at Porth Abergeirch on Penrhyn Llŷn, the other at Porth Trecastell (Cable Bay) in Anglesey, leading to relay stations at Nefyn and Llanfair Pwllgwyngyll respectively.

It is in the field of wireless technology that Gwynedd plays an important role both in terms of development and in terms of archaeological survival. Sir William Henry Preece of Caernarfon (1834-1913) originated his own wireless system in 1892, but his most important contribution in this field was persuading the Post Office to sponsor the experiments of Guglielmo Marconi (1874-1937). Much of Marconi's work on radio transmission was done in Wales. He proved that the curvature of the earth was not an obstacle for wireless telegraphy over great distances. On 21 May 1901, Marconi's post at 66 Queen's Park, Holyhead picked up the first ever ship-to-shore radio message from the Atlantic, from the SS *Lake Chaplain*, the first ship equipped with wireless, travelling from Liverpool to Nova Scotia, and later that year Marconi transmitted the first wireless signal in Morse code to cross the Atlantic, from Poldhu in Cornwall.

In 1914 Marconi opened a substantial wireless transmitting station at Waunfawr (SH 5330 6076), in use until 1939, when it was superseded by Marconi Co. short-wave services, as well as a receiving station at Tywyn, which closed in 1923. Little remains at Tywyn beyond 'Marconi Bungalows' at SH 5950 0019, but the buildings at Waunfawr survive little altered, now in use as an indoor climbing centre. As

101 The Marconi station at Waunfawr.

well as the main complex, the sites of the masts are evident (Figure 101).

The archaeology of visual telegraphy and wireless communication is particularly well represented in Gwynedd, though the Waunfawr station deserves a higher profile. The early 20th century in particular is a period when technical developments in this field need to be considered in an international context, including Marconi's stations

---

* For the history and archaeology of the Liverpool to Holyhead telegraph, see Large, F., *Faster than the Wind* (Avid Publications, 1998). See also Wilson, G., *The Old Telegraphs* (Chichester: Phillimore, 1976).

in Cornwall, Ireland and New Jersey, as well as other early wireless sites. This was a system which evolved into one of the defining technologies of the second phase of the industrial revolution as iron, coal and textiles had defined its first phase.*

4.6 Settlement

4.6.1 Housing

Industrialisation led to changes in the way people were housed in Gwynedd, but little is known of the origins of the dominant housing styles and their relationship to each other. This chapter discusses the validity of accepted categories of 'vernacular' and 'industrial' housing, and suggests that the two have much in common.

Earlier chapters have described the houses erected for workers in particular industries. Some of these make no attempt to acknowledge a regional idiom, for instance the railwaymen's houses at Bangor (p. 163) or the neo-Alpine foresters' chalets erected in several locations (p. 114). Others, such as slate quarrymen's barracks (pp. 67-8), are little different from other forms of workers' housing in Gwynedd. This chapter examines the mass of low-status housing in the area. It is an extensive resource; at the beginning of the 21st century the majority of people living in the region inhabit houses built between 1800 and 1900 – from when, in other words, the classic industrial revolution moved into its stride – whatever the type of settlement (see pp. 212-21). Analysis of house-type and of the relationship between different types has the potential to explain much about the regional dimension of industrialisation.

Two types of house predominate. One appears firmly in the 'vernacular' or 'cottage' tradition, typically single-storey or half-lofted, direct-entry and double-fronted, stone-built, with gabled end walls and a chimney in one or both gables (Figure 102). Often these are free-standing, sometimes they are built as rows or short terraces. Houses such as these are found as barracks in slate quarries, and as the homes of small-holders, of farm labourers and of quarrymen; they are even, sometimes, to be found in towns, on back-streets where the pressure to rebuild in a more recognisable late-Victorian form was forgotten or ignored. Often they are built roughly of whatever material lay to hand, though sometimes the use of squared stone, the detail of the joinery and perhaps a self-conscious architectural touch suggest the involvement of an estate manager and his workmen rather than a jobbing mason or self-build. They are very similar in many ways to other vernacular houses found all over Wales, in parts of England, Ireland and in Scotland.† Buildings of this type, such as the 'Anglesey barracks' at the Dinorwic slate quarries (SH 5895 6022 SAM), or Cae'r Gors in Rhosgadfan on the Moel Tryfan commons (SH 5065 5733), the childhood home of the novelist Kate Roberts, retain a capacity to humble in their evocation of the frugal, hard-working yet intensely literate culture which brought them into being. These were the dwellings of a people 'in league with the stones of the field', using simple proportions with a fine

---

* For a useful summary, see Williams, H., *Marconi and his wireless stations in Wales* (Llanrwst: Gwasg Carreg Gwalch, 1999).

† Aalen, F.H.A., Whelan, K. and Stout, M., *Atlas of the Irish Rural Landscape* (Cork: Cork University Press, 1997), pp. 146-7.

102 The classic vernacular cottage – Ty'n Llwyn near Rhosgadfan.

restraint to blend with their *locale* of rock, thatch, mud and slate, and it is not surprising that the strongest tradition of enquiry into their origins and evolution has been in terms of 'folk life' (see pp. 21-2).*

By contrast, the other common type, the uniform terrace which dominates the new industrial villages and towns of Gwynedd, regional variations on the two-up-and-two-down of Lancashire, are damned for precisely the opposite reason – for their environmental insensitivity. In 1953 Tom Rolt considered that the terraces which made up the slate quarry village of Abergynolwyn (Figure 103), built nearly ninety years earlier, were:

> ... as dark, as dour and as incapable of concession to their surroundings as those which were terracing the valleys of the Rhondda and the Ebbw ... it looks as though a section has been arbitrarily chopped out of a mean street in an industrial city and transplanted in the abortive hope that it might take root and grow.†

103 An industrial village – Abergynolwyn.

---

* The classic text is Iorwerth Peate's *The Welsh House*, published in 1940 and reprinted in 2004; see also Lord, P., 'The Genius Loci Insulted', *Gwenllian* (Llandysyl: Gomer, 1994), pp. 141-2.
† Rolt, L.T.C., *Railway Adventure* (London: Constable, 1953), p. 18.

For Rolt, and for many others, regionally distinctive vernacular architecture had evidently been under threat from this sort of housing for many years; by extension, the suburban developments of the late 19th and 20th centuries, and the social housing of the 20th, might be thought only to represent the later stages of a process that had begun in the mid-Victorian period.

It is axiomatic that all over Britain the arrival of mass transport in the 19th century spelt the end for 'vernacular' architecture, and its replacement by standardised 'industrial' housing; yet within any landscape undergoing rapid social and economic change, the relationship between different modes of building will be fluid, and the changes and continuities which they reveal, a rich source of evidence. Terraced houses in Gwynedd take as many different forms as cottages, some of them are as distinct to particular localities, and they are to be found in as wide a variety of locations. For this reason, it is worth not only tracing these different building types but also examining the validity of those well-worn categories, the 'vernacular' and the 'industrial'.

The results of such an inquiry can only be provisional for the simple reason that serious archaeological study of post-1700 low-status dwellings in Gwynedd has been very limited indeed. Hitherto, typologies have been established from documentary sources rather than examination of the material evidence, with the result that houses are often assumed to be much older than they necessarily are,[*] and existing studies are skewed very firmly towards vernacular buildings, since in practice industrial archaeologists, no less than folk-life enthusiasts, tend to be beguiled by them.[†] Terraced houses, on the other hand, have been little studied for a combination of several reasons – because of a belief (largely unstated) that they are of no interest, or because they are still inhabited or because they have disappeared under a thick layer of concrete or tarmacadam.

However inadequate base-line information may be, there is certainly no lack of specific conceptual models which might inform such a study, and outline its possible scope. In 1985 the Nuffield Foundation funded a study of the Ironbridge Gorge which examines the industrial-vernacular matrix as a major historical source for industrialisation.[‡] A study of the copper-smelting town of Swansea in South Wales is less explicitly theoretical but illustrates effectively the sheer variety of housing during the town's boom years, where, as workers raised cabins on the waste, the great minister-architect William Edwards was not only laying out planned terraces but building blocks of flats, amongst the first since the Roman empire.[§] Other explorations have identified social and economic agents of change in the evolution of housing stock (p. 18).

It is where 'historical archaeology' reigns – in the USA, and to some extent the English-speaking world outside America – that the archaeology of low-status dwellings has been taken seriously, though with the interesting difference that these concentrate

---

[*] Documentary sources such as parish registers will confirm the existence of a house on the site, and all too often this is assumed to be the one which survives.

[†] See for instance, the archives of the Snowdonia National Park Study Centre (Plas Tan y Bwlch) annual 'Practical Industrial Archaeology' course, also the present author's *Cae'r Gors: Archaeological, Historical and Cultural Assessment* (for Cyfeillion Cae'r Gors: Report 41) and 'Landscape, Economy and Identity: A Case Study in the Archaeology of Industrialisation' in Barker, D. and Cranstone, D., *The Archaeology of Industrialization* (Leeds: Maney, 2004), pp. 35-52.

[‡] Alfrey, J. and Clark, C., *The Landscape of Industry: Patterns of Change in the Ironbridge Gorge* (Routledge: London and New York, 1993).

[§] Hughes, S., *Copperopolis* (Aberystwyth: RCAHMW, 2000); Fisk, M.J., *Housing in the Rhondda 1800-1940* (Cardiff: Merton Priory Press, 1996).

more on artefactual evidence and less on the house itself. A few examples must suffice. A major study of Lowell, Massachusetts, the first planned industrial town in the USA, initiated in 1985 by Anne Beaudry and Stephen Mrozowski, identified *inter alia* the 'strategies of resistance' by which workers in a highly paternal organisation evaded company prohibitions on alcohol and public smoking through the evidence of finds – hidden bottle caches, for instance, and the many pipe stems that were excavated. The variety and context of artefacts recovered in the 1991 dig at New York's Five Points district suggested that this notorious area was far more prosperous and far more 'respectable' than either contemporaries or posterity would allow, in a rapidly-changing and multi-ethnic environment, nevertheless still far removed from the timeless world of Wales cherished by students of folk-life.*

This point is worth stressing, because Gwynedd had its own 'Five Points'. Very little survives (*eg* Glanrafon – SH 5792 7205) of the notorious and insanitary terraces erected in Bangor in the 1840s to house not only the city's own poor, a class largely dependent on ecclesiastical charity, but also a transient population caught between the expanding textile-processing and coal-producing economies of Lancashire and the collapsing agricultural economy of Ireland.† They have the same claim to be regarded as 'industrial' archaeology, and their inhabitants to the respect of posterity, as the cottages of Calvinist quarrymen. The homes of the fortunate and the prosperous also deserve attention; industrial undertakings built houses for foremen and other 'key workers' alongside those of the less skilled, but industrial economies also required the work of a service bourgeoisie of teachers, clergy, surveyors and lawyers. Or what, for instance, of Garth Terrace in Porthmadog (SH 6583 3829), with its spacious houses and their Italianate decoration, which might have housed local professionals but were in fact the *tai capteiniaid*, the homes of the master mariners who performed the vital role of shipping Ffestiniog slate? These were men skilled in the work of hands, more so even than the locomotive drivers who brought the slates down on the first leg of their long journey, but unlike the engine-men they were also minor capitalists. The distinctions between 'workers' housing' and 'middle-class housing' may not hold up well in Gwynedd.

With these reservations in mind, let us attempt to trace the changes which took place within our time-frame in the houses and interiors of Gwynedd, particularly those which were inhabited by the men and women who lived at the sharp end of social, economic and technical change. The story is a complicated one, and it is wise to postpone discussion of social infrastructure and spatial morphology until later sections (see *4.6.2*, pp. 195-210 and *4.6.4*, pp. 212-21).

Clearly, workers' housing existed in Gwynedd long before 1700. The region's urban settlements were small and unsuccessful, but undoubtedly included alongside the town houses of merchants and professionals, the dwellings and *ateliers* of craftsmen and the homes of labourers. Yet we know practically nothing of them; Lewis Morris' 1720s perspective drawing of Aberffraw, the settlement on Anglesey which had grown up

---

* Mayne, A. and Murray, T. (eds), *The Archaeology of Urban Landscapes: Explorations in Slumland* (Cambridge: Cambridge University Press, 2001) includes studies from the USA, from England (Sheffield) and from Canada, South Africa and Australia.

† The 1851 census identifies one tiny house, in Robert Street, as occupied by no fewer than 26 lodgers, mostly Irish, whose occupations include beggar, hawker and chimney sweep. See Jones, P.E., 'The Bangor Local Board of Health, 1850-83', *TCHS* 37 (1976), pp. 87-132.

on the site of a court of the princes of Gwynedd, identifies by name only the houses of the clergy, a wealthy farmer's house and the pubs, though it is quite possible that some of the smaller dwellings he shows, typically double-fronted and single-storey, would have housed landless craftsmen and workers.* The few smaller farmhouses and the even fewer cottages that do survive in Gwynedd from the 18th century appear to preserve and adapt the basic proportions and organisation of the regional sub-Medieval farm-house (see p. 106).

Sadly, the earliest examples of landlord-built cottages for industrial workers have probably all vanished. In 1810 the Rev. Walter Davies 'Gwallter Mechain' (1761-1849), a particularly well-informed and conscientious individual who was responsible for carrying out the Board of Agriculture's reports for Wales, within Gwynedd identified only Lord Penrhyn as having constructed cottages for either agricultural or industrial workers. Between 1790 and 1800 his lordship had built 40 cottages 'containing 63 dwellings, many of them having double apartments ... The architect, giving full scope to fancy, has studiously varied the plan of each cottage.'† Their precise location is unclear but they may have been built in the vicinity of Ogwen Bank (SH 6259 6553), the bijou cottage built to accommodate the family on trips up the valley, and Pen isa'r Nant, the estate's ornamental dairy farm (p. 101). It is not clear whether any survive.‡ Nevertheless, the words 'architect' and 'plan' suggest that, whatever form these took, they were radically different from whatever homes labourers were building for themselves.

We know a little more about the copper mining and smelting area of Mynydd Parys and Amlwch on Anglesey. The earliest surviving houses from the boom period of 1768 to 1800 are five examples from a number built along the eastern perimeter of the harbour at Porth Amlwch (Figure 104). These derive from the farmhouse plan – one is a substantial double-fronted two-storey dwelling, the others, at least in their original form, single-fronted and two storeys in height, built to unusual box-like proportions. Some of these may be shown on a map of 1780, others perhaps date from 1783.§ Less than 1km away, in Amlwch itself, another architectural idiom prevailed; from the 1760s onwards miners settled around the parish church of St Eleth (SH 4423 9295) and the adjacent bishop's court, now

104 A survivor from the 1780s – one of a former row at Porth Amlwch.

---

* Wiliam, D.W. (ed.), *Braslunian Lewis Morris o Eglwysi, Tai a Phentrefi ym Môn* (privately published, 1999).

† Davies, W., *General View of the Agriculture and Domestic Economy of North Wales* (London: Richard Phillips, 1810), pp. 84-5. Davies' work was begun before the end of the 18th century – see Thomas, D., *Agriculture in Wales During the Napoleonic War* (Cardiff: University of Wales Press, 1963), pp. 34, 157.

‡ It is possible that they were spread out along Lord Penrhyn's road from Bangor to the quarry and to Capel Curig, between Ogwen Bank (SH 6259 6552) and Hen Durnpike (SH 6102 6763), part of which has been covered by the workings of Penrhyn quarry. This would make sense in that it would advertise his Lordship's social concern for any visitors making their way to Ogwen Bank. CRO: X/Plans/RD/2 (a road map of 1817) shows cottages here. UWB: Penrhyn Maps 202 (a highly stylised plan of an intended canal to Penrhyn quarry, 1799) shows dwellings which probably correspond with these near the route of the proposed canal; they are typically double-fronted with a single chimney above the central front door. It is possible that one of these survives, much altered, at SH 6104 6755.

§ UWB: Llwydiarth Esgob 638 (map of 1780) and 27-50 (building leases). An archive photograph in Hope, B.D., *A Commodious Yard: The Story of William Thomas & Sons Shipbuilders of Amlwch 1858-1920* (Wrexham: Bridge Books, 2005), p. 198, when more were standing, shows that there was little attempt to achieve a uniform style.

demolished, along an existing pattern of lanes which still forms the outline of the settlement. Surviving houses are probably much later in date than this, since parish records for 1780 confirm that new houses were typically made up of two rooms, with no upper storey, mainly thatched, and that they measured no more than 3.6m by 4.5m (12ft by 15ft) – not only very small indeed but unusually proportioned, if the records are accurate.* A plan of the Parys copper mines dated 1786 shows single- and double-fronted single-storey cottages, built both singly and as short terraces.†

105 An industrial vernacular? – a row of c.1830 at Drws y Coed copper mine.

The cottages which survive at the Drws y Coed copper mine (Figure 105 – SH 542 534 and SH 546 536), where migrant workers from Parys were accommodated from around 1830, may perpetuate the double-fronted Parys type. Here, the two terraces, one of three dwellings, one of five, and the detached cottages, each represent the same basic plan of a single door in the long wall and two rooms.‡

This design is reproduced in several ways. Though none of the single-roomed dwellings on Mynydd Parys survives, a few remain elsewhere – for instance in the village of Tal y Sarn at SH 4926 5317, where it is as if one of the Drws y Coed cottages has simply had one room removed. More commonly, the design is elaborated rather than simplified. Most of the surviving cottages within this tradition have a *croglofft* ('hanging loft'), whereby a first floor is inserted into the smaller of the two rooms to provide extra sleeping space. This type is commonly met both in an industrial and a rural context, not only in Gwynedd but elsewhere in Wales, particularly in the west. The date of their introduction is hard to determine, since the limited archaeological excavation that has been carried out on these dwellings suggests that a surviving *croglofft* may well have gone though several phases of adaptation in the course of the 19th century – Cae'r Gors in Rhosgadfan is the most famous of such dwellings, but by the time the future novelist Kate Roberts went to live there in 1895 the original single-cell house of 1827 had had a loft added, and a catslide extension put on.§ An example on Penrhyn Llŷn incorporates a date-stone of 1812, and it is unlikely on present evidence that many are much earlier than this.¶

The *crog-lofft* becomes one of the most easily recognisable and widespread variant of the cottage house-type in the emerging industrial economy of Gwynedd. In 1857 the short-lived Bangor and Portmadoc Slate and Slab Company Ltd constructed 36 *crog-lofftydd* in rows each with a nominal quarter-acre of land, along three parallel roadways on the slopes of Cwm Ystradllyn (SH 5612 4542) – all had been abandoned

---

* Rowlands, J., *Copper Mountain* (Llangefni: Anglesey Antiquarian Society, 1981), pp. 131-4.
† UWB: Bangor mss 31603, copy of a plan dated 1786 (original in Liverpool University).
‡ Lowe, J., *Welsh Industrial Workers Housing 1775-1875* (Cardiff, 1989) p. 11, CRO: Vaynol papers 6871.
§ Gwyn, D., *Cae'r Gors: Archaeological, Historical and Cultural Assessment*.
¶ Judith Alfrey, pers. comm.

by 1871.* Some examples were either adapted to form a full loft or were built that way, effectively giving the dwelling the same number of rooms and the same degree of privacy as a standard two-up-two-down, though preserving the vernacular proportions. An example is the terrace 'Pen yr Incline' in Cwm Penmachno, probably built in the late 1850s (SH 7539 4728).† Around 1862 the basic *crog-lofft* design was used by the Penrhyn estate on Mynydd Llandygái (SH 600 654), each with a narrow plot of land.‡ The uniform design and detailing, and the standard of workmanship, strongly suggest that these houses were constructed by estate employees rather than the tenants (see pp. 216-17).§

106 *Cottage ornée* – an estate-built dwelling near Trefriw.

107 *Cottage ornée* – 'R uncorn' ('one-chimney') in Blaenau Ffestiniog, built in 1825.

Estate-built dwellings such as Mynydd Llandygái often incorporate elements that could not be resourced locally, such as some use of brick, as well as stone. As we have seen (p. 107), some estates went further and built cottages with 'neo-vernacular' details that are meant to suggest a fairy-tale rather than an architect's office – some of those on the Gwydir estate have round-plan chimneys with ornamental capping, and protruding 'oven-chimneys' in the gable (Figure 106 – SH 7894 6100).¶ The *cottage ornée* even appears in Blaenau Ffestiniog, where there survives a central chimney dwelling with a pyramidal roof, clearly intended for four quarry families each to inhabit a corner. This was built in 1825 on behalf of Lord Newborough by John Hughes, whom we have encountered on p. 102. The style derives ultimately from a Renaissance

---

* These were described as 'a sort of Johannesburg for the quarrymen' – evidently a shorthand for a wild and lawless community. See Williams, R., *Cofiant a Phregethau y diweddar Barch. Griffith Roberts, Carneddi* (Caernarfon: Cwmni'r Wasg Genedlaethol Gymreig, 1896), p. 16, and 1871 census.
† Date based on 1861 census and CRO: X/Plans/R/21.
‡ Lowe, *op. cit.*, p. 62.
§ Lowe, J., *op. cit.*, pp. 62-3; Roberts, J. ('Pedr'), *Traethodau ar Waen Gynfi* (Ebenezer: W.R. Hughes, 1869), p. 7. Lowe identifies these as the houses let out on a notorious system of leasing which specified that the quarrymen were to build the houses themselves but that the leases were to revert to the Penrhyn estate after 30 years, a state of affairs which David Lloyd George exploited to the full in his attacks on Gwynedd's landed establishment. It is hard to see that these were anything other than estate-built. Were the quarrymen required to pay for, though not themselves to build, a house of estate pattern, alongside their other burdens?
¶ Alfrey, J., 'Rural Building in Nineteenth-Century North Wales: The Role of the Great Estates', *Archaeologia Cambrensis* 147 (2001 for 1998), plate 16 and p. 25.

gentry pattern, and was used elsewhere on the estate and on its periphery (Figure 107 – SH 4511 5588).*

The earliest purpose-built workers' terraces to survive are those constructed by William Madocks as he set about draining the Traeth Mawr. Madocks' aim was not merely to complete the enclosure of the land vested in him by parliament but to create a sophisticated urban community, which he hoped would, in the fullness of time, serve as a staging-post on a highway from London to the proposed packet port for Dublin at Porth Dinllaen. Many, perhaps most, of the dwellings he built survive and, typically of Madocks, they are to a variety of different designs. At the south-eastern end of the cob, he built a regency-style two-storey barrack block (SH 5848 3791), now part of the Festiniog Railway's works, and at the north-western end a terrace of small houses, though again two-storey, with distinctive round-headed windows which are believed to date from 1809 (SH 5722 3849).† Tremadoc itself is built around a square dominated by its Italianate town hall-theatre and enclosed by architecturally unified double-fronted town-houses. On the edges of this town he built several terraces – again, all of them different. Contiguous with the town hall but along London Street are a few houses which follow the distinctive Irish fashion of having the front door at first-floor level, reached by steps, above a road-level basement.‡ Along Dublin Street is a terrace of single-fronted one-and-a-half-storey houses where the dormers have distinctive catslide pediments, a pattern found on some Merioneth farmhouses (Figure 108). A little beyond the town is a terrace of one-up, one-down houses erected for workers in his textile mill, probably around 1807.

108 Dublin Street, Tremadoc.

If these are indeed the earliest terraces in the area, they made their appearance significantly later than in other industrialising parts of the United Kingdom – architecturally unified workers' terraces are recorded in the Ironbridge Gorge from the 1780s and in Tameside from 1790§ – yet it was to be many years before Madocks' innovations found a parallel within the area. Typically, nucleated industrial settlements in Gwynedd begin with individually-constructed dwellings which abut on to each other. An example survives at Deiniolen where houses of different sizes and shapes are jumbled along the side of the road built in 1811 to cart slate

---

* Smith, P., *Houses of the Welsh Countryside*, pp. 228-9.
† The late Rev. Stephen Twycross, pers. comm.
‡ Others are to be found at Gaerwen on Telford's post road.
§ Alfrey, J. and Clark, C., *op. cit.*, p. 184; Nevell, M. and Walker, J., *Tameside in Transition* (Tameside Metropolitan Borough Council, 1999), p. 13.

from the Dinorwic quarries. Many of these date from comparatively late in the 19th century, but some, despite the pebble-dash liberally smoothed on them in recent years, are visibly the work of the 1820-1830s, built by local contractors. Round the corner from them is Rhes Fawr ('big row' – SH 5792 6308), built between 1832 and 1838, a terrace of 14 two-storey houses, with only one room on each floor.* The builder was David Griffith of Caernarfon who gave his name to the terrace Treddafydd ('David's town') in the quarry village of Pen y Groes – SH 4709 5352), 14.5km away. This dates from 1837-8, and preserves some of the original heavy slates and small window frames (Figure 109).†

These two terraces provide an intriguing, and all too rare, glimpse into the scale of operations of a local speculative builder. The majority of surviving examples date from later – from the expanding economy of the 1860s and 1870s – and are often built under systems of controlled leasing from the landowners, with the result that documentation is more apt to survive. Local materials are generally used even after the national railway system had extended its reach into comparatively rural areas, though brick becomes increasingly common as a structural material. Interestingly, strong local architectural patterns emerge rather than vanish from the mid-19th century. The Tremadoc estate, which included the growing harbour town of Porthmadog, favoured an interpretation of the regency style which Madocks had introduced to the area in the 1790s – it is not clear to what extent this represents the wishes of the estate or the pre-eminence of a local firm of builder-architects. It is characterised by overhanging eaves, and by an often elaborate pattern of drip-mouldings. At Blaenau Ffestiniog distinctive three-storey terraces, often with pointed dormer pediments over round-headed windows, survive in profusion, particularly in the centre of the town, and contrast markedly with the earlier vernacular dwellings on the edges. The three-storey style extends down the valley, and jostles with the Porthmadog style in the villages in between (Figure 110).

109 Treddafydd, Pen y Groes – the industrial row comes to Gwynedd.

Other styles did not catch on. The 'American style' houses in Pen y Groes (Figure 111) may have their parallels in the mid-West, but not elsewhere in Gwynedd. Sir Edmund Buckley's two facing rows at Dinas Mawddwy, built around 1870, blend local stonework with Alpine detail and overhanging roofs to create a village worthy of its mountain setting (SH 8591 1421).‡ More rustic are the dwellings which make up the village of Nantlle, provided by the Unitarian management of Pen yr Orsedd quarry

---

* Lowe, *op. cit.*, p. 44; 'Pedr', *op. cit.*, p. 75.
† UWB: Carter Vincent 2828-9.
‡ Alfrey, *op. cit.*, plate 11, p. 210.

(SH 5100 5337). The same family, the Darbishires, held sway over the stone quarries of Penmaenmawr, where housing begins with the 'New York cottages' of the early 1840s at SH 7161 7627, through the solid ranges of two-up-and-two-down houses to the splendid Arts-and-Crafts-inspired dwellings constructed at the very end of the 19th century on St David's Street (Figure 112 – SH 7152 7614).*

110 Contrasting styles – a Porthmadog-style terrace (nearer the photographer) and a Ffestiniog-style terrace in the village of Penrhyndeudraeth.

Unsurprisingly, the terrace design is far more likely than the cottage to make use of non-local building materials. The use of Welsh roofing slate is near-ubiquitous, but brick, often from around Ruabon in north-east Wales, becomes increasingly common as a walling material, as does pine rather than oak for roof-timbers.

The simultaneous existence of contrasting modes of building over nearly seventy years suggests a complex social and economic dynamic to industrialisation in the area (Figure 113). There seems no reason to doubt that the vernacular cottage represents a smaller version of the typical two-unit end-chimney storeyed farmhouse which became common in Gwynedd in the 16th century, though with a number of important changes. Cottage windows were inserted in a vertical rather than horizontal axis, as had in fact become increasingly common with farmhouses during the 17th century

111 When Pen y Groes people say they live 'in the American style' they are confirming not a taste for manhattans and shark-finned Cadillacs but that they live in this row of houses on County Road.

112 St David's Street, Penmaenmawr – Arts-and-Crafts inspired dwellings.

---

* Davies, I.E., 'A History of the Penmaenmawr Quarries', *TCHS* 35 (1974), p. 40.

113 Contrasting styles – pre-railway cottages built of local materials and late 19th-century town houses built of Ruabon brick in Bala.

but, unlike them, cottages built in the early 19th century did not have a first floor nor even a *croglofft*.* Because there are few pre-19th-century low-status dwellings, it is difficult to trace the line of descent, but the changes are explicable in terms of what is understood of the way traditional building styles evolve, whereby design is based on existing practice rather than written plans, and change is brought about by disassembling existing forms into component parts and re-assembling them in different ways. By this analysis, the one-room dwelling becomes an option within a single mode of practice – as simply one half of a two-unit plan.†

That there are so few low-status dwellings earlier than the first two decades of the 19th century may itself be a form of negative evidence – these years may represent the 'vernacular threshold' when even the comparatively poor might accumulate wealth and capital to build, rent, or commission homes that were going to last. Changes in the archaeological evidence also suggest a more varied dynamic to housing and to the regional economy in this period, even though documentation is not always forthcoming. The archives of estates or industrial undertakings tend to confirm when and where they erected houses, or allowed houses to be built on their behalf, even if details are lacking. However, the activities of those who operated outside this system can often only be gleaned from the material evidence. How many surviving dwellings were ever 'home-made homes' is not clear; even a squatter on the commons might hire a mason to build his home,‡ and a unified row or terrace on a freehold certainly implies a class of professional builder, with the resources available to build to rent. It is telling that cottages should have appeared from the very early 19th century in very different contexts, not only to house industrial workers as well as farm-labourers but also on both estates and on common land, in towns and villages as well as in the countryside. It may also be significant that even early survivors of the type contrast markedly with the ground plans of earlier small dwellings, which are often innocent of any attempt at a right-angle, even when they share the same basic approach to the provision of shelter and privacy. From this early period, cottages in fact share some of the characteristics more normally applied to 'industrial' dwellings and to polite architecture – for instance, a tendency, or need, to build in greater numbers, the habit of building in groups, often rows or terraces, a growing standardisation, and a conscious and recognisable aesthetic.

In Gwynedd, these rural-derived forms predominate in the earliest phases of industrialisation, before standardised industrial housing takes over. This is common

---

* Smith, *op. cit.*, p. 266.
† Discussion in Alfrey and Clark, pp. 175-80.
‡ Wiliam, E., *Home-made Homes: Dwellings of the rural poor in Wales* (Cardiff: National Museum of Wales, 1988), p. 12.

where factories and mines develop in areas with an existing tradition of farming,* and contrasts with the experience of newly-colonised areas, such as the American West or Australia, where contemporary idioms and materials such as galvanised iron and weatherboarding are evident as soon as shafts are sunk and spoil is heaped.

Just as it has been argued that the cottage derives from the medieval hall-house, so it has been suggested that the industrial terrace, as it is found all over the United Kingdom, adopts the proportions of the Hanoverian dwelling.† This holds good for the more standardised housing of the 1860s and 1870s, but as the terrace evolved through its early stages, in Gwynedd at least, it went through many changes and assumed many different forms. That a vernacular building style can underlie a terrace built to house the poorer members of society is demonstrated by the houses on Dublin Street in Tremadoc, with their echoes of older Merioneth farmhouses, and it is arguable that the vernacular process of adaptation of existing models by the subtraction of elements created the single-fronted terraced house from the townhouse model in the first place. The variety this represents is well illustrated in the town of Aberdyfi, near the southern limit of Gwynedd, where Copperhill Street includes not only a series of 18th-century dwellings of this pattern but partially hides an extraordinary survivor, a backyard 19th-century row, now uninhabited, 'Railway Court'. The basic conception is the same, though the 18th-century dwellings are larger and are all individually built, whereas 'Railway Court' is effectively one structure.‡ The two-up-two-down terraced house represents the most effective use of space in a crowded environment, though the option of a double-fronted house remained where resources were greater. What precedents were available to a builder like David Griffith in the 1830s are not at all clear, whether he had also built other types of dwelling, and whether he could have based Treddafydd and Rhes Fawr on what he might have seen had he gone to Liverpool or elsewhere. What is possible to suggest is that the terraces he erected might be the result of a traditional or 'vernacular' process of adaptation even though they exemplify manifestly 'industrial' characteristics.

Whatever the origin of the terrace design as it evolved in Gwynedd, by the late 19th century the basic conception was increasingly following national (British) models even when distinct regional or local signatures remained evident. The 20th century largely eroded these altogether, with the result that it becomes difficult to speak of any distinctively Gwynedd style of building for working people, despite the conscious adoption of faux-vernacular styles for middle-class and elite dwellings by Herbert Luck North and Clough Williams-Ellis.§ Planning regulations specifying the use of slate as a roofing material preserved something of the sense of regional identity in housing constructed from the 1960s though the use of slate blocks as a rustic walling material, commonplace since the 1970s, had no precedent in terms of domestic accommodation.

Several of these housing developments which ignored regional styles in favour of nationally-available models are interesting in themselves. At Dolgarrog, the Aluminium

---

* For instance at Le Creusot in France (see Alfrey and Clark, p. 172), and even under the Soviet five-year plan at Magnitogorsk – see Kotkin, S., *Magnetic Mountain: Stalinism as Civilisation* (University of California Press, 1995).

† Smith, *op. cit.*, pp. 226, 266.

‡ One of the houses on the street bears a plaque reading 'Built By/Anne Owen/Widow/AD/1733' (SH 6138 9603). 'Railway Court' is at SH 6141 9605.

§ Hughes, H. and North, H.L., *The Old Cottages of Snowdonia* (Bangor: Jarvis and Foster, 1908); Haslam, R., *Clough Williams-Ellis* (London: Academy Editions, 1996).

114 Contrasting styles – both in terms of design and ways in which modernisation has been carried out: Bontnewydd.

Corporation constructed rows of semi-detached cottages between 1911 and 1919, then from 1924 to 1926 50 semi-detached houses of a distinctly suburban type were built by the Shropshire-based Abdon Clee Stone Quarry Company who also erected similar houses in Neasden (north London) and Wolverhampton as well as on their doorstep in Ditton Priors.* These were made up of reinforced concrete frames into which concrete blocks were dropped, though, following the onset of 'concrete cancer', the majority of the Dolgarrog examples have had their exterior walls replaced by the expedient of propping up the tile roofs and replacing them with breeze blocks. Several local authorities set about constructing social housing, though the most enterprising policy was the one adopted by the city of Bangor. From 1905 to 1968, 1,612 houses, 64 maisonettes and 219 flats were constructed as part of 24 separate housing schemes. Maesgeirchen, initiated in 1939 (SH 589 718 C), the only one in Gwynedd to make use of the typical pattern of circuses and curving avenues, was the least successful for being remote from the main settlement and because of the failure to create adequate social infrastructure.†

Despite the scale of building over the last hundred years, the region preserves its 19th-century 'signature', with the result that Gwynedd has, in the main, avoided problems such as have befallen Ireland, where patchy but growing prosperity led to the loss of vernacular buildings in favour of strident and inappropriate new-build.‡ However, the management of low-status dwellings has become a controversial subject. As a declining population and industrial collapse lowered house-prices, places that had been mono-cultural and Welsh in speech were transformed into an exotic and novel variety of community – as homes for social service referrals, for people committed to alternative lifestyles, or for weekenders. Similar pressures were experienced in other parts of Britain, though, if nothing else, they ensured the viability of some settlements that might otherwise have simply fallen into ruin. In some cases, second-home-owners, with their greater capital, have sustained, or exaggerated, traditional features

---

* Jones, E. and Gwyn, D., *Dolgarrog: An Industrial History* (Caernarfon: Gwynedd Archives Service, 1989), pp. 84-91, 98-101; Trinder, B., *The Industrial Archaeology of Shropshire* (Chichester: Phillimore, 1996), p. 26.
† Jones, P.E., *Bangor 1883-1983: A Study in Municipal Government* (Cardiff: University of Wales Press, 1986), p. 269.
‡ Aalen, Whelan and Stout, *op. cit.*, pp. 240-3.

in a prettified way that echoed the estates' conscious evocation of the vernacular in the 19th century. Elsewhere, picture windows, flat-roof extensions, and the plastic-framed conservatories that became popular in the 1990s have changed the existing character of buildings.* Conservation professionals, aware of the fragility of the resource, and of the importance particularly of rural dwellings, tried to change mind-sets, conscious that confrontation would be counter-productive. The problem was compounded by a crass County Council policy, which made it possible as late as the 1990s to award grants to cover stone-built houses in pebbledash, thereby at once effacing traditional character and trapping damp within the structure. If the argument was at least set out for buildings in the vernacular tradition, no such pleading has so far been carried out for Gwynedd's industrial terraces – unlike the situation in England at the time of writing (2006), where central government and national heritage organisations set themselves on opposed courses on the issue of what has come to be called 'low-demand housing'.

4.6.2 Social infrastructure and communal buildings

Population-growth, the nucleation of settlement where often there had only been fields or moorland, and the growing intellectual self-confidence and purchasing power of working people in Gwynedd in the industrial period led to significant changes in the organisation of social infrastructure and in the provision of communal buildings.

Social and economic changes from 1700 onwards not only created a need for housing provision as described in *4.6.1.* on a larger scale, and of a different type, than had prevailed hitherto. A fitful but expanding economy and the changing expectations of working people themselves, as well of those who benefited from their labour, also called into being new forms of social infrastructure.

Gwynedd, of course, was not unique in this respect. It is the common experience of all developing societies, a fact which industrial archaeologists have recognised. Some have bravely offered a framework within which to analyse their role within the broader industrial landscape, in which, in one way or another, issues of patronage and sponsorship, resistance and control rise to the surface. Not surprisingly, these have had a muted reception; theoretical musings, in which the names of Marx, Heidegger or Giddens loom large, bewilder all but the most cerebral of archaeologists, a breed temperamentally happier out of the library and looking at the field evidence. Some argue that communal and infrastructural buildings are not the province of the industrial archaeologist at all, an objection that reflects the production/consumption divide which is supposed to distinguish the industrial archaeologist from the post-medievalist. Many practitioners feel uneasy at the move away from the 'functional' interpretation of industrial archaeology towards a social archaeology (see pp. 18-20), and it is undeniable that the shop and the workhouse, still less the chapel and the hospital, are not 'productive' environments in the same sense as a mine or a factory (and should not, on this analysis, form part of the present study). But there are powerful, if so far diffuse, arguments for considering social infrastructure and communal buildings as

---

* Cadw, *Anheddau Bychain Gwledig yng Nghymru/Small Rural Dwellings in Wales* (Cardiff: Cadw, 2003).

part of the industrial landscape – arguments, moreover, that might inform discussion of the broader questions about the purpose and scope of industrial archaeology. In the first place, there is now an argument from custom – enough studies have emphasised its importance that on this basis alone it seems perverse to ignore it. Secondly, the sheer cheek-by-jowl nature of many industrial communities requires it. Not only in Gwynedd, but in much of the developing world, workshop, mine and railway operated in unsalubrious proximity to hovel, truck-shop and meeting-house (see p. 220). Lastly, just as the variety and form of housing are eloquent of the dynamic of industrialisation, so are the ways in which those who participated in this evolving society spent their surplus and their leisure time; so are the ways in which they were sustained when they lost their health or their employment.

Part of the problem of constructing an intellectual framework is that the field evidence appears so entirely familiar and that theory seems both complicated and reductive. This fundamental problem is well illustrated by the way in which places of worship have traditionally been understood. In Wales as a whole, the Anglican (Episcopalian protestant) church is frequently equated with the landed elite and industrialists, and the chapels (Wesleyans, Calvinistic Methodists, Baptists and Congregationalists, as well as some smaller sects) with the workers. Churches of the establishment thereby embody hegemony and control, and dissenting chapels self-determination, like the settlements established by quarrymen on the moors and commons (see pp. 215-16) – or at best the concessions of a governing class prepared to trade the sobriety and steadiness of plebeian dissent for the rejection of patrician religious control. In Gwynedd, the distinctions are more elusive; by Hanoverian times, practically all the major landowners were indeed nominally Anglicans, but there were among them differences in religious allegiance. The Toryism of the Bulkeleys of Baron Hill was so high that they were widely suspected of being Jacobites, and in the 19th century 'Young England' and the Oxford Movement perpetuated High Church and Romanising tendencies. By contrast, some neighbouring families wistfully recalled the Commonwealth, long after zealous Puritanism had declined into comfortable Whiggery. Capel Newydd of 1770 in Llangian on Penrhyn Llŷn (SH 2858 3091), now the oldest functioning chapel in Gwynedd, was sponsored by the principal local landowner – a naval officer and ostensible churchman, though the descendant of Cromwellians and husband of an evangelical Englishwoman from John Bunyan's Bedfordshire.* In the town of Bala, Simon Lloyd, though both an ordained churchman and principal landowner, was sympathetic to the Methodists and gave them every support. Capitalists and industrial managers were by no means exclusively Anglicans. In the 1820s dissenting businessmen found common cause with the Jewish banker Nathan Meyer Rothschild, whose Royal Cambrian Company promoted grandiose schemes for mining throughout the area. Samuel Holland, a major figure in the development of the slate industry at Blaenau Ffestiniog, was a Unitarian, as a generation later were the Darbishire family, who played an important role in the slate and stone industries of the region. Outside the great estate-dominated workings at Penrhyn and Dinorwic, many slate quarries were effectively run as extensions of particular chapels, such as Dorothea in the Nantlle valley, managed by the famous Methodist minister John Jones Tal y Sarn.

---

* Ellison, D.B., *Hammer and Nails: Capt. Timothy Edwards Nanhoron* (Caernarfon: Gwynedd Archives Service, 1997), p. 94.

115 Glanogwen church, Bethesda (courtesy Gwynedd Archives Service: CRO: XS/2406/2).

The last spate of church building in Gwynedd until the 19th century had been before the Reformation, and the diocese of Bangor evidently considered that provision for worship was adequate until industrialisation.* At Amlwch, the medieval church was replaced in 1800 by a neo-Classical building of decidedly Protestant form, itself remodelled by Henry Kennedy, the diocesan architect, in 1867 (SH 4421 9290). Blaenau Ffestiniog was provided with an unpretentious Anglican place of worship in 1842 (SH 6976 4590), but the new churches for the burgeoning industrial settlements which Kennedy turned out from the 1850s to the 1870s were designed to impress, with tall spires and ritualistic internal fittings, in the hope of winning back congregations which had largely turned to the chapels, not by competing with dissent on its own terms but through ceremony and spectacle. Glanogwen in the quarry town of Bethesda (SH 6252 6672), consecrated in 1855 and built at the expense of the Penrhyn family, is a High Church showcase (Figure 115).

Although the 19th century saw new church-building in Gwynedd, it was nothing compared with the proliferation of nonconformist chapels. Long dismissed as a 'hideous box', and a blot on a beautiful landscape, Welsh chapels began to be perceived more sympathetically in the last decades of the 20th century, when they attracted the

---

* For instance, Holyhead, Clynnog and Aberdaron churches and Bangor cathedral were all substantially rebuilt in the late 15th and early 16th centuries. After the reformation, only Llandudwen church was substantially rebuilt, in 1595, though transepts were added to several other churches. St Mary's Dolgellau was built in 1716. See RCAHMW *Caernarvonshire* and RCAHMW: *County of Merioneth* (London: HMSO, 1921) and RCAHMW: *An Inventory of the Ancient Monuments in Anglesey* (1937).

116 Hen Gapel near Blaenau Ffestiniog at the beginning of the 20th century – from *Hanes Ysgolion Sabbothol Blaenau Ffestiniog*.

attention of architectural historians and the archaeological community. Most chapels that survived in use into the late 20th century or which remain is use today have been recorded, either by the RCAHMW or by voluntary groups. They have come to be understood as exuberant, original designs, and as a symbol of the confidence and independence of the ordinary people of Wales in establishing their own social and religious structures. An instinctive reaction that their tremendous number, their huge size and their variety of affiliation is entirely out of keeping with the scale of population is amply borne out by the statistics – by 1905 there were no fewer than 179,500 seats in churches and chapels in Caernarvonshire, for a total population of 127,000 (a provision of 141 per cent); in Merioneth there were 77,500 seats for a population of 49,000 (a provision of 158 per cent).* Though these figures are exceptional even by Welsh standards, they form part of a pattern of growth in radical Protestantism in the western world in the 18th and 19th centuries, a second, post-Enlightenment, reformation. They offer parallels with the expanding towns of England and of north America, as the confessional state evolved into an alternative social model that recognised diversity and individual conscience, and contrast markedly with the experience of industrial communities of Central Europe and the Urals, where churches might be many, but tended to serve different ethnic groups rather than different confessions, and where state-sponsored faith lost little of its grip until the upheavals of the 20th century.

In Gwynedd, as in Wales as a whole, though protestant dissent assumed various names and forms, its architectural style differed little from connection to connection but did evolve markedly over the years. Only a handful of 18th-century chapels survive. Both Capel Newydd in Llangian and Hen Gapel ('old chapel' – SH 7115 4260 – Figure 116) of 1785 in the parish of Ffestiniog, now a private house, are unpretentious buildings which made a virtue of their own plainness, the former very similar to a

---

* In Wales as a whole the provision was 74 per cent. Roberts, D., 'Y Deryn Nos a'i Deithiau', *Cof Cenedl* 3 (1988), p. 165.

barn, the second very similar to a cottage dwelling. The first architecturally self-conscious chapel in Wales is Peniel in Tremadoc (SH 5624 3989 – Figure 117), completed in 1810, based on Inigo Jones' classical Covent Garden chapel of 1638. Peniel also included innovations such as a raked floor so that the congregation could see the preacher better. It stands nearly opposite the undistinguished Anglican church consecrated in 1806 (SH 5623 4004), which does have the claim to fame of being the first Gothic revival church in Wales.

117 Capel Peniel, Tremadoc.

Both church and chapel at Tremadoc were built under the sponsorship of William Alexander Madocks, owner of the Tremadoc estate, and though Peniel was eventually to become the type for the great majority of Welsh chapels, it was to be many years before the basic plan – a façade facing the street, an ornamented front and plain side walls – became standard. As towns grew in the 19th century, such a building could fit conveniently into a burgage- or building-plot, and enabled the maximum impact at street level with the minimum cost. There were variations. The long-wall façade type took up more space along the street but less depth; here the pulpit was typically placed against an interior long wall rather than in the gable facing the entrance. Bozrah, in the copper miners' village of Pen Sarn on Anglesey (SH 4599 9039), is built on a square plan, perhaps following the Revelation of St John, 'The City of the Lord shall lie Four-square, and the breadth shall be no greater than the width'.

As the various denominations grew in self-confidence, the architecturally 'learned' chapel became the norm rather than the exception, with both individuals and firms based both within the region and within the Welsh diaspora of Liverpool competing for contracts to design and build these structures. Surviving chapels for the most part date from between 1860 and 1900, and are often third- or fourth-generation structures, a fact which is frequently announced on a tablet set into the gable, along with the chapel's name. The design of Welsh chapels in general offers a remarkably close parallel with those of Cornwall, despite the fact that there is practically no evidence for architects or builders from Wales working in Cornwall nor vice versa. Cornish mine managers may have influenced the design of the small side-entry English Wesleyan chapel at Amlwch (SH 4435 9305), a plain building of 1831, with pointed gothick windows, part of a diaspora of Cornish industrial chapels which extends to the highlands of Mexico and to Southern Australia.* It is likely that circulation of *The Builder* and *The Evangelical Magazine* made it possible to draw on patterns of Protestant architecture that had been established in Scotland and Ireland over many years, though much work

---

*   The prolific minister-architect Thomas Thomas of Glandore, Swansea, who designed many hundreds of Welsh chapels, including a considerable number in Gwynedd, also contracted for chapels in England though not in Cornwall. See Jones, A., *Welsh Chapels* (Stroud: Alan Sutton, 1996), pp. 91-5 and Lake, J., Cox J. and Berry, E., *Diversity and Vitality: The Methodist and Nonconformist Chapels of Cornwall* (Cornwall Archaeological Unit, Truro, 2001).

remains to be done.* In any event, Gwynedd chapels are remarkably eclectic. Classical or Romanesque styles were favoured over high-church Gothic, though architects, builders and congregations were much less constrained by prevailing canons of correctness than church architects. The brick-built Bethania in Bethesda is 'Swansea Lombardic' (SH 6199 6697); Siloam in Bontnewydd has something of a German church about it (SH 4831 5994); Peniel chapel (SH 4519 9312) in Porth Amlwch, built in 1898-1900 to the design of the architect Richard Davies of Bangor on the site of an earlier chapel of 1850, is an exercise in 'Arts and Crafts' classical (Figure 118). Many chapels constitute a religious complex in their own right, with a schoolroom, a vestry, a caretaker's house, sometimes even stabling, within the precinct. Interiors are lavish, making extensive use of decorated plasterwork, encaustic tiles and pitch-pine fixtures, focusing on a lofty pulpit, dominating a communion table and a deacons' bench, known in Welsh as the *sêt fawr* ('great seat'). The plain internal arrangements of early dissent nowhere survive.†

118 Peniel, Porth Amlwch.

Places of worship for non-Protestant Christian denominations are extremely rare, and mosques and synagogues effectively unknown.‡ There was no influx of Irish labour into extractive industries in Gwynedd, unlike the coal-fields of south Wales and of Lancashire, and none of the multi-ethnic mix of Cardiff or Swansea. Holyhead alone had a resident Catholic community of any size, though as we have seen (p. 185) Bangor played host to many Irish men, women and children as they tramped between home and the north of England. All the same, Catholicism re-established itself even in such Protestant communities as Blaenau Ffestiniog in the 20th century, and a workers' church was established nearby at Gellilydan (SH 6867 3989) for Irishmen building the Trawsfynydd nuclear power station (p. 144). Perhaps because of the low level of Irish-born population, and despite the vehement anti-Catholicism of Gwynedd in the 1820s, the area never acquired Orange Lodges or Brunswick clubs.§

As well as places of worship, graveyards represent an important form of social evidence, one which has seen comparatively little analysis. These are frequently associated with a parish church, less commonly with a chapel, and sometimes form a separate civic amenity. Inscriptions have been meticulously recorded by local and family history societies, and industrial archaeologists have found in dated gravestones

---

* An important start has been made with a study published by Stephen Hughes of the RCAHMW on the prolific minister-architect Thomas Thomas of Glandore (Swansea); see Hughes, S., 'Thomas Thomas, 1817-88: the first national architect of Wales', *Archaeologia Cambrensis* 152 (2003), pp. 69-166. Thirty-five probable or definite Thomas chapels have been identified in Gwynedd.

† Capel Newydd, for instance, has hinged box pews which may be 19th-century work – RCAHMW *Caernarvonshire (West)*, p. 58.

‡ The exceptions are a mosque built on Anglesey by a member of the Stanley family, who converted to Islam, and a recent conversion of a chapel in Llandudno Junction.

§ Though Welshmen were active in the Orange Order in Liverpool – pers. comm., Dr Wil Griffith, UWB.

a reasonably reliable way of dating the introduction of sawing machinery in slate quarries, but comparatively little work has been carried out on the ways in which social identities have been sustained or changed through burial practices. Within Gwynedd, slate is the material of choice for headstones from the late 18th century to the mid-20th. It is remarkable that English largely yields to Welsh as the language of inscription in the 19th century. Latin is very occasionally used, for instance on a clergyman's resting-place. As elsewhere in Wales, it is common to record the place of residence of the deceased on the stone. Early gravestone motifs include winged cherubim, which last well into the 19th century when they are largely replaced by symbols such as a broken column, the martyr's palm or clasped hands. More ostentatious monuments might indicate social aspiration, such as the angel statue over the remains of William Evans (1846-93) in Penmachno's Calvinistic Methodist graveyard, the base of which duly records that he was *Goruchwyliwr Chwarel Rhiw Fachno* ('Manager of Rhiw Fachno Quarry' – SH 7895 5062). Or they might consolidate status, such as the slate pyramid (presumably Masonic) tomb over the grave of several generations of the Wyatt family in Llandygái churchyard (SH 6004 7098). Within the church itself is the most lavish of monuments to an industrialist, Richard Westmacott's memorial to Richard Pennant, 1st Lord Penrhyn, consisting of a sarcophagus flanked by a quarryman in a toga and a peasant woman with her distaff, with a frieze in which *putti* quarry slate and teach each other the alphabet (SH 6006 7099 – Figure 119).*

119   Richard Westmacott's memorial to the 1st Lord Penrhyn.

Understanding the archaeology of worship and commemoration is crucial to understanding the experience of the people of Wales, and of Gwynedd, as they experienced the great changes of the 18th and 19th centuries. The chapels in particular should warn us against any notion that they formed a deracinated and exploited proletariat and that they were locked into an inevitably antagonistic relationship with the patrician classes. Chapels do represent an entirely new monument class within the area, one that only emerges in the late 18th century – much later than in many parts of England – and all but the very earliest are manifestly 'industrial' buildings not only in the sense that they served populations working in new callings and to new methods, but also in that their design and realisation increasingly depended on industrial

---

*   The National Trust, *Penrhyn Castle* (London: The National Trust, 1991), pp. 14, 18. Eric Hobsbawm pointed out that these must be the earliest sculptured proletarians – in 'Man and Woman: Images on the Left', republished in *Uncommon People* (London: Abacus, 1999), p. 135.

processes and on distribution systems which in fact encompassed the western world. Most significantly, from an archaeologist's point of view, they exemplify (paradoxically for Protestant places of worship) the consumerism of late 19th-century society and the resources which even industrial and rural congregations could command. There is an important change in social priorities and potential between the 18th-century barn chapel built from field stones, Merioneth oak and slates quarried from a local outcrop, and the chapel built a hundred years later to an architect's plans, with trusses of Canadian pine and a vast Leeds-built organ behind the pulpit.

Consumerism and resource-management have both become to a limited extent part of the vocabulary of industrial archaeologists as well as of Post-Medievalists and Historical Archaeologists in recent years,* and form useful tools in the analysis of infrastructural buildings as well as of houses. These terms logically lead to analysis of the archaeology of retailing, which offers a number of perhaps surprising parallels with the archaeology of religious dissent – in, for instance, its first appearance at the end of the 18th century, and its growth in scale and in architectural pretension from about 1860 onwards (see Appendix 2). Just as the archaeology of the chapel confirms an increasingly industrialised and shrinking world, the needs and priorities of a population increasingly affected by industrialisation are as apparent in the architecture and provision of the shop – a site-type very easily taken for granted by archaeologists.

The quarry village of Tal y Sarn demonstrates just how very tight could be the economic network of chapel, workplace and retail outlet in Gwynedd, giving the local elite a remarkable degree of control over the community's standard of living, as well

120 Chapel and shop, Tal y Sarn, 1820s; from Owain, O.Ll., *Cofiant Mrs. Fanny Jones Talysarn* (1906).

their morals. The Rev. John Jones of Tal y Sarn not only presided over the community's Calvinists, but managed Dorothea slate quarry and owned a shop, run by his formidable wife Fanny. John Jones's first shop and chapel of 1824 have long been engulfed by slate waste tips, though a sketch published in the early 20th century shows a double-fronted two-storey house with an additional range tacked on to the gable which may have been a warehouse, standing immediately adjacent to the 'barn' type chapel where he ministered (Figure 120). A new shop built a few minutes' walk away in the 1850s (SH 4924 5320) survives, albeit in ruinous condition, a two-storey dwelling built over the formation of the horse-drawn Nantlle Railway, complete with a trap-door and pulley to a cellar where wagons could be taken off the rails and stored.† Nearby, as if to underlie that God and Mammon could never be separated for long, at least not in Wales, John Jones'

---

* See Nevell, M. and Walker, J., *The Archaeology of Twentieth Century Tameside* (Ashton-under-Lyne, Tameside Metropolitan Borough Council with University of Manchester Archaeological Unit, 2004), pp. 35-60.

† Thomas, O., *Cofiant y Parchedig John Jones Talsarn* (Wrexham: Hughes and Son, 1874), p. 142; Owain, O. Ll., *Cofiant Mrs Fanny Jones Talysarn* (Caernarfon: Cwmni y Cyhoeddwyr Cymreig, 1906), plate opposite p. 65.

memorial chapel was erected in 1874.

Nor does the story end there. Almost opposite John Jones' shop stands one of the comparatively few examples within the area of a shop on the 'department store' model, the 'Gogerddan Stores', built in 1877 (SH 4923 3532 – Figure 121). The front is narrow, but the building is both high and deep, as if it had been designed for a town where land-values were high rather than for the periphery of a quarry village. It once had a central staircase, long gone, from which the various retail sections could be accessed by means of galleries along three sides, reaching up to a tailors' attic.* These by no means had the monopoly of local trading, since smaller 'front room' shops can be identified in the village by a discontinuity in the stonework of the front, or by a lintel for a larger window. None remains in business.

121 Gogerddan Stores at Tal y Sarn.

John Jones was by no means unique in Wales in being a Methodist minister and a shop-keeper. Ships' captains and quarry managers also appear as owners and managers of the few retail outlets that operated in the late 18th to mid-19th centuries. Whatever the means by which people provided themselves with food (see *4.2.3*, pp. 127-33), consumer goods continued to be bought from chapmen and at fairs until often after the Second World War. The 'Cambrian Pill Depot' (SH 5617 4015) on the corner of the square in Tremadoc is amongst the oldest surviving shops in the region; above the doorway a slate plaque (a recent replacement) announces the shopkeeper's name, Robert Isaac Jones, and the date of its foundation, 1839, in a building which has something of the proportions of a warehouse. Most shops otherwise are probably no older than the mid-19th century, the crucial period when consumer items began to be produced in factories for distribution throughout the United Kingdom. The typical Victorian shop is found throughout both the new and the pre-Industrial towns of Gwynedd, often much changed but still recognisable – most commonly a single central door flanked by two display windows, sometimes with a separate side door, giving access to the private quarters to the rear and on the upper floors. Pwllheli preserves many fine examples. So does Porthmadog, including Kerfoot's (SH 5667 3885 – Figure 122), on the department store staircase model, in business on the same site since 1874 – smaller stores such as these are less subject to the need to install lifts and escalators which have changed the internal appearance of larger establishments.

A different type of commercial establishment was the market hall, which grew out of, but is sometimes difficult to distinguish from, the older pattern of market

---

* Wyn Griffith, J.L., *Spring of Youth* (Swansea: Christopher Davies, 1971), p. 51. Griffith describes the shop as 'strangely like a chapel: across the road, and elevated above it, there was a real chapel, and it made Siop Fawr ['big shop'] with its plate-glass windows look slightly garish, of doubtful virtue.' – *ibid*.

house or covered market (see pp. 132-3). Only three were built in Gwynedd. Porthmadog's was constructed in 1846, extended in 1875, when a second storey and a clock-tower were added, and further embellished with an iron canopy and external iron steps in 1902. This preserved something of the Medieval pattern in the ground-floor arches, but these led to lock-up shops rather than an open market space. Blaenau Ffestiniog's was completed in 1864, and extended in 1870. Not only did both rent out retail space on a long-term basis to traders, but also offered a wide variety of functions in the public rooms, including film shows and political meetings.* The last was probably Tywyn's, constructed, on the evidence of its date-stone, in 1897 (SH 5878 0091).

The economic sluggishness of Gwynedd since 1900 has limited further growth in retailing. The art-deco Woolworth's chain store in Bangor and the adjacent Wellfield shopping centre (SH 5826 7219) illustrate changes in town-centre shopping that were common throughout Britain, as does the retail zone along the road that leads from here to Caernarfon. Though the goods these sell – computers, sportswear and car-parts – would have beggared the Victorian imagination, it is in the mid-19th century, in Gwynedd as in much of the western world, that working people entered the consumer society.†

122 Staircase in Kerfoot's Ltd, Porthmadog (Crown Copyright: NA/CA/90/33 – 1990/24).

Enjoyment of surplus, of consumer choice and of leisure is evident within the historic environment in many forms. Though the omnipresence of church or chapel amply confirms their centrality in the lives of the working people of Gwynedd, other forms of communal building are apparent. Band-rooms survive in the quarry villages of Tal y Sarn (1897 – SH 4897 5305) and Llanrug (1920s – SH 5332 6338), their walls adorned with faded sepia prints of long-dead performers in elaborate Ruritanian

---

* Morris, M., *Porthmadog: Llanw Ddoe/Yesterday's Tide* (Caernarfon: Gwynedd Archives, n.d.), pl. 54; Owain, S. ab, *Neuadd y Farchnad, Blaenau Ffestiniog: Cipdrem ar ei Hanes* (Blaenau Ffestiniog: Cyfeillion Neuadd y Farchnad, 1995). It was in the Blaenau market hall that David Lloyd George was first told to prepare himself for Westminster.

† Charting the period and the extent to which working people entered a 'consumer' society is always problematic – whether in the late 19th century, with consumer choice, or between the wars, with film-going, wireless sets, even holidays. See Schollier, P., 'Goods and Stores for the Workers, The Shaping of Mass Retailing in Late 19th-century Ghent', in Barker D. and Cranstone, D. (eds), *The Archaeology of Industrialization* (Leeds: Maney, 2004), pp. 257-67.

123 Star Stores, Dolgellau – this advertising print of the early 20th century brings out the old and the new in retailing. Goods are still delivered by cart and fair-days dominate the local economy but the telegraph is also now an established fact. The shop, originally built as a house in 1800, remains externally little altered in 2006 (courtesy Gwynedd Archives: DRO ZM/1052/4).

uniforms. Interestingly, entertainments popular in other parts of Britain, such as the Music Hall, made no impact whatsoever in Gwynedd. Village memorial halls were erected after the First World War, providing a non-denominational centre for community activities. These were often equipped with a stage, sometimes also found in chapel schoolrooms. Otherwise, with the single exception of Madocks' theatre at Tremadoc, which doubled as a market hall (see p. 132), no provision was made for dramatic entertainment within the area until the 20th century.* One slate quarry in Blaenau Ffestiniog

---

* The old satirical Welsh 'interludes' were performed in the open air. Schoolroom and memorial hall performances were mainly for recitation or singing, sometimes for an improving 'drama', often with preparation for the eisteddfod in mind. 'Theatre' as such only made an impact on regional culture after 1945, when supportive but utterly bewildered parents from quarry villages would sit through performances of Ionesco, Anouilh or Saunders Lewis put on by their offspring at the university.

124 The Cwmorthin quarry reading room of *c.*1841.

erected a *darllenfa* (reading room) for its workmen in about 1841, a remarkable regency-style structure parallel to, and facing the course of, the Festiniog Railway, with a bow window (SH 6844 4499 – Figure 124). What the impetus was to build this unusual structure is not clear. Some quarry barracks included a reading room, though these were in no sense architecturally pretentious buildings, and there is nothing to equal the magnificent miners' institutes that were a feature of British coalfields. One particularly remote quarry above Blaenau Ffestiniog provided not only accommodation for families and a school but also a library of sorts (p. 68).* Otherwise direct provision of infrastructure was rare in the slate industry. Libraries were provided by local government, as elsewhere in the Atlantic isles. The London and North Western Railway provided its workers at Bangor with an institute, now a club, but the only industrial undertaking which took it upon itself to provide recreational space and social centres was the aluminium works at Dolgarrog. As with the very similar aluminium-producing town of Kinlochleven in Scotland, these may have reflected the practice of continental firms such as Michelin and Renault, but the end results did not always do the Aluminium Corporation much credit – the football pitch was a thin layer of soil laid on tetanus-inducing pieces of scrap-iron, and the swimming pool was a tatty affair shielded by corrugated iron where the changing hut was an old railway carriage. What was unusual at Dolgarrog was that provision was made for both men and women, reflecting the newness of the industry, the fact that work-practices were radically different from the prevailing norm and that many of the employees had no deep roots in the area.†

In most of Gwynedd, however, the only other social centre was a purely masculine one, the public house, a structure-type whose morphology and architecture has received very little attention indeed from the archaeological community. Pre-19th-century taverns tend to be indistinguishable from contemporary private dwellings and often it is only the house name which suggests its former use – Ty'n Llan ('house in the churchyard') is often an indicator, as is the sign-name surviving in the modern address. Several present and former pubs rejoice in the name 'The Ring', which may be no more than an attempt to pronounce the English word 'inn' in Welsh (*yr inn*).

Pubs which survive from the later 19th century were very often built as commercial hotels and reflect the growth of the railway system. Appropriately, their architecture reflects the easily availability of building materials from outside, such as the *Queen's* at Porthmadog (SH 5661 3923 – Figure 125), with its polychromatic brickwork and ostentatious decoration. Watering-holes for working men are common in nearly all

---

* Jones, G.R., *Rhiwbach Slate Quarry* (privately published, 2005), pp. 45, 50, 182, 196-8.
† Jones, E. and Gwyn, D., *Dolgarrog: An Industrial History* (Caernarfon: Gwynedd Archives Service, 1989) and Fairweather, B., *A Short History of Kinlochleven* (Glencoe Folk Museum, n.d.).

125 *Queen's Hotel*, Porthmadog.

the industrial towns, though Tan y Grisiau, Llandygái and Nantlle are innocent of them because of the social concerns of their landlords. The growing opposition of the religious and political establishment of Gwynedd to drink prevented them from growing in scale or number, though in the early 21st century they enjoy a popularity which the chapels certainly do not. None ever achieved, or sought to emulate, the splendour of an Irish pub, with its rich interior decoration, but instead tended to be slightly paler reflections of licensed premises in the north of England.

Mention should also be made in this context of structures intended for the care and supervision of those on whom an expanding economy did not confer long-term benefit. Several early hospitals were built specifically for workers in a particular industry, such as those associated with slate quarries (*4.1.1*, pp. 42-69) or the now-demolished sailors' hospital at Holyhead, built by the Stanley family. Hospitals have proved to be a particularly fragile monument-category, given changes in medicine and in state provision. In Bangor the site of the Caernarvonshire and Anglesey Hospital is now occupied by a supermarket, and the splendid St David's Hospital was demolished in 2004, with minimal recording. Clough Williams Ellis' Heroes' Memorial Hospital of 1925 survives at Blaenau Ffestiniog (SH 7021 4556). Mental health problems were treated at the Denbigh hospital in north-east Wales, a structure now shorn of a purpose and facing an uncertain future.

A hardly less emotive structure-type was the workhouse, of which several examples were erected in the light of the 1834 Poor Law Amendment Act, intended to assist the destitute through supervised institutions. The Caernarfon workhouse of 1837 (SH 486 615), now Eryri Hospital, is the largest survivor, built on a cruciform plan to an unusual design with its slate-clad frontage and formal garden area to the front of the building. Dolgellau (SH 733 177), Pwllheli (SH 371 351) and Minffordd (SH 603 387) also survive, also as hospitals; the latter preserves the grilles in the casual ward through which tramps had to pass the stone they had broken in order to claim a bed for the night. Bala workhouse (1839-41, SH 925 358) has become a shop. It has a T-plan entrance block fronting a two-storey octagonal hub with accommodation wings to each side; a large rectangular block stands towards the rear of the site. Unusually it was built on the main street; most workhouses were deliberately kept on the periphery of the town. The town's later workhouse building on a different site has been demolished, as have Valley (1852), Conwy (1837) and Llanrwst (1837) workhouses.

For the most part, the remaining forms of institutional building – prisons and schools – are even less frequently studied by industrial archaeologists. It is the French tradition of philosophical enquiry that has seen these as central to industrialisation, whereby a capitalist economy requires and creates a coercive political anatomy. Prisons and reformatories were notoriously similar to workhouses in several respects, as Michel Foucault was only one of many to point out. Industrial schools in particular borrowed many of their architectural signatures and, if Foucault is to be believed, the institutional 'technology of subjection' reflects the accumulation of capital in an industrialising society.* A more pragmatic approach, stressing trends in economic and social history, is set out in Hughes' magisterial *Copperopolis*, so far the only detailed archaeological study of schools in an industrial context.† Certainly, education, as the primary institutional means of social reproduction, should merit the attention of industrial archaeologists, even where its link with industry is not obvious. Before local government assumed responsibility for education, most Gwynedd schools were sponsored by churches or by chapels or landowners rather than industries; however, it was often the chapel Sunday Schools, with their emphasis on discussion and framing an argument, that paradoxically provided the most effective training for a developing economy, rather than the Gradgrind preoccupation with basic literacy and numeracy available elsewhere.‡ The workplace itself was a major education-provider until the late 20th century through the provision of apprenticeships. There is a strong case to be made for regarding the University College of North Wales at Bangor as part of the 'productive landscape' on this basis in that attempts were made, with little success, to introduce courses in slate quarrying.§ More durably, the college also set up courses in forestry and electrical engineering and, as we have seen (p. 98), it took over and ran a farm at Abergwyngregyn as part of its agriculture course.

Perhaps one curious industrial signature in an educational building deserves mention; the County Secondary School in Amlwch (now Ysgol Syr Thomas Jones, SH 4375 9213), in the shadow of the Parys copper mines, the first comprehensive school in Britain, built between 1948 and 1953 to the designs of N. Squire-Johnson, the local authority architect, includes a rock-dressed masonry tower designed to echo a Cornish engine-house such as the one which survives at the mine.¶

The relationship between the archaeology of industrial sites and of social infrastructure is clearly complicated and multi-faceted, and is central to the debate as to the future scope of industrial archaeology – whether it continues to be focused on a functional interpretation, and what relationship it comes to have with other forms of enquiry. Whilst on the one hand workshop, mine and railway are indeed inextricably linked with hovel, truck-shop and meeting-house, infrastructural provision introduces problems of categorisation and analysis which hitherto have sat more comfortably with the theoretical focus of landscape archaeology (pp. 17-18) and of American historical archaeology (p. 19). However, to take a point made by one scholar recently, we have in the archaeology of towns and villages 'an awesome level quantity of evidence that

---

* Foucault, M., *Discipline and Punish: The Birth of the Prison* (trans. of *Surveiller et Punir: Naissance de la Prison* by Alan Sheridan) (New York: Vintage Books 1995), pp. 219-20.

† Hughes, S., *Copperopolis: Landscapes of the Early Industrial Period in Swansea* (Aberystwyth: RCAHMW, 2000), pp. 241-54. See also Hughes, S., 'Institutional Buildings in Worker Settlements', in *Understanding the Workplace: A Research Framework for Industrial Archaeology in Britain* (IAR 27 1 – May 2005), pp. 153-61.

‡ Evidence is necessarily anecdotal, but certainly the best of the Sunday Schools associated with the chapels emphasised not just reading of the Bible but also discussion and debate, often on secular topics, whereby young people learnt how to marshal arguments rather than merely imbibe facts, skills which stood them in good stead in entirely different contexts. Out of these grew organisations such as the WEA.

§ Wiliams, J.G., *The University College of North Wales: Foundations 1884-1927* (Cardiff: University of Wales Press, 1985), pp. 192-5.

¶ Pers. comm., Judith Alfrey.

is recognisable and capable of being understood if we have the analytical tools with which to examine it'.* Systems of enquiry that can encompass not only communal buildings but also housing, artefactual evidence and the whole question of settlement morphology need not replace site-specific and functional studies but do open the possibility of a more comprehensive archaeology of the industrial, or industrialising, world. The present study also underlines that baseline research, and chronologies to establish what is typical and what is likely to be exceptional, are still desperately needed for site-types that are all too often taken for granted.

These are also site types that are under particular pressure. An over-abundance of social infrastructure resulting from the comparatively short period of industrial-era prosperity in Gwynedd poses its particular problems. Because shops and banks need to present an attractive modern ambience, handsome Victorian buildings are disfigured by inappropriate fronts, which will invariably appear infinitely more dated than the original within a few years. Interiors of the 19th century have all but gone. Blaenau's market hall remains shut up until a future can be found for it, and high-street shops are under great pressure from out-of-town supermarkets. However, without a doubt, it is the nonconformist chapel which poses the most serious problem of management, one which is compounded by a partial failure to recognise its architectural merits and its place within a town or village street-scape (see p. 220).

126 The movement of capital: Williams and Hughes' bank in Caernarfon was built on the site of a town house belonging to a local landowning family.

Those that remain places of worship are exceptionally well cared-for, and the conservatism of most congregations in liturgy and worship has meant that there is little pressure for change to the fabric of the building. In many cases, the chapels themselves have been demolished, thereby releasing space for car-parking, and services have been held in the schoolroom. The greatest threat they face is the seemingly remorseless decline in religious attendance, which seems common to most of western Europe. Failures to unite the Methodists, Wesleyans, Baptists and Independents in a Free Church of Wales have meant that the prospect of perhaps three in every four chapels in Wales immediately becoming redundant has receded, but dry-rot and the age-profile of congregations ensure that the problem will be spread out over the years to come. As examples, Bethesda, the Independent chapel which gave its name to the slate-quarry village of which it was the original nucleus, was intelligently and sympathetically converted by the architect Geraint Evans into a block of flats, which has at least preserved the front (SH 6232 6667). Less successful was the conversion of a Tal y Sarn chapel into business units (SH 4905 5317), in a way which altered the

---

* Trinder, B., '18th- and 19th-Century Market Town Industry: An analytical model' in *IAR* 24 2 (November 2002), pp. 75-89.

façade into a cruder version of the original, covered with the apparently obligatory pebble-dash, and installed aluminium safety rails where once there had been wrought-iron. *A holl harddwch merch Sïon a ymadawodd â hi.**

4.6.3 Artefacts and interiors

Artefacts and domestic interiors have received some attention, in particular the rich tradition of slate-carving associated with Dyffryn Ogwen.

There has been little analysis of artefacts on the 'historical archaeology' model in a Gwynedd context, for several reasons. One is that this approach has still to make headway in the United Kingdom, partly because comparatively few industrial period buildings have been demolished, so there is little possibility of recovering artefacts through excavation.† Another is the remarkable conservatism of domestic interiors in the region, where well into the 1960s many people were still living in rooms that had barely changed since the end of the 19th century. Excavation and recording may seem an expensive way of confirming what people feel they already know. When the National Museums and Galleries of Wales reconstructed a row of slate-quarrymen's houses at Llanberis in 1998-9 to mirror the way of life of past generations, there was no difficulty recreating the interiors of 1969 or even 1901 from lumber rooms and attics, though the furnishings of 1861 were a little more problematic.‡ The interiors were chosen to illustrate changing mores as well as changing economic circumstances – whereas a print of the Rev. Henry Rees adorns the wall in 1900, a paperback copy of *Lady Chatterley's Lover* is part hidden under the bed-blanket in 1969, a recreation of a particular 'strategy of resistance' to prevailing cultural patterns that invites comparison with the beer bottles and clay pipes that Professors Beaudry and Mrozowski unearthed in Lowell (see p. 185). For that matter, beer bottles were uncovered in an excavation carried out at a barracks at Blaen y Cwm slate quarry, in contexts that suggest they were thrown out of doors and windows once their contents had been consumed, a state of affairs which contrasts markedly with the picture of the frugal and pious workman cherished by many.§

One regionally distinct feature which has been studied in some detail is the tradition of slate-carving. It was common until the later years of the 20th century to see a carved slate fan in the window of many houses in the quarrying areas, a testament to the extent to which the slate-splitter identified with his employment as well as to his skill in producing very fine work. (The fans consist of many small strips of slate to the same intricate pattern splayed around a central pin.) Smaller versions of these are now offered for sale in tourist outlets but they seem largely to have vanished from their former pride of place amongst the families of those who made them. More remarkable still are the extraordinary carved slate fireplaces, which seem to have originated in Dyffryn Ogwen, though they have been found in the other Gwynedd

---

* Lamentations, 1:6.
† Williams, G.H., 'Caernarvonshire House Interiors', *TCHS* 39 (1977) pp. 60-92 is an important study of 'pre-Industrial' interiors, based on a study of probate records.
‡ Hywel, E. ap, *Welsh Slate Museum, Llanberis; Guide* (Cardiff: National Museums and Galleries of Wales, 2002), pp. 41-4; pers. comm., Dr Dei Roberts, Bangor.
§ Unpublished excavation carried out by the late Dafydd Price, Dolau Las.

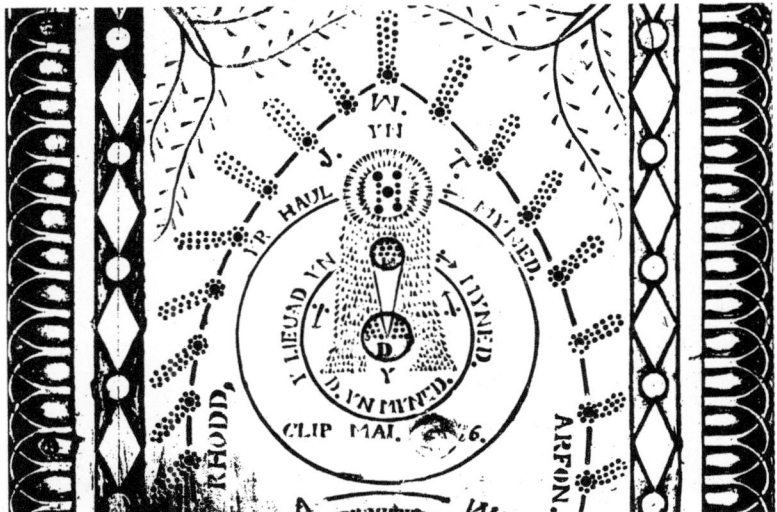

127 A detail of a rubbing of the Bryn Twrw astronomical slates.

quarrying districts and around Llangollen, in north-east Wales, whither Gwynedd quarrymen went in the 1860s and 1870s. The Dyffryn Ogwen examples, insofar as they are dated, were all carved between 1834 and 1843. More research is required to see if the dates and the names which often appear with them record marriages, or a move into a new house. Many show, in heavily stylised form, local scenes, such as the Menai bridge, or St Anne's church (the only visual record we now have of this building). One depicts a corner-cupboard containing a rum bottle (and remained in place even when the family became total abstainers); others show plant pots, wine glasses and clock faces, suggesting that those carved them enjoyed, or aspired to, a standard of living that encompassed consumer choice. Pride of place goes to the astronomical slates of Bryn Twrw, Tregarth, a visual representation of Halley's comet and the eclipse of 1836. These are known to reflect the work of John William Thomas 'Arfonwyson' (1805-40), a locally-born quarryman and schoolteacher who became Supervisor at the Greenwich Observatory, and were carved by Thomas and William Jones (1808-40, 1815-55) of Bryn Twrw (Figure 127).[*]

The carved slates may have declined in popularity with the availability of commercially-produced slate 'marble' fireplaces in the 1840s, in which a pattern was achieved by treating a block with an enamel, heating it in an oven then painting it with water and mordants, polishing and reheating. Fireplaces such as these often included decorated encaustic tiles, and survive in their numbers not only within the region but in England as well.[†] The kilns in which they were prepared were generally to be found within specialist slab mills. One set survives preserved at the Inigo Jones Slate Works at Groeslon (SH 4708 5511), and another has been excavated and recorded at Hafodlas slate quarry (SH 779 562).[‡]

[*] Caffell, G., *Llechi Cerfiedig Dyffryn Ogwen/The Carved Slate of Dyffryn Ogwen* (Cardiff: National Museum of Wales, 1983). It is likely that examples noted outside Dyffryn Ogwen are a little later.
[†] Jones, G.R., *Hafodlas Slate Quarry, Betws y Coed* (privately published, 1998), pp. 107-9, 164. See also patent specification 8383 of 1840.
[‡] Jones, *op. cit.*, pp. 190-2.

4.6.4 The morphology of settlement

Industrialisation altered existing patterns of settlement and created completely new ones. Their evolution and distinctive character provide evidence for the social dynamics of industrialisation.

Previous chapters have analysed the way in which workers were housed in the industrial period and their distinctive social infrastructure. The present chapter attempts to analyse the shape these communities took on the ground, the settlement patterns which grew up, and the changes which took place to them. It is a complicated story, involving both changes to established settlement as well as the creation of completely new ones (Map 15).

At the beginning of the 18th century Gwynedd remained, much as it had been 500 years earlier, a rural environment dominated by the houses of its landlords and the farmhouses of their tenants. The urban sector was represented by the towns of Bangor (traditionally a *dinas* or city by virtue of its cathedral status), Conwy, Newborough, Beaumaris, Nefyn, Criccieth, Pwllheli, Harlech, Caernarfon, Bala, Llanrwst and Dolgellau. These last two, founded before the Conquest, enjoyed some measure of success, but none could be described as thriving, and Criccieth and Harlech almost passed out of existence in the 16th and 17th centuries. All of them were very small, and some were tiny. Beaumaris and Conwy were still largely made up of half-timbered houses, of which one or two examples might also have been found in Caernarfon. Elsewhere, stone predominated. Sometime before 1742 the surveyor Lewis Morris sketched at Holyhead a cluster of houses catering for travellers making their way to and from Ireland, and at Aberffraw a settlement that had grown up on the site of the court of the princes of Gwynedd.* However, anything recognisable as a 'village' in English terms was a rarity.

Most of these settlements grew significantly within the period 1700-2005, though at different rates, and for different reasons, and it is hard to disentangle the factors which governed their development from those which brought into being specifically industrial settlements. Bala was built up on the grid-pattern inherited from its first, largely unsuccessful, medieval royal foundation by its principal landowner, Simon Lloyd, who granted leases to fellow Methodist sympathisers from the late 18th century. A parallel development was Llangefni, on Anglesey. Methodist preaching won its converts hereabouts partly because of the lack of patrician control over the nearby commons of Rhostrehwfa and Rhosmeirch, to such an extent that, when the Bulkeley estate started laying out houses here, the new settlement found itself with a *raison d'être*; if Bala, with its lake and college, was the Geneva of Wales, Llangefni became the Sublime Porte of Calvinism. The cathedral city of Bangor, despite being stuck with a narrow and winding main street, was able to benefit from its location on the main road along the north Wales coast even before the building of the Telford road, and from the patronage of Dean and Chapter on the one hand and of the Penrhyn estate on the other.

Harlech and Criccieth had to wait for the coming of the railway in 1867 before they began to develop, and then it was primarily as holiday centres rather than as industrial settlements. Pwllheli benefited from its new port facilities in the early 19th century and

---

* Wiliam, D.W. (ed.), *Brasluniau Lewis Morris o Eglwysi, Tai a Phentrefi ym Môn* (privately published, 1999).

Map 15 Settlement after 1700.

(Settlements that are largely Medieval in origin are lightly shaded; industrial-era settlements are darkly shaded.)

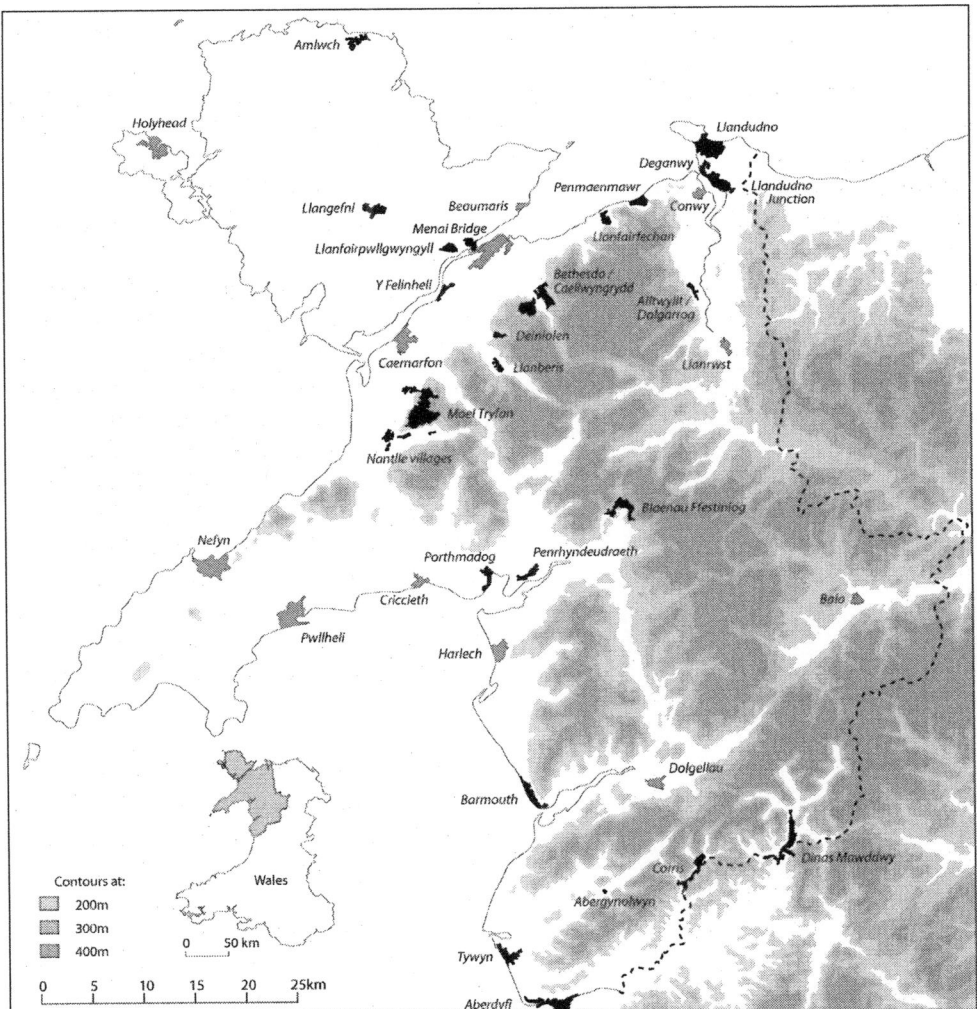

later from the railway, but only acquired its extensive 'West End' development from 1894, after the land had been purchased by Solomon Andrews, a Cardiff entrepreneur. Here, long straight avenues distinguish it in plan from the medieval borough just as surely as its multi-storeyed hotels in concrete or yellow Penybont brick from northeast Wales ignored local architectural idiom. It was equipped not only with a bandstand where the 'Welsh Ladies' Orchestra' performed but also a velodrome, reflecting the current international craze for cycling. Andrews was also responsible for a much smaller, largely abortive, development at Arthog.* Rhosneigr on Anglesey was developed by the Palethorpe family of sausage-making fame, and Fairbourne by 'self-raising flour' McDougall. The one large-scale holiday settlement conceived from new was the only one to have been sponsored by a member of the landed elite – Llandudno, by the

---

* Andrews, J.F., *Keep Moving: the Story of Solomon Andrews* (privately published, 1976), pp. 102-21.

Mostyn family, after earlier plans to make it a packet harbour for Ireland or a port for Wrexham coal had come to naught.* Industrial workers could occasionally benefit from such developments; at Penmaenmawr, sett-makers in the quarry would also run boarding-houses.† Butlin's holiday camp at Pwllheli, now 'Hafan y Mor', provided employment for many Gwynedd residents, though its facilities were vastly different from what was available to, or sought by, quarrymen and farm workers in Gwynedd.‡ Holidaymakers offered a good return on capital investment.

Significantly, the settlements which manifested little or no growth, or which might even have shrunk, were Beaumaris, Aberffraw, Newborough and Nefyn, none of which ever acquired a railway. Even so, any implied stagnation needs to be qualified. Beaumaris lost its role as the principal town of Anglesey to the upstart settlement at Llangefni, partly because the Telford road bypassed it and made the old (and very dangerous) crossing of the Traeth Lafan redundant. But it was served by the steam packet from Liverpool from 1822, and a sign of the town's vitality is the construction of a range of town houses by Hansom (of 'cabs' fame) on the Green in 1833.§ Aberffraw, once the 'oak door' of the medieval kingdom of Gwynedd, a settlement which made perfect strategic sense in the context of the 13th century and none by the 19th, had long been bypassed by the march of time.

Newborough was an Anglo-Norman foundation, though built adjacent to a Welsh royal court, and had a mayor and a borough charter despite consisting of only two short streets. In the 19th century it was sustained by its menfolk going to sea, generally on Liverpool ships, and the women weaving the plentiful local marram-grass. Nefyn was also a town whose origins lay in an Edwardian borough and a Medieval Welsh court. Until well into the 19th century, its modest prosperity was based on fishing, and when this came to an end, due partly to refrigeration of fish services on the main line railways, Nefyn mariners perpetuated their calling by service in the merchant marine. Men from these two places were more likely to know their way round Kowloon or Cairo than to the nearest Gwynedd market town, and it was the rhythms of international trade and the demands of productive economies which in fact sustained these apparently 'pre-industrial' settlements.

Industrialisation, both elsewhere in Britain and throughout the world, therefore had a profound, if indirect, impact on those towns in Gwynedd which long predated 1700, as well as calling into being some new tourist developments. What of the specifically industrial settlements, those built to house workers in the new industries? In particular, now that we have had the opportunity to examine their houses, their social infrastructure and the interiors which characterise them, can we establish their morphology and can we identify the interplay of social and environmental factors which gave them their form?

Two things impress from the start. First of all, much survives largely unaltered from the late 19th century. Not only, as suggested in *4.6.1*, does the region preserve its 19th-century architectural signature, but the essential shape of settlement is also little

---

* Even at Llandudno there had been a small community of copper-miners and fishermen.
† Davies, I.E., 'A History of the Penmaenmawr Quarries', *TCHS* 35 (1974), p. 40.
‡ For the context to Hafan y Mor, see Stratton, M. and Trinder, B., *Twentieth Century Industrial Archaeology* (London: Spon, 2000), pp. 193-4.
§ Dodd, A.H., *The Industrial Revolution in North Wales* (Cardiff: University of Wales Press, 1971; repr. by Bridge Books, 1990), p. 129; Cowell, J., *Beaumaris A Pictorial History* (privately published, 2005), p. 9.

changed – the effect of the economic stagnation of the 20th century. To this extent, just as low-status houses in their own right form an eloquent archaeological resource, the patterns in which they are laid out and the spatial relationships they create can tell us much about the way in which this particular region experienced industrialisation.

Secondly, the sheer variety of entirely new settlement pattern is remarkable, ranging from abortive rows of cabin-like dwellings on un-hospitable moorlands to towns which ultimately merited UDC status. Above all, it was mineral extraction which brought them in to being, and it is striking that an economic activity which even at its height employed no more than about 16,000 men should have had so profound a landscape impact. In part this is because miners and quarrymen, particularly in the old Caernarvonshire, remained rooted in the soil. In the words of one historian, '… a good number of hands skilled in gauging rock and wielding chisel and mallet could also perform with a long scythe in one of the bands that on July mornings would, standing in line, swathe their way through hilly hay fields.'*

Quarrymen would not only help with the harvest on neighbours' and relatives' farms but would sometimes have smallholdings of their own. Throughout the Atlantic isles, examples can be found of dual-economy settlements, perhaps typical of marginal landscapes where neither agriculture nor industry (as traditionally defined) could be certain of granting a sure and sustainable livelihood. In Cardiganshire the revival of lead mining in the 19th century sustained the pastoral economy of the uplands.† Similar settlements existed in the coal-producing areas of South Wales, in the lead-mining areas of the Pennines and in the early textile industry of Lancashire and Cheshire.‡ The Alltwyllt ('wild hill') near Dolgarrog in the Conwy valley is one such, a hillside of about 43 hectares (100 acres) covered in a patchwork of winding donkey-paths and of cottages with irregularly-shaped garden-fields (SH 765 679). Local tradition claimed that its first settlers were descended from the famous Medieval banditti of Dinas Mawddwy, the *Gwylliaid Cochion* – improbable, but providing a ready-made origin-myth for a marginal community of sulphur miners, slate quarrymen, basket-makers, river-fishermen and captains of the boats that plied up and down the Conwy.§

A much larger but in many ways similar development was the partial enclosure (approximately 586 hectares [1,449 acres] out of a total of 1,531 hectares [3,782 acres]) from 1798 onwards of the Moel Tryfan commons, an upland area south of Caernarfon which had been quarried for slate since the Medieval period (pp. 36, 42 – SH 519 559 C). This was the landscape which nurtured Kate Roberts (1891-1985), a quarryman's daughter, one of the finest Welsh novelists of the 20th century, whose writing returns time and time again to her formative years here.¶ Moel Tryfan had another chronicler also in Gilbert Williams (1874-1966), a primary school headmaster who even as a youth had started questioning his older neighbours about the encroachments of the

---

* Jones, R.M., *The North Wales Quarrymen* (Cardiff: University of Wales Press, 1982), p. 19.
† Vaughan, C., 'Lluestai Blaenrheidiol', *Ceredigion* 5 (1966), p. 247.
‡ Pollard, S., *Marginal Europe: The Contribution of Marginal Lands Since the Middle Ages* (Oxford: Clarendon Press, 1997), pp. 221-54.
§ Owen, J., 'Yr "Allt Wyllt," Talybont', undated column (?1930s) from *North Wales Weekly News*.
¶ Roberts, K., *Y Lôn Wen: darn o hunangofiant* (Denbigh: Gwasg Gee, 1960). Another native of the area, Richard Hughes Williams, 'Dic Tryfan' (1878?-1915), a pioneer of the short story, published *Straeon y Chwarel* ('Quarry Tales') in the early years of the 20th century – see *DWB*.

very early 19th century, and about traditions that went back much further.* Their origins have affected their environment, in that Kate Roberts' memory is perpetuated in a look-out point on the commons, ironically an attempt to tidy up a waste dump, and Williams is commemorated in a social housing estate called 'Bro Gilbert'.† Partly because of the interest both these writers showed in their origins, and partly because of the remarkable story of how the settlements came to be established on the Crown commons without warrant or permission and later defended against patrician control,‡ this is by far the best known of the dual-economy settlements of Gwynedd.

It is roughly triangular in plan, still bounded by the mountain wall – though here and there the course of the wall clearly accommodates an assart made at unrecorded times into the common land. To its north-east it falls steeply to the rural defile of the Gwyrfai valley. To its south it falls to the Nantlle valley, an area which in the 19th century saw intense industrialisation as slate veins were opened out, and where the villages of Pen y Groes, Tal y Sarn, Nantlle and Drws y Coed came into being. To the west it slopes more gently to the Arfon plain. As we have seen (p. 108), the dominant pattern is a dispersed settlement of smallholdings centered on a *crog-lofft* dwelling, with little in the way of outbuildings. The field boundaries themselves are straight and well laid-out – the enclosures were unofficial, but they were evidently not a free-for-all, and there was clearly an understood sense of who might claim what amount of land and what their rights and obligations were in respect of neighbours. Here and there, short two-up-two-down terraces stand by themselves in small enclosures, removed from other buildings, and ribbon developments of houses unassociated with anything larger than a garden have created several small nucleations, the villages of Fron, Rhosgadfan, Rhostryfan and Carmel.

The Moel Tryfan enclosures represent a landscape of cultural assertion and defiance, though in some respects they are very similar to the dual economy settlements created by the Penrhyn and Vaynol estates for their own quarrymen, where the purpose was explicitly social control, by rooting families in the soil rather than creating a landless proletariat. Those created by the Penrhyn estate on Mynydd Llandygái in the Ogwen valley (SH 6060 6547 – see p. 188) are characterised by rows of near-identical *crog-lofftydd* with long strip gardens, covering 173.5 hectares (429 acres), laid out in stages on what had been a potato patch from the Napoleonic wars until *c*.1862. The Vaynol estate was slightly less controlling, since the surviving houses are to different patterns and are associated with a more varied field system. These cover approximately 500 hectares (1,200 acres) out of a total of 1,091 upland hectares (2,695 acres) of the parish of Llanddeiniolen allotted to the Vaynol estate by an enclosure award of 1814.

In fact, many slate quarrymen and their families seem to have been more than happy to form a landless proletariat, unencumbered by either a leased or freehold smallholding. They created several remarkable nucleated communities which survive as classic examples of 19th-century industrial settlements. The most famous of these lie barely 2.5km away from Mynydd Llandygái, and are still instantly recognisable in a

---

* CRO: W. Gilbert Williams papers. Williams' fascination with Moel Tryfan was only matched by his profound lack of historical interest in the rest of the world.

† Untranslatable, but 'Gilbert's patch' is probably the nearest in meaning to the Welsh.

‡ See Gwyn, D., 'The Failed Enclosure: Common and Crown Land on Mynydd Cilgwyn', *TCHS* 2001, pp. 81-97; 'The Industrial Town in Gwynedd: a Comparative Study', *Landscape History*, 2002, pp. 71-89; 'Landscape, Economy and Identity: A Case Study in the Archaeology of Industrialisation', *Proceedings of the Conference of the Association for Industrial Archaeology and the Society for Post-Medieval Archaeology* (2004), pp. 35-52.

description of them as they were in 1853 penned by that erratic genius Robert Roberts *Sgolor Mawr* (1834-85), as he looked back over his youth in North Wales from the gold-fields of Ballarat:

> There was no other employment except quarrying: all the inhabitants were directly or indirectly dependent upon that industry. All the land for many miles around belonged to Colonel Pennant: the only exception consisted of two long strips which skirted the mountain on one side of the valley of the Ogwen. These irregular strips were the property of a bonnet laird in the neighbourhood and were leased in lots for building. On these two portions, therefore, the greater part of the population was located: about a thousand on the smaller and upper division, near the parish church, and three or four times that number on the larger portion near the Ogwen valley. The Holyhead and Shrewsbury Road ran through the latter division and formed its main street, a wide but winding thoroughfare, and the only street, properly so called, in the whole village. The rest of the houses were built all around, with great contempt for regularity: each house was built wherever a patch of tolerably level ground could be found facing any point of the compass which its builder might fancy.*

Bethesda (SH 622 667 C), and its satellite to the north, Caellwyngrydd (SH 623 681 C), were then manifestly new settlements, only a generation old, raw and unregulated. In the more than 150 years since the young Mr Roberts trudged up the post road to take up his teaching duties, Caellwyngrydd has barely changed at all, with its narrow road heading straight up the hill and its radiating spinal rows – an object-lesson in how to fit rows of houses within the wandering boundaries of a mountain field (Figure 128). Bethesda, however, has expanded; though quite a few of those that Roberts would have seen survive, most of the houses are late 19th-century. The centre of the town† is older, less regularly laid out and is dominated by smaller housing; most of the infrastructure, in the form of the larger chapels, the parish church and the principal hotel, lies on the periphery. Roberts provides a clue as to why this should be; the original settlement was the property of the 'bonnet laird', and it was here that the quarrymen chose to make their homes, rather than accepting the dwellings built for them (and the control thereby implied) by the Penrhyn estate. It is significant that the settlement took its name from the Independent chapel originally built right up against the boundary in the 1820s, by the side of Telford's road. In any event, Colonel Pennant (Lord Penrhyn from 1866) clearly accepted a *fait accompli* from when he took over the running of his estate, and was prepared to act as patron to the community when it needed to expand on to his land. The principal Methodist chapel, Jerusalem, was erected on the edge of the settlement as it then was in 1842, and the ritualist Glanogwen church nearby in 1855. Housing nearby is to a significantly higher standard than the surviving cottages in the older part of Bethesda (Figure 129).

Just as the Penrhyn and Vaynol estates' dual economy settlements are almost mirror-images of each other, so are the nucleated villages established in defiance of them. Deiniolen (SH 579 632 C) is surrounded by the Vaynol estate's enclosures but was created on a freehold that remained unaffected by the Llanddeiniolen enclosure act. The older houses, some of them so small that they may well date back to the 1820s,

---

* Roberts, R., *A Wandering Scholar: The Life and Opinion of Robert Roberts* (John Burnett and H.G. Williams, eds) (Cardiff: University of Wales Press, 1991), p. 274. *Sgolor Mawr* 'great scholar'; Roberts, born a Methodist, ordained an Anglican, was variously a cleric, gold-miner, journalist, lexicographer and schoolmaster, before alcohol- and drug-addiction finished him off.

† Bethesda was awarded Urban District Council status in 1894.

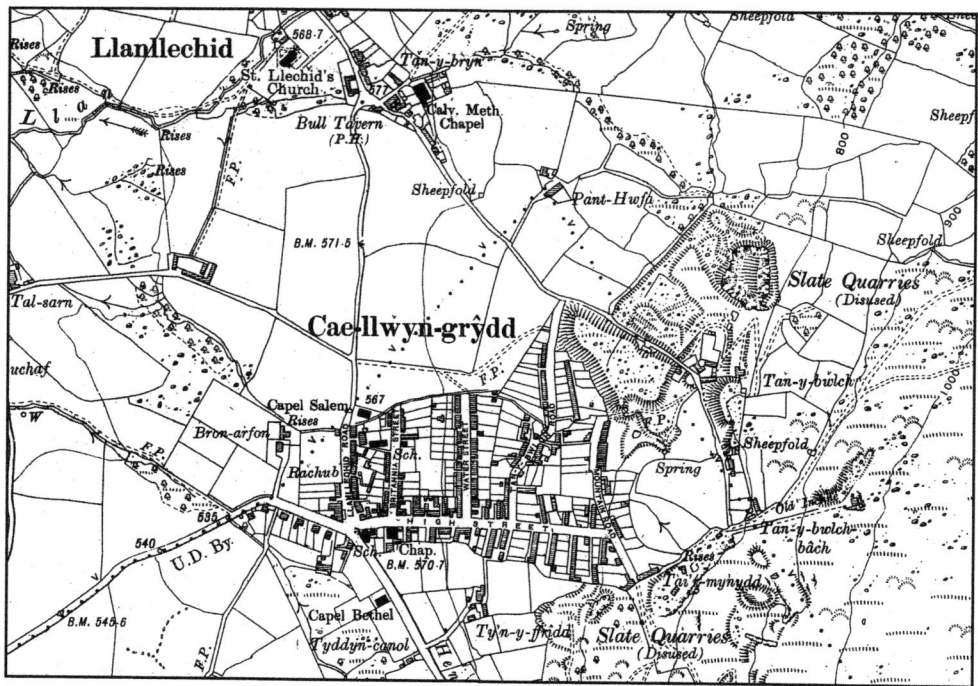

128 Caellwyngrydd is a quarry village visibly constrained by pre-industrial field boundaries.

129 Different land-ownership, different settlement pattern; the land to the west of Pen y Bryn road in Bethesda formed part of a freehold and is characterised by earlier and less planned development; to the east the land formed part of the Penrhyn estate, and is given over to planned housing and to infrastructural development.

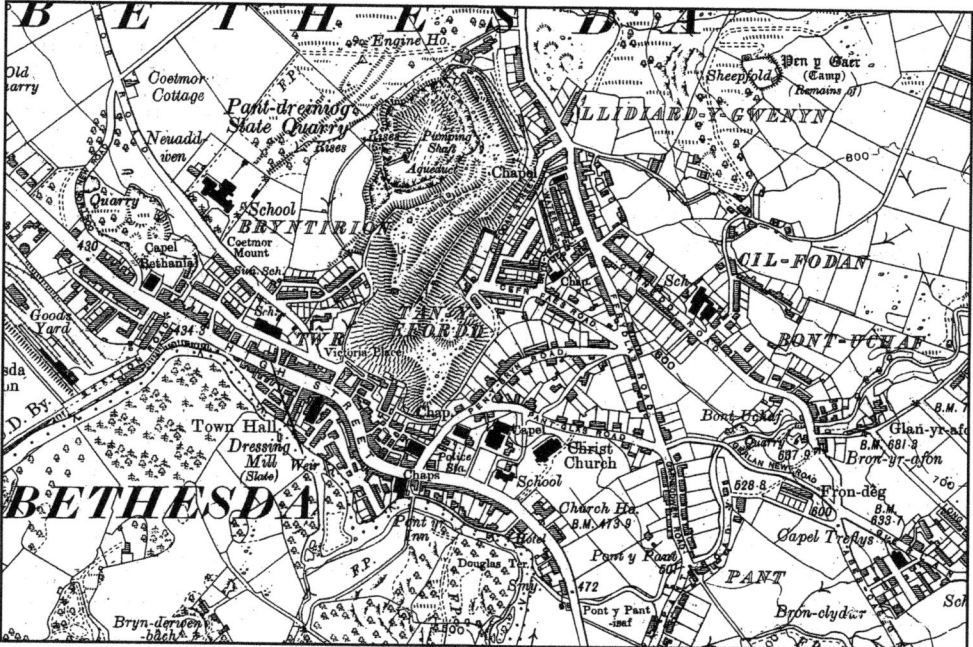

are strung out along the road to Dinorwic slate quarry, with Ebenezer chapel at one end – exactly as at Bethesda, right on the periphery of the freehold, as if announcing to the world that here at least the writ of a wealthy man did not run. Rhes Fawr, David Griffith's row of the 1830s, is built along a side road nearby (p. 190). More substantial houses, and the village's Carnegie library, are found on the periphery, on Vaynol land, as are the Llandinorwic church of 1856-7 and the Methodist Capel y Waun of 1868-9, some 300m away from the village centre, prominent in their isolation on the moor, vying with each other for the souls of the faithful and apparently waiting for the village to grow and encompass them.

The morphology of other quarrymen's settlements seems less ideologically charged. Pen y Groes and Tal y Sarn in the Nantlle quarrying area, one of the valleys to the south of the Moel Tryfan commons, are both settlements which evolved in the early 19th century along turnpike roads and the course of the Nantlle Railway (p. 156). Pen y Groes (SH 471 531 C) evolved from a workshops at the junction of the old road to Clynnog and the cart-track up to the quarries (see p. 135), and Tal y Sarn (SH 490 531 C) from a decision by the owner of the Coedmadog freehold to turn a few fields over to building.

A strict control of urban development was not purely a function of Tories and churchmen such as the owners of the Penrhyn and Vaynol estates. The harbour town of Porthmadog was owned by the Tremadoc estate, created by the Foxite radical William Alexander Madocks and sustained by his agent John Williams. Porthmadog is in many respects an unlikely port town, lacking the squalid dives that characterised even small rural harbours – at least until they become coffee-shops or restaurants. Its wide straight streets arranged in a diamond pattern reflect the fact that not only was it a completely new development of the 1820s but that it was built on reclaimed land, with no pre-existing proprietorial patterns to worry about – and that the agent was in a sufficiently strong position to insist that the first winding lane that ran down to the beach should be straightened out. Porthmadog houses are remarkably uniform in style, though it is not clear whether this reflects the hand of the estate or the preferred style of one or two active local firms of builder-architects (p. 190). It seems to be one of the earliest places to have acquired a recognisable 'industrial zone', based not on the availability of water-supply nor on an ancient system of tenure but established – one can surmise – as a result of deliberate policy. The use of steam plant rather than water-power lessened the environmental constraints on developing a town's service infrastructure in that sites such as gasworks, factories and corn mills could be set up near rail access, typically on the settlement's periphery. At Porthmadog, these sites were all located within a narrowly-defined area to the east of the town, whereas at Caernarfon they followed the course of the river.

If Bethesda and Deiniolen began life as demotic settlements which forced themselves on the controlled patrician world, and Porthmadog represents a town laid out and successfully managed by an estate, Blaenau Ffestiniog shows that these forces could operate in different ways again. Memorably described as 'a last Lhasa-like citadel of mountainlocked Celtic tradition',[*] this former community of slate-quarrymen and their families has the highest rainfall of any town in the United Kingdom, imparting a sense of gloom which is heightened by the massive tips of slate waste which dominate

---

[*] Wilson, D., editorial, *Festiniog Railway Magazine* 34 (Autumn 1966), p. 1.

it. Pre-industrial patterns of land-ownership in the uplands (the *blaenau*) of the parish of Ffestiniog were varied – they included two patrician estates, Newborough and Oakeley, and several freeholds, the property of local squireens, or as Robert Roberts would have it, 'bonnet lairds'. As quarrying developed in the early years of the 19th century, the dominant form of settlement was a ribbon development along pre-industrial roads and sheep tracks, or indeed, along the 'metropolitan corridor' that was the Festiniog Railway (p. 156), often with front doors facing the track. The patrician families were clearly prepared to extend their patronage to this upstart settlement from the beginning, since Mrs Oakeley gave land for an Anglican church in 1842, but only became directly involved in sponsoring the community from the late 1860s, when rows of terraced houses were let out on controlled leases. To this day, Blaenau Ffestiniog is a curious mixture of ribbon development dating in the main from the 1820s to the 1860s, characterised by cottage dwellings, and the better-quality terraced housing (see p. 190 – mainly on Oakeley and Newborough land) from the 1860s to the 1890s. A remarkable feature of this second phase of development is the provision of highly planned urban squares, complete with gardens and bandstand, in which nonconformist chapels occupy a prime site, much as an Anglican church might have been located in a Georgian townscape such as Bath or Dublin.

Certainly, by the late 19th century the layout of some towns makes it possible to speak of a 'new establishment', Liberal in politics and nonconformist in religion.* At Porthmadog, chapels are located on or near the main street, whilst the Anglican church is tucked away (though admittedly on a hillside) on the edge of the town. Even in the Anglican city of Bangor, dissent asserted itself in defiance of the establishment; a Methodist chapel at SH 5821 7253 is said to have been designed to rival the cathedral and to have been equipped with a tower for this very reason (naturally such assertion was never committed to paper); alas for the godly, it has since become a block of flats, whereas the sacraments are still administered on St Deiniol's acre as they have been since post-Roman times. Church-builders no less than dissenters were aware of the effect of location; in the Ogwen valley it is striking how the spire of Glanogwen church lines up with the (earlier) Telford road on the approach to Bethesda from the south, and the spire of St Anne's contrives to dominate the area to the north.

Where patrons of industrial settlements were even-handed in their support for different denominations or had no strong confessional affiliations, the results are equally distinctive. The Unitarian Darbishire family developed the stone-quarrying town of Penmaenmawr from the late 19th century onwards. It came to be generously endowed with churches and chapels of every confession, all soundly built out of the local stone and with brick detailing. As we have seen, the earliest industrial nucleus of Penmaenmawr is a row of four cottages of the 1840s known as 'New York' (SH 7161 7627) where Telford's post road crosses the quarry incline, and it was around here that the Darbishires promoted socially mixed housing, including St David's Street (see p. 191) as well as the drill hall, the co-op., a school and a Masonic hall – a reversion, though in a very planned sort of way, to the mixture of the productive and the infrastructural which characterises earlier industrial communities (p. 196).

---

* Chapels in pre-industrial settlements often occupy undistinguished plots on back streets, reflecting the location of an original meeting room or rented loft, though where the present building might be an imposing third or fourth replacement for the original humble structure. Even in Methodist Bala, Capel Tegid (SH 9271 3591) is tucked away from the main thoroughfare, though its spire dominates the entrance to the town from the west.

Large-scale 20th-century estates, whether speculative build or social housing, inevitably reflect non-regional concepts of urban planning, built around regular street-patterns or patterns of circuses and crescents. These arise from the Garden City movement, with its conscious rejection of the straight uniform streets and cramped terraces of the planned industrial settlement, and which in turn harks back to late 18th-century landscape design translated into urban terms, whereby the townscape was subservient to the lineaments of the country. By the time estates such as Maesgeirchen (SH 5889 7182) and Ysgubor Goch (SH 4860 6260) were built, these principles had effectively been forgotten in developments where a geometric pattern is imposed on the natural environment, and it is the early 19th-century laneways and settlements which appear as the landscape's true organic outgrowths. It is these that predominate in the historic environment of Gwynedd, not the confining regularity of the late 19th century nor the palliatives of the 20th.

The fact that industrial settlements in Gwynedd have survived largely unchanged over a hundred years is remarkable in itself, but its inevitable corollary has been a stagnant society and a landscape that is unvalued. The poet R. Williams Parry (1884-1956) famously lamented how the mean landscape of industry had blighted his native Nantlle valley, where once gods and heroes had walked 'in the splendour of the morning of the world'.* It is only very slowly that industrial settlements have come to be recognised as valuable historic environments in their own right.

4.7 The Twentieth Century

4.7.1 Warfare, industrialisation, the command economy and beyond

Gwynedd played comparatively little strategic role in the conflicts of the 20th century, and little remains of the majority of productive sites established to meet wartime needs. The 'command economy', which war conditions required and which were sustained long after 1945, had more effect but the later 20th century has seen profound changes.

Two world wars during the 20th century, and the 'cold war' with the Soviet Union and its satellites from 1945 to 1989, obliged the parliamentary democracies to take an active role in industry. Even so, this state of affairs was foreshadowed before the end of the 19th century by encouragement to, or even direct sponsorship of, strategically vital industries, evident even in a peripheral area such as Gwynedd (pp. 98, 111), and reflects a far older and widespread need for governments to control supplies of *materiel*. Warfare itself, or its prospect, has been one of the most powerful incentives to industrialisation. German expansionism from the 18th century into the 20th can be readily analysed in terms of access to raw materials and industrial capacity – to the coal of Silesia and the Saarland, the iron-ore of Alsace, the mines and workshops of Moravia and the oil of Roumania and Iran. In the west, Roosevelt's 'arsenal of democracy' applied Fordist principles to war-production and enabled first Britain,

---

* Parry, R.W., 'Y ddôl a aeth o'r golwg' in *Cerddi'r Gaeaf* (Denbigh: Gwasg Gee, 1952), p. 1 ('Y ddôl a ddaliai Pebin/ Yn sblander bore'r byd').

then Russia, to withstand the aggressor. The Soviet five-year plans, harsh and wasteful as they were, enabled a country racked by civil war and famine a generation earlier to hold the line against Hitler's guns in 1941 and to evolve into a super-power.

Even though the end of the 20th century has seen a return throughout much of the developed world to the rhetoric of the minimal state, the role of government and of central agencies is still strong. In Gwynedd, this now might mean the Welsh Assembly in Cardiff, the London parliament or the European Union, and for this reason it seems appropriate to consider the industries of the war years along with those developed since 1945, even though for the very recent period it is difficult to measure their historical impact or to assess their archaeology.

Warfare, needless to say, affected Gwynedd profoundly. Young men and women found themselves far from home, carrying out tasks utterly different from those to which they had been brought up – to say nothing of being instructed, commanded and sworn at in a language many of them barely understood, often in circumstances of great personal danger, more commonly of profound discomfort and tedium. The innocence of Victorian Wales was very comprehensively shattered between 1914 and 1945, and the old verities gradually ceased to have the same meaning. The memorials to those who were killed are the common cenotaph or the statue of a grieving soldier. Only in the village of Nantlle is there a departure from type, in a slate plaque along one side of which are panels showing the work of the quarry, complete with blondins, a slate mill and locomotives (SH 5104 5338). On the other side are panels showing soldiers in the trenches, a continuity between work and war that is unusual in public commemoration.*

Industries met wartime needs in a variety of ways, some of which have already been described. At Dolgarrog, the production of aluminium was strategically important in both world wars, though developments post-1945 have swept away most of its archaeology (p. 125). As *4.1.5* and *4.1.6* have outlined, more intensive agricultural and silvicultural practices were also pursued during the war years. Purely defensive sites do not form part of the present study,† but some of them were to have an industrial 'afterlife', such as the RAF stations at Llandwrog (SH 435 585) and Mona (SH 415 760), which became civilian airfields, and the naval training base at Penychain (SH 435 365), which became the Butlin's camp after the war. RAF Penrhos survived as a single-strip civilian airfield, and as the *Dom Polski*, a home for Polish refugees, still (2006) very much in being and surely amongst the last Second World War displaced persons' camps in Europe.‡

---

* The memorial was originally set up in Pen yr Orsedd quarry nearby but was moved to the Methodist chapel in Nantlle (SH 5106 5337). The sculptor is not recorded but is believed to have been female – possibly Mary-Elizabeth Thompson (see p. 23). Continuity between work-duty and imperial duty is stressed by some First World War poets, and the sculpture may reflect the military ethos of the Darbishire family – see *4.6.2*.

† Gwynedd's position on Britain's western coast did not altogether isolate it from strategic considerations. The first defensive structures to be erected in Gwynedd since the Edwardian castles in the 13th and 14th centuries were the work of Thomas Wynn, later 1st Lord Newborough. Fort Williamsburg (SH 4603 5508) was erected in the park at Glynllifon between *c.*1761 and 1776, and Fort Belan on the coast nearby at the mouth of the Menai Straits (SH 4405 6095) pre-1776. Second World War defensive works such as the 'dragon's teeth' along the beach at Fairbourne reflect the possibility that German forces might seize the Irish Free State as a spring-board for an invasion. Of the RAF stations, Valley remains in use, Llandwrog retains many of its wartime buildings in re-use, and some remains survive at Pwllheli and Llanbedr.

‡ RAF Penrhos entered Welsh nationalist consciousness with the pacifist arson attack in 1938 alluded to in Chapter 1, carried out by a minister of the gospel, an academic and a schoolteacher. It is an irony that this area should have been almost entirely Polish in speech from the war into the 21st century.

Wartime exigencies affected the existing productive landscape in a number of ways. A factory complex near Beaumaris (SH 608 776) built flying boats until 1945, thereafter motor torpedo boats, mine sweepers and lifeboats, ending its working life turning out dustcarts and the lifting gear for wheely-bins in the 1990s. Parts of both Penrhyn and Dinorwic slate quarries were given over to the manufacture of aircraft components as part of this scheme. At Dinorwic existing buildings and rail tunnels in August 1940 were taken over by the North East Coast Aircraft Company (NECACO), a subsidiary of Rollason Aircraft Services, after Rollason's Croydon factory had been bombed. The front fuselage sections of Avro Lancaster bombers were assembled in the large corrugated-iron slate mills which had been erected a few years before. The Llanberis site was completely destroyed after the quarry's closure by the creation of the pumped storage scheme, though a subsidiary factory adjacent to the site of one of Caernarfon's corn mills (SH 491 620) remains in use for various purposes – welding, producing tissue paper and for car body repair. The Conwy Morfa was one of the principal sites given over to the manufacture of the Mulberry harbours for the D-day landings, though archaeologically little remains to be seen of this huge project, the brainchild of a Welsh engineer, Iorys Hughes. One of the harbours survives, partially submerged, off Arromanches in Normandy.[*] However, in Welsh terms, the centres of war production were Bridgend in Glamorgan, with its huge armaments factory, the Dee estuary, with its long-established tradition of engineering, and the Ministry of Supply's no 34 ordnance factory, which survives as the Wrexham Industrial Estate, near the English border. This belongs indirectly to the Gwynedd story, as it recruited many of its workers from the Bala-Dolgellau area.

It is transport and storage facilities that survive from this period, rather than production sites. The cold storage depot at Llandudno Junction (SH 8082 7755) was one of 50 built for the Ministry of Food between April 1941 and February 1942, of which at least seven survived until recently. These were light-weight steel structures, 65m by 35m (214ft by 120ft) in plan, 'almost unfenestrated Cubist structures, constructed of low-cost Fletton-type bricks, around insulated steel frames.'[†] At Glynrhonwy slate quarry at Llanberis, a bomb-store, later a bomb-disposal site, operated until 1956. A honeycomb concrete structure survives in the lowest of the quarry's pits (SH 5699 6101), much overgrown, complete with bakelite light fittings. The decision to store the National Gallery's collection at Manod slate quarry above Blaenau Ffestiniog bequeathed an extraordinary and most untypical door across the mouth of the adit (SH 7308 4556), looking as if part of a gigantic suburban garage had been grafted onto a Welsh mountainside, leading to air-conditioned chambers where the paintings were kept.[‡]

The years 1939 to 1945 confirmed the extent to which the state had assumed the powers of social patronage and economic command which had once been the prerogative of a regional elite, and there is an aptness that some of Gwynedd's wartime inward investment came about through the influence of David Lloyd George, whose early career had been based on the need to dethrone the great landowners. The election of the Labour government of Clement Attlee in 1945, and the broad acceptance by

---

[*] Jones, R.C., *Bless 'Em All: Aspects of the War in North West Wales 1939-45* (Wrexham: Bridge Books, 1995).
[†] Stratton, M. and Trinder, B., *Twentieth Century Industrial Archaeology* (London and New York: E. and F.N. Spon, 2000), p. 113.
[‡] McCamley, N.J., *Saving Britain's Art Treasures* (Barnsley: Leo Cooper, 2003), pp. 104-14.

both Conservative and Labour parties of the economic role of the state until the premierships of Margaret Thatcher (1979-90) and of Tony Blair (1997 to date), ensured that *dirigisme* dominated economic thinking for a generation after the war.

The Attlee government's nationalisation of coal and steel had no direct impact on Gwynedd; the most visible changes in industrial ownership were the new liveries and crests applied to railway stations, locomotives and rolling stock. The slate industry remained in private hands. Government policy to minimise social disruption led to a decision to retain the Dolgarrog aluminium works on its old site, even though there was no particular reason why the factory should remain in a comparatively remote area of the United Kingdom once the high-energy reduction process had ceased. A more direct government role in industrial development also raised the stakes for Members of Parliament as regional patrons. Particularly since 1688, MPs had been expected to represent individual constituents' interest through access to ministerial patronage but in the 20th century the prizes grew to be much greater than (for instance) securing a constituent's son a clerkship or his daughter a position as a nurse. Henry Haydn Jones' purchase of Bryneglwys slate quarry and of the Talyllyn Railway in 1911 doubtless secured his place in the House of Commons as Merioneth's representative, even though they represented a drain on his purse for as long as he lived, but Cledwyn Hughes could fairly claim that the establishment of the aluminium plant near Holyhead (see p. 126) had transformed the economy of his entire constituency. Smaller scale 'Advance' factories were attracted to the region, such as Ferodo in Caernarfon (SH 4983 6538), which remains in production.

An impressive example of the dual role of government and private initiative was what became from 1947 the Hotpoint washing machine factory at Llandudno Junction (SH 8029 7774). The first stage was built in 1940 to manufacture aircraft components, to the designs of the local architect Sidney Colwyn Foulkes (1885-1971) and reflected the architectural principles of his friend Frank Lloyd Wright. Foulkes also designed the extensions of *c.*1959-60.* It was demolished post-2000, after cursory photographic recording; the failure to carry though more detailed archaeological study confirms the sense in which industrial structures that are recent or that do not have a strong regional identity are as apt to be taken for granted by archaeologists as by non-professionals.

The manufacture of domestic appliances reflected the new post-war prosperity and surplus; more recently, Gwynedd has reflected a world-wide move into knowledge-based industry. The software technology centre located near Bangor represents the sort of development that brings a gleam to the eye of vice-chancellors in nearby universities, who sense the growth of hi-tech industries in attractive modern buildings within their purview. Whether, and to what extent, the establishment of Technium CAST (Centre for Advanced Software Technology) marks a departure in Gwynedd remains to be seen, but it is representative of a new type of industry, the result of private initiative but made possible by grant-aid from the European Union, drawn down with the assistance of the Welsh Development Agency.

It is perhaps still too near at hand to attempt objective valuation of the industrial archaeology of the post-socialist state, yet sooner or later strategies will be required to assess and understand its material remains. The experience of Wales in general, and Gwynedd in particular, will be relevant here. Throughout the 1980s and 1990s, Wales

---

* Uncatalogued newspaper cutting, Colwyn Foulkes Collection, Conwy Archive Service.

was used as a test bed for both interventionist and minimalist policies by Secretaries of State who represented very different strands of thinking in the governing Conservative party.* The Welsh Development Agency, initially established under a Labour government in 1975, was expanded greatly by Margaret Thatcher in 1988 to attract inward investment under the chairmanship of Dr Gwyn Jones (born 1948) until his downfall five years later. In the valleys of South Wales, the pace of economic change seemed for a while to be relentless; new roads and retail developments came near to obliterating historic landscapes of coal-mining and iron production. Less could be seen of its work, for good or ill, in Gwynedd, though some of its grant aid has more recently gone towards community use and small businesses, often with a 'craft' focus, which have given a new life to redundant industrial buildings.† Remarkably, it was this same Conservative administration, committed to the free market and to a central role for business, that first adopted the vocabulary of urban regeneration, following the 1981 riots in Liverpool and elsewhere. By 1989 it had also begun to speak of sustainable development ('development that meets the needs of the present without compromising the ability of future generations to meet their own needs'), following the appointment of Professor David William Pearce (1941-2005) as Special Advisor to the Secretary of State for the Ministry of the Environment. Pearce's *Blueprint for a Green Economy* led ultimately to Britain's landfill tax, the European Union's emissions trading scheme and the mechanisms for international pollution offsets.‡ Another indirect result of his work was that Wales became the first country in the world to write sustainable development into its constitution.§ Environmental management has as a consequence become an economic activity in its own right in Gwynedd. Both the Countryside Council for Wales and the Environment Agency are based in Bangor; academics teach Countryside Management at the University; the Snowdonia National Park operates from Penrhyndeudraeth. A post-modernist gloss on the present study might argue that it owes much to the landscape management 'industry', which has not only created a potentially receptive context for discussion, but has also provided the author with employment and income, as consultant and university teacher. Less contentiously, the adaptation of 19th-century buildings as field-studies centres, for schools and local authorities is a marked feature of the modern Gwynedd landscape.¶ These reflect an elite interest in the landscape of Gwynedd that has its origins in the travellers of the late 18th century and in individuals affected by the Romantic movement such as Madocks. This grew particularly through university climbing clubs in the Victorian period, but has been to a great extent democratised by the direct involvement of local education authorities.

What is clear is that definitions of 'industry' and the material evidence associated with it are changing rapidly and that industrial archaeology needs to develop strategies

---

* The interventionist Peter Walker (born 1932), was Secretary of State for Wales from 1987 to 1990. The free-marketeer John Redwood (born 1951) held the post from 1993 to 1995.
† As well as the workshops at Glynllifon, other examples are the former quarrymen's barracks at Nantlle (SH 5082 5339), which now accommodates a photographer and a stockist of model railway items and also serves as a village meeting place, and Penrhyn quarry's slab mills, in which a car repair business is based.
‡ Obituary, *Guardian*, 22 September 2005; Pearce, D., Markandya, A. and Barbier, E.B. on behalf of the London Environmental Economics Centre, *Blueprint for a Green Economy* (London: Earthscan, 1989).
§ Government of Wales Act 1998 (chapter 38), 121.
¶ Rhyd y Creuau near Betws y Coed (SH 8023 5709) is now the Drapers' Field Studies Centre, one of 16 field studies centres in the Atlantic isles. Plas Tan y Bwlch (SH 6554 4063) is now the Snowdonia National Park Studies Centre.

130 Changing technology; Penrhyndeudraeth has been networked for internet access. The Festiniog Railway and its locomotive in the background represent an earlier type of networking.

to understand these changes if it wishes to write the long story. Software technology is one example. Though it represents a radical change from characteristic steam-age site-types that are still evident in Gwynedd (Figure 130), it arguably represents a form of *atelier*-based skill that enables comparisons to be drawn with much earlier phases of manufacture. Yet, in terms of style and manner, it has much more in common with another regional economic activity to which the word 'industry' is also regularly applied, the creation of entertainment media. The BBC has been broadcasting from Bangor since 1935,* but in recent years Caernarfon has become the focus of active Welsh-language television and pop businesses. Some operate out of purpose-built modern structures, such as Barcud, on the Caernarfon industrial estate. Cwmni Sain's studios, however, are based in the former Women's Auxiliary Air Force Institute at RAF Llandwrog; its neighbouring businesses include a car-breaker's and a second-hand furniture store – typical post-industrial uses. Like the band-rooms and chapels in the quarry villages, the media also have their own infrastructure – the rationale behind *y Galeri*, a theatre-café-bar-gallery space built on the old public quay in Caernarfon in 2005, has been *inter alia* to provide a location for networking (SH 4789 6312). Just as the roles of the state and of private enterprise have not only changed but also redefined themselves in recent years, so the words 'production' and 'consumption' have taken on meanings unfamiliar to the industrial archaeologist. This in turn raises the question of whether industrial archaeology will have anything to say about the material evidence for the present and the immediately forseeable future. We must now return to consider the questions with which this study began.

---

* Morgan, D. (ed.), *Babi Sam: yn dathlu can mlynedd o ddarlledu o Fangor, 1935-85: atgofion a gobeithion pen blwydd* (Bangor: BBC, 1985).

Chapter 5

PERSPECTIVES

5.1 An Industrial Revolution?

The archaeology of the productive landscape within Gwynedd from 1700 points strongly to the process of industrialisation as an all-embracing change that can truly be called a revolution.

The previous chapter has outlined the ways in which the archaeology of the productive landscape in Gwynedd changes over the period from 1700 to the present day. As it has shown, the overwhelming evidence from the material data confirms that from the late 18th century Gwynedd enters a transformative period. The evidence allows us to make some judgements about the pace of change, and about the social agents who drove change, and to make some broad comparisons with other areas of the world.

The most powerful and immediate evidence is the landscape itself. Though industrial sites in the established sense do not utterly dominate the historic environment as they do in parts of, for instance, Lancashire or the Saarland, they are nevertheless omnipresent in the landscape and some slate quarries and copper mines cover large areas.* If we take the comparatively broad view of what constitutes industrial archaeology that has informed this study, then the landscape as a whole is manifestly one that has been changed by, and within the time-frame of, the classic industrial period. Even though the area remained primarily rural, agriculture itself went through profound changes which did not occur in isolation from other sectors. There are few places in Gwynedd where the historic environment has not been radically changed by human activity of the last two or three hundred years, even if only in the shape of field-walls or peat-diggings.

The landscape evidence confirms the scale of change; analysis of site-evidence, which may include documentary sources, enables us to estimate when these changes took place. Beginning our survey in 1700 suggests that, in Gwynedd, there is very little evidence for a long period of proto-industrial growth – a negative result, perhaps, but a result nonetheless.

The conclusion seems inescapable that the pace of change quickens around 1770, when copper mining assumes importance. Even so, the story here is one of localised and short-term economic growth rather than sustained development. Change is only rapid and sustained from the 1820s to the 1870s, when Gwynedd completes the shift from a subsistence economy to a world economy. Every sector begins to see change, every pre-existing monument type evolves a completely different form and many new ones appear for the first time.

---

* As noted in *4.1.1*, slate quarries constitute approximately 30 km^2 of the surface of the region (0.75 per cent of the total area of the region = 3,979km^2); the metalliferous mines cover a significantly smaller area.

However, using traditional industrial archaeology to quantify the pace at which change took place is difficult; this is one of the areas where simply accumulating technical data from site-specific surveys is not always particularly illuminating. Again, it is the landscape evidence and the regional 'story' that provide the context. For instance, the appearance of the steam engine, as a characteristic 'industrial' technology, is often held up as an eloquent measure of a region's progress, yet, as we have seen, in an area such as Gwynedd, with its fast-flowing streams, water was always likely to remain the prime-mover of choice wherever possible, through such ambitious, and comparatively late, technologies as the suspension wheel at Dinorwic quarry, and the water-balance shafts at Penrhyn (pp. 54-5) to the pumped storage schemes of the late 20th century (p. 144). Even though the first Gwynedd steam engines, at Penrhyn Du in 1779 and at Mynydd Parys in 1790 (pp. 90-1), are not remarkably early examples, it would be wrong to see the slow development of steam and the late survival of industrial water power as evidence *per se* of technical or economic backwardness, so much as of rational response to what the area offered in terms of energy-generation. The late introduction of other site-types is perhaps more telling. Archaeological study and documentary sources confirm the use of the stamp mill in Gwynedd by 1768, long after it had become established in Cornwall and mid-Wales (p. 85). A similar tale is told by the comparatively late arrival of such other characteristic technologies as the industrial road (1780s – p. 147) and the overland railway (1801 – p. 156).

Basic social provision is only identifiable a little later – industrial workers' housing from the very late 18th century, terraces from about 1807 (*4.6.1*, pp. 182-95). Again, it is necessary to sound a note of caution. A monument type such as 'nonconformist chapel' by itself can only tell us so much; though the oldest surviving example in Gwynedd dates from 1770, its context is entirely rural. Chapels survive in industrialising areas from 1785, but perhaps the telling developments here are the replacement of the unadorned chapel of early dissent by the 'learned' and architectural designs that first appear in 1810 but only become common after 1860, and the vast growth in numbers and in seating capacity which begins around the same time (p. 198). Other sectors have still not had the benefit of the level of study which would make it possible to chart the appearance of particular monument types – we know comparatively little about the archaeology of farm buildings in this period, and cannot yet, for instance, chart with any confidence the emergence of the planned farmstead (p. 106).

The social groups who drove change appear to be varied. Powerful landed interests were undoubtedly crucial in most of the productive sectors in the early stages, though fluid, landless capital becomes increasingly important from the mid-19th century. Only the archaeology of the textile industry confirms that this, at least in part, was in the hands of fairly humble members of society. In the slate- and stone-industries, there is evidence that quarrymen were able to retain some element of autonomy within their workplace despite managerial initiatives. The slate-quarry communities, in their very different ways, also suggest that working people could retain a great deal of control over where and how they lived, and how they might choose to organise their leisure time. The worker-created communities of Bethesda, Deiniolen and Moel Tryfan were above all places where the landlord's writ did not run. Blaenau Ffestiniog followed a different dynamic, but here, perhaps most clearly, the new elite of middle-class radical dissenting Wales is visible in the town's neatly laid-out squares.

What is perhaps surprising is how early on the state figures as an agent in industrialisation, even in an area such as Gwynedd. Long before the nationalisation of the commanding heights of the economy under the Attlee administration, central government is taking an active role particularly in agriculture and in forestry, and civic socialism is building houses. The biggest industrial developments in Gwynedd in the 20th century were, not surprisingly, state initiatives. Industrial archaeology has tended to focus on private enterprise, perhaps unconsciously and perhaps because the privately-owned single site is a more manageable concept than a vast state-owned monolith; yet if it is to do justice to the nature, extent and complexity of industrialisation, the archaeology of the socialist state and of the corporate state and their successors needs to figure.

Industrialisation may have been late in coming, even patchy in its development, but it nonetheless represents a fundamental and – once it had started – rapid change in the way this region organised its human society. The people of Gwynedd have inherited a revolution.

5.2 Archaeology or Heritage Management?

Archaeology and heritage management have traditionally been seen as separate disciplines; the following section argues that they need to be further integrated and understood in relation to each other.

If industrialisation in Gwynedd was, as is suggested here, a defining and all-embracing force, then questions arise – how should this legacy best be approached and who particularly among the inheritors might assume, or retain, responsibility for it? These are fundamental to understanding of heritage and of the historic environment.

Chapter 3 outlined the particular intellectual circumstances by which the archaeology of the modern period has come to be studied, and chapter 4 has indicated the variety of interest-groups which have come to assume responsibility for research or active conservation within this region. Traditionally the material evidence for the past was examined by professional archaeologists, sometimes with advice from amateurs, and, if considered to be of sufficient importance, was protected by legislation. More recently, as 2.5 describes, within Wales as a whole, landscape archaeologists have identified areas that are considered to be of particular importance and described them on a published *Register*, a non-statutory document but a material consideration in the planning process. Professional training in heritage management is offered by several universities in Britain, including Bangor – though tellingly, here archaeology is taught in the History Department, and Heritage Management in the School of Business and Regional Development. Many archaeologists have increasingly come to regard themselves as 'managers of heritage', particularly after the introduction in the UK of Planning Policy Guidance notes 15 and 16 not only expanded the opportunities for developer-funded recording but also placed the onus on archaeological contractors to recommend mitigatory measures where archaeology is likely to be destroyed. The Welsh regional archaeological trusts and independent archaeological contractors offer advice on the management of the archaeological resource as well as excavation and recording. Heritage remains therefore to a great extent in the care and protection of a professional cadre.

In Gwynedd, as elsewhere in the United Kingdom, voluntary bodies interest themselves in areas where official agencies have no remit or manifest a bureaucratic slowness in recognising just what their remit might include. Some have become statutory consultees, mainly the ones whose interest is national (or supra-national, given that Wales, Scotland, England and Northern Ireland are increasingly considered separate national areas) – the Association for Industrial Archaeology, the Vernacular Architecture Group, the Georgian Society, and the Thirties Society. All have done much to enlarge understanding of the historic environment. The opportunity which some of these special-interest groups have had to contribute to policy, and the influence they have brought to bear, has meant that state-sponsored heritage bodies, local and central government and even universities throughout the United Kingdom have become responsive to new trends in archaeology to a remarkable degree. This offers a marked contrast with the situation in many countries in continental Europe, where archaeology is rigidly managed by state-run universities and state-run museums.*

As well as these, there are other voluntary bodies which have little thought of influencing policy outside their own area of interest. As we have seen, within Gwynedd this includes informal associations of people who interest themselves in old agricultural machinery (p. 105), or organisations with a very specific remit indeed, such as the Ffestiniog Railway Society (p. 160). Not all of these organisations will even think of themselves as concerned with 'heritage' at all – a volunteer fitter on the Festiniog Railway, down for his fortnight-long annual stint, will regard the task of returning a faulty locomotive to service as an engineering challenge rather than a heritage issue.† These various groups confirm the vitality of the sector at popular and voluntary level, and also emphasise that what constitutes 'archaeology' and 'heritage', and opinion as to how it should be managed, is an intensely subjective matter, no matter how professionals may attempt to put an objective gloss on it.

However, many elements of the historic environment, particularly those of the 18th century onwards, operate outside any effective controls, whether in Gwynedd or elsewhere. In part the problem arises from the common human failure to recognise that the familiar and the everyday can be significant, and in much of Wales the historic environment struggles against a perception that 'heritage' is purely about people and language, or abstractions such as class-conflict. The very strong sense of 'place' amongst Welsh people – or Welsh-language Wales at any rate – does not help particularly, because 'place' becomes, as for Iorwerth Peate, an 'immortal essence' that cannot be changed unless by eradication of the language-based culture. This state of affairs is summed up by the tale of the chapel deacons, who on being taxed by the relevant government agency with having demolished a listed building, replied in all earnestness that they had not demolished the chapel – on the contrary, they had built a new one in its place!

Some types of feature or site are neglected, or not considered as having a heritage value, because they have few academic partisans and have not yet developed a network of amateur devotees – terraced housing, for instance. In England at the present time

---

* A trivial but telling detail from one of the German *lander* is that officials of its museum service are not allowed to offer cups of coffee to visiting colleagues unless they are from another state jurisdiction or if they have a PhD.

† For an academic study of the heritage railway volunteer, see Wallace, T., '"Working the Train Gang": Alienation, Liminality and Communitas in the UK Preserved Railway Sector', *International Journal of Heritage Studies* 12 3 (May 2006), pp. 218-33.

(2006), English Heritage has publicly countered the government's argument that terraced houses have had their day; in Wales, their supporters are few and far between. The converse also has its problems; as we have seen, one particular site-type which has been recognised and extensively researched by a wide range of individuals, groups and agencies is the slate quarry – yet one can discern a sense, even now, that this 'identity-archaeology' is a means of proclaiming, or allying oneself with, a sense of Welshness. Even here, different agenda are apparent; it is not long since the quarries were treated largely as brownfield sites by officialdom, and grants were being made available to landscape them. Many local councillors continue to argue that slate tips should be removed even when a national organisation, the Countryside Council for Wales, has identified them as essential components of important historic landscapes on the *Register*. Cottage dwellings remain a controversial and unresolved issue, with arguments flaring up over appropriate planning policy.

This in turn underlines that we cannot maintain a distinction between 'archaeology' and 'heritage management'. Recognition of the material evidence for the recent past as 'archaeology', indeed as 'heritage', is the first stage of management. This ideally should involve academic institutions paying more serious attention to it, as well as voluntary organisations coming to terms with their role as custodians in a broader public interest rather than purely as defenders of their own particular concerns. Archaeological study, particularly intrusive techniques involving excavation, involves considerable resources of time and money, and is only undertaken (or should only be undertaken) after careful consideration of all the options. This is itself a form of heritage management, and will inform conservation, access and interpretation, as well as restoration and replication where these are options.

5.3 A period discipline or a thematic discipline?

Though a strong case can be made for 'industrial archaeology' as a thematic discipline rather than as a period-specific discipline, the archaeology of productive and processing sites in Gwynedd displays a fundamental change in character that is coeval with changes in other sectors from the mid-18th century. This is adduced as argument that industrial archaeology is a period-specific discipline and should use appropriate methods of analysis.

Even if we feel entitled to speak of a Gwynedd 'industrial revolution' starting in the late 18th century, the question arises as to whether this particular region strengthens the case for regarding industrialisation as an essentially distinct and separate phase of human activity, one which characterises the last few hundred years, or for regarding it as an intensification of a process which began much earlier. By extension, we may also ask whether industrial archaeology requires unique skills that are not as applicable to the Roman or Medieval period as to the 19th century.

Gwynedd poses this question in a particularly acute way as it is one of the comparatively few areas of the Atlantic isles where an 'industrial' activity can be identified in the age of its first farmers; at Penmaenmawr modern quarrying takes place adjacent to the axe factory which flourished in the third millennium BC, and at Mynydd Rhiw the refilled pits of an even earlier site survive (pp. 34, 71). Archaeometallurgy has confirmed that some lead and copper mines in Gwynedd began life in Prehistory, and that the Great Orme in particular was worked on a very extensive scale (pp. 79-80). Pre-18th-century quarrying is generally understood through slates and stones found in archaeological deposits rather than from the production sites themselves, but some Medieval quarry sites have at least been identified, and there remains the possibility of discovering others and of carrying out detailed study on selected examples.

Yet, if anything, it is not the continuity in the Gwynedd landscape of broad site-types such as 'quarry' and 'mine' that are most striking, but the changes in their characteristics, As we have seen, these gather pace in the late 18th century – much later, as we have seen, than in some other parts of the world, so clearly other regional studies would tell a different story. These changes, moreover, are not only coeval with the appearance of the new site-types discussed in 5.1 but also with different types of evidence. Above all, paper sources are available in greater number and in more detailed fashion; written sources from this stage onwards increasingly reflect the concerns of plebeians as well as of patricians. Cartographic and other visual sources become vastly more abundant and, for the 20th century onwards, oral history is also an option. Clearly, analysis requires a methodology which can integrate these sources with the material record, which in turn suggests that industrial archaeology should be approached primarily as a period-specific discipline.

Yet the question goes deeper. In the first place, these different forms of evidence are available for other forms of post-1700 archaeology as well. Secondly, and related, the tendency to regard industry as somehow a separate 'theme' within archaeology ignores the significance of the fundamental changes which took place in other sectors at the same time, and which are clearly related to industrialisation. The present study has chosen to consider agriculture as part of industrial archaeology on the basis that it is also a 'productive' sector. Even if the premises for doing so set out on p. 96 can be contested, it is unarguable that the agricultural sector went through fundamental change from the late 18th century onwards, and that increased productivity was vital to feed growing industrial populations – not only in Gwynedd but within all areas of the world that experienced industrialisation as well as many that did not, but which relied on export trade. Irish farming, particularly dairying, from the 18th century onwards depended not only on its trade with Britain but with British colonies in the West Indies. The rapid entry of the prairies and grasslands of the USA, Canada, Argentina, Australia and New Zealand into the global economy in the 19th century not only took place in order to feed a growing industrial workforce but also relied on new technology – refrigeration as well as steam railways and steam ships. Crucially, it also fundamentally changed the balance of power away from the landed interest in western Europe, which in turn led to increased investment in non-landed modes of income-generation; industrialisation became a self-reinforcing process. In the 20th century both Stalin and Mao Zedong disastrously sought to reform their agricultural sector to serve the needs of a rapidly-growing industrial economy.

Other categories of the archaeological thesaurus that are only indirectly 'productive' were also changed radically by industrialisation. Even in Gwynedd, which has been only indirectly touched by war since the mid-17th century, industrial sites cannot be considered in isolation from defensive sites. Here, as in many other parts of the world, industrial sites have come into being to serve military needs or have become a military objective. Schooling, and provision for religious observance, as p. 208 notes, served the needs of industrial society at many different levels, as did changes in the pattern of recreation; the massive popularity of football by the end of the 19th century, though it cut across class boundaries, would not have been possible without the concentration of working-class men in manufacturing towns. The historical connection between particular teams and particular industries is strong, not only in Britain but all over the world, often as a consequence of British workers taking the sport with them.*

The argument that industrial-period archaeology can only be understood in the context of industrialisation-as-transformative-process in turn provides support for a period-based, rather than a thematic, approach. This is once again strengthened by the ways in which economic activity has involved into different forms of 'industry' in which digital communications and entertainment media are barely visible in landscape terms but are transforming social organisation.

5.4 Industrial Archaeology, Post-medieval Archaeology, Historical Archaeology, an Archaeology of Capitalism or an Archaeology of Industrial Society?

There are many labels for the archaeology of the post-Medieval period. It is argued that study of the archaeology of the productive landscape of Gwynedd post-1700 suggests that an archaeology of industrial society *offers the most coherent way of integrating material evidence for this period.*

This study set itself the task of examining the evidence that Gwynedd offers of the range of site-types, and their landscapes contexts, that make up the presently-accepted definition of 'industrial archaeology' in order to analyse whether this can be regarded as a coherent area of study, or whether in fact it points to the inadequacy of this category. The answer must be that the early focus of industrial archaeology, on primary sites, on processing and on distribution, and on the machines which made these possible, did indeed form a coherent area of study, even if a very narrow one. Once industrial archaeology moved beyond this functional interpretation, as it began to do in the 1990s, and started to examine its own intellectual assumptions, it moved into an area that is more diffuse, less capable of easy definition, but also more interesting and rewarding.

This perhaps leads to the most important point that has emerged from this study of Gwynedd – and it must be emphasised that the forensic purpose of this study has been no rhetorical device. The evidence of this one region as it has been analysed here suggests that maintaining a distinction between what has traditionally been regarded as industrial archaeology and other forms of material evidence for the recent past becomes progressively more difficult to sustain intellectually.

The reasons why this is so have been set out on a sector-by-sector basis in chapter 4, but now is the time to attempt to draw these threads together. Clearly, productive site-types or landscapes such as slate quarries or copper mines pose no intellectual

---

* See Hobsbawm, E., 'Mass-Producing Traditions: Europe 1870-1914' in Hobsbawn, E. and Ranger, T. (eds), *The Invention of Tradition* (Cambridge: Cambridge University Press, 1983), pp. 263-307.

problem in this respect – these were what had defined industrial archaeology from the beginning. The nature of the challenge is better illustrated by the 'infrastructural' site-types that industrial archaeology has learnt to encompass. The wide variety of workers' housing in Gwynedd identified in *4.6.1* should discourage facile attempts to distinguish between the homes of those who produced and of those who consumed; as we have seen, the captains' houses at Porthmadog, and the houses of prosperous tenant-farmers all accommodated people who worked with their hands and possessed a great range of skills, but they neither physically resemble nor can be easily accommodated into a received notion of 'industrial housing'. Even where housing is on the site of a mine or a mill or nearby, and clearly intended for key workers – where it can, in other words, easily be intellectually accommodated into an archaeology of production – evidence derived from artefacts recovered from within them is generally considered testament to what a working family could consume, despite the fact that these are themselves 'productions', and a potentially valuable source for the relationship between craft- and factory-production, as well as for distribution systems. Furthermore, for a mine-captain or mill-manager, maintaining dedicated houses for workers was often a necessity but was also itself a means of generating revenue from rents, just as running a truck-shop might be.

On the simplest level, the argument is strengthened rather than weakened by considering the archaeology of holiday settlements as different as Llandudno and Butlins. The former, as noted on pp. 213-14, was developed by the Mostyn estate when copper-mining had gone into terminal decline and when plans for building a dock for Wrexham coal had come to nothing; a middle-class holiday resort was simply one more means of ensuring a return on property. Butlins holiday camp at Pwllheli is a more authentically proletarian landscape of consumption (for all its earlier attempts to appeal to wider social groupings), and is crucial to the experience and the identity of English working families who came on holiday there. *4.6.1* suggests (p. 185) that the houses in Bangor which sheltered destitute Irish families making their way to the textile mills and coal mines of Lancashire cannot be separated from 'industrial archaeology' under whatever name; neither, on this reckoning, can places where the newly-affluent working class of the post-1945 generation sought recreation. If worker *mentalité* extends beyond the immediate discourse of 'work' then it must encompass the experience and enjoyment of free time and of rest in the 20th century, just as it already includes the radical politics and often opiate forms of religious identity available to working people in the nineteenth.

Religious buildings illustrate in a similar way the problems of maintaining a distinction between the industrial or 'productive' landscape and the wider built heritage. The religious power of the state declined markedly in Gwynedd from the 18th century, as in much of western Europe, though a state church remained in being in Wales until 1920. In its place, at least until the late 20th century, came a variety of confessional allegiances, whose built heritage reflects the evolution of protestant assumptions about worship and liturgy that formed part of a shared culture throughout the Atlantic isles and to much of the transatlantic world and which dates back to the reformation. However, if anything, the evidence suggests that, compared with other parts of the United Kingdom, Gwynedd is likely to prove less diverse in terms of the heritage of worship than other regions dominated by traditional industry such as

Yorkshire, where Catholicism became revitalised with immigration from Ireland in the 1850s and where Islam powerfully established itself a century later. In any case, the study of industrial workers' places of worship cannot be accomplished on the basis of 'industrial archaeology' alone, but needs to accommodate the insights of the mature discipline of church archaeology as well as to develop new strategies for understanding non-Christian structures.

As the state relinquished its power in religion, it assumed powers in other areas. The present study has identified schools, reading-rooms, libraries and hospitals that were constructed by, and for the exclusive use of workers in, a particular industry; these invite cross-sectoral comparison with state-sponsored infrastructure, which might also have to include prisons and workhouses.

There is no serious argument for returning to the earlier functional interpretation of industrial archaeology; to do so would be for the industrial-archaeological community to turn its back on what has proved to be one of the most intellectually rewarding developments in recent years in favour of a 'comfort zone' in which all the issues of authenticity (see p. 15) can be elided rather than challenged. This is not for one moment to suggest that the focus must move away from machines, mines, mills and factories to houses, shops and chapels but does argue that all site-studies will benefit from a more holistic archaeology of the modern world. The challenge is to accommodate and refine existing approaches rather than to devise wholly new intellectual strategies.

If further research elsewhere suggests that Gwynedd is typical rather than exceptional, and that there is a sufficient level of change in the archaeological record in the 18th century to merit a distinct archaeological approach across the board – one perhaps that acknowledges the importance of documentary sources and other forms of non-material evidence – then it is important to give some thought to the focus it might bring to bear. There is no shortage of titles which archaeologists have sought to apply to the study of this period, as chapter 2 has suggested, but the name itself will be more than a mere label – the associations and the assumptions that the label brings with it will affect, for good or ill, the way in which we come to develop understanding of this period in the years to come. This is a question separate from, though related to, consideration of the methodologies that have been under discussion in recent years – whether the 'Manchester methodology', or habitus, or structuration theory.

The case is made here that the archaeology of Gwynedd, as one distinct region of the world, confirms significant social and intellectual disjunction in the early 16th century and again from the late 18th century onwards – at the Reformation and at the Enlightenment, as it happens, remote though the area was from the epicentres of these great events in history. The 16th century saw the evolution of both the town-house and the distinctive regional farm-dwelling, as well as an increasing number of elite-sponsored features, such as bridges and private chapels. 'Post-Medieval' is an appropriate label, for instance, for Plas Mawr, Robert Wynne's magnificent late 16th-century house at Conwy (see *3.3.3*, pp. 38-40). Its location within an Edwardian *bastide* town, and its spatial relationship with the Edwardian castle illustrate both continuity and change. Conwy castle had not entirely outlived its usefulness when Plas Mawr was built, as it was to be garrisoned during the civil war; yet it already belonged to a manifestly older world, one which Robert Wynne and his like had largely supplanted. On the other hand, to identify Trawsfynydd nuclear power station as 'post-Medieval' is to strip the term of meaning. Furthermore, a label such as this is liable to confuse discussion of industrialisation in its international aspect. The present study should have confirmed that the phenomenon of industrialisation has to be understood in its world-wide context even from a regional perspective, but it is important to remember that in many places, mines, factories, warehouses and railways did not evolve gradually within a landscape, or a 'world-view', that had once been 'Medieval'. Thomas Arnold, the Headmaster of Rugby School, famously observed 'feudality is gone for ever' the first time he saw a train tear through the English Midlands, but when the first steam locomotive made its way across new-laid rails in Wyoming in 1867, bringing in its wake a rash of clap-board saloons and stores, it was not the Medieval world that was thus being consigned to oblivion but the hunter-gatherer culture of the Cheyennes. Since only in the Atlantic isles and continental Europe can we speak of 'Post-Medieval Archaeology', it is evident that Post-Medievalists' claims to the 19th century, and to the world-wide phenomenon of industrialisation, are liable to cause intellectual difficulty.

Paradoxically, the American term 'Historical Archaeology' also poses similar problems. If this is, as some scholars suggest, the archaeology of literate society, then this label is not particularly appropriate for the 16th century onwards. Many members of the elite were literate long before, as the growth of secular literature suggests, and though the Reformation may have enlarged the numbers of those who could read and write, the real change comes from the late 18th century onwards, beginning with basic literacy for reading the bible but moving by the Victorian period into the world of mass literacy – of building accounts, grocers' bills, guide books, instruction manuals and popular encyclopaedias as well as novels and plays. On this basis, 'Historical Archaeology' would have a strong claim to be a more appropriate name for what is often now called the 'Industrial and Modern period' but it should be dated from the 18th century rather than the 16th.

It has been suggested that an 'archaeology of capitalism' might offer a more comprehensive basis for understanding the material evidence for the modern world. Industrial archaeology's long-standing focus on individual work-places and work-place types implicitly fostered an assumption that production is typically a process variously of partnership and conflict between labour and capital, and that this duality of plebeian and patrician explains much of industrial archaeology. In Gwynedd, as we have seen, a purely 'capitalist' phase for the archaeology outlined here might only cover the period 1800 to 1900. For other regions of the world, the dates might have to be redrawn, but the story is common enough. Even a consumer society need not be entered and experienced through capitalism but through co-operatives and other socialist experiments – what one scholar has gone so far as to call 'red commodification'.*

Perhaps the most intellectually coherent title is 'the archaeology of industrial society'. It avoids period-specific labelling and encompasses not only productive and processing sites, as agents of transformation (the original focus of industrial archaeology), but also the landscapes of consumption associated with them, as well as the areas outside the developed world that did not experience full-scale industrialisation at first hand but found themselves yoked into a world economy. If this is so, and if

---

* See p. 204; Schollier, P., 'Goods and Stores for the Workers, The Shaping of Mass Retailing in Late 19th-century Ghent', in Barker, D. and Cranstone, D. (eds), *The Archaeology of Industrialization* (Leeds: Maney, 2004), p. 265.

this title were to gain acceptance, it is possible that as archaeologists we might begin to grasp the true significance of industrialisation, and thereby begin to identify, even in measure to comprehend, the forces that have shaped the global community.

5.5 Regional Meaning and International Significance

Understanding regional realities is crucial to understanding the broader picture of industrial society, just as specific areas can only be properly analysed within the context of world systems.

Economic and labour historians have long accepted that industrialisation has strong regional dimension. Yet to what extent does a regional analysis of the archaeology of industrialisation enable us to comprehend a wider world? 'Regional' is a word of which university faculties in Britain are now very wary; it sounds little better than 'parochial' and lacks the grant-drawing associations of 'international' (see 2.4, p.17). Yet there is little chance of painting the broader picture without an appropriate focus, and there certainly is a clear and immediate sense in which the industrial archaeology of this region is internationally significant. This is in the commonly-understood sense of the way that individual technical systems proved to be applicable far beyond Gwynedd's borders. Many of these were responses to the area's challenging topography – Telford's roads and suspension bridges, Stephenson's Chester to Holyhead railway and tubular bridges, the Festiniog Railway, the Liverpool signal systems and Marconi's wireless stations. Other technical systems have skilfully exploited topography in ways which have also been emulated all over the world – the early alternating current electricity distribution systems and their hydro-stations, and the pumped storage schemes at Tan y Grisiau and Llanberis.

What is more important is that Gwynedd demonstrates that no story is ever likely to be purely 'regional'. Exports of copper ore, particularly from 1768-9, when Parys went into production, tied in the economy of Gwynedd with that of the Swansea smelters – an industry that already depended on the merchant capital of Bristol and the ores of Cornwall and which in the years to come was to extend its reach to Cuba, Chile, Wisconsin and Australia. Gwynedd's slate quarries dominated the world production of this roofing material and were regarded collectively throughout Europe as the industry leader. The major extractive industry of this region forms part of the archaeology of buildings all over the world. Furthermore, exports of slate enabled Gwynedd ships to participate in other inter-continental trades – salt from Cadiz to Labrador, phosphates from the Dutch Antilles, homeward journeys with fruit and olive oil from the Levant, grain from Morocco or timber from Canada. Other Gwynedd quarries produced at a smaller scale for niche markets – setts for town streets, manganese for weapons of war. Whilst hitherto, the archaeology of industrial society has been considered in too narrow a way, it is essential that the regional dimension be understood for what it is. The search for raw materials and the means by which to process them is by no means less important now that the western world has partly managed to offload them onto other cultures, since questions of topography, climate and human society will always ensure that these retain a regional dimension in all but the smallest mono-cultural polities. An understanding of the regional dynamic is therefore crucial not only to understanding the historical basis of industrialisation but also to comprehending the experiences of de-industrialisation, and the trauma of developing economies as they continue to undergo the process.

5.6 Conclusions

The archaeology of Gwynedd demonstrates that the process of industrialisation can be a rapid one. It is little exaggeration to state that the region as a whole went from a subsistence economy to a world economy within the space of a century, from 1770 to 1870, and that within some localities the change was much more sudden. In terms of our understanding of the past, this confirms that industrialisation was, and is, a process that can follow a very different set of dynamics from one area to another.

However, more detailed study of (for instance) the archaeology of farming has the potential at least to modify this statement. There is much that is unknown, unacknowledged or insufficiently analysed. To accomplish this task to the fullest extent not only requires a broader and more holistic view of what constitutes the archaeology of the recent past, but must also comprehend the very many agencies involved in studying it, and in managing it. Such a task would be worth taking further in this particular region because of the remarkable variety and eloquence of the recent past in Gwynedd. The present study has also confirmed what was outlined as a possibility in 2.6, that Gwynedd's relationship with the other countries of the Atlantic isles and beyond might offer a particularly illuminating archaeological study.

Accomplishing this task will require an informed debate amongst the various constituencies as to the scope and focus of study of the archaeology of the recent past, one that should not by any means be confined to Gwynedd but which should draw on, and inform, understanding of other regions. Analysis of the historic environment of Gwynedd has led the present author to argue in favour of an *archaeology of industrial society*, yet it may be that similar studies of other regions will tend to different conclusions. The need for regional studies has grown, not receded. They are required not only in the Atlantic isles but in all parts of the world which industrialisation has touched.

Industrialisation is the most profound change in human society since the establishment of agriculture. It underlies a restless, conflict-ridden world. It has brought human society near to the brink of destruction and to within sight of irreversible change to our ecology. We cannot understand how we live without a close study of its material remains, and without an evolving understanding of the assumptions by which we undertake the study. Only then will the narrative of industrialisation be written. Only then will we begin to comprehend the world we inhabit.

Envoi

To make the journey to Gwynedd is to follow one of several routes. For generations of Irish men and women, Holyhead mountain and the long breakwater formed the first sight of the country which was to be their new home. For the present author, returning at the end of each term from post-graduate work in Dublin in the 1970s, it was still possible to see, or at least to imagine, the historical traumas which had inured a population to the reality of exile, as the accents of Roscommon and Mayo mingled with the measured Welsh of seamen in dark blue jerseys. Now, Ireland has grown prosperous, and the ferry terminal has the impersonal grandeur of an airport. It is Wales that seems impoverished.

Other familiar routes, both of them in the 'heroic' tradition of engineering, are Thomas Telford's post road, from the English border through Llangollen, or Robert Stephenson's Chester to Holyhead railway. The first springs its surprises gradually, as the landscape becomes steadily more mountainous, the second more suddenly, as the train crosses the river Conwy through Stephenson's wrought-iron tubular bridge right by King Edward's castle – the mountains close in, and 'heritage', natural and human, becomes omnipresent.

A route that few take lies across the narrow 'waist' of Wales, from the English border in the Severn valley to the headwaters of the Dyfi in Gwynedd, a distance of only 37km. It follows no heroic engineering work and passes no battlemented castle, but it is in some ways the most instructive. To make this journey is to travel from the 17th century to the 19th. The half-timbered village of Berriw has changed little since the reign of the Stuarts, and sits firmly within the lowland zone of England, even though it is nominally in Wales. So does its neighbour town, the 'Welsh pool' at the navigable head of the Severn, where Hanoverian and Victorian façades have only hidden some of its distinctive black and white box-framed buildings. The journey west from here into Wales leads not into a timeless or 'traditional' archaeological landscape; if anything, the reverse. The watershed, the point where streams begin to flow into Cardigan Bay rather than into England, is the point where the landscape becomes wilder and more mountainous, yet Dinas Mawddwy at the western end of this journey, just within the borders of Gwynedd, is a stone-built village of the 1860s and '70s. A slate quarry, long closed down, clings to the hillside. It is more distinctively Welsh in appearance and more modern in conception than the half-timbered houses that we have left behind. The creation of a Manchester capitalist who fancied himself as a Tory squire and clearly an 'industrial period' settlement, its industrial development – its stop-go lead-mining and quarrying for slate, its loss-making branch line – was nevertheless not a success. As it was, Welshpool's long story of trade and exchange, extending back long before the classic 'Industrial' period, has provided a more secure basis for prosperity than the sudden influx of capital that Sir Edmund Buckley brought from Lancashire to the Gwynedd mountains in 1856. Perhaps Dinas Mawddwy is typical. Industrialisation in Gwynedd was patchy, dependent on external sources of capital, and its success limited. Yet the extraordinary and rapid transformation of this peripheral region at once opened it out to a world economy and, paradoxically, re-fortified the strong, fastness-like identity of Gwynedd.

Appendix 1

BATEMAN'S CLASSIFICATIONS OF LANDHOLDING

The following statistics are taken from John Bateman, *The Great Landowners of Great Britain* (New York: Leicester University Press, 1971 – original London, 1883), who prepared a comprehensive outline of British landholdings as they were in the 1870s. His research is particularly of value as dating from the period before the agricultural depression of the later 19th century and from a time when social prestige and political power were still largely identified with land. His calculations do not include rentals from town properties or other building property nor from minerals other than coal. Bateman's definitions are as follows:

- *Peers* included peeresses and peers' eldest sons. It was at this time still exceptionally rare for a peer not to own an extensive landed estate.
- *Great landowners* are commoners with estates of 3,000 acres or more if the rental reaches £3,000 p.a.
- *Squires* are owners of estates of between 1,000-3,000 acres and such estates as would be included in the previous categories if the rental reached £3,000 p.a.
- *Greater yeomen* are owners of estates of between 300 and 1,000 acres.
- *Lesser yeomen* are owners of estates of between 100 and 300 acres.
- *Small proprietors* are owners of land of between one and 100 acres.
- *Cottagers* own less than one acre of land.

The number of peers is given for each county according to the location of their principal seats. Therefore, 16,684 acres of Merionethshire could be owned by peers though no peer had his principal country dwelling in the county.

ANGLESEY

No. of owners	Class	Acres	Percentage
3	Peers	31,339	18.7
8	Great landowners	66,175	39.5
6	Squires	10,200	6.1
31	Greater yeomen	15,500	9.2
86	Lesser yeomen	14,620	8.7
955	Small proprietors	20,421	12.2
3,015	Cottagers	234	0.1
37	Public bodies	3,447	2.1
	Waste	5,678	3.4
Total: 4,141		**167,614**	

CAERNARVONSHIRE

No. of owners	Class	Acres	Percentage
4	Peers	102,470	32.4
10	Great landowners	100,861	32.0
19	Squires	32,300	10.2
42	Greater yeomen	21,000	6.6
96	Lesser yeomen	16,320	5.2
1,407	Small proprietors	23,527	7.5
4,610	Cottagers	373	0.1
52	Public bodies	4,382	1.4
	Waste	14,563	4.6
Total: 6,240		**315,796**	

MERIONETH

No. of owners	Class	Acres	Percentage
0	Peers	16,684	5.5
12	Great landowners	128,593	42.4
37	Squires	168,800	55.7
96	Greater yeomen	48,000	15.8
135	Lesser yeomen	22,950	7.6
346	Small proprietors	14,244	4.7
1,044	Cottagers	212	0.1
25	Public bodies	3,174	1.0
	Waste	416	0.1
Total: 1,695		**303,073**	

SUMMARY TABLE OF ENGLAND AND WALES

No. of owners	Class	Acres	Percentage
400	Peers	5,728,979	16.6
1,288	Great landowners	8,497,699	24.6
2,529	Squires	4,319,271	12.5
9,585	Greater yeomen	4,782,627	13.9
24,412	Lesser yeomen	4,144,272	12.0
217,049	Small proprietors	3,931,806	11.4
703,289	Cottagers	151,148	0.4
14,459	Public bodies	1,443,548	4.2
	Waste	1,527,624	4.4
Total: 973,011		**34,523,974**	

Though the three counties of Anglesey, Caernarvonshire and Merioneth do not exactly conform to the boundaries of this study, they confirm the way in which landed power lay within Gwynedd in the late 19th century. They confirm for instance the hold of the wealthiest echelons of British society over Caernarvonshire where nearly a third of all the land is owned by peers of the realm. In Merionethshire, by contrast, peers had little influence, great landowners little more than in Caernarvonshire, but squires and greater yeomen were much more strongly represented. Squires in particular owned nearly a seventh of Merioneth compared with little more than a tenth of Caernarvonshire and less than one-sixteenth of Anglesey.

Appendix 2

GROWTH OF RETAILING

	Booksellers, bookbinders, publishers	Boot and shoe makers	Butchers	Chemists and druggists	China, glass, earthenware dealers	Confectioners	Drapers and milliners	Dressmakers	Grocers and dealers in sundries	Hairdressers	Hatters	Tailors and drapers	Toy dealer	Watch and clockmakers	Linen and woollen drapers
Porthmadog and Tremadoc															
1828		2		} + 5 unspecified 'shopkeepers' {			1					2		§	
1850	1	7	6	2					14	3		8		2	
1868	3	10	7	4	1			5	28	2		9		1	12
1883	2	14	10	3	2	3		6	29	3	1	11		2	13
Dolgellau															
1828	2	4	3						10*			5		2	
1850	7	21	8	2					21	4		10		3	
1868	6	17	9	3	4			5	36	2		8		5	
1883	10	14	8	2	6	7	12		31	2		11	4	2	6
Penmachno															
1868		1	1		1	1			5			2			
1883			1			2			11			3			6

These figures derived from the relevant Trade Directories illustrate the growth of retailing within Gwynedd. Porthmadog and Tremadoc were settlements that grew rapidly in the early years of the 19th century, and Dolgellau was an established borough. Penmachno, a 'wretched village', does not appear at all until 1868, but by the end of the 19th century it is almost on the verge of becoming a small town.

*   Grocers and drapers – also includes druggists.

BIBLIOGRAPHY

Aalen, F., Whelan, K. and Stout, M., *Atlas of the Irish Rural Landscape* (Cork: Cork University Press, 1997)
Abbott, R., 'Chronicles of a Caernarvonshire Ironworks', *TCHS* 17 (1956) pp. 86-94
— *Vertical Boiler Locomotives and Railmotors Built in Great Britain* (Oxford: Oakwood Press, 1989)
Agricola, G., trans. Hoover H. and Hoover, L.H., *De Re Metallica* (New York: Dover, 1950)
Alfrey, J., 'A New Look at Conservation Values', *Heritage in Wales* 12 (1999), pp. 13-17
— 'Rural Building in Nineteenth-Century North Wales; The Role of the Great Estates', *Archaeologia Cambrensis* 107 (2001 for 1998), pp. 199-216
Alfrey, J. and Clark, C., *The Landscape of Industry: Patterns of Change in the Ironbridge Gorge* (Routledge, 1993)
Alfrey, J. and Putnam, T., *The Industrial Heritage: managing resources and uses* (London and New York: Routledge, 1992)
Anderson, V.R. and Fox, G.K., *An Historical Survey of the Chester to Holyhead Railway* (Poole: Oxford Publishing Company, 1984)
Andrews, J.F., *Keep Moving: the Story of Solomon Andrews* (privately published, 1976)
Angerstein, R., *R.R. Angerstein's Illustrated Travel Diary, 1753-1755* (trans. Torsten and Peter Berg) (London: Science Museum, 2001)
Anon., *Artist yn y Chwarel/An Artist in the Quarries* (Cardiff: Welsh Arts Council, 1981)
Anon., *The Dinorwig power station: papers presented at a major achievement symposium* (London: The Institution of Mechanical Engineers, 1985)
Anon., *Beamish; The North of England Open-Air Museum* (Jarrold Publishing, 2003)
Arnold, M., *The Study of Celtic Literature* (London: Smith, Elder and Co., 1891)
Ashton, T.S., *The Industrial Revolution* (London: Oxford University Press, 1948)
Bailey, M.R. and Glithero, J.P., *The Engineering and History of Rocket* (London and York: National Railway Museum, 2000)
Bailey, M.R. (ed.), *Robert Stephenson – The Eminent Engineer* (Aldershot: Ashgate, 2003)
Baldwin Locomotive Co., *Illustrated Catalogue of Baldwin Locomotives, Burnham, Parry, Williams & Co., Philadelphia* (London: reprint of J.B. Lippincott and Co. edition of 1881, Bishopsgate Press Ltd, 1983)
Barnwell, P.S. and Giles, C., *English Farmsteads 1750-1914* (Royal Commission on the Ancient and Historic Monuments of England, 1997)
Bartram, M., *The Pre-Raphaelite Camera: Aspects of Victorian Photographs* (London: Weidenfeld and Nicolson, 1985)
Bassett, T.M. and James, G., 'Coalmining in Anglesey', *TAAS* (1969-70), pp. 137-63
Bateman, J., *The Great Landowners of Great Britain* (New York: Leicester University Press, 1971 – original London, 1883)
Beazley, E., *Madocks and the Wonder of Wales* (Aberystwyth: P&Q, 1985)
Bennett, J. and Vernon, R.W., *Mines of the Gwydyr Forest Parts 1-6* (Knutsford: Gwydyr Mines Publications, 1989-1995)
— *Metal Mines of Llanengan* (Warrington: Gwydyr Mines Publications, 2002)
Bennett, J. and Williams, C.J., 'Pearl Shaft Engine House, Mona Mine, Parys Mountain', *TAAS* (2000), pp. 40-42
Bezant Lowe, W., *The Heart of Northern Wales* (privately published, 1927)
Bick, D., *The Old Copper Mines of Snowdonia* (Newent: the Pound House, 1985)
— 'The Beam-Engine House in Wales', *IAR* 12 1 (Autumn 1989), pp. 84-93
— 'Evolution of the Pre-Cornish Beam Engine House', *IAR* 21 2 (Autumn 1999), pp. 134-5
Bielenberg, A. (ed.), *Irish Flour Milling: A History 600-2000* (Dublin: Lilliput, 2003)
Bingley, W., *North Wales, including its Scenery, Antiquities, Customs etc* (London, 1804)
Bogue, A.G., 'An Agricultural Empire' in *The Oxford History of the American West* (New York and Oxford: Oxford University Press, 1996), pp. 275-313

Boon, G.C., 'A Temple of Mithras at Caernarvon – Segontium', *Archaeologia Cambrensis* 109 (1960), pp. 136-72
Boyd, J.I.C., *Narrow Gauge Railways in North Caernarvonshire* (Oxford: Oakwood Press, 1981)
— *Narrow Gauge Railways in North Caernarvonshire Volume 2 The Penrhyn Quarry Railways* (Headington: Oakwood Press, 1985)
— *Narrow Gauge Railways in North Caernarvonshire Volume 3* (Oxford: Oakwood Press, 1986)
— *The Talyllyn Railway* (Oxford: Wild Swan, 1988)
Bradley, R. and Edmonds, M., *Interpreting the Axe Trade – production and exchange in Neolithic Britain* (Cambridge, 1993)
Bradley V.J., *Industrial Locomotives of North Wales* (London: Industrial Railway Society, 1992)
Brayshay, M. and Williams, A., 'North Snowdonia: an upland landscape under pressure' in Whyte, I.D. and Winchester, A.J. (eds), *Society, Landscape and Environment in Upland Britain* (Society for Landscape Studies supplementary series 2, 2004), pp. 125-39
Briggs, C.S., *Towards a Research Agenda for Welsh Archaeology* (Oxford: Archaeopress, 2003)
Broadberry, S. and Gupta, B., *Cotton Textiles and the Great Divergence: Lancashire, India and Shifting Competitive Advantage* (London: discussion paper 5183, Centre for Economic Policy Research, 2005)
Bromwich, R., *Trioedd Ynys Prydein: The Triads of the Isle of Britain* (Cardiff: University of Wales Press, 2006)
Brown, C. and M., *The Clockmakers of Llanrwst* (Wrexham: Bridge Books, 1993)
Cadw, *Anheddau Bychain Gwledig yng Nghymru/Small Rural Dwellings in Wales* (Cardiff: Cadw, 2003)
Cadw, ICOMOS UK and the Countryside Council for Wales, *Register of Landscapes of Outstanding Historic Significance in Wales* (Cardiff, 1998)
— *Conwy Gwynedd & The Isle of Anglesey: Register of Landscapes, Parks and Gardens of Special Historic Interest in Wales: Part 1 Parks and Gardens* (Cardiff, Cadw, 1998)
— *Register of Landscapes of Special Historic Interest in Wales* (Cardiff, 2001)
Caffell, G., *Llechi Cerfiedig Dyffryn Ogwen/The Carved Slates of Dyffryn Ogwen* (Cardiff: National Museum of Wales, 1983)
Cameron, A., *Slate from Coniston* (Barrow in Furness; Cumbria Amenity Trust Mining History Society, 1996)
Cannadine, D., 'Engineering History, or the History of Engineering? Rewriting the Technological Past', *Transactions of the Newcomen Society* 74 2 (2004), pp. 163-80
Chapman, C., *A Guide to Parliamentary Enclosures in Wales* (Cardiff: University of Wales Press, 1992)
Clapham, J., *Economic History of Modern Britain* (Cambridge: Cambridge University Press, three vols, 1926-38)
Clayton, D., 'A North Wales Locomotive Mystery', *Industrial Railway Record* 126 (September 1991), pp. 310-18
Cockshutt, E., 'The Parys and Mona Copper Mines', *TAAS* 1960, pp. 1-25
Colley, L., *Britons: Forging the Nation 1707-1837* (New Haven and London: Yale University Press, 1992)
Cossons, N., 'A Perspective on the Nature of Industrial Collections', in Dollery, D. and Henderson, J. (eds), *Industrial Collections: Care and Conservation* (Cardiff and London: Council of Museums in Wales and The United Kingdom Institute for Conservation, 1997), pp. 9-15
Coulls, A., 'The Ephemeral Archaeology of the Miniature Railway', *IAR* 25 1 (May 2003), pp. 31-41
Cowell, J., *Beaumaris A Pictorial History* (privately published, 2005)
Cozens, L., Kidner, R.W. and Poole, B., *The Mawddwy, Van and Kerry Branches* (Usk: Oakwood Press, 2004)
Craig, M., *Dublin 1660-1860* (Dublin: Allen Figgis, 1980)
Crankshaw, W.P., *Report on a Survey of the Welsh Textile Industry made on Behalf of the University of Wales* (Cardiff: University of Wales Press, 1927)
Cranstone, D., 'After Industrial Archaeology', in Casella E. and Symonds, J. (eds), *Industrial Archaeology: Future Directions* (New York: Springer, 2005), pp. 77-92
Crew, P., 'The Copper Mines of Llanberis and Clogwyn Goch', *TCHS* 37 (1976), pp. 58-79
Crew, P. and Williams, M.C., 'Dol y Clochydd', *Archaeology in Wales* 24 (1984), pp. 83, 25 (1985), pp. 54-5 and 26 (1986), p. 68
Crocker, A. and G., 'The Gunpowder Mills at Tyddyn Gwladys, near Dolgellau', *Melin* 12 (1996), pp. 2-25
Davidson, A., 'Tidal mills on Anglesey', *Melin* 16 (2000), pp. 29-50
Davies, E., *The North Wales Quarry Hospitals and the Health and Welfare of the Quarrymen* (Caernarfon: Gwynedd Archives Service, 2003)
Davies, I.E., 'A History of the Penmaenmawr Quarries', *TCHS* 35 (1974), pp. 27-72
Davies, I.E., 'The Manufacture of Honestones in Gwynedd', *TCHS* 37 (1976), pp. 80-86

Davies, W., *A General View of the Agriculture and Domestic Economy of North Wales* (London: 1810)
Dibble, K., *Nant-y-Gamar* (privately published, no date)
Dinn, J., 'Dyfi Furnace Excavations 1982-87', *Post-Medieval Archaeology* 22 (1988), pp. 111-42
Dodd, A.H., *A History of Caernarvonshire* (Wrexham: Bridge Books, 1990)
— *The Industrial Revolution in North Wales* (Wrexham: Bridge Books, rep. 1990)
Donelly, T., 'Structural and Technical Changes in the Aberdeen Granite Quarrying Industry 1830-1880', *IAR* 3 3 (1979), pp. 228-42
Down, C.G., 'Narrow Gauge Wagons: Penmaenmawr Quarries', *Industrial Railway Record* 64 (February 1976), pp. 174-7
— 'Narrow Gauge Wagons: The Britannia Foundry', *Industrial Railway Record* 92 (March 1982), pp. 401-7
— 'The Britannia Foundry, Portmadoc' (Festiniog Railway), *Heritage Group Journal* 56 (Winter 1998-9), pp. 5-25
Doyle, W., *The Oxford History of the French Revolution* (OUP, 1990)
Ebenezer, E., *Fron-Goch and the birth of the IRA* (Llanrwst: Gwasg Carreg Gwalch, 2006)
Edwards, T. ('Twm o'r Nant'), *Pedair Colofn Gwladwriaeth* (Caerfyrddin: Jonathan Harris, 1810)
Electricity Council, *Electricity Supply in the United Kingdom* (London, 1982)
Ellis, B., *The History of Halkyn Mountain* (Halkyn: Helygain, 1998)
Ellison, D.B., *Hammer and Nails: Captain Timothy Edwards of Nanhoron* (Caernarfon: Gwynedd Archives Service, 1997)
Evans, C., *The Labyrinth of Flames: work and social conflict in early industrial Merthyr* (Cardiff: University of Wales Press, 1993)
Evans, J., *Topographical and Historical Description of Anglesey* (London, 1810)
Evans, K., 'A Survey of Caernarvon, 1770-1840 Part 1A', *TCHS* 32 (1971), pp. 32-71
Fairweather, B., *The 300-Year Story of Ballachulish Slate* (Glencoe: Glencoe and North Lorn Folk Museum, n.d)
Farrington, T.B., *Cowlyd Waterworks* (Conway and Colwyn Bay Joint Water Supply District, 1904)
Firbanks, T., *I Bought a Mountain* (London: Harrap, 1953)
Fisk, M.J., *Housing in the Rhondda 1800-1940* (Cardiff: Merton Priory Press, 1996)
Forestry Commission Booklet 28, *Gwydyr Forest in Snowdonia: A History* (London: HMSO, 1971)
Forestry Commission Guide, *Cambrian Forests* (London: HMSO, 1975)
Foster, C. and Cox, S.H., *Ore and Stone Mining* (London: Charles Griffin, 1910)
Foucault, M., *Discipline and Punish: The Birth of the Prison* (trans. of *Surveiller et Punir: Naissance de la Prison* by Alan Sheridan), (New York: Vintage Books 1995)
Geddes, R.S., *Burlington Blue-Grey: A History of the Slate Quarries, Kirkby-in-Furness* (privately published, 1975)
Gerhold, D., *Carriers and Coachmasters: Trade and Travel before the Turnpikes* (Chichester: Phillimore, 2005)
Gerrard, S., 'The Medieval and Early Modern Cornish Stamping Mill', *IAR* 12 1 (Autumn 1989), pp. 9-19
Godwin, F. and Toulson, S., *The Drovers' Roads of Wales* (London: Whittet Books, 1994 repr.)
Gould, S., review of Cossons, N., *Perspectives on Industrial Archaeology (2000)*, *IAR* 23 1 (May 2001), p. 67
Greenhill, B., *The Evolution of the Wooden Ship* (London: Batsford, 1988)
Greenly, E., *The Geology of Anglesey* vol. 2 (Memoir of the Geological Survey, 1919)
Griffith, M., 'Manganese Mining at Rhiw in Llŷn between 1827 and 1945', *TCHS* 50 (1989), pp. 41-65
Guise, B. and Lees, G., *Windmills of Anglesey* (Painscastle: Attic Books, 1992)
Gwyn, D. and Jones, E., *Dolgarrog: An Industrial History* (Caernarfon: Gwynedd Archives Service, 1989)
Gwyn, D., 'Valentia Slate Slab Quarry', *Cumann Seandáloichta is Staire Chiarrai/Journal of the Kerry Archaeological and Historical Society* 24 (1995 for 1991), pp. 40-57
— 'From Blacksmith to Engineer: Artisan Technology in North Wales in the Early Nineteenth Century', *Llafur* 7 (1999), pp 51-65
— 'Hoisting Machinery in the Gwynedd Slate Industry', *Transactions of the Newcomen Society* 71 22 (2000), pp. 190-94
— 'Transitional Technology – the Nantlle Railway' in *Early Railways* (London: the Newcomen Society, 2000), pp 46-62.
— '"Ignorant of all science": Technology transfer and peripheral culture, the case of Gwynedd, 1750-1850', *From Industrial Revolution to Consumer revolution: international perspectives on the archaeology of industrialisation* (The International Committee for the Conservation of the Industrial Heritage, 2001 for 2000), pp 39-45
— 'The Failed Enclosure: Common and Crown Land on Mynydd Cilgwyn', *TCHS* 62 (2001), pp. 81-97
— 'The Industrial Town in Gwynedd: a Comparative Study', *Landscape History*, 2002, pp. 71-89
— 'An Early High-Pressure Steam Engine at Cloddfa'r Coed', *TCHS* 63 (2002), pp. 26-43

— 'A Welsh Quarryman in County Tipperary: Further Light on Griffith Parry', *North Munster Antiquarian Journal/Irisleabhar Ársaíochta Tuadh-Mhumhan* 43 (2003), pp. 105-9

— 'Partnerships and Priorities for the Industrial and Modern Period' in Briggs, C.S. (ed.), *Towards a Research Agenda for Welsh Archaeology* (Oxford: Archaeopress, 2003), pp. 179-86

— 'Publishing and Priority in Industrial Archaeology' in Casella, E. and Symonds, J. (eds), *Industrial Archaeology: Future Directions* (New York: Springer, 2005), pp. 121-34

— 'The Landscape Archaeology of the Vale of Ffestiniog', *IAR* 27 1 (May 2004), pp. 129-36

— 'Landscape, Economy and Identity: A Case Study in the Archaeology of Industrialisation' in Barker, D. and Cranstone, D., *The Archaeology of Industrialization* (Leeds: Maney, 2004), pp. 35-52

Gwyn, M., *Continuity and Change in Women's Lives in Gwynedd 1937-1947* (Bangor: Women's Studies Monograph Series, 2002)

Hague, D.B., *Lighthouses of Wales* (Aberystwyth: RCAHMW, 1994)

Hammond, J. and B., *The Village Labourer 1760-1832* (London: Green, 1911)

— *The Town Labourer 1760-1832* (London: Longmans, Green and Co., 1917)

— *The Skilled Labourer 1760-1832* (London: Longmans, Green and Co., 1919)

Harris, J.R., *The Copper King: Thomas Williams of Llanidan* (Ashbourne: Landmark Publishing, 2003)

Harrison, R. (ed.), *Independent Collier: the coal miner as archetypal proletarian reconsidered* (New York: St. Martin's Press, 1978)

Hartley, R.F., 'The Tudor Miners of Coleorton, Leicestershire', *Mining Before Powder* (Peak District Mines Historical Society 12 3, Summer 1994 and Historical Metallurgy Society Special Publication), pp. 91-101

Haslam, R., *RIBA Drawings Monographs no. 2: Clough Williams-Ellis* (London: Academy Editions, 1996)

Hay, G.D. and Stell, G.P., *Monuments of Industry* (Edinburgh: Royal Commission on the Ancient and Historical Monuments of Scotland, 1986), pp. 176-80

Hays, Rh.W., *A History of the Abbey of Aberconway* (Cardiff: University of Wales Press, 1957)

Hayter, H., 'Holyhead New Harbour', *Minutes of the Proceedings of the Institute of Civil Engineers* 44 (1875-6), pp. 95-130

Heaney, S., *Death of Naturalist* (London: Faber and Faber, 1966)

Henderson, J.M., 'Aerial Suspension Cableways', *Proceedings of the Institution of Civil Engineers* 108 (1904), pp. 186-204

Hewison, R., *The Heritage Industry: Britain in a Climate of Decline* (London: Methuen, 1987)

Hills, R. and Gwyn, D., 'Three Engines at Penrhyn Du, 1760-1780', *Transactions of the Newcomen Society* 75 1 (2005), pp. 17-36

Hilton, G.W., *American Narrow Gauge Railroads* (Stanford: Stanford University Press, 1990)

Hilton, T., *John Ruskin: The Later Years* (New Haven and London: Yale University Press, 2000)

Hindley, P.G., 'The Penmaenmawr Quarry Inclines', *Industrial Railway Record* 86 (September 1980), pp. 173-94

Hobsbawm, E., 'Mass-Producing Traditions: Europe 1870-1914' in Hobsbawm, E. and Ranger, T. (eds), *The Invention of Tradition* (Cambridge: Cambridge University Press, 1983), pp. 263-307

— 'Man and Woman: Images on the Left', republished in *Uncommon People* (London: Abacus, 1999)

Hooke, D., 'Place-names and vegetation History as a key to Understanding Settlement in the Conwy Valley' in *Landscape and Settlement in Medieval Wales* (Oxford: Oxbow Monograph 81, 1997), pp. 79-95

Hope, B.D., *A Curious Place: An Industrial History of Amlwch (1550-1950)* (Wrexham; Bridge Books, 1994)

— *A Commodious Yard: The Story of William Thomas & Sons Shipbuilders of Amlwch 1858-1920* (Wrexham: Bridge Books, 2005)

Hubbard, E., *The Buildings of Wales: Clwyd* (London: Penguin Books, University of Wales Press, 1994)

Hughes, E. and Eames, A., *Porthmadog Ships* (Caernarfon: Gwynedd Archives Service, 1975)

Hughes, H., *Immortal Sails* (Prescot: T. Stephenson and Sons, 1977)

Hughes, H.D., *Hynafiaethau Llanllechid a Llandegai* (Bethesda, 1866)

Hughes, S., *The Archaeology of the Montgomeryshire Canal* (Aberystwyth: RCAHMW, 1989)

— *The Archaeology of an Early Railway System: The Brecon Forest Tramroads* (Aberystwyth: RCAHMW, 1990)

— *Copperopolis: Landscapes of the Early Industrial Period in Swansea* (Aberystwyth: RCAHMW, 2000)

— 'Institutional Buildings in Worker Settlements', in *Understanding the Workplace: A Research Framework for Industrial Archaeology in Britain; IAR* 27 1 (May 2005), pp. 153-61

— 'Thomas Thomas, 1817-88: the first national architect of Wales', *Archaeologia Cambrensis* 152 (2003), pp. 69-166

Hughes, S., Malaws, B. *et alii*, *Collieries of Wales* (Aberystwyth: RCAHMW, n.d.)

Hughes Williams, R., *Straeon y Chwarel* (Caernarfon: Cwmni y Cyhoeddwyr Cymreig, 1914)

Huntley, J., *Railways on the Screen* (Shepperton: Ian Allan, 1993)

Hyde-Hall, E., *A Description of Caernarvonshire* (Caernarfon: Caernarvonshire Historical Society, 1956)

Hywel, E. ab, *Welsh Slate Museum, Llanberis; Guide* (Cardiff: National Museums and Galleries of Wales, 2002)
Ince, L., *Neath Abbey and the Industrial Revolution* (Stroud: Tempus, 2001)
Isherwood, G., *Cwmorthin Slate Quarry* (Gwernaffield: Adit, 1982)
Jackson, B.L., *Isle of Portland Railways volume 1 The Admiralty and Quarry Railways* (Oakwood Press, 1999)
Jackson, G., *The History and Archaeology of Ports* (Tadworth, 1983)
Jarvis, A., 'Introduction: The present state of the History of Ports' in Jarvis, A. (ed.), *Port and Harbour Engineering* (Ashgate, 1998), pp. xiii-xxxiv
Jenkins, D., *Hywel Dda: The Law* (Llandysul: Gomer, 1990)
Jenkins, J.G., *The Welsh Woollen Industry* (Cardiff: National Museum of Wales, 1969)
— *Life and Tradition in Rural Wales* (London: J.M. Dent and Sons, 1976)
— *The People's Historian Professor Gwyn A. Williams (1925-1995)* (Aberystwyth: Centre for Advanced Welsh and Celtic Studies, 1996)
Jones, A., *Welsh Chapels* (Stroud: Alan Sutton, 1996)
Jones, B., *Etholiadau'r Ganrif* (Y Lolfa, 1999)
Jones, E., *Stiniog* (Caernarfon: Gwasg Gwynedd, 1988)
Jones, E.J., 'The Enclosure Movement in Anglesey (1788-1866)', *TAAS* 1926, pp. 31-89
Jones, G.P., 'The Slate Quarries of the Nantlle Valley', *Stationary Power* 2 (1985), pp. 47-73
Jones, G.R., *Hafodlas Slate Quarry Bettws-y-Coed* (privately published, 1998)
— *Rhiwbach Slate Quarry* (privately published, 2005)
Jones, G.T., *The Fords of Anglesey* (Bangor: Canolfan Ymchwil Cymru, 1992)
Jones, O., *Cymru: Hanesyddol, Parthedigol, a Bywgraphyddol* (London, Glasgow and Edinburgh, 1875)
Jones, P.E., 'The Bangor Local Board of Health, 1850-83', *TCHS* 37 (1976), pp. 87-132
— *Bangor 1883-1983: A Study in Municipal Government* (Cardiff: University of Wales Press, 1986)
Jones, R. and Reeve, C.G., *A History of Gas Production in Wales* (Wales Gas Printing Centre, n.d.)
Jones, R.C., *Bless 'Em All: Aspects of the War in North West Wales 1939-45* (Wrexham: Bridge Books, 1995)
Jones, R.M., *The North Wales Quarrymen 1874-1922* (Cardiff: University of Wales Press, 1981)
Jones R.M. and Lovecy, J., 'Slate Workers in Wales, France and the United States: A Comparative Study', *Industrial Gwynedd* 3 (1998), pp. 8-16
Kellow, M., *Application of Hydro-Electric Power to Slate Mining* (London, 1907)
— 'Autobiography of the late Ex-Alderman Moses Kellow', *The Quarry Managers' Journal*, January 1944-December 1945
Kent, J.M., 'The Delabole Slate Quarry', *Journal of the Royal Institution of Cornwall* new series 5, part 4 (1968), pp. 317-23
Kotkin, S., *Magnetic Mountain: Stalinism as Civilisation* (Berkeley, London: University of California Press, 1995)
Lake, J., Cox, J. and Berry, E., *Diversity and Vitality: The Methodist and Nonconformist Chapels of Cornwall* (Cornwall Archaeological Unit, Truro, 2001)
Large, F., *Faster than the Wind* (Wirral: Avid Publications, 1998)
Laun, J. van, *Early Limestone Railways* (London: The Newcomen Society, 2001)
Lewis, M.J.T., *Early Wooden Railways* (London: Routledge and Kegan Paul, 1970)
— *Sails on the Dwyryd* (Maentwrog: Plas Tan y Bwlch, 1989)
— 'Archery and Spoonerisms: The Creators of the Festiniog Railway', *JMHRS* 13 part 3 (1996), pp. 263-76
— *Millstone and Hammer: The Origins of Water Power* (Hull: The University of Hull, 1997)
— 'New Light on Ty Mawr Ynysypandy', *Industrial Gwynedd* 3 (1998), pp. 34-49
— 'Railways in the Greek and Roman World' in *Early Railways* (London: The Newcomen Society, 2001), pp. 8-19
— *Blaen y Cwm and Cwt y Bugail Slate Quarries* (Gwernaffield: Adit, 2003)
— 'Bar to Fish-Belly: The Evolution of the Cast-Iron Edge Rail' in *Early Railways 2* (London: Newcomen Society, 2003) pp. 102-17
Lewis M.J.T. and Denton, J., *Rhosydd Slate Quarry* (Shrewsbury: Cottage Press, 1974)
Lewis, M.J.T. and Rattenbury, G., *Merthyr Tydfil Tramroads and their Locomotives* (Oxford: Railway and Canal Historical Society, 2004)
Lewis, M.J.T. and Williams, M.C., *Pioneers of Ffestiniog Slate* (Maentwrog: Snowdonia National Park Study Centre, 1987)
Lindsay, J., *A History of the North Wales Slate Industry* (Newton Abbot: David and Charles, 1974)
— *The Great Strike: A History of the Penrhyn Quarry Dispute of 1900-1903* (Newton Abbot: David and Charles, 1987)
Linnard, W., *Welsh Woods and Forests: A History* (Llandysyl: Gomer Press, 2000)
Lloyd, L., *The Port of Caernarfon, 1793-1800* (privately published, 1989)

— *Pwllheli: The Port and Mart of Llŷn* (privately published 1991)
— *De Winton's of Caernarfon 1854-1892* (Harlech: privately published, 1994)
Lord, P., *Gwenllian* (Llandysyl: Gomer, 1994)
— *Industrial Society* (Cardiff: University of Wales Press, 1998)
Lowe, J., *Welsh Industrial Workers Housing 1775-1875* (Cardiff, 1989)
Lycett-Smith, R., 'Cambrian Timber Trestle Bridges and Viaducts in 1994: A Photographic Survey', *Historical Model Railway Society Journal* 15 7 (1994-6), pp. 208-17
McCamley, N.J., *Saving Britain's Art Treasures* (Barnsley: Leo Cooper, 2003)
MacDermott, E.T., *History of the Great Western Railway 1833-1863 volume 1* revised C.R. Clinker (London: Ian Allan, 1964)
McElvogue, D., 'The Forgotten ways; evidence for water-borne transport in Nant Peris, Gwynedd', *Industrial Gwynedd* 4 (1999), pp. 5-15
Manning, I., 'Broad Gauge Rolling Stock at Holyhead Breakwater', *Industrial Gwynedd* 3 (1998), pp. 17-22
Marshall, D., *A History of Railway Locomotives Down to the Year 1831* (London: Locomotive Publishing Company, 1953)
Marshall, J., *The Lancashire & Yorkshire Railway*, vol. 2 (Newton Abbot: David and Charles, 1970)
Martin, T., *Halfway to Heaven: Darjeeling and its Remarkable Railway* (Chester: Rail Romances, 2000)
Matts, R.S., 'A Century of Timber Management at Baron Hill, Anglesey, 1734-1835' (Diploma dissertation, UWB, 1977)
Mayne, A. and Murray, T. (eds), *The Archaeology of Urban Landscapes: Explorations in Slumland* (Cambridge: Cambridge University Press, 2001)
Mills, M., *Greenwich Marsh – The 300 years before the dome* (London: Docklands Forum, 1999)
Monmouthshire County Council: *Addasu Adeiladau Fferm Hanesyddol yng Nghmyru/ Converting Historic Farm Buildings in Wales* (Cardiff, 2004)
Moore-Colyer, R., *Welsh Cattle Drovers* (Ashbourne: Landmark Publishing, 2002)
Morgan, D. (ed.), *Babi Sam: yn dathlu can mlynedd o ddarlledu o Fangor, 1935-85: atgofion a gobeithion pen blwydd* (Bangor: BBC, 1985)
Morgan, K.O., *Rebirth of a Nation: Wales 1880-1980* (Oxford: Oxford University Press, 1981)
Morris, M., *Porthmadog: Llanw Ddoe/ Yesterday's Tide* (Caernarfon: Gwynedd Archives Service, n.d.)
Morrison, T.A., *Goldmining in Western Merioneth* (Llandysul: Gomerian Press for Merionethshire Historical and Record Society, 1975)
Morriss, R., *The Archaeology of Railways* (Stroud: Tempus, 1999)
Nash-Williams, V.E., *The Roman Frontier in Wales* (Cardiff: University of Wales Press, 1969 –second edition, revised Michael G. Jarrett)
National Trust, *Penrhyn Castle* (London: The National Trust, 1991)
Neale, A., 'Broad Gauge at Holyhead', *Industrial Gwynedd* 2 (1997), pp. 18-25
Neaverson, E., *Medieval Castles in North Wales: A Study of Sites, Water Supply and Building Stone* (London: Hodder and Stoughton, University Press of Liverpool, 1947)
Nevell, M. (ed.), *From Farmer to Factory Owner: Models, Methodology & Industrialisation. Archaeological Approaches to the Industrial Revolution in North West England* (Council for British Archaeology, University of Manchester Archaeology Unit and Chester Archaeology, 2003)
Nevell, M. and Walker, J., *The Archaeology of Twentieth Century Tameside* (Ashton-under-Lyne, Tameside Metropolitan Borough Council with University of Manchester Archaeological Unit, 2004)
Nevell, M., Roberts, J. and Champness, B., 'Excavating the Iconic: The Rediscovery of the Fairbottom Bobs Colliery Pumping Engine', *IAR* 26 2 (November 2004), pp. 83-93
Newman, R., *The Historical Archaeology of Britain c. 1540-1900* (Stroud: Sutton, 2001)
Nicholson, C., 'Easdale Island, Argyll', *IAR* 5 2 (Spring 1981), pp. 163-4
Owain, O. Ll., *Cofiant Mrs Fanny Jones Talysarn* (Caernarfon: Cwmni y Cyhoeddwyr Cymreig, 1906)
Owain, S. ab, *Neuadd y Farchnad, Blaenau Ffestiniog: Cipdrem ar ei Hanes* (Blaenau Ffestiniog: Cyfeillion Neuadd y Farchnad, 1995)
— 'Hen Felinau Plwyf Ffestiniog (2)', *Rhamant Bro* 24 (Gaeaf 2005), pp. 26-7
Owen, G. (ed. Miles, D.), *Description of Pembrokeshire* (Llandysul: Gomer Press, 1994)
Owen, T.M., 'Y Drol Gyntaf', *Medel* 3 (1986), pp. 21-6
— 'Iorwerth Peate a Diwylliant Gwerin', *Trafodion Anrhydeddus Gymdeithas y Cymmrodorion/ Transactions of the Honourable Society of Cymmrodorion* new series 5 (1995), pp. 62-79
Palmer, M., 'Industrial Archaeology: a thematic or a period discipline?', *Antiquity* 64 (1990), pp. 275-85
Palmer, M. and Neaverson, P., *Industry in the Landscape 1700-1900* (London: Routledge, 1994)
— *Industrial Archaeology: Principles and Practice* (London and New York: Routledge, 1998)
Parliamentary Papers, *Royal Commission to Enquire into Harbours of Refuge* (British Parliamentary Papers 1847 411 LXI.1)

Parry, G., 'Owen Charles Jones, Gosodwr Peiriannau Oel', *Fferm a Thyddyn* 5 (Calan Mai 1990), p. 16
Parry, J.G., 'Terfysgoedd Ŷd yng Ngogledd Cymru 1740-58', *TCHS* 39 (1978), pp. 74-107
Parry, R.W., *Cerddi'r Gaeaf* (Denbigh: Gwasg Gee, 1952)
Pearce, D., Markandya, A. and Barbier, E.B., on behalf of the London Environmental Economics Centre, *Blueprint for a Green Economy* (London: Earthscan, 1989)
Peate, I., *The Welsh House* (published 1940 as vol. LXVII of *Y Cymmrodor*; reprinted Lampeter: Llannerch Press, 2004)
Pollard, S., *Marginal Europe: The Contribution of Marginal Lands Since the Middle Ages* (Oxford: Clarendon Press, 1997)
Postal Directory for Caernarvonshire and Anglesey (New Brighton: 1886)
Price, E., 'The Smaller Industries in the XIX Century' in *Atlas of Caernarvonshire* (Caernarfon: Gwynedd Rural Council, 1976), pp. 176-9
Pritchard, O., *Hanes Methodistiaid Calfinaidd Nefyn 1757-1926* (Pwllheli: D. Caradog Evans, n.d.)
Quartermaine, J., Trinder, B. and Turner, R., *Thomas Telford's Holyhead Road: The A5 in north Wales* (CBA Research Report 135, 2003)
Raistrick, A, *Industrial Archaeology: An Historical Survey* (London: Eyre Methuen, 1972)
Ransom, J.P.G., *Narrow Gauge Steam: its origins and world-wide development* (Yeovil: Oxford Publishing Company, 1996)
RCAHMW, *An Inventory of the Ancient Monuments in Anglesey* (1937)
– *Caernarvonshire: Inventory of Caernarvonshire* (London: HMSO; volume 1 – East [1956]; volume 2 – Central [1960]; Volume 3 – West [1964])
Reed, M.C., *The London and North Western Railway* (Penryn: Atlantic Transport Publishers, 1996)
Rees, A, *Cyclopaedia, or Universal Dictionary of Arts and Sciences* (Newton Abbot: David and Charles, 1972)
Rees, D.M., *Mines, Mills and Furnaces: an introduction to Industrial Archaeology in Wales* (London: HMSO, 1969)
– *The Industrial Archaeology of Wales* (Newton Abbot: David and Charles, 1975)
Rees, T. and Thomas, J., *Hanes Eglwysi Annibynol Cymru* 3 (Liverpool: 1873)
Richards, A.J., *A Gazetteer of the Welsh Slate Industry* (Capel Garmon: Gwasg Carreg Gwalch, 1991)
—— *Slate Quarrying in Corris* (Llanrwst: Gwasg Carreg Gwalch, 1994)
—— *Fragments of Mine and Mill in Wales* (Llanrwst: Gwasg Carreg Gwalch, 2002)
Richards, M., 'Dŵr', in Richards, M. (ed.), *Atlas Môn* (Cyngor Gwlad Môn, 1972), p. 145
Riden, P., *A Gazetteer of Charcoal-fired Blast Furnaces in Great Britain in use since 1660* (Cardiff, Merton Priory Press, 1993)
Roberts, D., 'Y Deryn Nos a'i Deithiau', *Cof Cenedl* 3 (1988), pp. 153-79
Roberts, G.R., *New Lives in the Valley: Slate Quarries and Quarry Villages in North Wales, New York and Vermont, 1850-1920* (New Hampshire: New Hampshire printers, 1998)
Roberts, K., *Y Lôn Wen: darn o hunangofiant* (Denbigh: Gwasg Gee, 1960)
Roberts, R., *A Wandering Scholar: The Life and Opinion of Robert Roberts* (John Burnett and H.G. Williams, eds) (Cardiff: University of Wales Press, 1991)
Rolt, L.T.C., *Railway Adventure* (London: Constable, 1953)
—— *Landscape with Canals* (London: Allen Lane, 1977)
Roose-Williams, J., *Quarryman's Champion: the Life and Activities of William John Parry of Coetmor* (Denbigh: Gwasg Gee, 1978)
Rowlands, J., *Copper Mountain* (Llangefni: Anglesey Antiquarian Society, 1981)
Rynne, C., *Technological change in Anglo-Norman Munster* (Barryscourt Trust and Cork County Council, 1998)
—— *The Industrial Archaeology of Cork City and its Environs* (Dublin: Stationery Office, 1999)
Sandby, P., 'The Iron Forge between Dolgelli and Barmouth in Merioneth Shire', *XII Views in North Wales* (London: 1776)
Schama, S., *Landscape and Memory* (London: Fontana, 1996)
Schmiechen, J. and Carls, K., *The British Market Hall* (New Haven and London: Yale University Press, 1999)
Schollier, P., 'Goods and Stores for the Workers, The Shaping of Mass Retailing in Late 19th-century Ghent', in Barker D. and Cranstone, D. (eds), *The Archaeology of Industrialization* (Leeds: Maney, 2004), pp. 257-67
Short, B., Watkins, C., Foot, W., and Kinsman, P., *The National Farm Survey of 1941–1943: State Surveillance and the Countryside in England and Wales in the Second World War* (Wallingford and New York: CABI, 2000)
Skempton, A.W., *Bibliographical Dictionary of Civil Engineers in Great Britian and Irelands Volume 1 1500 to 1830* (London: Institution of Civil Engineers, 2002)

Smith, A., *The Wealth of Nations* (London: Methuen, 1904)
Smith, N., *A History of Dams* (Secaucus, New Jersey: Citadel Press, 1972)
Smith, P., *Houses of the Welsh Countryside* (London: HMSO, 1988)
Smith, W., 'Summit-Level Tunnel of the Bettws and Festiniog Railway', *Proceedings of the Institution of Civil Engineers* 73 3 (1882-3), pp. 150-77
Soulsby, I., *The Towns of Medieval Wales* (Chichester: Phillimore, 1983)
Stanier, P., *Quarries of England and Wales: an historic photographic record* (Truro: Twelveheads Press, 1995)
Stephenson, D., *The Governance of Gwynedd* (Cardiff: University of Wales Press, 1984)
Stratton, M. and Trinder, B., *Twentieth Century Industrial Archaeology* (London: Spon, 2000)
Sutherland, J., 'Iron railway bridges', in Bailey, M.R. (ed.), *Robert Stephenson - The Eminent Engineer* (Aldershot: Ashgate, 2003), pp. 301-35
Sutton's Directory of North Wales (Manchester: 1889)
'Sylwedydd', *Chwarelau Dyffryn Nantlle a Chymdogaeth Moel Tryfan* (Cylchwyl Lenyddol Rhostryfan, *c.* 1889)
Symonds, J., 'Experiencing Industry: Beyond Machines and the History of Technology' in Casella, E. and Symonds, J. (eds), *Industrial Archaeology: Future Directions* (New York: Springer, 2005), pp. 33-57
Taylor, A.J., *The Welsh Castles of Edward I* (London and Ronceverte: Hambledon Press, 1986)
Thomas, B., 'Iron-making in Dolgellau', *JMHRS* 9 (1981-4), pp. 474-5
Thomas, C., 'The Corsygedol Estate in an Age of Improvement', *JMHRS* 6 (1971), pp. 303-10
Thomas, C., *Quarry Hunslets of North Wales* (Usk: Oakwood, 2001)
Thomas, D., *Hen Longau Sir Gaernarfon* (Caernarfon: Caernarvonshire Historical Society, 1952)
— *Agriculture in Wales During the Napoleonic War* (Cardiff: University of Wales Press, 1963)
Thomas, D.W., *Hydro-Electricity in North Wales* (Llanrwst: Gwasg Carreg Gwalch, 1997)
Thomas, O., *Cofiant y Parchedig John Jones Talsarn* (Wrexham: Hughes and Son, 1874)
Thomas, W.N., *The History of the Gas Industry in Pwllheli* (privately published, Pwllheli, 1976)
Thorburn, J.A., 'Stone Mining Tools and the Field Evidence for Early Mining in Wales' in Crew, P. and Crew, S. (eds), *Early Mining in the British Isles* (Maentwrog: Plas Tan y Bwlch, 1990)
Timberlake, S., 'Archaeological and Circumstantial Evidence for Early Mining in Wales' in Ford, T. D. and Willies, L., *Mining Before Powder* (Peak District Mines Historical Society Bulletin vol. 12 3, Historical Metallurgy Society Special Publication), pp. 133-43
Timmins, G., *The Last Shift: the Decline of Handloom Weaving in Nineteenth Century Lancashire* (Manchester: Manchester University Press, 1993)
Trinder, B., *The Industrial Revolution in Shropshire* (Chichester: Phillimore, 1973, 1981, 2000)
— *The Making of the Industrial Landscape* (London: J.M. Dent and Sons, 1982)
— *The Industrial Archaeology of Shropshire* (Phillimore: Chichester, 1996)
— '18th and 19th-Century Market Town Industry: An analytical model', *IAR* 24 (November 2002), pp. 75-89
— *The Most Extraordinary District in the World': Ironbridge and Coalbrookdale* (Chichester: Phillimore, 2005)
Trinder, B. and Cossons, N., *The Iron Bridge* (Chichester: Phillimore, 2002)
Tucker, D.G., 'The Slate Quarries of Easdale, Argyllshire, Scotland', *Post-Medieval Archaeology* 10 (1976), pp. 118-30
Vaughan, C., 'Lluestai Blaenrheidiol', *Ceredigion* 5 (1966), pp. 246-63
Vernon, R.W., 'Conservation of Mining Sites in the Gwydyr Forest Area of the Snowdonia National Park', *IAR* 12 1 (Autumn 1989), pp. 77-83
Wallace, T., '"Working the Train Gang": Alienation, Liminality and Communitas in the UK Preserved Railway Sector', *International Journal of Heritage Studies* 12 3 (May 2006), pp. 218-33
Watts, M., *The Archaeology of Mills and Milling* (Stroud: Tempus, 2002)
Wiliam, D.W. (ed.), *Brasluniau Lewis Morris o Eglwysi, Tai a Phentrefi ym Môn* (privately published, 1999)
Wiliam, E., 'The Vernacular Architecture of a Welsh Rural Community, 1700-1900: The Houses of Mynytho', *TCHS* 36 (1975), pp. 173-93
— 'The Corn Mills of Llyn in the Fourteenth Century', *Melin* 2 (1986), pp. 26-31
Williams, C.J., *Great Orme Mines: British Mining History No. 52* (Keighley: Northern Mine Research monograph, 1995)
— *Metal Mines of North Wales: a collection of pictures* (Wrexham; Bridge Books, 1997)
Williams, D.H., *The Welsh Cistercians* (Leominster: Gracewing, 2001)
Williams, E., *The Day Before Yesterday* (Beaumaris, 1988)
Williams, E.A., *Hanes Môn yn y Bedwaredd Ganrif ar Bymtheg* (Eisteddfod Gadeiriol Môn, 1927)
Williams, G., 'Ffatri Laeth Rhydymain', *Llen y Llannau* (1997), pp. 31-49
Williams, G.H., 'Caernarvonshire House Interiors', *TCHS* 39 (1977) pp. 60-92
— 'Estate Management in Dyffryn Conwy, c. 1685', *Transactions of the Honourable Society of Cymmrodorion*, 1979, pp. 31-74

— 'Farming in Stuart Caernarvonshire', *TCHS* 42 (1981), pp. 49-79
Williams, G.J., *Hanes Plwyf Ffestiniog* (Wrexham, 1882)
Williams, H., *Marconi and his wireless stations in Wales* (Llanrwst: Gwasg Carreg Gwalch, 1999)
Williams, J.G., 'The Quakers of Merioneth During the Seventeenth Century', *JMHRS* 8 2-3 (1978-9), pp. 122-56
— *The University College of North Wales: Foundations 1884-1927* (Cardiff: University of Wales Press, 1985)
Williams, J.Ll., 'Two Powder Magazines in the parish of Llanllechid, Bethesda', *Industrial Gwynedd* 2 (1997), pp. 7-17
— '"A Kind of Sheffield of the Stone Age" – Samuel Hazzledine Warren's excavations of a Neolithic Axe Factory on the Graiglwyd, Penmaenmawr, 1919-1921', *TCHS* 59 (1998), pp. 7-34
Williams, J.Ll. and Jenkins, D., 'Dwr a Llechi ym Mhlwyf Llanllechid, Bethesda – agweddau ar ddatblygiad diwydiant yn Nyffryn Ogwen', *TCHS* 54 (1993), pp. 29-62
— 'Tair Chwarel ym Mhlwyf Llanllechid, Bethesda', *TCHS* 55 (1994), pp. 47-70
— 'Rhai Nodiadau Ychwanegol ar Chwarel Bryn Hafod y Wern', *TCHS* 56 (1995), pp. 87-107
— 'Tair Chwarel ym Mhlwyf Llanllechid, Bethesda Rhan II', *TCHS* 57 (1996), pp. 65-84
Williams, M.C., 'An Early Mathews Dressing Machine in the Ffestiniog Quarries', *Archaeology in Wales* 25 (1985), pp. 53-4
— *The Slate Industry* (Princes Risborough: Shire Publications, 1991)
Williams, M.C. and Lewis, M.J.T., *Gwydir Slate Quarries/Chwareli Gwydir* (Penrhyndeudraeth: Snowdonia National Park Study Centre, 1989)
Williams, R., *The History and Antiquities of Aberconwy* (Denbigh: Thomas Gee, 1835)
Williams, R., 'Hunangofiant Chwarelwr', *Cymru* 16 (1890)-19 (1900)
Williams, W., *Mwyngloddio ym Mhen Llŷn/The Llŷn Peninsula Mines* (Llanrwst: Gwasg Carreg Gwalch, 1995)
Wilson, G., *The Old Telegraphs* (London: Phillimore, 1976)
Wood, D. and Field, V., *The Vincent Family Diary: Gentry Life in Victorian Bangor* (privately published, 2002)
Woodward, G., 'Hydro Electricity in North Wales, 1880-1948', *Transactions of the Newcomen Society* 69 2 (1997-98), pp. 205-35
Wyn Griffith, J.L., *Spring of Youth* (Swansea: Christopher Davies, 1971)
Wynn, J., *History of the Gwydir Family and Memoirs* (Llandysul: Gomer Press, 1990)
Zeller, T., '"The Landscape's Crown" Landscape, Perceptions and Modernizing Effects of the German Autobahn System, 1934 to 1941', in Nye, D.E. (ed.), *Technologies of Landscape: From Reaping to Recycling* (Amherst, Massachusetts: University of Massachusetts Press, 1999), pp. 218-38

Art galleries:

Walker Art Gallery, Liverpool

Archival and archaeological collections:

Birmingham City Library
Caernarfon Record Office
Clwyd-Powys Archaeological Trust, Historic Environment Record
Conwy Archives
Dolgellau Record Office
Gwynedd Archaeological Trust, Historic Environment Record
Hawarden Record Office
Llangefni Record Office
National Library of Wales
Patent Library
The National Archives, Kew
RCAHMW, National Monuments Record
Scottish Record Office
Snowdonia National Park Study Centre
University of Wales, Bangor, Department of Manuscripts
West Glamorgan Record Office

Academic theses and dissertations:

Johnstone, F., 'The Archaeological and Agricultural Significance of the Multicellular Sheepfolds of Snowdonia' (B.A. thesis, University of Manchester, 1998)
Jones, G.P., 'The Economic and Technical Development of the Slate Industry in the Nantlle Valley' (PhD thesis, University of Wales, Bangor, 1996)

Newspapers and periodicals:

Baner ac Amserau Cymru
Caernarvon and Denbigh Herald
Y Clorianydd
The Electrical Review
Y Faner
(Festiniog Railway) *Heritage Group Journal*
Festiniog Railway Magazine
The Guardian
The Manufacturer
The Miller
Mining Journal
North Wales Chronicle
North Wales Gazette
North Wales Weekly News
Planet
The Times
Times Literary Supplement
Welsh Highland Heritage

Websites:

www.steam-up.co.uk/dsf2k2/u4748_dsf2k2.htm
http://news.bbc.co.uk/1/low/wales/4097496.stm
www.oldglory.co.uk/archive/12May04/ft.1.htm
www.page27.co.uk/nwales/nwgoods.htm
http://news.bbc.co.uk/2/hi/uk_news/wales/north_west/3122269.stm
www.publications.parliament.uk/pa/cm200405/cmselect/cmwelaf/329/4031702.htm
http://hen.gwynedd.gov.uk/adrannau/economaidd/ffeithiau/agriculture

INDEX

compiled by Auriol Griffith-Jones

Note: Page numbers in *italics* refer to illustrations; those in **bold** refer to Appendices

Aber, railway station 162
Aberconwy, monastery 31
Aberdyfi 172, 193; wharf 168, 170
Aberfan coal mine, disaster (1966) 25, *26*
Aberffraw 212, 214; housing 185–6
Abergavenny 32
Abergwyngregyn, cheese factory 130
Abergynolwyn, industrial housing 183, *183*
Aberllefenni slate quarry 55, 61
Abt, Dr Roman 161
Afon Ddu (river) 126
Agricola, Georgius, *De Re Metallica* (1556) 11
agricultural buildings, barns 103–4, *103*, 104, *104*, 131; building materials 104, *104*, 106; field-house 104
agricultural colleges 98
agricultural improvement 97, 104–5
agriculture 8, 96–110, *99*, 215; archaeological study of 96, 110, 232; cattle 29, 39, 100–1, 129; early modern 38–9; enclosure 97, 107–8, 217; future of 109–10; grain 29, 103; land quality 38, 102–3; livestock markets 131; machinery 39, 104–5; parks 99–100, 102; patrician estates 8–9, 38–9, 97; sheep 29; transhumance 38, 101, 109, *see also* food industry
Alexandra (Cors y Bryniau) slate quarry *50*
Alfrey, Judith and Clark, Catherine, *The Landscape of Industry* 18
aluminium (bauxite), imports 125, 126–7
Aluminium Corporation Ltd 125
aluminium smelting 3, 125–7, *126*, 140, 222, 224
Alwen reservoir 141
Amlwch, County Secondary School 208
Amlwch Industrial Heritage Trust 91, 92, *see also* Port Amlwch
Amlwch Light Railway 139
Anafon valley, sheepfolds *108*
Andrews, Solomon 213
Angerstein, Reinhold, travel diary (1753-55) 11
Anglesey 29, 30, 71; agriculture 29; brick-making 116; coal mines 92–6; parliamentary enclosure 97; tidemills 128, *see also* Holyhead
Anglesey, Marquess of 102
Anglesey Aluminium 126
Anglesey Central Railway 87
Anglesey Mining plc 92

Anglican (Episcopalian) Church 196, *see also* churches and chapels
Anglo-Norman period, roofing slates 36
Anti-Corn Law League 33
archaeology, Post-Medieval 19–20, 233, 235–6; theories of 19–20; trends in 229–30, *see also* industrial archaeology
architecture *see* churches and chapels; housing
Ardudwy manganese mine 91–2
Arfon coastal plain 29
Arnold, Matthew, *On the Study of Celtic Literature* 21
Arnold, Thomas 236
artefacts, domestic 210–11
Arthog, development 213
Arthurian legend 21
Ashton, T.S. 13
Assheton Smith, Thomas, Vaynol 61
Associated Ethyl Co. Ltd 139
Association for Industrial Archaeology 230
Aston, Michael (Mick) 17
Attlee, Clement, Prime Minister 223–4
Avery, Thomas, Delabole quarry, Cornwall 56
Awdry, Revd Wilbert Vere 160

Baker, William 163
Bala 37, 207, 212; market hall 132–3, *132*; powered loom 119; sluices 141
Bala Lake Railway 165
Baldwin, Archbishop 36
band-rooms 204–5
bandstands 213
Bangor 197, 207, 212, 225; covered market 133; gasworks 142; housing 185; industries 129, 130, 135; Methodist chapel 220; *Penrhyn Arms Hotel* 147; public quay 172; railway station 162; shops 204, *see also* University College of North Wales
Baptist church 32, 196
Barmouth 142, 164
barns 103–4, *103*; tithe 131
Baron Hill estate 37, 39, 99, 105, 109
'barracks', slate workers' accommodation 67–8, *67*, 182, 210
Bath University, History of Technology centre 15
Battersby, J.H. 24
Bayly, Sir Nicholas 93, 146

255

BBC, in Bangor 226
Beamish Open Air Museum 4, 17
Beaumaris 37, 212, 214; docks 166, 223
Beazley, Elizabeth 178
Beckett, Paul 109
Beddgelert, Augustinian canons of 36; Sygun copper mine 82, 85, 86
Belan, harbour 175
Beresford, Maurice 17
Berriw 239
Berw colliery 95, *95*
Bethesda 1, 137, 217, *218*; chapels 200, 209, 217; Glanogwen church 197, *197*, 217, 220; toll-house 149
Betws y Coed, Waterloo Bridge 150, *151*
Bick, David 85
Birmingham University, industrial archaeology 15
Blaen y Cae slate quarry 57
Blaen y Cwm, slate quarry barracks 210
Blaenau Ffestiniog 25, 27, 135, 219–20; Anglican church 197; Catholic community 200; *cottage ornée* 188, *188*; Cwmorthin reading room 206, *206*; Hen Gapel 198–9, *198*; hospitals 67, *67*, 207; market hall 204, 209; powered loom 119; railway 164;
   slate mines 4, 41, *48*, 55, *see also* Oakeley slate mine
   terraced housing 190; wartime storage of National Gallery collection 223
Blaenavon, World Heritage Site 27
blast furnaces 124–5
blondin ropeway *see* ropeways
Bodnant, ornamental park 100
Bodorgan, railway station 162
Bodorgan estate 101, 109
Bodwrda, brick building 115
Bodwrda, Hugh 115
Bontnewydd 130, 200; housing *194*
Boston, Lord 177
Boswell, M.A., road builder *148*
Bourdieu, Pierre 19
Boyd, James 157
Braich yr Oen copper mine 87–8
Braichllwyd stone crushing mill 75
breweries 130
brick-making 115–17, *115*, *117*; kilns 116, 117
bridges, iron 102; Llanrwst 38, *38*; railway 163–4, *163*; suspension 150–1, *151*, 152; Trefriw *147*
Britannia railway bridge, Menai Strait 163–4, *163*
Brithdir, Roman lead-smelting hearths 35, 80
British language 31
bromine extraction 139
Bronze Age, Great Orme workings 79–80, 232; mining sites 34, 80, 82
Brunel, I.K. 156
Brunlees, Sir James 58
Bryn Twrw astronomical slates 211, *211*
Bryn y Gefeliau, Roman fort 36
Bryncir, livestock market 131
Bryneglwys slate quarry 56, 224

Brynkir Woollen Mill 122
Brynyfelin bridge 137
Buchanan, Angus 15
Buckley, Sir Edmund, at Dinas Mawddwy 106, 131, 190, 239; Hendre Ddu 105–6
Bulkeley family, Baron Hill 37, 39, 196
Burgess, Cefyn 109
Bwlch y Ddeufaen, road over 146, 148
Bwlch y Plwm 35

Cader Idris 29
Cadw (Welsh Historic Monuments) 26, 152
Caellwyngrydd, settlement 217, *218*
Caergeiliog, toll-house 149
Caernarfon 37, 212, 219; bank 209, *209*; brewery 130; brickworks 116, 117; Brunswick Ironworks 136–7; carriers from Chester 146; county record office 5, 97; covered market 133; Ferodo factory 224; gasworks 142; harbour offices 170; quays 166–7, 168, 169, 171–2; *Royal Hotel* 148; timber yard 114; warehouses 132; workhouse 207
Caernarvonshire 33, 97
Calvinistic Methodists 32, 196
canals 14, 179
Capel Curig 149; *Royal Hotel* 147
carbon anodes, manufacture of 125, 127
Cardiff, University of Wales 22
Cardigan Bay 29, 71, 239
Carmel 216
Carneddau 29
castles, Edwardian 31, 37
Catherine and Jane Consols mine 90, 91
Cefn Du, telegraph station 180
Cemaes 116; harbour 29
Cemlyn canal 179
chain incline *see* ropeways
chapels *see* churches and chapels
chapmen 203
charcoal production 111–13
Charles, Prince of Wales, investiture (1969) 3
Chartism, Monmouthshire 33
chemical industry 139
Chester and Holyhead Railway 41, *148*, 174, 179, 239
China, slate from 42, 61
china clay deposits 116
Christianity, early 31, 178, *see also* monasteries
Church of England *see* Anglican Church
churches and chapels 196–202, 228, 234; Anglican 196–7, *197*, 199; Catholic 200; chapel design 198–200; graveyards 200–1; influence of chapels 32–3, 130; position in settlements 217, 219, 220; redundant 209–10, *see also* Dissenters
Cilgwyn slate quarry 36
clock-making 37
clog-making 113
Clogau gold mines 88
Clogwyn y Fuwch slate quarry 46
Clough family 37

Index

Clwt y Bont, rail route 157
Clynnog Trefor, granites 70
coaching inns 149, *150*, *see also* public houses
coal, Anglesey 29, 92–6; for smelting 86, 87
coal mines 25, 92–6, *93*; extraction methods 94–5; Medieval 92–3, *94*; nationalisation 224
coastlines 29
Cobb, Richard 22
Coed y Brenin 111, 138; blast furnace 124; ore mines 78, 80
Coedmadog slate quarry, beam engine 65
Coleg Harlech 24
communal buildings *see* public (communal) buildings
Congregationalist church 32, 196
conservation, of industrial heritage 14–15, 229–31
Conservative Party 33–4, 224, 225
Conway and Colwyn Bay Joint Water Supply 140
Conwy 37, 130, 207, 212; aqueduct *141*; public wells 140; quay 166; railway bridge 163, 164; suspension bridge 150–1, 152
Conwy castle 128, 235
Conwy Morfa, Mulberry harbours 223
Conwy, River 30
Conwy valley 29; brick-making 116
Cook, William 181
Cooke, R.T. 138
copper, Bronze-Age production 34, 232; monastic extraction 36; Roman production 34–5; storage bins at ports 168, *168*
copper mines 78, 80, 232; extraction methods 81–2, 84–5; inclines and railways 87–9; precipitation ponds 82, 84, *84*; pumping systems 89–90, *see also* Drws y Coed; Great Orme; Llanberis; Mynydd Parys
copper-smelting 80–1, 84, 112
corn mills 127–9
Cornwall 78; beam engines 65; Delabole slate quarry 56, 66, 69; engine houses 90–1; mining engineers 134, 137
Corris, slate quarries 42, 44
Cors Ddygái, Anglesey 92
Cors y Bryniau (Alexandra) slate quarry *50*
Corsygedol estate, barn 103
Cossons, Sir Neil 16
cottages, agricultural 106–7; *crog-lofftydd* type 107, 108
Countryside Council for Wales 225, 231
creameries and cheese factories 130, *130*
Cremlyn, stationary engine 105
Creuddyn peninsula 71, 128
Crewe, Peter 89
Criccieth 37, 212
Croesor slate quarry 52, 63
Cwm Bychan estate 99
Cwm Bychan mine, ropeway 88, *89*
Cwm Ciprwth copper mine 89, *90*
Cwm Dyli, hydro-power station 143
Cwm Eigiau slate quarry 68
Cwm Penmachno, Pen y Incline terrace 188
Cwm Pennant, Prince of Wales slate quarry 60
Cwm y Glo 111–12
Cwm Ystradllyn, *crog-lofft* cottages 187–8; dam 140
Cwmdwyfor copper mine 88
Cwt y Bugail slate quarry 62; steam engine 64–5
Cyffty copper mine 91
Cymer Abbey 31, 36, 166

dairies, estate 100–1, *see also* creameries
dams 126, 140–1, 143, 145; pumped storage hydro schemes 144, *145*
Darbishire family 191, 196, 220
Darby, Abraham (I) 9, 124
Dargan, William, engineer 151
Darjeeling-Himalayan Railway 158, *158*
Davies, Oliver 79
Davies, Richard, architect 200
Davies, Walter 117
Davies, Rev. Walter (*Gwallter Mechain*) 186
De Winton, Union ironworks, Caernarfon 51, 72, 101, 135–6, *136*, 137
de Winton, Jeffreys Parry 136
Dearborn, Michigan, industrial museum 13–14
Dee, River 29, 141
Deganwy, railway quay 168, 172
Deiniolen, chapels 219; housing 190, 217, 219; Llandinorwic church 219
Denbigh 37
Deutsches Museum von Mesiterwerken der Naturwissenschaft und Technik (1903) 13
Dibnah, Fred 109
Dickens, Charles 13
Diderot, Denis, *Encyclopédie* (1751-65) 11
Diffwys, Ffestiniog, slate quarries 49–50, 58, 59–60, 62
Dinas Mawddwy 42, 106, 131, 239; estate-built housing 190–1; Medieval bandits (*Gwylliaid Cochion*) 215
Dinorwic slate quarry, Llanberis 3, 4, 23, *23*, 42; Anglesey barracks 68, 182; Australia mill 60; compressor houses 66; engineering workshops 26; extraction method 43, *48*; hospital 67; landscaping *45*; pumped storage hydro scheme 144; railway 49, *52*, 156; railway workshops 61, *62*, 63; Vivian quarry, inclined plane 54, *54*; wartime industry 223
Disraeli, Benjamin, Prime Minister 13
Dissenters 32–3; numbers 198, *see also* churches and chapels; Methodists
distillery, Frongoch 130–1
docks, quays and harbours 72, 73, 76, 166–75, *167*; access to 170–2; buildings 170, *170*, 172; Cemaes 29; mineral quays 167–72; public quays 172; Pwllheli 172, 212–13; rail access 171–3; ship-building yards 172; storage facilities 168–9, *see also* Holyhead; Porthmadog
Dodd, A.H. 119; *The Industrial Revolution in North Wales* 25–6
Dol Hendre scheme 98

Dol y Clochydd, blast furnace 124
Dolaucothi gold mine 80, 85
Dolgarrog 121, 206, 215; aluminium smelting 125–6, *126*, 140, 222, 224; housing 194, 215; power station 143, *143*
Dolgarrog canal 179
Dolgellau 37, 39, 130, 212; cloth weaving 37, 119–20; county record office 5, 97; gasworks 142; market hall 132; shops *205*, **243**; woollen mills 121; workhouse 207
Dolgun, ironworking 124
Dolmelynllyn estate 100
Dolwen, electricity station 142–3
Dom Polski refugee camp 222
Dorothea slate quarry, Nantlle 3, 23, *47*, 61; chapel 196; pumping engine 49, 65
droving 39, 131, 146
Druidism, Anglesey 30
Drws y Coed 216; chapel *2*
Drws y Coed copper mine 80, 84, 85; miners' village 91, 187, *187*; stamp mill 85, *85*, 134
Dwyryd estuary 30, 170, *171*
Dwyryd, river, woodland 111
Dyffryn Ardudwy, droving road 146
Dyffryn Ogwen slate quarries 42; slate fireplaces 210, 211
Dyfi, blast furnace 124–5
Dyfi Junction railway 164
Dyfi valley 29, *see also* Aberdyfi
Dyson, Jonathan 177

Easdale, Scotland, slate quarries 65
Edison, Thomas Alva 13
Edward I, King 31
Edwards, John 135
Edwards, Richard, farm machinery manufacturer 105
Edwards, Thomas *see* Twm o'r Nant
Edwards, William 184
Eglwysbach, blast furnace 124
Egryn, manganese mine *83*
eisteddfodau 32
Elan valley reservoir 141
electricity supplies 142–5; for metal processing 125, 126; nationalisation 143; nuclear power stations 3, 126, 127, 144–5, 235–6; thermal power stations 144; to farms 105, 142; transmission systems 143–4, *143*
Elias, Rev. John 33
Ellis, Tom, MP 33
emigrants 39, 98
enclosure 107–8; Moel Tryfan commons 215–16; for ornamental parks 100; parliamentary 97, 217
Engels, Friedrich 13
England, and Act of Union (1536) 31; and development of towns in Wales 37
English Heritage 16, 231
Enlightenment 11
Environment Agency 225

environmental management 225
estates, patrician 8–9, 38–9, 97–8, *99*; dairies 100–1; planned complexes 106; strategic locations 99; survival of 109; woodland planting 111; workers' cottages 106–7, 188, 190–1, 216–17; workshops 65, 101–2, *102*, 109, *see also* Baron Hill; Newborough; Penrhyn; Plas Newydd; Vaynol
Europe, industrialisation 11–12, *12*
Euston, station arch 14–15
Evans, Ann-Catrin 109
Evans, William, monument 201
excavators, slate mines 49
explosives, manufacture 137–8; for slate quarrying 45, *46*

Fairbourne 162, 213
fairs *see* markets and fairs
farmhouses 106, 186; and cottage styles 191–2, 193
Felin Fawr 61; slate mill building 58, 63
Felin Isaf, watermill 128
fertilizers, artificial 139
Festiniog Flour and Corn Mill 129
Festiniog Railway 4, 135, 151, 156, 157–61; Boston Lodge 135, 138, 157, 160; civil engineering 157; explosives store 138; Fairlie locomotive *158*; Minffordd yard 159; restoration of 159–60
Festiniog Railway Society 230
Ffestiniog 111, 147
Ffestiniog slate quarries 42, 43, 44, 46; inclined plane 53; mill buildings 58; railway 49; steam engines 64–5
Firbanks, Thomas, *I Bought a Mountain* 105
First World War 221
fishing, Nefyn 214
flannel (woollen cloth) 118–19
Foel Ispri, copper and gold mines 78
'folk-life' 15; Welsh studies 21
food industry 127–33; breweries 130–1; corn mills 127–9; dairying 129–30; imports 132, 133; slaughterhouses 131; soft drinks 131; specialist 131
Ford, Henry 13
Forestry Commission 111
forestry, and timber trade 110–15, *112*; harvesting methods 113–14; state intervention 111
forges 36, 124
Foulkes, Sidney Colwyn, architect 224
foundries 134–5, 150
Francis, John and Thomas 60
Free Wales Army 3
French Revolution 32–3
Fron 216
Frongoch, distillery 130–1
fulling mills 119, 121, 122
Fyfe, John, Aberdeen 56

Gadlys, lead-smelting 80
Garth Shale Company, Mochdre stone quarry 76

gas supplies, estate gasworks 101; public 142
Gaskell, Elizabeth 13
Gellilydan, Catholic church 200
gentry, native Welsh 31, 32, 38, 39
Georgian Society, The 230
Gerddibluog farm, buildings 103
Giddens, Anthony 19
Gilfach Ddu, slate quarry workshops 61, *62*, 63, *see also* Welsh Slate Museum
Giraldus Cambrensis 36–7
Glan y Bala, slate quarry manager's house 68
Glanllyn estate, experimental nationalisation of 98
Glanrafon slate quarry 68
Glasdir copper and gold mine 86, *87*
Glaslyn 30, 41; copper mine 78, 87
Glaslyn, river 179
Gloddfa Ganol Slate Mine Mountain Tourist Centre 68
Glynllifon 101, 109, 175; agricultural college 98; estate workshops 65, 101–2, *102*, 109; ornamental park 100, 111
Glynrhonwy, slate quarries 43
Golborne, James 177
gold mines 78, 86, *87*, 88; Dolaucothi 80, 85; Gwynfynydd 88, 92, 138; Tyddyn Gwladys 138
Gorsedda Junction and Portmadoc Railways 88
Gorseddau (Gorsedda) slate quarry 58
government, local 34; role of 148, 221, 229
Graig Ddu, slate quarry 42
gravestones, inscriptions 201; slate 58, 69, 201
Great Orme, Bronze-Age workings 79–80, 232; copper mines 34, 35, 79–80, 89–90; Penmorfa adit 85; telegraph station 180, *180*; Tramway 161–2; washing floors 85
Green, E.R.R., *The Industrial Archaeology of County Down* 15
Greenfield, James 68
Greenfield valley, copper-smelting 80–1
Griffith, David, builder 190, 193, 219
Groeslon, Inigo Jones Slate Works 60, 211
Gryffudd ap Cynan 31
Gryn, manganese mine *83*
Guest, Lady Charlotte 32
Gwalchmai, toll-house 149
gwaliau (slate trimming sites) 57–8, *58*
Gwydir estate 99
Gwydir ore-fields 78, 86
Gwydir Uchaf 38, 39
Gwydyr Forest 111, 114
Gwynedd xvii, 34, 239; history 21, 31; industrial archaeology in 20–1; industrial character of 7, 225–6, 227–9; place in industrial history 237–8; pre-modern history 30–4; pre-modern industry 34–9, *35*; rate of industrialisation 238, 239; topography 29–30, *30*, 239
Gwynfynydd gold mine 88, 92, 138
Gwyrfai valley 216

Hadfield, Charles 14

Hafna copper mine 85, 86, 91
Hafod y Llan slate quarry 63
Hafodlas slate quarry 60, 62, 211
Hague, Douglas 26
Hammond, John and Barbara 13
Hansom, Joseph 214
harbours *see* docks, quays and harbours
Harlech 37, 166, 212
harp manufacture 37
Harrison, Thomas 152
Hartley, Jesse 178
Hartwell, Max 13
Hazledine, William 150
Henblas estate, barn 103
Henderson's of Aberdeen, blondin cableways 56
Hendre Ddu 105–6; slate quarry 68
Hendre Isaf, toll-house 149
Hildred, Falcon 122
hill-top settlements 34
Hills, Charles Henry 139
Historical Archaeology, use of term 236
Hobsbawm, E.J. 13
Hofal Wen reservoir 140
Holland, Samuel, MP 33, 196
Holyhead 29, 41, 71, 212; aluminium smelting 3, 126–7, 224; breakwater 162, 174–5; brickworks *115*, 116; covered market 133; harbour 172–5, *174*; hotels 173, *174*; Marine Yard 135, 173–4, *174*; Memorial Arch 152; sailors' hospital 207; station 131, 162, 163, 173; telegraph station 180; Telford's road to 41, 146, 148–52, *148*; Valley Foundry 135
Holyhead Steam Mills 129
horse-haulage 51, 156
Hoskins, W.G. 17
hospitals 207; on-site slate quarry 67, *67*
hotels, railway 163; on turnpike roads 147–8
housing 182–95, 228, 234; 'American style' 190, *191*; brick-built 191; *cottage ornée* designs 188–9, *188*; *crog-lofftydd* (half loft) type 107, 108, 187–8; estate cottages 106–7, 188; farmhouses 106, 186, 191–2, 193; for forestry workers 114, 182; half-timbered 212; industrial (workers') 182, 183, 184, 185, 193; interiors 210–11; miners' 91–2; modern changes and 'improvements' 194–5; national models 193, 194; planning policies 195, 231; post-war social 194; railwaymen's 163, 182; semi-detached 194; slate workers' 67–8, *67*, 182; speculative builders 190, 192; terraced 183, 184, 189–91, *189*, *190*, *191*; vernacular (cottage) tradition 182–3, *183*, 192, 193; weavers' cottages 118; workers' 8, 77, 189–90, *189*
Hughes, Cledwyn, MP 126, 224
Hughes, Iorys 223
Hughes, John (John y Gôf), blacksmith and engineer 102, 135, 188
Hunslet Engine Company, Leeds 51, *52*
hydro-electric schemes 3, 101, 143; for aluminium smelting 125

hydro-power turbines, on farms 105; Llechwedd slate quarry 63–4, *63*

inclined planes, on Penrhyn Quarry railroad 157; slate quarries 53–5, *53*, *54*; stone quarries *71*, 72–3, *73*; water-balance systems 53–5, *55*
industrial archaeology 13–16, 228–9; beginnings of 4, 14–15; dating of 235–7; development of 17–20; functional sites 41, 233–4, *235*; infrastructural sites 234; museums 13–14; periodic–thematic debate 231–3; publications 15–16; relationship to conservation 13–14, 229–31; societies 14; trends in 6–7, 11, 27–8, 233–7; as university discipline 15–16; Wales 20–7, 78–9
Industrial Archaeology Review 15
industrial heritage, conservation of 14–15, 229; management of 16–17, 229–31
industrialisation 13, 196; influence of warfare on 221–3, 232–3; international significance 237–8; perceptions of process of 11–14, 227–9; regional dimension of 237–8; role of government in 221, 229; on rural estates 8–9, 96, 100, 101–2, *102*; social archaeology of 6, 228, 234; and starting date 9, 231–2; and urban settlement 214
industries, ancillary 134–9; modern 3, 224–6; pre-modern 34–9, *35*
information technology 224, 226, *226*
Inland Waterways Association 14
inns *see* public houses
internal combustion engines 105; in slate quarries 65
International Committee for the Conservation of the Industrial Heritage, The 16
Iolo Morgannwg *see* Williams, Edward
Ireland 151, 238–9; and Holyhead 148, 152, 172; Howth harbour 172, *173*; Valentia slate quarry 69
Iron Age, iron-smelting 34, 80; mining sites 80
iron industry, South Wales 125
iron ore diggings 179
iron-smelting 113, 123–4; blast furnaces 124–5; Iron Age 34, 80
Ironbridge 14, 18; Ironbridge Gorge Museum 4, 16
ironworks 102, 135–7, *136*, *see also* De Winton
Iwan, Dafydd 3

James of St George, Master, castle-builder 37
Jenkins, J. Geraint 119
Johannesburg Consolidated Investment 82
John y Gôf *see* Hughes, John
Jones, Dr Gwyn 225
Jones, Sir Henry Haydn, MP 24, 224
Jones, Iorwerth *4*, *5*
Jones, Rev. John, Methodist minister, Tal y Sarn 196, 202–3
Jones, John, Pen y Cae, slate manager in Ireland 69

Jones, John Maurice, woodland planting 111
Jones, Merfyn, *The North Wales Quarrymen* 22–3
Jones, Owain Gethin 164
Jones, Rhydderch, *Fo a Fe* (drama) 23–4
Jones, Richard, Ty Cerig 132
Jones, Robert Isaac 203
Jones, Thomas and William, slate carvers 211
Journal of Industrial Archaeology 15
J.W. Greaves Welsh Slate 42

Kellow, Moses, Croesor quarry 52, 63, 69
Kendall family 125
Kennedy, Henry, church architect 197
knitting 119

Labour Party, in Wales 22, 33–4
labourers, agricultural 106–7; Irish 200
Lancashire, copper-smelting 80
landowners 33, 111, 196; radical opposition to 96, 98; and settlement development 217, 220; woollen mills 121; and workers' housing 186
landownership, Bateman's classification **241–2**; patterns of 97–8
landscapes, industrial 17–18; 'productive' 8–9, 232; *Registers* 26–7, 42
laundries, on estates 100
lead mines 80, 88; on Gwydir estate 38, 78; Llanymynech 80; Parc 82, 88; prehistoric 232
lead smelting 125; Roman 35, 80
Leicester University, School of Archaeology 16, 18
Leicestershire, coal mining 94, 95
Lewis, Michael 24, 157; *Early Wooden Railways* 15–16
Lewis, Saunders 2
Lewis, Thomas 'Palestina' 129
Liberation Society 33
libraries and reading rooms 206
Liddell, Henry, Dean of Christ Church 85
limekilns 75, *75*; Port Penrhyn 102, 117
limestone, Anglesey 29, 70
Lindsay, Jean 23
Lindsay, Robert Bertie, 4th Earl of 39
literacy 236
literature, Welsh prose 32
Liverpool, telegraph 180; water supply 140
Liverpool Bay 29
Llam Carw, chemical works 139
Llanaber, agricultural research 110
Llanbedr y Cennin, agricultural research 110
Llanbedrog stone quarry 76
Llanberis 42, 210; hydro scheme 3; *Royal Victoria Hotel* 147–8, *see also* Dinorwic quarry
Llanberis copper mine 80, 84, 135; wartime bomb store 223
Llanddeiniolen, enclosure act 217
Llandderfel, powered loom 119
Llandecwyn, wood felling 111
Llandudno 130, 131; holiday development 213–14, 234; power station 144; shipping 167–8

Llandudno Junction 165, *165*, 224; brickworks 116; wartime food depot 223
Llanduwchllyn, public handpump 139, *140*
Llandwrog, public drinking fountain 139; RAF station 222, 226
Llandygái, churchyard 201
Llanegryn, handlooms 119
Llanengan, lead mines 80
Llanfachreth, Cymer Abbey forge at 36
Llanfaes 37
Llanfaethlu, telegraph station 180
Llanfairfechan, brewery 130
Llanfairpwllgwyngyll 149, 152, 181
Llanfrothen 111, 147, 178
Llangefni 5, 97, 131, 214; Glanbia cheese factory 130, *130*; hand-loom weaving 119
Llangian, Capel Newydd 196, 198
Llangybi, St Cybi's well 139
Llanneilian, telegraph station 180
Llannerch y Medd, hand-loom weaving 119
Llanrug, band-room 204
Llanrwst 37, 131, 165, 212; bridge 38, *38*; knitting industry 37, 119; lead mine 90, 91; market hall 133; workhouse 207
Llechwedd slate mines 4, 42, 60; electric locomotives 52–3, *52*; hydro-power station 63–4, *63*; ropeways 56–7
Lledr valley 117, 152
Lledwigan stone quarry, limekilns 75, *75*
Lletty Lloeger inn 146
Llidiart Yspytty, ironstone mine 179
Lliwedd copper mine 85, *85*
Lloyd George, David, Prime Minister 32, 33, 96, 130, 223
Lloyd, Simon, Bala 196, 212
Llwyn Du, Medieval bloomery 123–4
Llyn Alaw, dam 140
Llyn Cefni, dam 140
Llyn Cowlyd reservoir 140, 143
Llyn Eigiau 126
Llyn Geirionydd, lead mine 86
Llyn Ogwen stone quarry 74
Llyn Padarn 144, 170
Llyn Ystradau, pumped storage scheme *145*
Llywelyn Fawr 31, 36
local history societies 5–6
locomotives, electric 52–3, *52*; Fairlie *158*; *Fire Queen* 156, *157*, 159; petrol-powered 52; preservation of 13, 24, *51*, 159; in quarries 51–3, *51*, *52*, 72, 137, 156
Lôn Isaf, toll-house 149
London Lead Company 80
London and North Western Railway (LNWR) 163, 174, 206
London Patent Office, Museum 13

McAlpine, Alfred, Penrhyn slate quarry 3
McAlpine Welsh Slate 42, 55, 61
McDougall family 213
Macmillan, Harold, Prime Minister 14

Madoc-Jones, Geraint, machinery merchant 78
Madocks, William Alexander, development of Porthmadog 219; textile mill 121–2, *121*; and Traeth Mawr 102, 178; Tremadoc church and chapel 199; workers' terraced housing 189–90, *189*, 190
Madryn, farm institute 98
Maenan abbey 166
Maenofferen slate quarry *53*, 63
Maentwrog 111; power station 143, *143*; *Tan y Bwlch Inn* (*Oakeley Arms*) 147
Maesgeirchen housing estate 221
Maesygarnedd farm, buildings 103
'Making of the English Landscape' series 17
Malltraeth marsh, Anglesey 92; sea-defence 176–8, *177*
maltings 130
Manchester University, Archaeological Unit 18
manganese mines 82, *83*, 91
Marchogion incline, drum-house 157
Marconi, Guglielmo 181
Maredudd ap Cynan 31
markets and fairs 146, 203; covered 133; livestock 131; market halls 132–3, *132*, 203–4
marl, Anglesey 38
Mawddach, estuary 30; valley 138
Mawddwy Railway 106
media, Welsh-language broadcasting 226
Melin Llynon, windmill 128
Melynllyn, stone quarry (hones) 74
Menai Bridge, timber warehouse 114
Menai Strait, Britannia railway bridge 163–4, *163*; suspension bridge 150, *151*
Merioneth 33, 97, 103
Merthyr Tydfil 27
Mesolithic period, Mynydd Rhiw axe factory 34, 231
metal processing industries 123–7; aluminium smelting 125–7, *126*; blast furnaces 124–5; Medieval bloomeries 123–4
metalliferous mining 78–92, *79*; engine houses 90–1, *90*; engines 89–91; extraction methods 81–2, 84–5; prehistoric 78; processing methods 85–7, *85*, *86*; Roman 34–6, 78, 80; smelting 86–7; stamp mills *85*; transport within and from 87–9; workshop buildings 85–6, *85*, see also copper; gold; iron ore; lead
Methodists 196, 212; political sympathies 33, see also Calvinistic Methodists; Wesleyan Methodists
Meyrick, Owen Putland, Bodorgan 177
Migneint, droving road 146
mills, corn 127–9; fulling 119, 121, 122; horizontal 127, 133; saw 101–2, 114; textile *118*, 119, 120, 121–2, *121*, see also watermills; windmills
millstones 129
miners, Cornish 78, 91; German 78
Minffordd 159, 207
mining, and agricultural holdings 108, 215;

Roman 34–6, 78, 80; South Wales 22, *see also* coal; copper; gold; iron; metalliferous mining; slate; stone
Minllyn slate quarry 59
Mochdre stone quarry 76, *76*
Moel Tryfan commons 215–16, 219; agricultural holdings 108; slate quarries 36, 62, 108, *see also* Nantlle-Moel Tryfan slate quarry; Rhosgadfan
Moel y Gest stone quarry 76
Mona, RAF station 222
Mona Inn 149, *150*
monasteries 31, 36, 38; Cistercian 36, 166
money economy, introduction of 37
Morgan, Dr William, Welsh translation of Bible 31
Morgan, William Pritchard 138
Morris brothers, Anglesey 32
Morris, Lewis, surveyor 185, 212
Mostyn family 106, 128*n*, 214
mountains, unenclosed 108
Murdoch, William 142
Museum of Welsh Life 119
museums 4, *5*, 13–14
Myddleton family 37
Mynydd Llandygái 49, 108; estate workers' housing 188, 216–17
Mynydd Parys (Anglesey), Bronze-Age hammerstones 82; copper mines 29, 34, 78, 80–2, *81*, 92; engine house 90–1; Mona mine 147, *147*; precipitation pits 82, 84, *84*; Roman workings 80; smelting 86–7, 125; workers' housing 186
Mynydd Rhiw, manganese mine 82, 89; prehistoric site 34, 231
Mynytho, agricultural cottages 107

Nanhoron estate 99, 109
Nanhoron stone quarry 76
Nannau estate 99, 109
Nannau family, of Nannau 39
Nant Gwrtheyrn, granite quarries 71, 75, 76
Nantlle 191, 216; war memorial 222
Nantlle slate quarries 68, 135; inclined planes 53, 54–5; Moel-Tryfan quarry 42, 43, 45; railway 156, 157; ropeway 56; steam engines 64–6, *see also* Dorothea slate quarry; Moel Tryfan commons
National Museum of Wales 21, 26, 122; re-erected buildings 119, 210
National Record of Industrial Monuments 15
National Trust 98, 109, 152
Neaverson, Peter and Palmer, Marilyn 18
Nefyn 181, 212; origins of 37, 214
Nevell, Michael 18
Newborough, Anglesey 128, 212, 214
Newborough estate, labourers' houses 107, 220
Newborough, Lord 121, 177, 188
Newcomen engines 9, 14, 65
Newcomen Society 14
Non-conformity *see* Dissenters
North, Herbert Luck 193

North Wales Power and Traction Company 143
nuclear power stations 3, 126, 127, 144–5, 235–6

Oakeley, William Edward 101, 111
Oakeley estate 220
Oakeley slate mine, Blaenau Ffestiniog 3, 42, 49, 68
ochre manufacture 139
Ogwen Bank 186
Ogwen valley 38, 41; slate quarries 62
Owen family, Clennenau 39
Owen, George, *Description of Pembrokeshire* (1602-3) 94–5
Owen, Sir Hugh, Bodeon 177
Owen, William 151

Padarn Country Park 111
Padarn railway 156, 157, *157*
Palethorpe family 213
Palmer, Marilyn 16, 18
pandai (pandy) (fulling mills) 119, 121
Pant yr Afon, railway sidings 159
Pant yr Ynn, textile mill 122; water-powered slate mill 58
Parc lead mine 82, 88
parks, ornamental 99–100, 102
Parliamentary constituencies 33, 224
Parnell, Sir Henry, MP 148
Parry, Gwenlyn, *Fo a Fe* (drama) 23–4
Parry, R. Williams 105, 221
Parry, William John 137–8
Pearce, Professor David William 225
peat, for smelting 87
Peate, Iorwerth Cyfeiliog 21–2, 230
Pen Cae, agricultural cottage 107
Pen isa'r Nant, model dairy farm 101, *101*, 186
Pen Sarn, Capel Bozrah 199
Pen Syflog, iron ore diggings 179
Pen y Bryn quarry 65, 68
Pen y Ffridd, slate mine 46
Pen y Groes 157, 216; housing 190, *190*, *191*, 219; workshops 123, 135
Pen yr Orsedd slate quarry 23, 57, *57*, 61, 66; first aid post ('hospital') 67; workers' housing 191
Penmachno 122, 147; shops **243**, *see also* Cwm Penmachno
Penmaen stone crushing mill 75
Penmaenbach, stone quarries 72
Penmaenmawr, churches and chapels 220; housing 191, *191*, 214, 220; roads and railways 76, *148*, 152, 162; stone quarries 71, *71*, 72–3, *73*, 75, 76–7; Stone-Age axe factory 34, 71, 231
Penmarian stone quarry 73, 75
Penmon Priory, holy well 139
Penmon stone quarries 71, 74, *74*; Dinmor Park 72, 76; Flagstaff quarry 75
Pennant, Colonel *see* Penrhyn, Lord
Penrhyn family 23, 197
Penrhyn, Edward Gordon, Lord (d.1886) 61, 217
Penrhyn, George Sholto, Lord (d.1907) 22

Index

Penrhyn, Edward Sholto, Lord (d.1927) 98
Penrhyn, Richard Pennant, 1st Lord 101, 147, 186; memorial 201, *201*
Penrhyn Arms Hotel, Bangor 147
Penrhyn castle 9, 102, 109, 115
Penrhyn Du lead mine 87, 90, *90*, 125, 134
Penrhyn estate 99, 100, *100*, 106, 216; gasworks 101; park 100, *100*, 111; Pen isa'r Nant model dairy farm 101, *101*; stationary steam engine 105; Ty'n y Hendre farm 106
Penrhyn Llŷn 8–9, 29, 91, 128
Penrhyn Mawr, coal mines 93, 95
Penrhyn slate quarries 3, 23, 42, *44*, 60; extraction method 43, 68; Felin Fawr foundry 61; hospital 67; inclined plane 53, 55, *55*, 100; landscaping 45; 'lord's road' to 147; output 44; railway *4*, 24, 50, 61, 156, 157; strikes (1900-1903) 5, 22; wartime aircraft components 223
Penrhyndeudraeth 90, 91, 138; housing *191*; internet technology 225, *226*
Pensarn, railway bridge 164
Pentre Berw, coal mines 87
Penychain, naval training base 222
Penydarren Ironworks 102
Perspectives on Industrial Archaeology (Science Museum) 7
Pihl, Carl Abraham, railway engineer 158
Pinkerton, Jonathan 177
pit-props, timber for 113
place, importance of 230
Plaid Cymru 33–4
plas, as centre of rural economy 98–9
Plas Berw, Anglesey 38
Plas Kynaston, foundry 150
Plas Mawr, Conwy 38, 235
Plas Newydd estate 99, 100, 106, 109
Plas Tan y Bwlch, Snowdonia National Park Study Centre 24, 109
Plas y Brenin Mountain Centre 147
Plynlimon 29
poetry, tradition of 32
political traditions 32–4
Pont Briwat, railway bridge 164
Pont Gethin, railway viaduct 164
Port Dinorwic (y Felinheli), quays 168, *169*, 171–2
Port Nigel, mine stack 91
Port Penrhyn 117, 168, 170, *170*; rail depot 157, 171–2
Porth Abergeirch, telegraph cable to 181
Porth Amlwch 27, 29, 114, 130; chemical works 139; *lôn felen* (yellow road) to 147, *147*; Peniel chapel 200, *200*; quays 168–9, *168*, 172; ship-building 113, 173; smelters 86, *86*, 125; workers' housing 186, *186*
Porth Dinllaen 41, 173
Porth Llanlleiana, brickworks 116
Porth Llwyd, river 126
Porth Neigwl 89
Porth Trecastell (Cable Bay), telegraph cable to 181

Porth Wen, brickworks 116–17, *117*
Porth Ysgo, manganese mine *83*, 89
Porthmadog 114, 132, 135, 219; Britannia foundry 105, 135; churches and chapels 220; corn-milling complex 128–9; gasworks 142; housing 185, 190, *191*, 234; market hall 204; *Queen's Hotel* 206, *207*; shops 203, *204*, **243**; slate quarries 42; Vulcan foundry (Union Ironworks) 135
Porthmadog harbour, buildings 170; quays 168, 169, 171–2; ship-building 113; stone exports 76
ports *see* docks, quays and harbours
Preece, Sir William Henry, wireless telegraph 181
Price, Roger, of Rhiwlas 139
Prichard, Robert 132
Prichard, Thomas 151
prisons 207–8
Pritchard, Dylan 26
Pritchard, Mr 121
'productive landscape' 8–9, 232
Protestantism 31–2, 196
Provis, John 150
Provis, William Alexander 150, 151, 177
public (communal) buildings 195–210; band-rooms 204–5; churches and chapels 196–202, 228; market halls 203–4; reading rooms and libraries 206; schools 208; shops 202–3, *202*, *203*, 204, *204*, *205*; theatre 205; village memorial halls 205–6; workhouses 207
public houses 149, 206–7; coaching inns 149, *150*; harbour inns 172
public utilities 139–45; gas and electricity 142–5; water supply 139–41
Puffin Island, telegraph station 180
pumping systems, copper mines 89–90; Roman waterwheel 34; slate mines 46, 49; water-pressure engines *46*
Pwllheli 37, 132, 212; bandstand 213; brewery 130; Butlin's holiday camp 214, 234; gasworks 142; harbour 172, 212–13; shops 203; workhouse 207

Quakers, at Dolgellau 39, 125; ironworkers 124
quarries *see* slate quarries; stone quarrying
quartz quarries 117
quartzite, for bricks 116
quays *see* docks, quays and harbours

railways 4, 153–66, *154*, *155*, 214; Amlwch Light Railway 139; to brickworks 116; buildings *157*; civil engineering for 156–7; for construction 162; at copper mines 88; definitions 154–5; on estates 102; to explosives factory 138; to farms 105; Hendre Ddu 105–6; horse-hauled 51, 156; to lay electricity cable 144; to mineral harbours 171–3; miniature 162; modern industrial use of 127; national 155, *155*, 162–5; preservation 14, 24, 159–61; rope-haulage systems 162; signals 165; from slate quarries 50–1, 171–3; within slate quarries 49–50, 51, *51*, 156; stone quarries

71–2, 76–7, *77*; *The Titfield Thunderbolt* (film) 14, 24; tourist 161–2, 165; track and rails 51, 72, 156; and water reservoirs 140; workshops 61, *62*, 63, *see also* Chester to Holyhead; Festiniog Railway; locomotives; Snowdon Mountain Railway; Talyllyn Railway; transport; Welsh Highland Railway
Rank Hovis McDougall 129
Rees, Abraham, *Cyclopaedia* (1802-19) 11–12
Rees, D. Morgan 26
Register of Landscapes of Outstanding Historic Interest in Wales (1998) 26–7, 42
Register of Landscapes of Special Historic Interest in Wales (2001) 27
Rendel, James Meadows 162, 174
Rennie, John 172–3
reservoirs 140–1
retailing, growth of **243**, *see also* shops
Rhinogydd 29
Rhiwbach slate quarry 65–6, *66*; school 68
Rhiwbryfdir viaduct 114
Rhos slate quarry, Capel Curig 55–6, *55*, 60, 66
Rhosgadfan 216; Cae'r Gors workers' cottages 182, *183*, 187
Rhosneigr, Anglesey 213
Rhostryfan 113, 216
Rhosydd, slate quarry 4
Rhyd y Gwystl, South Caernarfon Creamery 130
Rhyd y Main creamery 130
Rhyd y Sarn, slate mill building 58; timber saw-mill 114
Rigby, Joseph and Charles, railway engineers 162, 174
Rix, Michael, industrial archaeology classes 15
roads 146–53, *149*; drovers' 39, 131, 146; garages and service stations 153; government-funded 148; Holyhead (Telford's) 41, 146, 148–52, *148*; impassable to wheeled traffic 146; *lôn felen* (yellow road) 147, *147*; *lôn goed* haulage road (Eifionydd) 105; modern 152–3; Roman 35–6; route from London to Dublin 148, 152, 239; timber haulage 113; trackways 146; tunnels 152; turnpikes 146, 147–8, *see also* bridges; transport
Roberts, Kate 182, 187, 215–16
Roberts, Robert, *Sgolor Mawr* 217
Rocket locomotive, preservation of 13
Rollason Aircraft Services 223
Rolt, L.T.C. (Tom) 14, 15, 183; and Talyllyn Railway 4, 24, 159
Roman occupation 30–1, 78, 166; mineral extraction 34–6, 78, 80
ropeways 113, 138; blondin 56, *57*, 71; chain incline 56, *57*; metalliferous mines 88–9; slate quarries 55–7, *57*; stone quarries 71, *76*
Rothschild, Nathan Meyer 196
Rowley, Trevor 17
Royal Air Force (RAF), wartime airfields 222
Royal Cambrian Company 196
Royal Commission on the Ancient and Historical Monuments of Wales 26

Royal Navy, visual telegraph systems 180
Ruabon 92, 93, 191
Ruskin, John 13
Russia 16
Rydal School, Colwyn Bay 79
Rynne, Colin, *The Industrial Archaeology of Cork City* ... 15

St Eilian's Colour Works 139
Sandby, Paul 124
Savery pump 9
saw-mills 101–2, 114
saw-tables, slate 59, *59*
saws, for cutting slate 58, 60–1; for stone cutting 74; for timber 114
schools 31, 33, 68, 208, 233
Science Museum 13
Scotland, slate quarries 56
Scottish Industrial Archaeology Survey 16
sea-defences 176–8
Second World War 15, 221–2; industry 222–3
Segontium Roman fort (Caernarfon) 35, 36; and church of St Peblig 36; wharves 166
settlements *213*; controlled development 219–21; dual economy 215–16, 217; industrial 215, 216–17; modern townscapes 221; morphology 212–21; nucleated villages 217, 219; urban 212–14
Severn, River 29
Sheffield Trades Historical Society 14
ship-building 37, 113, 172; Porth Amlwch 113, 173; wartime 223
shipping 76, 87; re-loading vessels 170–1
shires 31
shops 202–3, *202*, *204*, *205*; department store 203, *203*; growth of retailing **243**; town centre 204, 209
Simon, Heinrich, mill engineer 129
slate, carving 210–11; for fireplaces 210–11; geology of 42–3; for roofing 36, 59, 61, 106, 191, 193
slate industry 224; Roman 36; worldwide 42, 68–9
slate quarries 1, 3, 23, 42–69, *43*; archaeology of 4, 45–6, 232; block processing 57–60, *58*, *59*; drainage and pumping 46, 49; extraction methods 43–6, 49–50; housing 67–8, *67*, 182; inclined planes 53–5, *53*, *54*; locomotive haulage 51–3, *51*, *52*; Medieval 232; mill buildings 58, *58*, 60, 61; power-transfer systems 65–6; railways 49–51, *51*, 156; re-worked waste 49; research into 25–6; rock loading and moving 49–51; ropeways 55–7, *57*; service buildings 67–8, *68*; steam engines 64–6; underground chambers 46, *48*; waste tips 45, *45*, 49, *50*; water power for 53–5, *55*, 58, 62–3, *63*
slaughterhouses 131
sluices, Bala 141; Traeth Mawr 178–9
Smiles, Samuel 12
Smith, Benjamin 68–9

Index

Smith, Stuart 16
smithies 61, 135
Smithsonian Museum 13, 15
Snowdon Mountain Railway 161, *161*
Snowdonia National Forest Park 111
Snowdonia National Park 98, 109; Study Centre 24, 109
Snowdonian massif 29–30; copper mines 78
snuff mill, Porth Amlwch 130
social infrastructure 195–6, 207–10, 228–9
Society for Industrial Archaeology (American) 15
Society for Post-Medieval Archaeology 6, 19
Society for the Promotion of Christian Knowledge 31
software technology 224, 226, *226*
Spillers, corn merchants 129
Spooner, Charles Easton 156
Spooner, James 151
Squire-Johnson, N., architect 208
Stanley embankment 149, 151
steam engines 9, 14, 134, 228; agricultural machinery 104–5; beam engines 65; coalfields 95; corn mills 129; metalliferous mines 90–1; slate quarries 64–6
steel-making 137
Stephenson, Robert 163
stocking trade 37, 120
stone, granites 70–1, 73; limestone (Anglesey) 29, 70; millstone (Anglesey) 36; for setts (paving blocks) 75, 76
Stone Age, Penmaenmawr axe factory 34, 71
stone quarrying 70–7, *70*; crushing mills 75; extraction methods 71–3, *71, 73*; limekilns 75; Medieval 71, 232; processing 73–5; transport 75–7; wharves for 168
Straphen, John 150
Strathclyde University 16
Suetonius Paulinus, Gaius 30
sulphur kilns 86
Swansea, copper-smelting 80, 84
Switzerland, mountain influences 161, *161*
Sygun copper mine 82, 85, 86
Sylvester, John, road builder 148

Tal y Cafn 171
Tal y Sarn 187, 204, 216, 219; chapel conversion 209–10; combined chapel and shop 202, *202*; Gogerddan Stores 203
Talyllyn Railway 14, *25*, 158, 224; restoration of 4, 24, 159
Talyllyn Railway Society 160
Talyllyn slate quarry 42
Talysarn slate quarry, Nantlle 68
Tan y Bwlch estate 99, 100, 101, 111
Tan y Grisiau 135; hydro scheme 3, 144; Pandy Moelwyn woollen mill 122
tanning, bark for 114
Tanyfynwent farm, agricultural institute 98
technology transfer, slate industry 68–9
telegraphy 179–82; electric telegraph 181;
telegraph stations (visual) 180–1; wireless 181–2
Telford, Thomas 146, 172–3; bridges 150–1; road to Holyhead 41, 146, 148–52, *148*
textile industry 118–23; factory production 118; knitting 119; mechanisation 119–20; spinning 119; technology and glossary 123; weaving 16, 37, 119; woollen mills *118*, 119, 121–2, *121*
Thatcher, Margaret, Prime Minister 224, 225
Thirties Society 230
Thomas, John William (*Arfonwyson*) 211
Thomas, Owen 136
Thompson, E.P. 22
Thompson, Francis, station buildings 162–3
Thompson, Mary Elizabeth 23
tidemills 128, 133
timber, uses of 112–14
Timmins, Geoffrey 16
toll-houses 149, *152*
Tonfanau stone quarry 72, 76
topography 29–30, *30*
tourism, archaeology of 234; holiday towns 212, 213–14; railways 161–2, 165; slate mines 68
Town and Country Planning Act (1947) 98
towns 37, *213*; *bastide* 31, 36, 37; development of 36–7, 212–14; earliest 31, 212
trackways 146
traction engines, agricultural 104
Trade Union movement 22
Traeth Bach 171
Traeth Coch, port 29
Traeth Dulas, Anglesey, brick-making 116
Traeth Mawr 87, 102, 164; harbour cob (sea-wall) 72, 178–9
tramways, Great Orme 161–2
transport 41, 96, 105–6; carriers 146; coaches 146, 153; passenger motor vehicles 153; slate by road 61; stone by road 75, 76; wheeled vehicles 38, 147, *see also* railways; roads
Trasbwll 126
Trawsfynydd 36, 143, 164; nuclear power station 3, 144, 145, 235–6
Trearddur Bay, windmill 128
Trefor 76; granite quarries 72, 75
Trefriw 122, 130; bridge *147; cottage ornée* 188
Tregarth, Bryn Twrw astronomical slates 211, *211*
Tremadoc 199, 203; Capel Peniel 199, *199*; Madocks' textile mill 121–2, *121*; Madocks' theatre 205; market hall 132; Roman *mansio* 178; shops **243**; tannery 114, 122; terraced housing 189, *189*, 190
Tre'r Gof, tidemill 128
Trinder, Barrie 16; *Making of the Industrial Landscape* 17–18; *The Industrial Revolution in Shropshire* 15
Tryweryn, Merionethshire, reservoir 2, 140–1
tunnels, railway 164; road 152
turnpikes 146, 147–8
Twll y Bwbach, wool spinning 119
Twm o'r Nant (Thomas Edwards) 131; *Pedair Colofn Gwladwriaeth* 97

Ty Gwyn copper mine *88*, 90
Ty Gwyn y Gamlas, grain warehouse 132, *132*
Tyddyn Gwladys gold mine 138; gunpowder works 138
Tyddyn Isa wharf *171*
Tyddyn Mawr, Medieval coal mines 94
Tyddyn y Gaib, quartz quarry 117
Tywyn 181, 204

United States, industrial archaeology in 13, 15, 16, 19; Quaker emigration to 39; slate quarries 69; study of workers' housing 184–5; telegraph communication with 180, 181
universities, extra-mural classes 5, 15
University College of North Wales at Bangor 5, 21, 25, 208; agricultural college 98, 208; archaeology and heritage conservation courses 229; School of Forestry 111
Uxbridge, Earl of 177

Vaenol stone quarry 76
Valley 162, 207
Vaynol estate 99, 217; barn 103, *103*; buildings conservation school 109; copper mines 80; dairy 100, 101; estate housing 216; slate quarry 61
Vernacular Architecture Group 230
Victoria and Albert Museum 13
Victoria County Histories 17
Vyrnwy dam 140–1

Wales 4–5, 32; and Act of Union (1536) 31; Assembly 4, 34; industrial archaeology 20–7; local government reform (1972) 34; and portrayal of Welsh identity 23–4, *23*; radical traditions in 22–3; Victorian 1–2, 6–7, *see also* Welsh language; Welsh nationalism
Walker, John 18
war memorials 222
Wardle, Colonel Gwilym Lloyd 122
warehouses, grain 131–2, *132*; timber 114
warfare, and industry 221–3, 232–3
water control systems 175–9, *176*
water power 105, 114, 135, 228; for electricity generation 143; for forges 124; for gunpowder works 138; Roman 34; for slate quarries 53–5, *55*, 58, 62–3, *63*; for woollen mills 120, 122
water supplies 126, 139–41; dams 140–1; pumping stations 140; reservoirs 140–1; wells 139–40
watermills 36, 127, 128
waterwheels *63*, 105, 135
Waunfawr, Marconi wireless station 181, *181*
WEA (Workers' Educational Association) 5, 22
weigh-bridge 149
wells, and handpumps 139–40
Welsh Crown Spelter Company 86

Welsh Development Agency 225
Welsh Highland Railway 136, 137, 160, *160*
Welsh Industrial and Maritime Museum, Cardiff 26
Welsh Labour History Society 22
Welsh language 2, 21, 24, 32, 135; broadcasting 226; origins 31
Welsh Mines Preservation Trust 91
Welsh nationalism 2–3, 23, 33–4
Welsh Slate Museum 4, 54, *62*
Welshpool 239
Wesleyan Methodists 32, 196
Westmacott, Richard, sculptor 201
Wheatstone, Charles 181
Williams, Archbishop 39
Williams, David, MP 33
Williams, Edward (*Iolo Morgannwg*) 32
Williams, Gilbert 215–16
Williams, Gwyn Alf 22
Williams, Sir Hugh 177
Williams, John, agent to Madocks 219
Williams, John, landscape gardener 102
Williams, Richard, Penrhyn estate survey (1804) 100
Williams-Ellis, Clough 161, 193, 207
Willoughby lead mine 88
Wilson, John 150
wind power, for slate quarries 66
windmills, Anglesey 105, 128
women, in copper mines 84–5
Woodcroft, Bennet 13
woollen cloth *see* textile industry
workhouses 207
workshops, engineering 26, 123, 135, 137; estate 65, 101–2, *102*, 109; mining 85–6, *85*; railway 61, *62*, 63
World Heritage sites 27
Wrexham Industrial Estate 223
Wyatt family, tomb 201
Wylfa, Anglesey, nuclear power station 3, 126, 127, 144–5
Wynn family 38, 175
Wynn, Sir John, Gwydir 37
Wynn, Sir Robert 38, 235
Wynn, Thomas 175
Wynnstay family 98

y Felinheli *see* Port Dinorwic
Yale Electric Power Company 142–3
Yeats, William Butler 3
Ynys Cyngar, wharf 170
Ynys y Pandy, slate mill building 58, *58*
Ysbyty Ifan 119, 144; estate 106, 109
Ysgubor Goch housing estate 221

Zola, Émile 13